D1241937

*Christianity through the
Thirteenth Century*

A volume
in
THE DOCUMENTARY HISTORY
of
WESTERN CIVILIZATION

CHRISTIANITY
THROUGH THE
THIRTEENTH CENTURY

edited by
MARSHALL W. BALDWIN

WALKER AND COMPANY
New York

First published in the United States of America in 1970
by the Walker Publishing Company, Inc.

Published simultaneously in Canada
by The Ryerson Press, Toronto.

Library of Congress Catalog Card Number: 72-122470
ISBN: 0-8027-2003-X
Printed in the United States of America

Volumes in this series are published in association
with Harper & Row, Publishers, Inc., from
whom paperback editions are available in Harper
Torchbooks

Contents

Preface

PART I   THE PATRISTIC HERITAGE   1

    THE ORGANIZATION OF THE EARLY CHURCH   10
  1. St. Clement of Rome, Letter to the Corinthians   10
  2. St. Ignatius of Antioch, Letters   13
  3. St. Irenaeus of Lyons, *Against Heresies*   18
  4. Canons of the Early Ecumenical Councils   20

    STATEMENTS OF FAITH   24
  5. The Creed of Nicea   24
  6. Pope Leo I, Letter to Flavian, Bishop of Constantinople   25
  7. The Creed of Chalcedon   27

    SACRAMENTS AND LITURGY   28
  8. The *Didache*   28
  9. Justin Martyr, *The First Apology*   30
 10. Hippolytus, *On the Apostolic Tradition*   34
 11. *The Apostolical Constitutions*   36
 12. Gregory the Great and the Liturgy   40
 13. Liturgical Hymns of the Patristic Period   42
 14. Sermon of St. John Chrysostom   47

    THE RESPUBLICA CHRISTIANA   50
 15. St. Augustine, *The City of God*   50

    MONASTICISM   68
 16. *The Rule of St. Benedict*   68

    THE BISHOP AS PASTOR   95
 17. Gregory the Great, The *Pastoral Rule*   95

PART II   THE CAROLINGIAN AGE   109

    ECCLESIASTICAL ORGANIZATION UNDER ROYAL AUTHORITY   115

18. Charlemagne, *Admonitio generalis*, Letter to Pope Leo III, Letter from Alcuin   115
19. Theodulf of Orléans, *Precepts* and *Hymn for Palm Sunday*   120
20. Ardo Smaragdus, *Life of Benedict of Aniane and Inda*   131
21. Halitgar's *Roman Penitential*   134

     CAROLINGIAN LITURGICAL DOCUMENTS   144
22. Charlemagne, *Epistola generalis*   144
23. Alcuin, *Preface* and Additions to the Roman Mass   145
24. Latin the Exclusive Liturgical Language of the West   149
25. Liturgical Interpretation: Symbolism and Allegory   152

     THE RE-EMERGENCE OF THE PAPACY   158
26. Pope Nicholas I, Letters   158

PART III   THE CENTRAL MIDDLE AGES (900–1150)
    164

     MONASTIC REFORM   170
27. Ulrich, Customs of Cluny   170
28. The Cistercian *Exordium*   177

     PAPAL REFORM   181
29. Pope Gregory VII, *Dictatus papae*   181
30. Pope Gregory VII, Letters   183

     CANON LAW   188
31. Gratian, *The Concord of Discordant Canons*   188

     THE THEOLOGY OF THE SACRAMENTS   205
32. Peter Lombard, *Four Books of Sentences*   205

     POPULAR RELIGION   217
33. Rodulfus Glaber, *Five Books of Histories*   217
34. Reports of Urban II's Speech at Clermont   225
35. *The Book of the Pilgrim*   229

     THE LITURGY: SEQUENCE, TROPE, AND DRAMA   237
36. The Sequence   237
37. The *Quem quaeritis* Trope   240
38. The *Quem quaeritis* "Play"   241

     ST. BERNARD OF CLAIRVAUX   243
39. Sermons on the Virgin Mary   243
40. *On Consideration*   247

PART IV   THE HIGH MIDDLE AGES (1150–1300)   276

POPE INNOCENT III   283
41. Letter to Archbishop Hubert of Canterbury   283
42. Letter to the Bishop of Ely   287

THE FOURTH LATERAN COUNCIL (1215)   292
43. Innocent III and the Fourth Lateran Council   293
44. Canons of the Council   299
45. Implementation of the Decrees: Robert Grosseteste   323
46. Eudes Rigaud's Record of Visitations   334

FRANCISCAN WRITINGS   344
47. *The Rule of 1223*   344
48. *The Rule of the Third Order*   350
49. *The Canticle of Brother Sun*   356
50. The *Stabat mater*   357
51. Jacopone da Todi, *Donna del paradiso*   358

DOMINICAN DOCUMENTS   363
52. Raymond of Peñafort, *Constitutions*   363
53. Provisions for the Friars Preachers at the University of Paris   367
54. Thomas Aquinas, *Summa theologica*   369
55. Thomas Aquinas, *Pange, lingua*   379

THE LITERATURE OF PROTEST   380
56. Robert Grosseteste, Memoranda   381
57. Humbert of the Romans, Passage from the *Opus tripartitum*   384
58. Bruno of Olmütz, Memorandum to Pope Gregory X   385
59. *The Gospel According to Marks of Silver*   389
60. Protest in Vernacular Poetry   391

PRIESTS AND LAYMEN   395
61. Sermon Literature   395
62. Jacobus de Voragine, The *Golden Legend*   397
63. *The Lay-Folks' Mass-Book*   400

Chronology   413
Index   416

Preface

The selections included in this volume have been chosen to illustrate the features most characteristic of Christianity in each of four periods: the early patristic age to the pontificate of Gregory the Great (d. 604), the Carolingian age, the period of European recovery from the tenth to the mid-twelfth century, and finally the period from about 1150 to 1300, sometimes called the High Middle Ages. Partly because of limitations of space, and partly because they are well covered by readily available translations, certain categories of Christian documents have been left out or given scant treatment. Such, for example, are the theological treatises which deal with controversies between the temporal and spiritual jurisdictions and the literature of Byzantine Christianity. What is offered here, therefore, might best be described as a selection of documents illustrating Christian life, largely in the West, in its varied and changing aspects. I have attempted to be as inclusive as possible, but often only one or two typical examples could be presented. To those who miss a favorite selection or to those who would like to have more, I can but suggest the only remedy appropriate to such frustrations, a wide and deep reading in the vast field of Christian literature.

Except where otherwise indicated, the translations have been prepared by the editor. For expert assistance in this task I am most grateful to Dr. Sara Sindel of the Department of Classics of Emory University.

M. W. B.

I

The Patristic Heritage

The foundation and early growth of Christianity coincided in secular history with the establishment of the Roman principate under Augustus, its gradual transformation into a monarchy and empire, its decline, and the first settlements of Germans on Roman soil. For the first three Christian centuries the Roman government, though not continuously persecuting, was officially hostile. By the early fourth century, although Christians were still far from a majority, Christian communities were to be found everywhere and governmental policy changed. Following the Edict of Milan, promulgated by the emperor Constantine in A.D. 313, the Church was able to establish itself on a permanent basis throughout the Roman world and to begin pushing beyond. By the time of the death of the emperor Theodosius (A.D. 395), simple toleration by the imperial government had become official support. Thus the empire of the late fourth and early fifth centuries was a Christian empire and its laws included provisions for ecclesiastical matters.

This same fifth century witnessed the occupation of large areas in the West by Germanic peoples. A temporary calm established by Theodoric, the Ostrogothic king (d. 526), was followed first by the partial reconquest of the West by the emperor Justinian (527–65), and then by the occupation of most of the interior of Italy by the Lombards. By the time of Pope Gregory the Great (590–604), Roman rule in Italy was restricted to Ravenna, Rome, Naples, parts of the south, and Sicily. Moreover, any semblance of jurisdiction over the kingdoms of the Franks in Gaul or of the Visigoths in Spain was rapidly disappearing; and Britain was irretrievably lost.

The consequences for Christianity of the transformation of the ancient Roman world were profound. For while the eastern provinces of the empire maintained the traditional forms of administration, the West, divided among the Germanic kingdoms, failed to preserve Roman governmental institutions. As a consequence, ecclesiastical dealings with the East followed a more or less traditional manner, while the problems of the West required an altogether different approach. Moreover, the cultural separation between the Greco-Oriental East, the "Byzantine" world as it was later designated, and the

Latin West was accentuated with the passing years. Nevertheless, it must be emphasized that despite increasing difficulties, Christendom retained its formal unity.

Among the developments of fundamental importance during this period was the growth of an ecclesiastical organization which gradually assumed the characteristics it was to maintain permanently. One essential feature of this organization was the position of the bishop as head of a congregation in a city. Bishops were regarded as the successors of the Apostles, consecrated by "the laying on of hands" in an unbroken line from their predecessors. They, in turn, were assisted by presbyters (priests) and deacons. The latter were often called "Levites" in early documents.

So much was Christianity in its early days an urban affair that a country dweller (*paganus*) was for long assumed not to be a Christian. But even after the faith had penetrated the rural areas, the bishop and his see remained the center of religious life. This was true not only of administrative concerns but also of public worship and preaching. Well into the early Middle Ages the bishop remained the "pastor" and his jurisdiction was a "parochia." He was the presiding functionary in the early eucharistic liturgy, and it was he who was expected to give a homily or sermon.

According to an early tradition, Rome enjoyed a primacy as the see established by St. Peter, whom Jesus had singled out in a special way (Matt. 16:18–19). Meanwhile, the Church had singled out four special jurisdictions known as patriarchates. These were centered in four cities which were so chosen because of association with the Christ (Jerusalem)[1] or with one of the Apostles (Alexandria, Antioch, Rome). Although both Antioch and Rome were associated with St. Peter, it was the latter see which came to be regarded as the "see of Peter" and the place of his primacy. The status of Constantinople posed a special problem. It was originally not a major see and its bishop was subject to the metropolitan archbishop of Heraclea. But because it was the capital city and the "new Rome" (as it came to be called), gradually, though not without opposition, Constantinople gained an ascendancy in the East as a patriarchate. Thus the political pre-eminence of the city resulted in its attaining metropolitan jurisdiction and eventually a position second only to that of Rome.

As the primitive Church expanded, and especially after the Edict of Milan, the simple administrative procedures of early days were progressively replaced by a more definitive organization. The minor episcopal sees which had been established in the first urban Christian communities tended to become grouped around a large urban center under the jurisdiction of a metropolitan archbishop.[2] And these arch-

1. Jerusalem was destroyed by the emperor Titus in A.D. 70. The patriarch resided in a new adjacent community called Aelia.
2. All metropolitans were archbishops. In later times certain archbishops were given the title without the specific metropolitan jurisdiction.

bishops summoned the bishops of the sees within their jurisdiction to periodic local councils.

On occasions of especial urgency, the entire Church acted as a body through the medium of a council of all the bishops. Beginning with the Council of Nicea (A.D. 325), seven of these assemblies of churchmen from the entire Christian world held during the early centuries have been recognized as "ecumenical" (universal) and their decrees (canons) accepted everywhere as official.[3] Occasionally certain decrees of important local councils were received and repeated by the general synods, and thus included in the growing body of ecclesiastical or canon law.

A problem of major importance which confronted the ecclesiastical authorities from the earliest times was the appearance of heresy. Heresy, or the deviation from the accepted or orthodox doctrine, resulted from the inevitable differences of opinion on the interpretation of the teachings which had been handed down from the time of Christ and the Apostles. Broadly speaking, the heresies of the fourth and fifth centuries fall into two categories. First are those which dealt with the Trinity or with the person and nature of Christ, the latter sometimes being called Christological heresies. The second problem was that posed by the attempt to understand and define the nature of man and his will in relation to Christian teaching on original sin and grace.

The significance of the first problem is clear, because any understanding or acceptance of the doctrine of man's redemption by Christ depends on what is believed of Christ's divinity and humanity. It was essential, therefore, that some official guidance be given in the form of an official definition at the Church's belief.

At the Council of Nicea (325) the Church dealt with the first major Trinitarian heresy, Arianism. Arius, from whom this heresy derived its name, was a bishop of Libya. He maintained that Christ, the Word (*Logos*),[4] had not existed from eternity and was not, therefore, coeternal with the Father. His teaching spread so widely that the emperor Constantine summoned the bishops of the entire Church to meet at Nicea. There Arianism was condemned and a definition of the Trinitarian doctrine, later known as the Nicene Creed, proclaimed that Christ was consubstantial with the Father. The original version of the creed of Nicea was given by Eusebius of Caesarea, who was present at the council. Later councils usually repeated the Nicene formula, and at the Council of Constantinople (381) the phrase concerning the Holy Spirit was somewhat elaborated. It is the version of Constantinople

3. The other councils were Constantinople (I; 381), Ephesus (431), Chalcedon (451), Constantinople (II; 553), Constantinople (III; 680–81), Nicea (II; 787).

4. *Logos*, or Word, as identified with Christ appears in the opening passage of St. John's gospel: "In the beginning was the Word, and the Word was with God, and the Word was God."

which came to be accepted in the West and is given here (Document 5).

Arianism persisted for some time and occasionally had governmental support. Eventually, however, it died out within the empire, largely owing to the strenuous efforts of such men as Athanasius of Alexandria (296–373) and with the assistance of orthodox emperors.

During the century following Nicea, and partly as a measure to combat Arianism, certain theologians maintained that Christ's two natures, the human and divine, amounted to two distinct personalities and that Mary was the mother of Christ, but not the Mother of God. Known as Nestorianism from its principal proponent, Nestorius, this doctrine was condemned by both the councils of Ephesus (431) and Chalcedon (451). The latter council also dealt with the Monophysite heresy which, in turn, arose as an opposition to Nestorianism. Monophysites held that Christ possessed a single combined nature both human and divine. In condemning this doctrine, the conciliar fathers accepted a letter from Pope Leo I (440–61). This letter, addressed to Flavian, bishop of Constantinople, and usually called the "Tome," is a document of first importance for two reasons. First, it provides a summary of the Church's teaching on the incarnation of Christ; and second, it is a major dogmatic pronouncement by a bishop of Rome. The council also added a definition of faith with a more precise terminology regarding the person and nature of Christ and the role of Mary as the Mother of God. Unlike Arianism, both Nestorianism and Monophysitism have persisted into modern times.

Early Christian public worship centered around certain ceremonies known as sacraments. The term "sacrament," derived from a Greek word meaning mystery, was most regularly used in the patristic period and in the Middle Ages as signifying a sacred sign or symbol. The number of sacraments was not officially fixed at seven until the Council of Trent, but by the twelfth century the number seven was already customarily accepted. Very early in the Church's history three sacraments—baptism, the Eucharist, and penance—came to be regarded as essential for all Christians. Then ceremonies developed surrounding each original simple rite. All these taken together, and especially the ceremonies associated with the Eucharist, constitute the liturgy or public worship of the Church.[5]

Baptism, the sacrament of initiation which cleansed the new Christian from the stain of original sin, is referred to many times in Scripture. Moreover, baptism came to be associated with the liturgy of the Eucharist, for catechumens (those preparing for baptism) were not permitted to remain for the most solemn part of the eucharistic service. It became customary, too, for new converts to be baptized during the pre-Easter ceremonies at the very end of Lent.

5. Both "liturgy" and "rite" can be used with a general connotation, but rite is also commonly associated with specific sees or areas, e.g., Roman rite, Byzantine rite.

The sacrament of penance was instituted to provide for the remission of sins committed after baptism. The penances, that is, the acts prescribed for penitents for the priest, were commonly severe and often involved long periods of fasting. Moreover, those who were guilty of serious sin were obliged to perform a public penance before they were permitted to participate with the body of the faithful in the liturgy of the Eucharist.

In the fourth century, according to a practice known as *exomologesis*, penitents were divided into four classes. First were the "weepers," who were required to remain outside the church, or in a portico or atrium sometimes provided for the purpose. Second were the "hearers," who remained in the narthex or vestibule of the church building with the catechumens and other non-Christians. All of this group left before the most solemn part of the liturgy. In the lower part of the nave or main area of the church's interior stood the "prostrators" or "kneelers," who remained somewhat longer and, before leaving, genuflected to receive the bishop's blessing. A fourth class of penitents included the co-standers, who remained for the entire service but were not permitted to make offerings or receive Holy Communion. It is, therefore, clear that penance was closely associated with the eucharistic liturgy and even had bearing on ecclesiastical architecture.

Public penance gradually died out after the patristic age, to be replaced by systems of private confession. But there are many references to it in patristic literature and occasional examples of it in much later times.

Around the Eucharist, the central act of Christian worship, the most solemn ceremonies of the Church's liturgy developed. This sacrament was derived from the gathering of Christ with His Apostles on the night before His death at which He "gave thanks" and pronounced the words "This is My body" and "This is My blood" over the bread and wine. The sacrament seems to have been associated at first with the Jewish tradition of a common meal and the offering of thanks. The sacrament proper then followed—first called the sacrament of "the breaking of bread." Doubtless, the ceremonies often took place in private homes.

In what is certainly an early, if not the earliest, description of the sacrament, in which St. Paul upbraids the Corinthians for improper behavior, he is presumably referring to the preceding common meal.[6] And he speaks of the entire ceremony as "the Lord's supper."

As Christian communities lost ties with their Jewish past, the common meal was dropped and the liturgy developed around the sacrament itself. Vestiges of the earlier association remained, notably the offering of thanks, which became the central prayer. And the sacrament came to be known as "Eucharist" from the Greek word for thanksgiving. Moreover, since the primary reason for offering thanks

6. I Corinthians 11.

was the redemption of mankind, Sunday, the commemoration of Christ's resurrection, was deemed the most appropriate day for the eucharistic liturgy. Indeed, an especially elaborate ceremonial developed around Easter Sunday and the hours preceding, during which, among other things, catechumens were baptized. Noticeable, too, is the association of the idea of sacrifice with the offering of thanks.

By the fourth century a well-developed liturgy of the Eucharist had appeared. Everywhere its essential features were the same. But although the principal usages gradually became stereotyped within the major patriarchates, local variants persisted for centuries. Moreover, even though Greek predominated as the liturgical language of the East, it never became universal. In Rome, Greek was used until the early third century. But Latin did become the universal liturgical language of the West, largely because the Celtic and German peoples had not yet developed a vernacular which was deemed sufficiently formed for liturgical use. From the words of dismissal "*Ite missa est*," the Eucharist in the West came to be called the mass.

Much of the liturgy was sung and the importance of liturgical chant in the history of music is well known. Closely associated with the liturgy, though not at first strictly a part of it, was the hymn. One of the Latin fathers, St. Ambrose of Milan (d. 397), himself a poet and composer of hymns, encouraged congregational singing on one occasion to assist in calming a crowd during a crisis in the city. And eventually certain hymns were in fact incorporated into the liturgy.

From the earliest times many Christians, feeling a call to greater sacrifice and devotion than that generally prescribed, have sought a life of self-denial apart from the ordinary affairs of the world. The experiments of such persons with both the eremitical or solitary life and the coenobitical or common life have contributed to an enduring tradition of Christian asceticism. What is particularly relevant here is the fact that the patristic age witnessed, under the leadership of such men as St. Basil of Cappadocia and St. Benedict of Nursia, the first development within the Christian world of a systematic common life under a rule which is the essence of monasticism.

Finally, in all these areas of religious activity, Christians, despite many differences in usage and practice, developed a strong sense of solidarity. Especially in the early years, Christians regarded themselves as pilgrims or wayfarers journeying toward the life to come. After toleration this solidarity began to manifest itself also in Christian attitudes toward the world and its institutions. Thus, although the sense of pilgrimage was never lost, there developed the concept of a terrestrial society of Christians, a *societas* or *respublica christiana*, a sort of religio-political commonwealth dedicated to the conduct of earthly affairs in such a way that all men might attain salvation.

The documents which illustrate these things are principally of two kinds: the decrees of ecclesiastical councils and the treatises or letters of the great ecclesiastical writers. The two are not unconnected.

Conciliar decrees are often brief, but the discussions which preceded their enactment commonly depended on the treatises or the personal intervention of those who by their sermons and writings were creating an impressive religious literature. Because these men have come to be known collectively as the "fathers of the Church," this literature is designated as patristic.

Although Gregory the Great (d. 604) and St. John of Damascus (d. 754) are usually included among the fathers, the majority lived in the period extending from the immediate post-apostolic age to the mid-fifth century. Aside from saintly life, the most important qualities distinguishing the fathers were freedom from heresy and excellence in the explanation and defense of doctrine. Unity of faith did not, however, preclude differences on matters of ecclesiastical policy, even of philosophical speculation and interpretation. Nevertheless, as they acquired the stamp of official approval, the works of the fathers came to be regarded as authoritative, to be cited by ecclesiastical councils and referred to constantly by subsequent generations.

Those writers who knew or were believed to have known the Apostles have been called the "apostolic fathers." As St. Paul and other Apostles had done, certain of these wrote to Christian communities to give instruction and advice. Their letters, therefore, present evidence of the teaching and organization of the infant Church in the period immediately following the passing of the Apostles. Somewhat later, but still mainly falling within the first two Christian centuries, were a group of writers known collectively as "apologists." These men addressed their words principally, though not exclusively, to opponents on the outside, the Roman government, non-Christian pagans, or Jews.

With the coming of toleration, and coinciding with the important heresies mentioned above, patristic literature increased markedly. The great age of the fathers, therefore, was the fourth and fifth centuries. It should be noted, too, that the first of the patristic writers were Greek, or at least products of the eastern Mediterranean. At home in the metaphysical subtleties of Greek philosophy, they were able to confute heresy as well as to present the Christian religion to the educated pagan. Somewhat later in time and owing much to their Greek forerunners were such men as St. Ambrose, St. Jerome, and St. Augustine, who represent the Latin tradition, and are known, together with Gregory the Great, as the Latin fathers.

A great part of the patristic literature deals with theological matters, for the Church was faced not only with the problem of defining the true faith but of explaining it and defending it in its various aspects in a manner understandable to the Greco-Roman and Judaic mentality. Although it has been possible to include in this collection only a few examples of theological discussion, the significance of this aspect of patristic thought must be recognized. In a sense it underlies all Christian literature, of whatever type.

It is impossible to overemphasize the importance of the patristic period in the total development of Christian culture. The writings of the fathers constitute what might be called the Christian classics. Throughout Christian history they have occupied a place not unlike that held by the secular Greek and Latin literature in the field of western learning.

Suggested Readings

The most useful history of the Church for the entire period is the multivolume series, A. Fliche et V. Martin, *Histoire de l'église* (Paris, 1934 ff.). Volumes I–X, XII, and XIII are applicable to the period covered here. A selected list of titles in English for Part I follows below.

GENERAL

Bainton, R. S., *Early Christianity* (New York, 1960).
Bull, N. J., *The Rise of Christianity* (London, 1967).
Carrington, P., *The Early Christian Church* (2 vols., London, 1957).
Davies, J. G., *The Early Christian Church* (New York, 1965).
Dudden, F. H., *Gregory the Great* (2 vols., London, 1905).
Hughes, P., *A History of the Church*, vol. I (New York, 1934).
Latourette, K. S., *A History of the Expansion of Christianity*, vol. I (New York, 1937).

LITURGY

Dix, Gregory, *The Shape of the Liturgy* (London, 1945).
Jungmann, J. A., *The Early Liturgy*, trans. F. A. Brummer (Notre Dame, Ind., 1959).
Raby, F. J. E., *A History of Christian-Latin Poetry from the Beginnings to the Close of the Middle Ages* (2nd. ed., Oxford, 1953).
Strawley, J. H., *The Early History of the Liturgy* (Cambridge, 1957).

THE FATHERS

Campenhausen, H. von, *The Fathers of the Greek Church* (London, 1963).
——, *The Fathers of the Latin Church* (London, 1964).
Ladner, G. B., *The Idea of Reform* (new ed., New York, 1967).

Rand, E. K., *Founders of the Middle Ages* (Cambridge, 1928).
Ward, M., *Early Christian Portrait Gallery* (London, 1959).

MONASTICISM

Daly, L. J., S.J., *Benedictine Monasticism* (New York, 1965).
Duckett, E., *The Gateway to the Middle Ages. Monasticism* (Ann Arbor, Mich., 1961).
Knowles, Dom D., *From Pachomius to Ignatius* (Oxford, 1966)
———, *The Monastic Order in England* (2nd, ed., Cambridge, 1963).

The Organization of the Early Church

1. St. Clement of Rome, Letter to the Corinthians

Clement was bishop of Rome in the last decade of the first century (c. 90–99). Although he was preceded by Linus and Cletus, there is reason to believe that Peter had designated him as successor. His Letter to the Corinthians, urging them to end a schism, is frequently cited as the earliest extant example of an authoritative instruction by a bishop of Rome. As the letter indicates, it was delivered by delegates who were expected to return with an answer. Clement's message was long and included many allusions to local matters and exhortations supported by scriptural quotations. Chapters 42–44 and 63–65 which are given here contain important references to usages in the primitive Church and especially to the position of bishops as successors of the Apostles. The translation is by F. X. Glimm, S.T.L., *The Apostolic Fathers*, Fathers of the Church (New York, 1947), pp. 42–44, 57, 58. Reprinted by permission of The Catholic University of America Press. (Notes have been omitted except for scriptural references.)

Chapter 42

1 The Apostles received the Gospel for us from the Lord Jesus Christ; Jesus Christ was sent from God. 2 Christ, therefore, is from God and the Apostles are from Christ. Both, accordingly, came in proper order by the will of God. 3 Receiving their orders, therefore, and being filled with confidence because of the Resurrection of the Lord Jesus Christ, and confirmed in the word of God, with full assurance of the Holy Spirit, they went forth preaching the Gospel of the Kingdom of God that was about to come. 4 Preaching, accordingly, throughout the country and the cities, they appointed their first-fruits, after testing them by the Spirit, to be bishops and deacons of those who should believe. 5 And this they did without innovation, since many years ago things had been written concerning bishops and deacons. Thus, the Scripture says

in one place: 'I will establish their bishops in justice and their deacons in faith' (cf. Isa. 60:17).

Chapter 43

1 And what wonder is it if they, who had been entrusted in Christ by God with such a work, appointed the persons we have mentioned? After all, the blessed man Moses, 'a faithful servant in all his house' (Num. 12:7) recorded in the sacred books all the things commanded him. And the other prophets followed him, testifying with him to the laws laid down by him. 2 For, when jealousy arose about the priesthood and the tribes quarreled, as to which of them should be honored with that glorious name, he commanded the chiefs of the twelve tribes to bring him rods inscribed with the name of each tribe (cf. Num: 17); and, taking them, he bound them, and sealed them with the rings of the chiefs, and put them away in the Tabernacle of Testimony on the table of God. 3 And, closing the Tabernacle, he sealed the keys as well as the doors. 4 And he said to them: 'Brethren, the tribe whose rod blossoms, this one has God chosen to be priests and to minister to Him.' 5 And, when morning came, he called together all Israel, six hundred thousand men, and showed the seals to the chiefs of the tribes, and opened the Tabernacle of Testimony, and brought out the rods; and the rod of Aaron was found not only to have blossomed, but also to be bearing fruit. 6 What do you think, beloved? Did not Moses know beforehand that this would happen? Certainly, he knew. But, that no disorder should arise in Israel, he acted thus to glorify the name of the true and only God, to whom be glory forever and ever. Amen.

Chapter 44

1 Our Apostles also knew, through our Lord Jesus Christ, that there would be contention over the bishop's office. 2 So, for this cause, having received complete foreknowledge, they appointed the above-mentioned men, and afterwards gave them a permanent character, so that, as they died, other approved men should succeed to their ministry. 3 Those, therefore, who were appointed by the Apostles or afterwards by other eminent men, with the consent of the whole Church, and who ministered blamelessly to the flock of Christ in humility, peaceably and nobly, being commended for

many years by all—these men we consider are not justly deposed from their ministry. 4 It will be no small sin for us, if we depose from the episcopacy men who have blamelessly and in holiness offered up sacrifice. 5 Blessed are the presbyters who have gone before, since they reached a fruitful and perfect end; for now they need not fear that anyone shall remove them from the place assigned to them. 6 For we see that, in spite of their good conduct, you have forced some men from a ministry which they fulfilled without blame.

Chapter 63

1 Confronted by so many and such great examples, therefore, we rightly should bow our necks and adopt an attitude of obedience, so that abandoning this foolish rebellion we may without blame reach the goal set before us. 2 For you will afford us joy and gladness if you obey what we have written through the Holy Spirit and get rid of the wicked passion of jealousy, according to the plea for peace and harmony which we have made in this letter. 3 We have sent trustworthy and prudent men, who have lived among us irreproachably from youth to old age; and they will be witness between you and us. 4 We have done this in order that you may know our entire preoccupation has been and remains that you may quickly achieve peace.

Chapter 64

1 In conclusion, may the all-seeing God and Ruler of the spirits and Lord of all flesh, who chose the Lord Jesus Christ and us through Him to be a special people (Num. 16:22; 27:15; Heb. 12:9; Deut. 14:2), grant to every soul upon whom His great and holy name has been invoked faith, fear, peace, patience, and long-suffering, self-control, purity and prudence, so that they may be well-pleasing to His name through our high priest and defender Jesus Christ, through whom be glory and majesty, power and honor, to Him, both now and for all ages. Amen.

Chapter 65

1 Send back to us quickly our delegates, Claudius Ephebus and Valerius Vito, together with Fortunatus, in peace with gladness, so

that they may speedily announce the peace and harmony which we have prayed for and desired, and that we also may more speedily rejoice at your good order. 2 May the grace of our Lord Jesus Christ be with you and with all those, in every place, who have been called by God through Him; through whom be glory, honor, power, and majesty to Him, and eternal dominion from eternity to all eternity. Amen.

2. St. Ignatius of Antioch, Letters

Ignatius of Antioch was the third to occupy the see once ruled by the Apostle Peter. He wrote several letters, all of them important in casting light on the organizations of the primitive Church, the primacy of Rome, and the functions of bishop, priest, and deacon. Both the letters given here, the Letter to the Trallians (para. 1–4) and the Letter to the Romans, were evidently written as Ignatius journeyed to Rome to the martyrdom which he was then anticipating and which took place around A.D. 107. The latter, especially, is a moving human document. The translation is by Gerald G. Walsh, S.J., from *The Apostolic Fathers*, pp. 102–103, and 107–112. Reprinted by permission of the Catholic University of America Press. (Notes omitted except for scriptural references.)

To the Trallians

Ignatius Theophorus to the holy Church which is in Tralles in Asia. Beloved as you are by God, the Father of Jesus Christ, elect and worthy of God, outwardly and inwardly at peace through the passion of Jesus Christ, in whom we have hope through our resurrection unto Him, I salute you in the fullness of God, as the Apostles used to do, and I wish you every joy.

1. By the will of God and of Jesus Christ your bishop, Polybius, has visited me here in Smyrna. He tells me that by nature more than by habit you are faultless in disposition and resolute in patience. In spite of the bonds I bear for Jesus Christ, he filled me with such consolation that in him I was able to behold your whole community. Accepting your spiritual benevolence through him, I thanked God to find, as I had heard, that you are imitators of God.

2. For it seems to me that, when you are obedient to the bishop

as you would be to Jesus Christ, you are living, not in a human way, but according to Jesus Christ, who died for us that by faith in His death you might escape death. You must continue, then, to do nothing apart from the bishop. Be obedient, too, to the priests as to the apostles of Jesus Christ, our hope—in whom we shall be found, if only we live in Him. And, as ministers of the mysteries of Jesus Christ, the deacons should please all in every way they can; for they are not merely ministers of food and drink, but the servants of the Church of God. They must avoid all reproach as they would beware of fire.

3. In the same way all should respect, the deacons as they would Jesus Christ, just as they respect the bishop as representing the Father and the priests as the council of God and the college of the Apostles. Apart from these there is nothing that can be called a Church. In such matters I am sure you feel as I do, for I have received a sample of your love in the person of your bishop who is here with me. His demeanor is a great lesson; his meekness is his power. I am sure that even the infidels esteem him. Because I love you I treat you gently; but on his behalf I could write more sharply. However, prisoner as I am, I have not felt myself in a position to command you as though I were an Apostle.

4. By the grace of God I am not lacking in wisdom; but I measure my words, lest my boasting should be fatal. I must, in fact, be more afraid than ever of paying attention to those who flatter me. Their words only serve to scourge me. I long to suffer, but I do not know if I am worthy. To most people my ardor is not apparent, but for my part it is becoming irresistible. My prayer is for humility, by which the prince of this world is overcome. . . .

To the Romans

Ignatius Theophorus to the Church on which the majesty of the most high Father and of Jesus Christ, His only Son, has had mercy; to the Church beloved and enlightened by the faith and charity of Jesus Christ, our God, through the will of Him who has willed all things that exist—the Church in the place of the country of the Romans which holds the primacy. I salute you in the name of Jesus Christ, the Son of the Father. You are a Church worthy of God, worthy of honor, felicitation and praise, worthy of attaining to God, a Church without blemish, which holds the primacy of the community of love, obedient to Christ's law, bearing the Father's name. To you who are united, outwardly and inwardly, in the whole of His commandment, and filled with grace, in union with God and with every alien stain filtered away, I wish every innocent joy in Jesus Christ, our God.

1. In answer to my prayer and beyond all I asked for, I have at last seen the faces I have longed to see. In chains as I am for Jesus Christ, I hope to salute you, if only it be His will to grant me grace to reach my goal. I shall know that the beginning is providential if, in the end, without hindrance, I am to obtain the inheritance. But I am afraid of your love; it may do me wrong. It is easy for you to have your way, but if you do not yield to me, it will be hard for me to reach God.

2. I would have you think of pleasing God—as indeed you do— rather than men. For at no later time shall I have an opportunity like this of reaching God; nor can you ever have any better deed ascribed to you—if only you remain silent. If only you will say nothing in my behalf, I shall be a word of God. But, if our love is for my body, I shall be once more a mere voice. You can do me no greater kindness than to suffer me to be sacrificed to God while the place of sacrifice is still prepared. Thus forming yourselves into a chorus of love, you may sing to the Father in Jesus Christ that God gave the bishop of Syria the grace of being transferred from the rising to the setting sun. It is good to set, leaving the world for God, and so to rise in Him.

3. Never have you envied anyone. You have been others' teachers. I trust that what you have taught and prescribed to others may now be applied by yourselves. Beg only that I may have inward and outward strength, not only in word but in will, that I may be a Christian not merely in name but in fact. For, if I am one in fact, then I may be called one and be faithful long after I have vanished from the world. Nothing merely visible is good, for our God, Jesus Christ, is manifest the more now that He is hidden in God. Christianity is not the work of persuasion, but, whenever it is hated by the world, it is a work of power.

4. I am writing to all the Churches to tell them all that I am, with all my heart, to die for God—if only you do not prevent it. I beseech you not to indulge your benevolence at the wrong time. Please let me be thrown to the wild beasts; through them I can reach God. I am God's wheat; I am ground by the teeth of the

wild beasts that I may end as the pure bread of Christ. If anything, coax the beasts on to become my sepulcher and to leave nothing of my body undevoured so that, when I am dead, I may be no bother to anyone. I shall be really a disciple of Jesus Christ if and when the world can no longer see so much as my body. Make petition, then, to the Lord for me, so that by these means I may be made a sacrifice to God. I do not command you, as Peter and Paul did. They were Apostles; I am a condemned man. They were free man; I am still a slave. Still, if I suffer, I shall be emancipated by Jesus Christ and, in my resurrection, shall be free. But now in chains I am learning to have no wishes of my own.

5. I am already battling with beasts on my journey from Syria to Rome. On land and at sea, by night and by day, I am in chains with ten leopards around me—or at least with a band of guards who grow more brutal the better they are treated. However, the wrongs they do me make me a better disciple. 'But that is not where my justification lies' (I Cor. 4:4). May I find my joy in the beasts that have been made ready for me. My prayer is that they will be prompt in dealing with me. I shall coax them to devour me without delay and not be afraid to touch me, as has happened in some cases. And if, when I am ready, they hold back, I shall provoke them to attack me. Pardon me, but I know what is good for me. I am now beginning to be a disciple; may nothing visible or invisible prevent me from reaching Jesus Christ. Fire and cross and battling with wild beasts [their clawing and tearing,] the breaking of bones and mangling of members, the grinding of my whole body, the wicked torments of the devil—let them all assail me, so long as I get to Jesus Christ.

6. Neither the kingdoms of this world nor the bounds of the universe can have any use for me. I would rather die for Jesus Christ than rule the last reaches of the earth. My search is for Him who died for us; my love is for Him who rose for our salvation. The pangs of new birth are upon me. Forgive me, brethren. Do nothing to prevent this new life. Do not desire that I shall perish. Do not hand over to the world a man whose heart is fixed on God. Do not entice me with material things. Allow me to receive the pure light. When I reach it, I shall be fully a man. Allow me to be a follower of the passion of my God. Let those who hold Him in their hearts understand what urges me, realize what I am choosing, and share my feelings.

7. The prince of this world is eager to tear me to pieces, to weaken by will that is fixed on God. Let none of you who are watching the battle abet him. Come in, rather on my side, for it is the side of God. Do not let your lips be for Jesus Christ and your heart for the world. Let envy have no place among you. And even, when I am come, if I should beseech you, pay no attention to what I say; believe, rather, what I am writing to you now. For alive as I am at this moment of writing, my longing is for death. Desire within me has been nailed to the cross and no flame of material longing is left. Only the living water speaks within me saying: Hasten to the Father. I have no taste for the food that perishes nor for the pleasures of this life. I want the Bread of God which is the Flesh of Christ, who was of the seed of David; and for drink I desire His blood which is love that cannot be destroyed.

8. I desire no longer to live a purely human life; and this desire can be fulfilled if you consent. Make this your choice, if you yourselves would be chosen. I make my petition in a few words. Please believe me; Jesus Christ will make it clear to you that I speak the truth, for He was the mouth without deceit through which the Father truly spoke. Beg for me that, through the Holy Spirit, I may not fail. I have not written to you after the manner of men, but according to the mind of God. If I die, it will prove you loved me; if I am rejected, it will be because you hated me.

9. Remember in your prayers that Church of Syria, which now, in place of me, has God for its pastor. Jesus Christ, along with your love, will be its only bishop. For myself, I am ashamed to be called one of them, for I am not worthy, being the last among them and, as it were, born out of due time (cf. I Cor. 15:8). If I reach God, I shall be some one only by His mercy. My spirit salutes you—and with it the love of the Churches which welcomed me in the name of Jesus Christ. They treated me as more than a passing pilgrim; for even the communities that did not lie along the route I was taking conducted me from city to city.

10. I am writing this letter to you from Smyrna by the hands of the Ephesians, who deserve all praise. Among many others who are with me there is my dear friend Crocus. I trust you have come to know those who went ahead of me from Syria to Rome for the glory of God. Please tell them that I am not far away. All of them are worthy of God and of yourselves. You will do well to help them in every way. The date of this writing is the ninth day before

the calends of September. Farewell, and persevere to the end in Jesus Christ.

3. *St. Irenaeus of Lyons*, Against Heresies

St. Irenaeus, one of the leading apologists, was a native of Smyrna in Asia Minor who traveled West to become priest and later, after a visit to Rome, bishop of Lyons, where he died a martyr in 202. His major work, *Against Heresies*, was written to refute various heretical doctrines which disturbed the Church of his time. In the passages cited here, Irenaeus explains the succession of bishops from the Apostles, with particular reference to Rome. This "apostolic succession" of the bishops was a doctrine of fundamental importance in the Church's belief about the authority of bishops. Irenaeus also refers to the letter of Clement (cited above) and mentions Polycarp (d. 156), another of the apostolic fathers, disciple of St. John and bishop of Smyrna.

The translation of sections from Book III is by A. Roberts and W. H. Rambaut, *Irenaeus*, Ante-Nicene Christian Library, vol. V (Edinburgh, 1898), pp. 260–264.

1. It is within the power of all, therefore, in every church, who may wish to see the truth, to contemplate clearly the tradition of the apostles manifested throughout the whole world; and we are in a position to reckon up those who were by the apostles instituted bishops in the churches, and [to demonstrate] the successions of these men to our own times; those who neither taught nor knew of anything like what these [heretics] rave about. For if the apostles had known hidden mysteries, which they were in the habit of imparting to "the perfect" apart and privily from the rest, they would have delivered them especially to those to whom they were also committing the churches themselves. For they were desirous that these men should be very perfect and blameless in all things, whom also they were leaving behind as their successors, delivering up their own place of government to these men; which men, if they discharged their functions honestly, would be a great boon [to the church], but if they should fall away, the direst calamity.

2. Since, however, it would be very tedious, in such a volume as this, to reckon up the successions of all the churches, we do put to confusion all those who, in whatever manner, whether by an evil

self-pleasing, by vainglory, or by blindness and perverse opinion, assemble in unauthorized meetings; [we do this, I say,] by indicating that tradition derived from the apostles, of the very great, the very ancient, and universally known church founded and organized at Rome by the two most glorious apostles, Peter and Paul; as also [by pointing out] the faith preached to men, which comes down to our time by means of the successions of the bishops. For it is a matter of necessity that every church should agree with this church, on account of its pre-eminent authority, that is, the faithful everywhere, inasmuch as the apostolical tradition has been preserved continuously by those [faithful men] who exist everywhere.

3. The blessed apostles, then, having founded and built up the church, committed into the hands of Linus the office of the episcopate. Of this Linus, Paul makes mention in the Epistles to Timothy. To him succeeded Anacletus; and after him, in the third place from the apostles, Clement was allotted the bishopric. This man, as he had seen the blessed apostles, and had been conversant with them, might be said to have the preaching of the apostles still echoing [in his ears], and their traditions before his eyes. Nor was he alone [in this], for there were many still remaining who had received instructions from the apostles. In the time of this Clement, no small dissension having occurred among the brethren at Corinth, the church in Rome despatched a most powerful letter to the Corinthians, exhorting them to peace, renewing their faith, and declaring the tradition which it had lately received from the apostles, proclaiming the one God, omnipotent, the Maker of heaven and earth, the Creator of man, who brought on the deluge, and called Abraham, who led the people from the land of Egypt, spake with Moses, set forth the law, sent the prophets, and who has prepared fire for the devil and his angels. From this document, whosoever chooses to do so, may learn that He, the Father of our Lord Jesus Christ, was preached by the churches, and may also understand the apostolical tradition of the church, since this epistle is of older date than these men who are now propagating falsehood, and who conjure into existence another god beyond the Creator and the Maker of all existing things. To this Clement there succeeded Evaristus. Alexander followed Evaristus; then, sixth from the apostles, Sixtus was appointed; after him Telesphorus, who was gloriously martyred; then Hyginus; after him, Pius; then

after him, Anicetus. Soter having succeeded Anicetus, Eleutherius does now, in the twelfth place from the apostles, hold the inheritance of the episcopate. In this order, and by this succession, the ecclesiastical tradition from the apostles, and the preaching of the truth, have come down to us. And this is most abundant proof that there is one and the same vivifying faith, which has been preserved in the church from the apostles until now, and handed down in truth.

4. But Polycarp also was not only instructed by apostles, and conversed with many who had seen Christ, but was also, by apostles in Asia, appointed bishop of the church in Smyrna, whom I also saw in my early youth, for he tarried [on earth] a very long time, and, when a very old man, gloriously and most nobly suffering martyrdom, departed this life, having always taught the things which he had learned from the apostles, and which the church has handed down, and which alone are true. . . .

There is also a very powerful epistle of Polycarp written to the Phillippians, from which those who choose to do so, and are anxious about their salvation, can learn the character of his faith, and the preaching of the truth. Then, again, the church in Ephesus, founded by Paul, and having John remaining among them permanently until the times of Trajan, is a true witness of the tradition of the apostles.

4. *Canons of the Early Ecumenical Councils*

The text is taken from the translation by H. R. Percival, *The Seven Ecumenical Councils*, The Nicene and Post-Nicene Fathers, second series, vol. XIV (New York, 1916), pp. 11, 13, 15, 17, 24, 31, 32, 35, and 176–178. Reprinted by permission of Charles Scribner's Sons, New York, and T. & T. Clark, Edinburgh.

Council of Nicea (325)

CANON IV

It is by all means proper that a bishop should be appointed by all the bishops in the province; but should this be difficult, either on account of urgent necessity or because of distance, three at least should meet together, and the suffrages of the absent bishops also being given and communicated in writing, then the ordination should take place. But in every province the ratification of what is done should be left to the metropolitan.

Canon V

Concerning those, whether of the clergy or of the laity, who have been excommunicated in the several provinces, let the provision of the canon be observed by the bishops which provides that the persons cast out by some be not readmitted by others. Nevertheless, inquiry should be made whether they have been excommunicated through captiousness, or contentiousness, or any such like ungracious disposition in the bishop. And, that this matter may have true investigation, it is decreed that in every province synods shall be held twice a year, in order that when all the bishops of the province are assembled together, such questions may by them be thoroughly examined, that so those who have offended against their bishop, may be seen by all to be for just cause excommunicated, until it shall seem fit to a general meeting of the bishops to pronounce a milder sentence upon them. And let these synods be held, the one before Lent (that the pure Gift may be offered to God after all bitterness has been put away), and let the second be held about autumn.

Canon VI

Let the ancient customs in Egypt, Libya, and Pentapolis prevail, that the Bishop of Alexandria have jurisdiction in all these, since the like is customary for the Bishop of Rome also. Likewise in Antioch and the other provinces, let the Churches retain their privileges. And this is to be universally understood, that if any one be made bishop without the consent of the Metropolitan, the great Synod has declared that such a man ought not to be a bishop. If, however, two or three bishops shall from natural love of contradiction, oppose the common suffrage of the rest, it being reasonable and in accordance with the ecclesiastical law, then let the choice of the majority prevail.

Canon VII

Since custom and ancient tradition have prevailed that the Bishop of Aelia [i.e., Jerusalem] should be honoured, let him, saving its due dignity to the Metropolis, have the next place of honour.

[The following two canons refer to the ancient practice of public penance]

Canon XI

Concerning those who have fallen without compulsion, without the spoiling of their property, without danger or the like, as happened during the tyranny of Licinius, the Synod declares that, though they deserve no clemency, they shall be dealt with mercifully. As many as were communicants, if they heartily repent, shall spend three years among the hearers; for seven years they shall be prostrators; and for two years they shall communicate with the people in prayers, but without oblation.

Canon XIV

Concerning catechumens who have lapsed, the holy and great Synod has decreed that, after they have passed three years as hearers, they shall pray with the catechumens.

Canon XV

On account of the great disturbance and discords that occur, it is decreed that the custom prevailing in certain places contrary to the Canon, must wholly be done away: so that neither bishop, presbyter, nor deacon shall pass from city to city. And if any one, after this decree of the holy and great Synod, shall attempt any such thing, or continue in any such course, his proceedings shall be utterly void, and he shall be restored to the Church for which he was ordained bishop or presbyter.

Canon XVI

Neither presbyters, not deacons, nor any others enrolled among the clergy, who not having the fear of God before their eyes, nor regarding the ecclesiastical Canon, shall recklessly remove from their own church, ought by any means to be received by another church; but that every constraint should be applied to restore them to their own parishes; and if they will not go, they must be excommunicated. And if anyone shall dare surreptitiously to carry off and in his own church ordain a man belonging to another, without the consent of his own proper bishop, from whom although he was enrolled in the clergy list he has seceded, let the ordination be void.

Council of Constantinople (381)

CANON II

The bishops are not to go beyond their dioceses to churches lying outside their bounds, nor bring confusion on the churches; but let the Bishop of Alexandria, according to the canons, alone administer the affairs of Egypt; and let the bishops of the East manage the East alone, the privileges of the church in Antioch, which are mentioned in the canons of Nice, being preserved; and let the bishops of the Asian diocese administer the Asian affairs only; and the Pontic bishops only Pontic matters; and the Thracian bishops only Thracian affairs. And let not bishops go beyond their dioceses for ordination or any other ecclesiastical ministrations, unless they be invited. And the aforesaid canon concerning dioceses being observed, it is evident that the synod of every province will administer the affairs of that particular province as was decreed at Nice. But the Churches of God in heathen nations must be governed according to the custom which has prevailed from the times of the Fathers.

CANON III

The bishop of Constantinople, however, shall have the prerogative of honour after the bishop of Rome; because Constantinople is New Rome.

Statements of Faith

---

5. The Creed of Nicea

From the translation by H. R. Percival, *op. cit.*, p. 163 (with minor alterations in accordance with modern English usage). Peprinted by permission of Charles Scribner's Sons, New York, and T. & T. Clark, Edinburgh.

We believe in one God, the Father Almighty, maker of heaven and earth and of all things visible and invisible. And in one Lord Jesus Christ, the only begotten Son of God, begotten of his Father before all worlds, Light of Light, very God of very God, begotten not made, being of one substance with the Father, by whom all things were made. Who for us men and for our salvation came down from heaven and was incarnate by the Holy Spirit and the Virgin Mary, and was made man, and was crucified also for us under Pontius Pilate. He suffered and was buried, and the third day he rose again according to the scriptures, and ascended into heaven, and sits at the right hand of the Father. And he shall come again with glory to judge both the living and the dead. Whose kingdom shall have no end.

And we believe in the Holy Spirit, the Lord and Giver-of-Life, who proceeds from the Father,[1] who with the Father and the Son together is worshipped and glorified, who spoke by the prophets. And we believe in one holy, catholic and apostolic Church. We acknowledge one baptism for the remission of sins, and we look for the resurrection of the dead and the life of the world to come. Amen.

1. The phrase, "and the Son," officially added in the West early in the eleventh century, was not admitted by the eastern Church.

6. Pope Leo I, Letter to Flavian, Bishop of Constantinople

This letter, known as the "Tome" of Pope Leo and accepted by the Council of Chalcedon (451), is an important elaboration of the theology of the incarnation of Christ. Eutyches (referred to here as "he") was the principal proponent of the heresy that came to be known as Monophysite. It failed to distinguish the two real natures, human and divine, in the second person of the Trinity. The letter is long and only certain key passages are given here. The translation is by W. Bright in H. R. Percival, *op. cit.*, pp. 255–256. Reprinted by permission of Charles Scribner's Sons, New York, and T. & T. Clark, Edinburgh.

. . . And he should not have spoken idly to the effect that the Word was in such a sense made flesh, that the Christ who was brought forth from the Virgin's womb had the form of a man, and had not a body really derived from his Mother's body. Possibly his reason for thinking that our Lord Jesus Christ was not of our nature was this—that the Angel who was sent to the blessed and ever Virgin Mary said, "The Holy Ghost shall come upon thee, and the power of the Highest shall overshadow thee, and therefore also that holy thing which shall be born of thee shall be called the Son of God;" as if, because the Virgin's conception was caused by a divine act, therefore the flesh of him whom she conceived was not of the nature of her who conceived him. But we are not to understand that "generation," peerlessly wonderful, and wonderfully peerless, in such a sense as that the newness of the mode of production did away with the proper character of the kind. For it was the Holy Ghost who gave fecundity to the Virgin, but it was from a body that a real body was derived; and "when Wisdom was building herself a house," the "Word was made flesh, and dwelt among us," that is, in that flesh which he assumed from a human being, and which he animated with the spirit of rational life. Accordingly, while the distinctness of both natures and substances were preserved, and both met in one Person, lowliness was assumed by majesty, weakness by power, mortality by eternity; and, in order to pay the debt of our condition, the inviolable nature was united to the passible, so that as the appropriate remedy for our ills, one and the same "Mediator between God and man, the Man Christ Jesus," might from one element be capable of dying and also from the other be incapable. Therefore in the entire and perfect nature of very man was born very God, whole in what was his, whole in what was ours. By "ours" we mean what the Creator formed in us at the beginning and what he assumed in order to restore; for of that which the deceiver brought in, and man, thus deceived, admitted, there was not a trace in the Saviour; and the fact that he took on himself a share in our infirmities did not make him a partaker in our transgressions. He assumed "the form of a servant" without the defilement of sin, enriching what was human, not impairing what was divine: because that "emptying of himself," whereby the Invisible made himself visible, and the Creator and Lord of all things willed to be one among mortals, was a stooping down in compassion, not a failure of power. Accordingly, the same who, remaining in the form of God, made man, was made man in the form of a servant. For each of the natures retains its proper character without defect; and as the form of God does not take away the form of a servant, so the form of a servant does not impair the form of God. . . .

. . .. Accordingly, the Son of God, descending from his seat in heaven, and not departing from the glory of the Father, enters this lower world, born after a new order, by a new mode of birth. After a new order; because he who in his own sphere is invisible, became visible in ours; He who could not be enclosed in space, willed to be enclosed; continuing to be before times, he began to exist in time; the Lord of the universe allowed his infinite majesty to be overshadowed, and took upon him the form of a servant; the impassible God did not disdain to be passible Man, and the immortal One to be subjected to the laws of death. And born by a new mode of birth; because inviolate virginity, while ignorant of concupiscence, supplied the matter of his flesh. What was assumed from the Lord's mother was nature, not fault; nor does the wondrousness of the nativity of our Lord Jesus Christ, as born of a Virgin's womb, imply that his nature is unlike ours. For the selfsame who is very God, is also very man; and there is no illusion in this union, while the lowliness of man and the loftiness of Godhead meet together. For as "God" is not changed by the compassion [exhibited], so "Man" is not consumed by the dignity [bestowed]. For each "form" does the acts which belong to it, in communion with the other; the Word, that is, performing what belongs to the Word, and the flesh carrying out what belongs to the flesh; the one of these shines out in miracles, the other succumbs to injuries. And as the Word does not withdraw from equality with the Father in glory, so the flesh does not abandon the nature of our kind. For, as we must often be saying, he is one and the same, truly Son of God, and truly Son of Man. God, inasmuch as "in the beginning was the Word, and the Word was with God, and the Word was God." Man, inasmuch as "the Word was made flesh, and dwelt among us." God, inasmuch as "all things were made by him, and without him nothing was made." Man, inasmuch as he was "made of a woman, made under the law." The nativity of the flesh is a manifestation of human nature; the Virgin's child-bearing is an indication of Divine power.

7. *The Creed of Chalcedon*

This is the final statement of faith promulgated by the Council of Chalcedon (451). The translation is by H. R. Percival, *op. cit.*, pp. 264–265. Reprinted by permission of Charles Scribner's Sons, New York, and T. & T. Clark, Edinburgh.

Following the holy Fathers we teach with one voice that the Son [of God] and our Lord Jesus Christ is to be confessed as one and the same [Person], that he is perfect in Godhead and perfect in manhood, very God and very man, of a reasonable soul and [human] body consisting, consubstantial with the Father as touching his Godhead, and consubstantial with us as touching his manhood; made in all things like unto us, sin only excepted; begotten of his Father before the worlds according to his Godhead; but in these last days for us men and for our salvation born [into the world] of the Virgin Mary, the Mother of God according to his manhood. This one and the same Jesus Christ, the only-begotten Son [of God] must be confessed to be in two natures, unconfusedly, immutably, indivisibly, inseparably [united], and that without the distinction of natures being taken away by such union, but rather the peculiar property of each nature being preserved and being united in one Person and subsistence, not separated or divided into two persons, but one and the same Son and only-begotten, God the Word, our Lord Jesus Christ, as the Prophets of old time have spoken concerning him, and as the Lord Jesus Christ hath taught us, and as the Creed of the Fathers hath delivered to us.

Sacraments and Liturgy

---

8. The Didache

One of the earliest descriptions of the rite of baptism and of the eucharistic liturgy is given in a short treatise by an unknown author which is commonly included among the writings of the apostolic fathers. This is the *Didache* or *The Teaching of the Twelve Apostles*, the manuscript of which was not discovered until the latter part of the nineteenth century. For a time it was thought that the *Didache* was the earliest Christian document, excluding the New Testament, but present opinion seems to favor a later date, perhaps around the middle of the second century. The translation of the parts given here is by F. H. Glimm, S.T.L., from *The Apostolic Fathers*, pp. 170–180 and 180–183. Reprinted by permission of the Catholic University of America Press. (Notes omitted except for scriptural references.)

Chapter 7

1 Regarding baptism, baptize thus. After giving the foregoing instructions, 'Baptize in the name of the Father, and of the Son, and of the Holy Spirit' (Matt. 28:19), in running water. 2 But if you have no running water, baptize in any other; and if you cannot in cold water, then in warm. 3 But, if the one is lacking, pour the other three times on the head 'in the name of the Father, and Son, and Holy Spirit.' 4 But, before the baptism, let the one who baptizes and the one who is to be baptized fast, and any others who are able to do so. And you shall require the person being baptized to fast for one or two days.

Chapter 8

1 But do not let your fast be with the hypocrites; for they fast on Monday and Thursday; but you shall fast on Wednesday and Friday. 2 And do not pray as the hypocrites,[1] but as the Lord directed in His gospel, 'Thus shall you pray: "Our Father in heaven, hallowed by Thy name, Thy kingdom come, They will be done on earth just as in heaven; give us this day our bread from above, and forgive us our debt as we also forgive our debtors, and lead us not into temptation, but deliver us from evil," ' for Thine is the power and glory forever. 3 Three times in the day pray thus.

Chapter 9

1 In regard to the Eucharist, you shall offer the Eucharist thus: 2 First, in connection with the cup, 'We give Thee thanks, Our Father, for the holy vine of David Thy son, which Thou hast made known to us through Jesus Thy Son; to Thee be glory forever.' 3 And in connection with the breaking of bread, 'We give Thee thanks, Our Father, for the life and knowledge which Thou hast revealed to us through Jesus Thy Son; to Thee be glory forever.' 4 As this broken bread was scattered upon the mountain tops and after being harvested was made one, so let Thy Church be gathered together from the ends of the earth into Thy kingdom, for Thine is the glory and the power through Jesus Christ forever. 5 But let no one eat or drink of the Eucharist with you except for those baptized in the name of the Lord, for it was in reference to this that the Lord said: 'Do not give that which is holy to dogs (Matt. 7:6).'

Chapter 10

1 But after it has been completed, give thanks in the following way: 2 We thank Thee, holy Father, for Thy holy name which Thou hast caused to dwell in our hearts, and for the knowledge and faith and immortality, which Thou hast made known to us through Jesus thy Son; to Thee be glory forever. 3 Thou, Lord Almighty, has created all things for Thy name's sake and hast

---

1. According to the translator this refers either to the Pharisees or to some Jewish converts who continued the practices of the Pharisees.

given food and drink to men for their refreshment, so that they might render thanks to Thee; but upon us Thou hast bestowed spiritual food and drink, and life everlasting through Thy Son (Wisd. 1:14; Eccl. 18:1; 24:8; Apoc. 4:11; Isa. 43:7; John 6:27). 4 For all things we render Thee thanks, because Thou art mighty; to Thee be glory forever. 5 Remember, O Lord, Thy Church, deliver it from all evil and make it perfect in Thy love and gather it from the four winds (Matt. 6:13; 24:31; John 17:15), sanctified for Thy kingdom, which Thou hast prepared for it; for Thine is the power and the glory forever. 6 Let grace come, and let this world pass away, 'Hosanna to the God of David (Matt. 21:9, 15).' If anyone is holy, let him come; if anyone is not, let him repent. Marantha,[2] Amen. 7 But allow 'prophets' to render thanks as they desire. . . .

Chapter 14

1 And on the Lord's day, after you have come together, break bread and offer the Eucharist, having first confessed your offenses, so that your sacrifice may be pure. 2 But let no one who has a quarrel with his neighbor join you until he is reconciled, lest your sacrifice be defiled (Matt 5:23 ff). 3 For it was said by the Lord: 'In every place and time let there be offered to me a clean sacrifice, because I am the great king'; and also: 'and my name is wonderful among the Gentiles (Mal. 1:11, 14).'

9. *Justin Martyr*, The First Apology

Another early description of the baptismal ceremonies is given by Justin Martyr, one of the most important of the apologists. Justin was born in Palestine of Greco-Roman parents, probably in the early years of the second century. He received an excellent education and, after much searching in Greek philosophy, especially in the works of Plato, became a Christian convert. Unlike most of the fathers, Justin remained a layman. He spent his life as a teacher and in fearlessly discoursing on matters of religion until he was put to death in Rome around A.D. 165. In his apologetical works Justin reasoned that the

2. I Cor. 16:22, an Aramaic phrase meaning "Lord, come."

Word, the divine Logos mentioned in the opening passage of St. John's gospel, which was to become incarnate in the Christ of the New Testament, had been made known to pagan philosophers as well as to Jewish prophets.

Justin also gives a description of the eucharistic liturgy which is especially important in that he presents it as it appeared shortly after the middle of the second century. The fact that Justin cites no fixed prayers indicates that the liturgy, at least as Justin knew it, had not yet become standardized. In form, however, it already contained certain essential features which were to remain in later days: an introductory part consisting of readings from Old and New Testaments, the offering of thanksgiving by the presiding official, the communion of the faithful. In the first part of the selection, where Justin is evidently describing a Eucharist which followed the baptism of catechumens, he speaks of these as joining the "brethren." This illustrates the strong sense of community which was evident in early Christian worship, as well as the custom of excluding nonbaptized persons and penitents from all but the introductory part of the liturgy. The chapters cited here are taken from the translation by Thomas B. Falls, *Saint Justin Martyr*, Fathers of the Church (New York, 1948), pp. 99–100 and 104–107. Reprinted by permission of the Catholic University of America Press. (Notes omitted except for scriptural references.)

Chapter 61

Lest we be judged unfair in this exposition, we will not fail to explain how we consecrated ourselves to God when we were regenerated through Christ. Those who are convinced and believe what we say and teach is the truth, and pledge themselves to be able to live accordingly, are taught in prayer and fasting to ask God to forgive their past sins, while we pray and fast with them. Then we lead them to a place where there is water, and they are regenerated in the same manner in which we ourselves were regenerated. In the name of God, the Father and Lord of all, and of our Savior, Jesus Christ, and of the Holy Ghost, they then receive the washing with water. For Christ said: 'Unless you be born again, you shall not enter into the kingdom of heaven (John 3:3).' Now, it is clear to everyone how impossible it is for those who have been born once to enter their mothers' wombs again. Isaias the Prophet explained, as we already stated, how those who have sinned and then repented shall be freed of their sins. These are his words: 'Wash yourselves, be clean, banish sin from your souls; learn to do well: judge for the fatherless and defend the widow; and then come and let us reason together, saith the Lord. And if your sins be as scarlet, I will make them white as wool; and if they be red as crimson, I will make them white as snow. But if you will not hear me, the sword shall devour you: for the mouth of the Lord hath spoken it (Isa. 1:16–20).' And this is the reason, taught to us by the Apostles, why we baptize the way we do. We were totally unaware of our first birth, and were born of necessity from fluid seed through the mutual union of our parents, and were trained in wicked and sinful customs. In order that we do not continue as children of necessity and ignorance, but of deliberate choice and knowledge, and in order to obtain in the water the forgiveness of past sins, there is invoked over the one who wishes to be regenerated, and who is repentant of his sins, the name of God, the Father and Lord of all; he who leads the person to be baptized to the laver calls him by this name only. For, no one is permitted to utter the name of the ineffable God, and if anyone ventures to affirm that His name can be pronounced, such a person is hopelessly mad. This washing is called illumination, since they who learn these things become illuminated intellectually. Furthermore, the illuminated one is also baptized in the name of Jesus Christ, who was crucified under Pontius Pilate, and in the name of the Holy Spirit, who predicted through the Prophets everything concerning Jesus. . . .

Chapter 65

After thus baptizing the one who has believed and given his assent, we escort him to the place where are assembled those whom we call brethren, to offer up sincere prayers in common for ourselves, for the baptized person, and for all other persons wherever they may be, in order that, since we have found the truth, we may be deemed fit through our actions to be esteemed as good citizens and observers of the law, and thus attain eternal salvation. At the conclusion of the prayers we greet one another with a kiss. Then, bread and a chalice containing wine mixed with water are presented to the one presiding over the brethren. He takes them and offers praise and glory to the Father of all, through the name of the Son and of the Holy Spirit, and he recites lengthy prayers of thanksgiving to God in the name of those to whom He granted such favors. At the end of these prayers and thanksgiving, all present express their approval by saying 'Amen.' This Hebrew word, 'Amen,' means 'So be it.' And when he who presides has celebrated the eucharist, they whom we call deacons permit each one present to partake of the eucharistic bread, and wine and water; and they carry it also to the absentees.

Chapter 66

We call this food the eucharist, of which only he can partake who has acknowledged the truth of our teachings, who has been cleansed by baptism for the remission of his sins and for his re-generation, and who regulates his life upon the principles laid down by Christ. Not as ordinary bread or as ordinary drink do we partake of them, but just as, through the word of God, our Savior Jesus Christ became Incarnate and took upon himself flesh and blood for our salvation, so, we have been taught, the food which has been made the eucharist by the prayer of His word, and which nourishes our flesh and blood by assimilation, is both the flesh and blood of that Jesus who was made flesh. The Apostles in their memoirs, which are called Gospels, have handed down what Jesus ordered them to do; that He took bread and, after giving thanks, said: 'Do this in remembrance of Me; this is My body.' In like manner, He took also the chalice, gave thanks, and said: 'This is My blood' (cf. Luke 22:19; Matt. 26:26–27; Mark 14:22); and to them only did He give it. The evil demons, in imitation of this, ordered the same thing to be performed in the Mithraic mysteries. For, as you know or may easily learn, bread and a cup of water, together with certain incantations, are used in their mystic initia-tion rites.

Chapter 67

Henceforward, we constantly remind one another of these things. The rich among us come to the aid of the poor, and we always stay together. For all the favors we enjoy we bless the Creator of all, through His Son Jesus Christ and through the Holy Spirit. On the day which is called Sunday we have a common assembly of all who live in the cities or in the outlying districts, and the memoirs of the Apostles or the writings of the Prophets are read, as long as there is time. Then, when the reader has finished, the president of the assembly verbally admonishes and invites all to imitate such examples of virtue. Then we all stand up together and offer up our prayers, and, as we said before, after we finish our prayers, bread and wine and water are presented. He who presides likewise offers up prayers and thinksgivings, to the best of his ability, and the people express their approval by saying 'Amen.' The eucharistic elements are distributed and consumed by those present, and to those who are absent they are sent through the deacons. The wealthy, if they wish, contribute whatever they desire and the collection is placed in the custody of the president. [With it] he helps the orphans and widows, those who are needy because of sickness or any other reason, and the captives and strangers in our midst; in short, he takes care of all those in need. Sunday, indeed, is the day on which we hold our common assembly because it is the first day on which God, transforming the darkness and [prime] matter, created the world; and our Savior Jesus Christ arose from the dead on the same day. For they crucified Him on the day before that of Saturn, and on the day after, which is Sunday, He appeared to His Apostles and disciples, and taught them the things which we have passed on to you also for consideration.

10. *Hippolytus*, On the Apostolic Tradition

As mentioned above, the eucharistic liturgy took different forms in the various parts of the Christian world, Syria, Egypt, Africa, Byzantium, Rome, etc. An important document known as the *Apostolic Tradition*, which is now believed to be the work of St. Hippolytus, presents a picture of the liturgy in Rome around the second decade of the third century. Here certain forms of prayer are given, but accompanied by the admonition that these precise words were not necessary. The *Apostolic Tradition* was originally composed in Greek, which was still the liturgical language of Rome. It was soon translated into Latin, gradually coming into use then in Rome and the West, and it is the Latin version which has survived. The work is highly important not only for the liturgy, but for many other aspects of third-century ecclesiastic life. The selection given here includes the offertory, where the bread and wine to be used later in the service are brought to the bishop; the prayer called the preface; and the *anaphora*, later called the canon in the West. The translation is by Gregory Dix, from Henry Chadwick (ed.), *The Treatise on the Apostolic Tradition of St.*

Hippolytus (rev. ed., London, 1968), pp. 6–9. Reprinted by permission of S.P.C.K., London.

The Liturgy

KISS OF PEACE

1. And (δέ) when he has been made bishop (ἐπίσκοπος)[1] let every one offer him the kiss of peace (εἰρήνη) saluting (ἀσπάζεσθαι) him, for he has been made worthy <of this>.

OFFERTORY

2. To him then let the deacons (διάκονος) bring the oblation (προσφορά) and (δέ) he with all the presbyters (πρεσβύτερος) laying his hand on the oblation (πρ.) shall say giving thanks (εὐχαριστῶν sic):
3. The Lord be with you. And the people (λαός) shall say: And with thy spirit. [*And the bishop shall say:*] Lift up your hearts. [*And the people shall say:*] We have them with the Lord. [*And the bishop shall say:*] Let us give thanks unto the Lord. [*And the people shall say:*] <It is> meet and right. And forthwith he shall continue thus:

CANON

4. We render thanks unto thee, O God, through Thy Beloved Child Jesus Christ, Whom in the last times Thou didst send to us <to be> a Saviour and Redeemer and the Angel of Thy counsel;
5. Who is Thy Word inseparable <from Thee>, through Whom Thou madest all things and in Whom Thou wast well-pleased;
6. <Whom> Thou didst send from heaven into <the> Virgin's womb and Who conceived within her was made flesh and demonstrated to be Thy Son being born of Holy Spirit and a Virgin;
7. Who fulfilling Thy will and preparing for Thee a holy people stretched forth His hands for suffering that He might release from sufferings them who have believed in Thee;
8. Who when He was betrayed to voluntary suffering that He might abolish death and rend the bonds of the devil and tread down hell and enlighten the righteous and establish the limit and demonstrate the resurrection:

1. The liturgy given here follows the consecration of a bishop.

9. Taking bread <and> making eucharist [*i.e.* giving thanks] to Thee said: Take eat: this is My Body which is broken for you [*for the remission of sins*]. Likewise also the cup, saying: This is My Blood which is shed for you.

10. When ye do this [ye] do My "anamnesis."[2]

11. Doing therefore the "anamnesis" of His death and resurrection we offer to Thee the bread and the cup making eucharist to Thee because Thou hast made us worthy to stand before Thee and minister as priests to Thee.

12. And we pray Thee that thou wouldest send Thy Holy Spirit upon the oblation of Thy holy Church Thou wouldest grant to all ⌈*Thy Saints*⌉ who partake to be united [*to Thee*] that they may be fulfilled with the Holy Spirit for the confirmation of <their> faith in truth,

13. that ⌈we⌉ may praise and glorify Thee through Thy [*Beloved*] Child Jesus Christ through whom glory and honour <be> unto Thee with <the> Holy Spirit in Thy holy Church now ⌈and for ever⌉ and world without end. Amen.

11. The Apostolical Constitutions

By the fourth century the general structure of the mass had already assumed the form which it was to maintain permanently. The essential element was the Eucharist itself, the rite of sacrifice, now divided into three parts: the offertory or oblation, which included the presentation of the bread and wine; the consecration; and, finally, the communion. The second part, which included the principal eucharistic prayers, also came to be divided into a preface which was sung and the prayers which were recited silently by the celebrant.

As is evident in the earliest descriptions of the eucharistic liturgy, the central rites of sacrifice and communion followed a preliminary service, sometimes called the Service of the Word of God or Fore-mass. Since catechumens were permitted to be present only at this portion of the service, it came to be known as the mass of the catechumens.

The Fore-mass included both prayers of petition and readings from Scripture. And although the order and number of these changed over

2. Remembrance or commemoration, but with the sense of recalling a past event as a present reality.

the years, the general idea of scriptural reading and prayer combined persisted. Further, these were normally followed by a homily given by the bishop.

The following selection taken from the *Apostolical Constitutions,* a document of Oriental origin dating from the early fourth century, illustrates the development of the Fore-mass. A second section gives an early form of the prayer known as the *Gloria,* which originated in the East as a morning hymn. Since the opening words, "Glory to God in the Highest," the angelic salutation to the newborn Christ, were deemed particularly appropriate to Christmas, it was inserted in the West after the first reading of the Fore-mass. Originally sung at Rome on Christmas Day only, its use as a regular feature of the Sunday mass developed gradually. The translation is by J. Donaldson, *The Apostolical Constitutions,* Ante-Nicene Christian Library, vol. XVII (Edinburgh, 1870), Book II, pp. 83–86 and Book VII, p. 205.

Chapter LVII

But be thou, O bishop, holy, unblameable, no striker, not soon angry, not cruel; but a builder up, a converter, apt to teach, forebearing of evil, of a gentle mind, meek, long-suffering, ready to exhort, ready to comfort, as a man of God.

When thou callest an assembly of the church as one that is the commander of a great ship, appoint the assemblies to be made with all possible skill, charging the deacons as mariners to prepare places for the brethren as for passengers, with all due care and decency. And first, let the building be long, with its head to the east, with its vestries on both sides at the east end, and so it will be like a ship. In the middle let the bishop's throne be placed, and on each side of him let the presbytery sit down; and let the deacons stand near at hand, in close and small girt garments, for they are like the mariners and managers of the ship: with regard to these, let the laity sit on the other side, with all quietness and good order. And let the women sit by themselves, they also keeping silence. In the middle, let the reader stand upon some high place: let him read the books of Moses, of Joshua the son of Nun, of the Judges, and of the Kings and of the Chronicles, and those written after the return from the captivity; and besides these, the books of Job and of Solomon, and of the sixteen prophets. But when there have been two lessons severally read, let some other person sing the hymns of David, and let the people join at the conclusions of the verses. Afterwards let our Acts be read, and the Epistles of Paul our fellow-worker, which he sent to the churches under the conduct of the Holy Spirit; and afterwards let a deacon or a presbyter read the Gospels, both those which I, Matthew and John, have directed to you, and those which the fellow-workers of Paul received and to you, Luke and Mark. And while the Gospel is read, let all the presbyters and deacons, and all the people, stand up in great silence; for it is written: "Be silent, and hear, O Israel." (Deut. 27:9) And again: "But do thou stand there, and hear" (Deut. 5:31). In the next place, let the presbyters one by one, not all together, exhort the people, and the bishop in the last place, as being the commander. Let the porters stand at the entries of the men, and observe them. Let the deaconnesses also stand at those of the women, like shipmen. For the same description and pattern was both in the tabernacle of the testimony and in the temple of God (cf. Deut. 23:1). But if any one be found sitting out of his place, let him be rebuked by the deacon, as a manager of the foreship, and be removed into the place proper for him; for the church is not only like a ship, but also like a sheepfold. For as the shepherds place all the brute creatures distinctly, I mean goats and sheep, according to their kind and age, and still every one runs together, like to his like; so is it to be in the church. Let the young persons sit by themselves, if there be a place for them; if not, let them stand upright. But let those that are already stricken in years sit in order. For the children which stand, let their fathers and mothers take them to them. Let the younger women also sit by themselves, if there be a place for them; but if there be not, let them stand behind the women. Let those women which are married, and have children, be placed by themselves; but let the virgins, and the widows, and the elder women, stand or sit before all the rest; and let the deacon be the disposer of the places, that every one of those that comes in may go to his proper place, and may not sit at the entrance. In like manner, let the deacon oversee the people, that nobody may whisper, nor slumber, nor laugh, nor nod; for all ought in the church to stand wisely, and soberly, and attentively, having their attention fixed upon the word of the Lord. After this, let all rise up with one consent, and looking towards the east, after the catechumens and penitents are gone out, pray to God eastward, who ascended up to the heaven of heavens to the east; remembering also the ancient situation of paradise in the east, from whence the first men, when he had yielded to the persuasion of the serpent, and disobeyed the command of God, was expelled. As to the deacons, after the prayer is over, let some of them attend upon the oblation of the eucharist, minstering to the Lord's body with fear. Let others of them watch the multitude, and keep them silent. But let that deacon who is at the high priest's hand say to the people, Let no one have any quarrel against another; let no one come in hypocrisy. Then let the men give the men, and the women give the women, the Lord's kiss. But let no one do it with deceit, as Judas betrayed the Lord with a kiss. After this let the deacon pray for the whole church, for the whole world, and the several parts of it, and the fruits of it; for the priests and the rulers, for the high priest and the king, and the peace of the universe. After this let the high priest pray for peace upon the people, and bless them, as Moses commanded the priests to bless the people, in these words: "The Lord bless thee, and keep thee: the Lord make His face to shine upon thee, and give thee peace." Let the bishop pray for the people, and say: "Save Thy people, O Lord, and bless Thine inheritance, which Thou hast obtained with the precious blood of Thy Christ, and hast called a royal priesthood, and an holy nation." After this let the sacrifice follow, the people standing, and praying silently; and when the oblation has been made, let every rank by itself partake of the Lord's body and precious blood in order, and approach with reverence and holy fear, as to the body of their king. Let the women approach with their heads covered, as is becoming the order of women; but let the door be watched, lest any unbeliever, or one not yet initiated, come in.

Chapter XLVII

"Glory be to God in the highest, and upon earth peace, good-will among men." (Luke 2:14) We praise Thee, we sing hymns to Thee, we bless Thee, we glorify Thee, we worship Thee by Thy great High Priest; Thee who art the true God, who art the One Unbegotten, the only inaccessible Being. For Thy great glory, O Lord and heavenly King, O God the Father Almighty, O Lord God, the Father of Christ the immaculate Lamb, who taketh away the sin of the world, receive our prayer, Thou that sittest upon the cherubim. For Thou only art holy, Thou only art the Lord Jesus, the Christ of the God of all created nature, and our King, by whom glory, honour, and worship be to Thee.

12. Gregory the Great and the Liturgy[1]

Precisely what Pope Gregory the Great himself contributed to the Roman mass is not easy to define. A sacramentary (*liber sacramentorum*), or book containing only the mass prayers recited by the priest or bishop, had been issued under the name of Pope Leo I and later under the name of Pope Gelasius (d. 496). Each edition seems to have been amplified subsequently, and the entire collection was revised and simplified by Gregory. But it has been shown that Gregory's book was intended for his own personal use and that both "Gelasian" and "Gregorian" sacramentaries remained in use. Gregory, it seems, did add certain phrases to the canon of the mass. The Venerable Bede (d. 735), the Saxon historian, describes it in his *Ecclesiastical History* as follows:[2] "And in the celebration of masses, he added three phrases full of great goodness and perfection: 'And dispose our days in thy peace, and preserve us from eternal damnation, and rank us in the number of thy elect, through Christ our Lord.'"

Gregory also altered the position of the Lord's Prayer and the manner of reciting the *Kyrie*, as he indicates in the following letter, dated 598, to Bishop John of Syracuse. This letter, it may be added, also brings out clearly Gregory's attitude, courteous and friendly but firm in his insistence on the primacy of the Roman see. The translation is by J. Barmby, *Selected Epistles of Gregory the Great*, Nicene and Post-Nicene Fathers, vol. IX (New York, 1898), pp. 8–9.

One coming from Sicily has told me that some friends of his, whether Greeks or Latins I know not, as though moved by zeal for the holy Roman Church, murmur about my arrangements [i.e. of divine service], saying, How can he be arranging so as to keep the Constantinopolitan Church in check, when in all respects he follows her usage? And, when I said to him, What usages of hers do we follow? he replied; you have caused Alleluia to be said at mass out of the season of Pentecost; you have made appointment for the sub-deacons to proceed disrobed, and for Kyrie Eleison to be said,

1. On Gregory, see below, p. 95. Gregory's name has traditionally been associated with what was to become the official chant of the Church. Apparently, his contribution consisted in a wise selection and rearrangement of existing Roman chants and in the founding of a *schola cantorum* at Rome.
2. Ed. Vida Scudder (London, 1910), p. 63.

and for the Lord's Prayer to be said immediately after the canon. To him I replied, that in none of these things have we followed another Church.

For, as to our custom here of saying the Alleluia, it is said to be derived from the Church of Jerusalem by the tradition of the blessed Jerome in the time of pope Damasus of blessed memory; and accordingly in this matter we have rather curtailed the former usage which had been handed down to us here from the Greeks.

Further, as to my having caused the sub-deacons to proceed disrobed, this was the ancient usage of the Church. But it pleased one of our pontiffs, I know not which, to order them to proceed in linen tunics. For have your Churches in any respect received their tradition from the Greeks? Whence, then, have they at the present day the custom of the sub-deacons proceeding in linen tunics, except that they have received it from their mother, the Roman Church?

Further, we neither have said nor now say the Kyrie Eleison, as it is said by the Greeks: for among the Greeks all say it together; but with us it is said by the clerks, and responded to by the people; and as often as it is said, Christe Eleison is said also, which is not said at all among the Greeks. Further, in daily masses we suppress some things that are usually said, and say on Kyrie Eleison, Christe Eleison, so as to devote ourselves a little longer to these words of deprecation. But the Lord's prayer (*orationem Dominicam*) we say immediately after the prayer (*mox post precem*) for this reason, that it was the custom of the apostles to consecrate the host of oblation to (*ad*) that same prayer only. And it seemed to me very unsuitable that we should say over the oblation a prayer which a scholastic had composed, and should not say the very prayer which our Redeemer composed over His body and blood. But also the Lord's Prayer among the Greeks is said by all the people, but with us by the priest alone. Wherein, then, have we followed the usages of the Greeks, in that we have either amended our own old ones or appointed new and profitable ones, in which, however, we are not shewn to be imitating others? Wherefore, let your Charity, when an occasion presents itself, proceed to the Church of Catana; or in the Church of Syracuse teach those who you believe or understand may possibly be murmuring with respect to this matter, holding a conference there, as though for a different purpose, and so desist not from instructing them. For as to what they say about the Church of Constantinople, who can doubt that it is subject to the Apostolic See, as both the most pious lord the emperor and our brother the bishop of that city continually acknowledge? Yet, if this or any other Church as anything that is good, I am prepared in what is good to imitate even my inferiors, while prohibiting them from things unlawful. For he is foolish who thinks himself first in such a way as to scorn to learn whatever good things he may see.

13. Liturgical Hymns of the Patristic Period

St. Ambrose, Hymn for Sunday Lauds

It was St. Ambrose of Milan (d. 397) who first gave impetus to the hymn as part of religious worship in the western part of the Christian world. St. Augustine in his *Confessions* describes the attempt of Justina, the mother of the emperor Valentinian and an Arian, to force Ambrose to surrender his church in Milan. He tells how "the devout people watched day and night in the church, ready to die with the bishop, their servant . . ." and goes on to say: "At this time was it here first instituted after the manner of the Eastern Churches, that hymns and psalms should be sung lest the people should wax faint through the tediousness of their sorrow."[1]

Ambrose composed hymns for congregational singing, and several were later adopted formally either in the public liturgy, or in the monastic hours. Since many other hymns soon appeared in the same iambic dimeter which he used, there is considerable doubt as to the genuineness of many of the so-called Ambrosian hymns.

In the following examples, some of the Latin is given in order to show the original rhythm. The Latin version and prose translation is taken from F. Brittain (ed.), *The Penguin Book of Latin Verse* (Baltimore, 1962), pp. 88–89, verses 1, 2, 5–8. Reprinted by permission of Penguin Books Ltd.

> *Aeterne rerum conditor*
> *Noctem diemque qui regis*
> *Et temporum das tempora*
> *Ut alleves fastidium,*

1. *Confessions,* IX, vii, trans. W. Watts, The Loeb Classical Library (London, 1925), p. 31.

Praeco diei jam sonat
Noctis profundae pervigil
Nocturna lux viantibus
A nocte noctem segregans.

Eternal founder of the world, who rulest night and day and givest changes in due season to relieve our weariness,

The herald of the day, ever watchful through the depth of night and as helpful as a light in the dark is to travellers, is sounding his call, marking off one night-watch from another.

Surgamus ergo strenue,
Gallus jacentes excitat,
Et somnolentos increpat,
Gallus negantes arguit.

Gallo canente spes redit,
Aegris salus refunditur,
Mucro latronis conditur,
Lapsis fides revertitur.

Let us therefore rise promptly. The cock rouses those who are asleep, rebukes the drowsy, and denounces those who will not get up.

When the cock crows hope returns, health is restored to the sick, the robber's sword is sheathed, and faith returns to backsliders.

Jesu, labentes respice
Et nos videndo corrige;
Si respicis, lapsus cadunt,
Fletuque culpa solvitur.

Tu lux refulge sensibus
Mentisque somnum discute
Te nostra vox primum sonet,
Et vota solvamus tibi.

Look on us, Jesus, in our wavering, and correct us by a glance; for if thou lookest on us our sins leave us and our guilt is washed away in tears.

Be thou a light, shine into our minds, and dispel sleep from our souls. May the first act of our voices be to sing of thee, and so may we pay our vows to thee.

Hymn for Compline

Ambrosian, author unknown (c. sixth century). The Latin version is taken from F. J. E. Raby (ed.), *The Oxford Book of Medieval Latin Verse* (Oxford, 1959), no. 36. Translated by J. M. Neale and others, *Hymns Ancient and Modern* (London, 1875), no. 15. The English translation retains the original meter.

> *Te lucis ante terminum*
> *rerum creator, poscimus*
> *ut solita clementia*
> *sis praesul ad custodiam.*

> Before the ending of the day,
> Creator of the world, we pray
> That Thou with wonted love wouldst keep
> Thy watch around us while we sleep.

> *Procul recedant somnia*
> *et noctium phantasmata,*
> *hostemque nostrum comprime*
> *ne polluantur corpora.*

> O let no evil dreams be near,
> Nor phantoms of the night appear;
> Our ghostly enemy restrain,
> Lest aught of sin our bodies stain.

> *Praesta, pater omnipotens,*
> *per Iesum Christum Dominum,*
> *qui tecum in perpetuum*
> *regnat cum sancto spiritu.*

> Almighty Father, hear our cry
> Through Jesus Christ our Lord most High,
> Who with the Holy Ghost and Thee
> Doth live and reign eternally.

Verses from the Hymn for Every Hour

Prudentius (Aurelius Prudentius Clemens, d.c. 405) wrote hymns with a rather specialized theological content. The verses cited here have long been in use as a Christmas hymn. The Latin version is from F. J. E. Raby, *op. cit.*, no. 20, translated by J. M. Neale and H. W. Baker, *op. cit.*, no. 56, verses 1, 3, 5.

Corde natus ex parentis ante mundi exordium,
alpha et omega cognominatus, ipse fons et clausula
omnium quae sunt, fuerunt, quaeque post futura sunt.

Of the Father's love begotten, ere the worlds began to be,
He is Alpha and Omega, He the source, the ending He,
Of the things that are, that have been, and that future years shall see.

Corporis formam caduci, membra morti obnoxia
induit, ne gens periret primoplasti ex germine,
merserat quem lex profundo noxialis tartaro.

He is found in human fashion, death and sorrow here to know,
That the race of Adam's children, doomed by Law to endless woe,
May not henceforth die and perish, in the dreadful gulf below.

Ecce quem vates vetustis concinebant saeculis,
quem prophetarum fideles paginae spoponderant,
emicat promissus olim; cuncta collaudent eum.

This is He Whom seers in old time chanted of with one accord;
Whom the voices of the Prophets promised in their faithful word;
Now He shines, the long expected; let creation praise its Lord.

Hymn on Christ's Passion

Venantius Fortunatus (d.c. 610) was born and educated in Italy.
Around 565—during the turbulent period of early Frankish history—
he undertook a pilgrimage to the shrine of St. Martin at Tours in
gratitude for that saint's intercession in healing an eye affliction. It was
at the monastery of the Holy Cross at Poitiers, not far off, that St.
Radegund had taken refuge from her husband, the bloodthirsty
Chlotar, who had murdered her brother. Fortunatus became bishop of
Poitiers toward the end of his life.

Fortunatus was one of the first poets to inject a frankly emotional
content into his hymns. Much of his verse is mediocre, but two hymns,
the *Vexilla regis prodeunt* ("Forth the royal banners go") and the
Pange lingua gloriosi, have become famous. The latter, of which verses
1, 2, 8, 9, and 10 are given here, forms part of the Good Friday liturgy.
Centuries later it directly inspired an equally famous hymn by Thomas
Aquinas, (cf. below, p. 379). The meter is trochaic tetrameter, a
meter which was used in Roman soldiers' songs. Latin version from
F. J. E. Raby, *op. cit.,* no. 54, translated by J. M. Neale, *op. c.,* no. 97,
verses 1, 2, 8, 9, 10.

Pange lingua gloriosi proelium certaminis
et super crucis tropaeo dic triumphum nobilem
qualiter redemptor orbis immolatus vicerit

Sing, my tongue, the glorious battle,
Sing the last, the dread affray;
O'er the Cross, the Victor's trophy,
Sound the high triumphal lay,
How, the pains of death enduring,
Earth's Redeemer won the day.

De parentis protoplasti fraude factor condolens
quando pomi noxialis morte morsu corruit,
ipse lignum tunc notavit, damna ligni ut solveret.

He, our Maker, deeply grieving
That the first-made Adam fell,
When he ate the fruit forbidden
Whose reward was death and hell,
Mark'd e'en then this Tree the ruin
Of the first tree to dispel.

Crux fidelis, inter omnes arbor una nobilis
nulla talem silva profert flore fronde germine,
dulce lignum, dulce clavo dulce pondus sustinens.

Faithful Cross, above all other
One and only noble Tree,
None in foliage, none in blossom,
None in fruit thy peer may be;
Sweetest wood, and sweetest iron;
Sweetest weight is hung on thee.

Flecte ramos, arbor alta tesa laxa viscera,
et rigor lentescat ille quem dedit nativitas,
ut superni membra regis mite tendas stipite.

Bend, O lofty Tree, thy branches,
Thy too rigid sinews bend;
And awhile the stubborn hardness,
Which thy birth bestowed suspend;
And the Limbs of Heav'n's high Monarch
Gently on thine arms extend.

Sola digna tu fuisti ferre pretium saeculi
atque portum praeparare nauta mundo naufrago,
quem sacer cruor perunxit fusus agni corpore.

Thou alone wast counted worthy
This world's ransom to sustain
That a shipwrecked race for ever
Might a port of refuge gain,
With the sacred Blood anointed
Of the Lamb for sinners slain.

14. *Sermon of St. John Chrysostom*

Sermons, whether delivered during a liturgical service or on some special occasion, constituted an important part of patristic literature. Virtually all of the great Greek and Latin fathers left to posterity sermons which are still prized. The following selection is part of a homily by St. John Chrysostom, the "golden-mouthed" (347–407), one of the most distinguished of the Greek fathers and one of the greatest preachers of the patristic age. While he was at Antioch, before he became bishop of Constantinople, he preached a famous series of sermons, *On the Statues*. These were occasioned by the violence of the city crowd protesting a threatened new tax. Statues of the emperor Theodosius and his wife were tumbled over, and afterwards the people were in great fear of governmental retribution. Eventually, the matter was settled peaceably. Chrysostom's reference to Lent in this sermon is important as indicating the development of this religious observation of the time preceding the great feast of Easter, a practice which had grown up during the fourth century. The translation is by W. R. W. Stephens, *The Works of St. John Chrysostom*, The Nicene and Post-Nicene Fathers, vol. IX (New York, 1889), pp. 471–72, 476, 481.

(From Homily XX) . . . At length the season is verging towards the end of the Fast, and therefore we ought the more earnestly to devote ourselves to holiness. For as in the case of those who run a race, all their circuits will be of no avail if they miss the prize; so neither will any advantage result from these manifold labours and toils with regard to the fast, if we are not able to enjoy the sacred Table with a good conscience. For this end are fasting and Lent appointed, and so many days of solemn assemblies, auditories, prayers, and teachings, in order that by this earnestness being cleansed in every possible way from the sins which we had contracted during the whole year, we may with spiritual boldness religiously partake of that unbloody Sacrifice; so that should this not be the result, we shall have sustained so much labour entirely in vain, and without any profit. Let every one, therefore, consider with himself what defect he hath corrected, what good work he hath attained to; what sin he hath cast off, what stain he hath purged away; in what respect he has become better. And should he discover that in this good traffic he has made any gain by the fast, and be conscious in himself of much care taken of his wounds, let him draw near! But if he hath remained negligent, having nothing to shew but mere fasting, and hath done nothing which is right besides, let him remain outside;[1] and then let him enter, when he hath purged out all these offences. Let no one rest on the fast merely; whilst continuing unreformed in evil practices. For it is probable, that he who omits fasting may obtain pardon, having infirmity of body to plead; but it is impossible that he can have an excuse who hath not amended his faults. Thou hast not fasted, it may be, on account of bodily weakness. Tell me for what reason thou art not reconciled to thine enemies? Hast thou, indeed, here to allege bodily infirmity? Again; if thou retainest envy and hatred, what apology hast thou then I ask? For no one in offences of this kind is able to take refuge in the plea of bodily infirmity. And this was a work of Christ's love toward man, viz. that the chief of the precepts, and those which maintain our life, should not be impaired in any degree through the weakness of the body.

But since we need to practise all the divine laws alike, and more especially that which bids us consider no man as an enemy, nor retain resentment long, but forthwith to be reconciled; suffer us today to discourse to you concerning this commandment. For as it is not to be imagined that the fornicator and the blasphemer can partake of the sacred Table, so it is impossible that he who hath an enemy, and bears malice, can enjoy the Holy Communion. And this with good reason. For a man when he has committed fornication, or adultery, at the same time that he hath accomplished his lust, hath also completed the sin; and should be willing by watchful living to recover from that fall, he may afterwards, by manifesting great penitence, obtain some relief. But he who is resentful worketh the same iniquity every day, and never brings it to an end. In the former case the deed is over, and the sin completed; but here the sin is perpetrated every day. What excuse can we then have, I ask, for delivering ourselves willingly to such an evil monster? How canst thou ask thy Lord to be mild and merciful to thee,

1. i.e., with the lowest order of penitents on the porch.

when thou hast been so hard and unforgiving to thy fellow-servant? . . .

Lo! I forewarn, and testify, and proclaim this with a voice that all may hear! "Let no one who hath an enemy draw near the sacred Table, or receive the Lord's Body! Let no one who draws near have an enemy! Hast thou an enemy! Draw not near! Wilt thou draw near? Be reconciled, and then draw near, and touch the Holy Thing!" Nor, indeed, is this my declaration. Rather it is that of the Lord Himself, Who was crucified for us. That He might reconcile thee to the Father, He refused not to be sacrificed, and to shed His blood! And art thou unwilling to utter a word, or make the first advance, that thou mayest be reconciled to thy fellow-servant? Hear what the Lord saith, concerning those who are in this disposition; "If thou bring thy gift to the altar, and there rememberest that thy brother hath aught against thee"—He does not say, "wait for him to come to thee," nor "speak with another as mediator," nor "entreat some other," but "do thou thyself make the advance toward him," For the exhortation is, "Go thy way, first be reconciled to thy brother (Matt. 5:23, 24)" O transcendent wonder! Does He Himself account it no dishonor, that the gift should be left unoffered, and dost thou think it a mark of disgrace to go first and be reconciled? And how can such a case, I ask, be deemed worthy of pardon? Were you to see a member of yours cut off, would you not use every exertion so that it might be reunited to the body? This do with regard to thy brethren; when thou seest them cut off from thy friendship, make all haste to recover them! Do not wait for them to make the first advance, but press onward, that thou mayest be foremost to receive the prize. . . .

Being mindful then of all these things, be urgent with all, for the speedy fulfilment of this precept. And tell me not, that you will do this by little and little; nor put it off till the morrow, for this to-morrow never finds an end. Forty days have already passed away. Should the Holy Easter pass away, I will thenceforward pardon no one, nor employ further admonition, but a commanding authority, and severity not to be despised. For this apology drawn from custom is of no force. Why may not the thief as well plead custom, and get free from punishment? Why may not the murderer and adulterer? Therefore I protest, and give warning to all, that if, when I have met you in private, and put the matter to the proof (and I will certainly put it to the proof), I detect any who have not corrected this vice, I will inflict punishment upon them, by ordering them to be excluded from the Holy Mysteries; not that they may remain always shut out, but that having reformed themselves, they may thus enter in, and with a pure conscience enjoy the Holy Table; for this is to be a partaker of the Communion! God grant that through the prayers of those who preside over us, as well as of all the saints, having corrected these and all other deficiencies, we may obtain the kingdom of heaven through the grace and loving kindness of our Lord Jesus Christ, with Whom to the Father, together with the Holy Spirit, be glory, honour, and adoration, now and ever, world without end. Amen.

The Respublica Christiana

15. St. Augustine, The City of God

St. Augustine of Hippo (354–430), the greatest of all the Latin fathers, was the son of a devout Christian mother, St. Monica, and a pagan father. Augustine passed from a nominal Christianity in his early days into a young manhood somewhat dissolute and wayward, but ever marked by an unremitting search for the meaning of existence. He was profoundly puzzled by the problem of evil, and for a time he adhered to the sect of Manichaeans. Through the study of Plato he obtained a deeper insight into the meaning of incorporeal reality. And Platonism, or Neoplatonism, remained a significant influence in his thinking. For a while he taught rhetoric at Milan. Finally, as he relates in his *Confessions*, a remarkable spiritual autobiography, the prayers of his mother were answered. Much influenced by St. Paul, and assisted by Ambrose of Milan, he regained his faith.

Shortly afterward (395), Augustine was made bishop of Hippo in North Africa. There the religious controversies into which he was plunged, together with his own amazing energy, produced an extraordinary flow of letters, sermons, and treatises. Although he did not know Greek, Augustine was a student of Greek philosophy, aware of its weaknesses as well as of its strength. He was, in fact, a philosopher in his own right; and he gave to Christian theology the stamp of his own genius. Augustine lived to see the Vandal invasions of Africa and died during the siege of Hippo.

At the age of fifty-nine Augustine undertook a task on which he spent most of the remaining years of his life and which he perhaps considered his most important work. The immediate occasion was the sack of Rome by the Visigoths under Alaric in 410. One Marcellinus, a Roman functionary and friend of Augustine, was troubled by the charge of pagans that the abandonment of Rome's ancient gods had been the cause of the disaster. The celebrated treatise, the *City of God*, which is Augustine's answer to this charge, is a long, diffuse, and occasionally confusing work. It is, however, much more than an answer to a specific charge concerning a single event of history. Rather, it represents the reflections of a Christian philosopher, theologian, and historian on the meaning of life, of time, and eternity. Thus, although the first ten books comprise a lengthy discussion of Roman history and pagan religion, their good as well as bad aspects, it is with Book XI that he begins his analysis of the two cities, or societies—that of God and that of man, the former inhabited by those destined for eternal life in heaven, the latter by those whose vision is limited to the things of time. On earth and in time the two societies are intermingled; ultimately their respective destinies diverge.

Generations of scholars have pondered Augustine's great work. In the early Middle Ages it contributed notably to the growth of the concept of the *respublica christiana*, still, as Augustine held, wayfaring on earth, but becoming increasingly identified with existing Christian society. However interpreted, the *City of God* is one of the classics of Christian literature. The following selections are taken principally from Parts III, IV, and V, *The Origin, the Development, and the End of the Two Cities*. The translation is by Gerald Walsh, S. J., Grace Monahan, O.S.U., and Daniel Honan, S.T.L., Fathers of the Church (Washington, D.C., 1952 ff.), vol. XIV, pp. 187–420 *passim;* vol. XXIV, 210–511 *passim.* Reprinted by permission of the Catholic University of America Press.

Book Eleven

CHAPTER I

The expression, 'City of God,' which I have been using is justified by that Scripture whose divine authority puts it above the literature of all other people and brings under its sway every type of human genius—and that, not by some casual intellectual reaction, but by a disposition of Divine Providence. For, in this Scripture, we read: 'Glorious things are said of thee, O city of God' (Ps. 86:3); and, in another psalm: 'Great is the Lord, and exceedingly to be praised in the city of our God, in His holy mountain, increasing the joy of the whole earth'; and, a little later in the same psalm: 'As we have heard, so have we seen, in the city of the Lord of hosts, in the city of our God: God hath founded it for ever' (Ps. 47:1–2, 9), and in another text: 'The stream of the river maketh the city of God joyful: the most High hath sanctified his own tabernacle. God is the midst thereof, it shall not be moved.'

Through these and similar passages too numerous to quote, we learn of the existence of a City of God whose Founder has inspired us with a love and longing to become its citizens. The inhabitants of the earthly city who prefer their own gods to the Founder of the holy City do not realize that He is the God of gods—though not, of course, of those false, wicked and proud gods who, because they have been deprived of that unchangeable light which was meant for all, are reduced to a pitiful power and, therefore, are eager for some sort of influence and demand divine honors from their deluded subjects. He is the God of those reverent and holy gods who prefer to obey and worship one God rather than to have many others obeying and worshiping them.

In the ten proceding Books, I have done my best, with the help of our Lord and King, to refute the enemies of this City. Now, however, realizing what is expected of me and recalling what I promised, I shall begin to discuss, as well as I can, the origin, history, and destiny of the respective cities, earthly and heavenly, which, as I have said, are at present inextricably intermingled, one with the other. . . .

Book Fourteen

CHAPTER I

I have already said, in previous Books, that God had two purposes in deriving all men from one man. His first purpose was to give unity to the human race by the likeness of nature. His second purpose was to bind mankind by the bond of peace, through blood relationship, into one harmonious whole. I have said further that no member of this race would ever have died had not the first two—one created from nothing and the second from the first—merited this death by disobedience. The sin which they committed was so great that it impaired all human nature—in this sense, that the nature has been transmitted to posterity with a propensity to sin and a necessity to die. Moreover, the kingdom of death so dominated men that all would have been hurled, by a just punishment, into a second and endless death had not some been saved from this by the gratuitous grace of God. This is the reason why, for all the difference of the many and very great nations throughout the world in religion and morals, language, weapons, and dress, there exist no more than the two kinds of society, which, according to our Scriptures, we have rightly called the two cities. One city is that of men who live according to the flesh. The other is of men who live according to the spirit. Each of them chooses its own kind of peace and, when they attain what they desire, each lives in the peace of its own choosing. . . .

CHAPTER 28

What we see, then, is that two societies have issued from two kinds of love. Worldly society has flowered from a selfish love which dared to despise even God, whereas the communion of saints is rooted in a love of God that is ready to trample on self. In a word, this latter relies on the Lord, whereas the other boasts that it can get along by itself. The city of man seeks the praise of men, whereas the height of glory for the other is to hear God in the witness of conscience. The one lifts up its head in its own boasting; the other says to God: 'Thou art my glory, thou liftest up my head.' (Ps.3:4)

In the city of the world both the rulers themselves and the people they dominate are dominated by the lust for domination; whereas in the City of God all citizens serve one another in charity, whether they serve by the responsibilities of office or by the duties of obedience. The one city loves its leaders as symbols of its own strength; the other says to its God: 'I love thee, O Lord, my strength.' (Ps. 17:2) Hence, even the wise men in the city of man live according to man, and their only goal has been the goods of their bodies or of the mind or of both; though some of them have reached a knowledge of God, 'they did not glorify him as God or give thanks but became vain in their reasonings, and their senseless minds have been darkened. For while professing to be wise' (that is to say, while glorying in their own wisdom, under the domination of pride), 'they have become fools, and they have changed the glory of the incorruptible God for an image made like to corruptible man and to birds and four-footed beasts and creeping things' (meaning that they either led their people, or imitated them, in adoring idols shaped like these things), 'and they worshiped and served the creature rather than the Creator who is blessed forever.' (Rom. 1:21–23) In the City of God, on the contrary, there is no merely human wisdom, but there is a piety which worships the true God as He should be worshiped and has as its goal that reward of all holiness whether in the society of saints on earth or in that of angels of heaven, which is 'that God may be all in all.' (I Cor. 15:28)

Book Fifteen

CHAPTER 1

. . . In regard to mankind I have made a division. On the one side are those who live according to man; on the other, those who live according to God. And I have said that, in a deeper sense, we may speak of two cities or two human societies, the destiny of the one being an eternal kingdom under God while the doom of the other is eternal punishment along with the Devil.

Of the final consummation of the two cities I shall have to speak later. Of their original cause among the angels whose number no man knows and then in the first two human beings, I have already spoken. For the moment, therefore, I must deal with the course of the history of the two cities from the time when children were born to the first couple until the day when men shall beget no more. By the course of their history, as distinguished from their original cause and final consummation, I mean the whole time of world history in which men are born and take the place of those who die and depart.

Now, the first man born of the two parents of the human race was Cain. He belonged to the city of man. The next born was Abel, and he was of the City of God. Notice here a parallel between the individual man and the whole race. We all experience as individuals what the Apostle says: 'It is not the spiritual that comes first, but the physical, and then the spiritual.' (I Cor. 15:46) The fact is that every individual springs from a condemned stock and, because of Adam, must be first cankered and carnal, only later to become sound and spiritual by the process of rebirth in Christ. So, too, with the human race as a whole, as soon as human birth and death began the historical course of the two cities, the first to be born was a citizen of this world and only later came the one who was an alien in the city of men but at home in the City of God, a man predestined by grace and elected by grace. By grace an alien on earth, by grace he was a citizen of heaven. In and of himself, he springs from the common clay, all of which was under condemnation from the beginning, but which God held in His hands like a potter, to borrow the metaphor which the Apostle so wisely and deliberately uses. For, God could make 'from the same mass one vessel for honorable, another for ignoble use.' (Rom. 9:21) The first vessel to be made was 'for ignoble use.' Only later was there made a vessel for honorable use. And as with the race, so, as I have said, with the individual. First comes the clay that is only fit to be thrown away, with which we must begin, but in which we need not remain. Afterwards comes what is fit for use, that into which we can be gradually molded and in which, when molded, we may remain. This does not mean that every one who is wicked is to become good, but that no one becomes good who was not once wicked. What is true is that the sooner a man makes a change in himself for the better the sooner he has a right to be called what he has become. The second name hides the first.

Now, it is recorded of Cain that he built a city (Gen. 4:17), while Abel, as though he were merely a pilgrim on earth, built none. For, the true City of the saints is in heaven, though here on earth it produces citizens in whom it wanders as on a pilgrimage through time looking for the Kingdom of eternity. When that day comes it will gather together all those who, rising in their bodies, shall have that Kingdom given to them in which, along with their Prince, the King of Eternity, they shall reign for ever and ever.

CHAPTER 2

A shadow, as it were, of this eternal City has been cast on earth, a prophetic representation of something to come rather than a real presentation in time. Yet this shadow, merely symbolic as it is and not the reality that is to be, is properly called the holy City. It was of these two cities, the one, as it were, in bondage to symbolic purpose and the other free, that the Apostle writes in the Epistle to the Galatians: 'Tell me, you who desire to be under the Law, have you not read the Law? For it is written that Abraham had two sons, the one by a slave-girl and the other by a free woman. And the son of the slave-girl was born according to the flesh, but the son of the free woman in virtue of the promise. This is said by way of allegory. For these are the two convenants: one indeed from Mount Sinai, bringing forth children unto bondage, which is Agar. For Sinai is a mountain in Arabia, which corresponds to the present Jerusalem, and is in slavery with her children. But that Jerusalem which is above is free, which is our mother. For it is written, "Rejoice thou barren, that dost not bear; break forth and cry, thou that dost not travail; For many are the children of the desolate, more than of her that has a husband." Now we, brethren, are the children of promise, as Isaac was. But as then he who was born according to the flesh persecuted him who was born according to the spirit, so also it is now. But what does the Scripture say? "Cast out the slave-girl and her son, for the son of the slave-girl shall not be heir with the son of the free woman." Therefore, brethren, we are not children of a slave-girl, but of the free woman—in virtue of the freedom wherewith Christ has made us free.' (I Gal. 4:21–31)

This exegesis, which comes to us with apostolic authority, opens up for us a way to understand much that is written in both Testaments, the Old and the New. We see that one portion of the world community became a symbol of the heavenly City and was 'in bondage' in the sense that its significance was not in itself but in serving to signify the other city. It was, in fact, founded, not for its own sake, but as the shadow of another substance, a shadow that was itself foreshadowed by a previous symbol. For, the symbol of this shadow was Sara's handmaid, Agar, with her son. It was because shadows were to cease when the light came that the free woman, Sara, symbol of the free City (to which, in turn, the shadow served as another kind of prelude), uttered the words: 'Cast out this slave-girl with her son; for the son of this slave-girl shall not be heir with my son Isaac' (Gen. 21:10), or, to use the Apostle's expression, 'with the son of the free woman.'

In the world community, then, we find two forms, one being the visible appearance of the earthly city (Gal. 4:30) and another whose presence serves as a shadow of the heavenly City.

Notice that it is nature, flawed by sin, that begets all the citizens in the world community, whereas nothing but grace, which frees nature from sinfulness, can bring forth citizens of the heavenly

City. The former are called 'vessels of wrath'; the latter, 'vessels of mercy.' (Rom. 9:22–23) This distinction was symbolized in the two sons of Abraham. One, Ismael, was born of the slave-girl whose name was Agar and he was born according to the flesh. The other, Isaac, was born of the free woman, Sara, according to the promise. Of course, both were sons of Abraham, but he begot the one by a law suggesting the order of nature, while the other was born in virtue of a promise which pointed to the order of grace. What is clear in the one case is human action; in the other, divine favor. . . .

CHAPTER 4

As for the city of this world, it is neither to last forever nor even to be a city, once the final doom of pain is upon it. Nevertheless, while history lasts, it has a finality of its own; it reaches such happiness by sharing a common good as is possible when there are no goods but the things of time to afford it happiness. This is not the kind of good that can give those who are content with it any freedom from fear. In fact, the city of man, for the most part, is a city of contention with opinions divided by foreign wars and domestic quarrels and by the demands for victories which either end in death or are merely momentary respites from further war. The reason is that whatever part of the city of the world raises the standard of war, it seeks to be lord of the world, when, in fact, it is enthralled in its own wickedness. Even when it conquers, its victory can be mortally poisoned by pride, and if, instead of taking pride in the success already achieved, it takes account of the nature and normal vicissitudes of life and is afraid of future failure, then the victory is merely momentary. The fact is that the power to reach domination by war is not the same as the power to remain in perpetual control.

Nevertheless, it is wrong to deny that the aims of human civilization are good, for this is the highest end that mankind of itself can achieve. For, however lowly the goods of earth, the aim, such as it is, is peace. The purpose even of war is peace. For, where victory is not followed by resistance there is a peace that was impossible so long as rivals were competing, hungrily and unhappily, for something material too little to suffice for both. This kind of peace is a product of the work of war, and its price is a so-called glorious victory; when victory goes to the side that had a juster cause it is surely a matter for human rejoicing, and the peace is one to be welcomed.

The things of earth are not merely good; they are undoubtedly gifts from God. But, of course, if those who get such goods in the city of men are reckless about the better goods of the City of God, in which there is to be the ultimate victory of an eternal, supreme, and untroubled peace, if men so love the goods of earth as to believe that these are the only goods or if they love them more than the goods they know to be better, then the consequence is inevitable: misery and more misery.

Book Nineteen

CHAPTER 10

. . . On earth we are happy, after a fashion, when we enjoy the peace, little as it is, which a good life brings; but such happiness compared with the beatitude which is our end in eternity is, in point of fact, misery. When we mortal men, living amid the realities of earth, enjoy the utmost peace which life can give us, then it is the part of virtue, if we are living rightly, to make a right use of the goods we are enjoying. When, on the other hand, we do not enjoy this temporal peace, then it is the function of virtue to make a right use of the misfortunes which we are suffering. By genuine Christian virtue we mean here that we refer not only all good things which are being rightly used, and all the right use we are making of blessings and misfortunes, but our very virtue itself to that End in which there will be a peace so good that no peace could be better, a peace so great that a greater would be impossible.

CHAPTER 11

Thus, we may say of peace what we have said of eternal life—that it is our highest good; more particularly because the holy Psalmist was addressing the City of God (the nature of which I am trying, with so much difficulty, to make clear) when he said: 'Praise the Lord, O Jerusalem; praise thy God, O Sion. Because he hath strengthened the bolts of thy gates, he hath blessed they children within thee. He hath placed peace in thy borders.' (Ps. 146:12-14) For, when the bolts of that city's gates will have been strengthened, none will enter in and none will issue forth. Hence, its borders [*fines*] must be taken to mean that peace which I am trying to show is our final good. Note, too, that Jerusalem, the mystical name which symbolizes this City, means, as I have already mentioned, 'the vision of peace.'

However, the word 'peace' is so often applied to conditions here on earth, where life is not eternal, that it is better, I think, to speak of 'eternal life' rather than of 'peace' as the end or supreme good of the City of God. It is in this sense that St. Paul says: 'But now being made free from sin, and become servants of God, you have your fruit unto sanctification, and the end life everlasting' (Rom. 6:22) . . .

<h2 align="center">CHAPTER 13</h2>

The peace, then, of the body lies in the ordered equilibrium of all its parts; the peace of the irrational soul, in the balanced adjustment of its appetites; the peace of the reasoning soul, in the harmonious correspondence of conduct and conviction; the peace of body and soul taken together, in the well-ordered life and health of the living whole. Peace between a mortal man and his Maker consists in ordered obedience, guided by faith, under God's eternal law; peace between man and man consists in regulated fellowship. The peace of a home lies in the ordered harmony of authority and obedience between the members of a family living together. The peace of the political community is an ordered harmony of authority and obedience between citizens. The peace of the heavenly City lies in a perfectly ordered and harmonious communion of those who find their joy in God and in one another in God. Peace, in its final sense, is the calm that comes of order. Order is an arrangement of life and unlike things whereby each of them is disposed in its proper place. . . .

God, the wise Creator and just Ordainer of all natures, has made the mortal race of man the loveliest of all lovely things on earth. He has given to men good gifts suited to their existence here below. Among these is temporal peace, according to the poor limits of mortal life, in health, security, and human fellowship; and other gifts, too, needed to preserve this peace or regain it, once lost—for instance, the blessings that lie all around us, so perfectly adapted to our senses: daylight, speech, air to breathe, water to drink, everything that goes to feed, clothe, cure, and beautify the body. These good gifts are granted, however, with the prefectly just understanding that whoever uses the goods which are meant for the mortal peace of mortal men, as these goods should be used, will receive more abundant and better goods—nothing less than immortal peace and all that goes with it, namely, the glory and honor of enjoying God and one's neighbor in God everlastingly; but that whoever misuses his gifts on earth will both lose what he has and never receive the better gifts of heaven.

Chapter 14

In the earthly city, then, temporal goods are to be used with a view to the enjoyment of earthly peace, whereas, in the heavenly City, they are used with a view to the enjoyment of eternal peace. Hence, if we were merely unthinking brutes, we would pursue nothing beyond the orderly interrelationship of our bodily part and the appeasing of our appetites, nothing, that is, beyond the comfort of the flesh and plenty of pleasures, so that the peace of body might contribute to peace of the soul. For, if order in the body be lacking, the peace of an irrational soul is checked, since it cannot attain the satisfaction of its appetites. Both of these forms of peace meanwhile subserve that other form of peace which the body and soul enjoy between them, the peace of life and health in good order. . . .

Chapter 17

While the homes of unbelieving men are intent upon acquiring temporal peace out of the possessions and comforts of this temporal life, the families which live according to faith look ahead to the good things of heaven promised as imperishable, and use material and temporal goods in the spirit of pilgrims, not as snares or obstructions to block their way to God, but simply as helps to ease and never to increase the burdens of this corruptible body which weighs down the soul. Both types of homes and their masters have this in common, that they must use things essential to this mortal life. But the respective purposes to which they put them are characteristic and very different.

So, too, the earthly city which does not live by faith seeks only an earthly peace, and limits the goal of its peace, of its harmony of authority and obedience among its citizens, to the voluntary and collective attainment of objectives necessary to mortal existence. The heavenly City, meanwhile—or, rather, that part that is on pilgrimage in mortal life and lives by faith—must use this earthly peace until such time as our mortality which need such peace has passed away. As a consequence, so long as her life in the earthly city is that of a captive and an alien (although she has the promise of ultimate delivery and the gift of the Spirit as a pledge), she has no hesitation about keeping in step with the civil law which governs matters pertaining to our existence here below. For, as mortal life is the same for all, there ought to be common cause between the two cities in what concerns our purely human living. . . .

Chapter 27

The City of God, however, has a peace of its own, namely, peace with God in this world by faith and in the world to come by vision. Still, any peace we have on earth, whether the peace we share with Babylon or our own peace through faith, is more like a solace for unhappiness than the joy of beatitude. Even our virtue in this life, genuine as it is because it is referred to the true goal of every good, lies more in the pardoning of sins than in any perfection of virtues. Witness the prayer of God's whole City, wandering on earth and calling out to Him through all her members: 'Forgive us our debts as we also forgive our debtors.' (Matt. 6:12)

This prayer is effective, not on the lips of those whose faith without works is dead (cf. James 2:17), but only on the lips of men whose faith works through charity (cf. Gal. 5:6). This prayer is necessary for the just because their reason, though submissive to God, has only imperfect mastery over their evil inclinations so long as they live in this world and in a corruptible body that 'is a load upon the soul.' (Wis. 9:15) Reason may give commands, but can exercise no control without a struggle. And, in this time of weakness, something will inevitably creep in to make the best of soldiers—whether in victory or still in battle with such foes—offend by some small slip of the tongue, some passing thought, if not by habitual actions. This explains why we can know no perfect peace so long as there are evil inclinations to master. Those which put up a fight are put down only in perilous conflict; those that are already overcome cannot be kept so if one relaxes, but only at the cost of vigilant control. These are the battles which Scripture sums up in the single phrase: 'The life of man upon earth is a warfare.' (Job 7:1)

Who, then, save a proud man, will presume that he can live without needing to ask God: 'Forgive us our debts'? Not a great man, you may be sure, but one blown up with the wind of self-reliance—one whom God in His justice resists while He grants His grace to the humble. Hence, it is written: 'God resists the proud, but gives grace to the humble.' (James 4:6; I Peter 5:5)

This, then, in this world, is the life of virtue. When God commands, man obeys; when the soul commands, the body obeys; when reason rules, our passions, even when they fight back, must be conquered or resisted; man must beg God's grace to win merit and the remission of his sins and must thank God for the blessings he receives.

But, in that final peace which is the end and purpose of all virtue here on earth, our nature, made whole by immortality and incorruption, will have no vices and experience no rebellion from within or without. There will be no need for reason to govern non-existent evil inclinations. God will hold sway over man, the soul over the body; and the happiness in eternal life and law will make obedience sweet and easy. And in each and all of us this condition will be everlasting, and we shall know it to be so. That is why the peace of such blessedness or the blessedness of such peace is to be our supreme good.

CHAPTER 28

On the other hand, the doom in store for those who are not of the City of God is an unending wretchedness that is called 'the second death,' because neither the soul, cut off from the life of God, nor the body, pounded by perpetual pain, can there be said to live at all. And what will make that second death so hard to bear is that there will be no death to end it.

Now, since unhappiness is the reverse of happiness, death of life, and war of peace, one may reasonably ask: If peace is praised and proclaimed as the highest good, what kind of warfare are we to think of as the highest evil? If this inquirer will reflect, he will realize that what is hurtful and destructive in warfare is mutual clash and conflict, and, hence, that no one can imagine a war more unbearably bitter than one in which the will and passions are at such odds that neither can ever win the victory, and in which violent pain and the body's very nature will so clash that neither will ever yield. When this conflict occurs on earth, either pain wins and death puts an end to all feeling, or nature wins and health removes the pain. But, in hell, pain permanently afflicts and nature continues to feel it, for neither ever comes to term, since the punishment must never end.

However, it is through the last judgment that good men achieve that highest good (which all should seek) and evil men that highest evil (which all should shun). . . .

Book Twenty-Two

CHAPTER 1

As I mentioned in the preceding Book, the present one is to be the last of the whole work, and is to deal with the eternal blessedness of the City of God. The word 'eternal' as here used means more than any period, however long, of centuries upon centuries which, ultimately, must have an end. It means 'everlasting' in the sense of the text which runs: 'Of his kingdom there shall be no end.' (Luke 1:33) It does not mean the kind of apparent perpetuity produced by successive generations which come and go by births and deaths. Such a perpetuity is merely perennial like the color of an evergreen that seems to continue forever because the new leaves, sprouting while the old ones wither and fall, maintain an unchanging density of foliage. On the contrary, in the eternal City of God, each and all of the citizens are personally immortal with an immortality which the holy angels never lost and which even human beings can come to share. This is to be achieved by the supreme omnipotence of the Creator, the Founder of the City. It is a realization which God, who cannot but keep His Word, has promised, and He has given abundant pledges of its fulfillment in the promises which He has already kept and in the uncovenanted blessings which He has already bestowed. . . .

CHAPTER 30

Who can measure the happiness of heaven, where no evil at all can touch us, no good will be out of reach; where life is to be one long laud extolling God, who will be all in all; where there will be no weariness to call for rest, no need to call for toil, no place for any energy but praise. Of this I am assured whenever I read or hear the sacred song: 'Blessed are they that dwell in thy house, O Lord: they shall praise thee forever and ever.' (Ps. 38:5) Every fiber and organ of our imperishable body will play its part in the praising of God. On earth these varied organs have each a special function, but, in heaven, function will be swallowed up in felicity, in the perfect certainty of an untroubled everlastingness of joy. Even those muted notes in the diapason of the human organ, which I mentioned earlier, will swell into a great hymn of praise to the supreme Artist who has fashioned us, within and without, in every fiber, and who, by this and every other element of a magnificent and marvelous Order, will ravish our minds with spiritual beauty.

These movements of our bodies will be of such unimaginable beauty that I dare not say more than this: There will be such poise, such grace, such beauty as become a place where nothing unbecoming can be found. Wherever the spirit wills, there, in a flash, will the body be. Nor will the spirit ever will anything unbecoming either to itself or to the body.

In heaven, all glory will be true glory, since no one could ever err in praising too little or too much. True honor will never be denied where due, never be given where undeserved, and, since none but the worthy are permitted there, no one will unworthily ambition glory. Perfect peace will reign, since nothing in ourselves or in any others could disturb this peace. The promised reward of virtue will be the best and the greatest of all possible prizes—the very Giver of virtue Himself, for that is what the Prophet meant: 'I will be your God and you shall be my people.' (Lev. 26:12) God will be the source of every satisfaction, more than any heart can rightly crave, more than life and health, food and wealth, glory and honor, peace and every good—so that God, as St. Paul said, 'may be all in all.' (I Cor. 15:28) He will be the consummation of all our desiring—the object of our unending vision, of our un-lessening love, of our unwearying praise. And in this gift of vision, this response of love, this paean of praise, all alike will share, as all will share in everlasting life.

But, now, who can imagine, let alone describe, the ranks upon ranks of rewarded saints, to be graded, undoubtedly, according to their variously merited honor and glory. Yet, there will be no envy of the lower for the higher, as there is no envy of angel for archangel—for this is one of the great blessednesses of this blessed City. The less rewarded will be linked in perfect peace with the more highly favored, but lower could not more long for higher than a finger, in the ordered integration of a body, could want to be an eye. The less endowed will have the high endowment of longing for nothing loftier than their lower gifts.

The souls in bliss will still possess the freedom of will, though sin will have no power to tempt them. They will be more free than ever—so free, in fact, from all delight in sinning as to find, in not sinning, an unfailing source of joy. By the freedom which was given to the first man, who was constituted in rectitude, he could choose either to sin or not to sin; in eternity, freedom is that more potent freedom which makes all sin impossible. Such freedom, of course, is a gift of God, beyond the power of nature to achieve. For, it is one thing to be God, another to be a sharer in the divine nature. God, by His nature, cannot sin, but a mere sharer in His nature must receive from God such immunity from sin. It was proper that, in the process of divine endowment, the first step should be a freedom not to sin, and the last a freedom even from the power to sin. The first gift made merit possible; the second is a part of man's reward. Our nature, when it was free to sin, did sin. It took a greater grace to lead us to that larger liberty which frees us from the very power to sin. Just as the immortality that Adam lost by his sin was, at first, a mere possibility of avoiding death, but, in heaven, becomes the impossibility of death, so free will was, at first, a mere possibility of avoiding sin, but, in heaven, becomes an utter inability to sin.

Our will will be as ineradicably rooted in rectitude and love as in beatitude. It is true that, with Adam's sin, we lost our right to grace and glory, but, with our right, we did not lose our longing to be happy. And, as for freedom, can we think that God Himself, who certainly cannot sin, is therefore without freedom? The conclusion is that, in the everlasting City, there will remain in each and all of us an inalienable freedom of the will, emancipating us from every evil and filling us with every good, rejoicing in the inexhaustible beatitude of everlasting happiness, unclouded by the memory of any sin or of sanction suffered, yet with no forgetfulness of our redemption nor any loss of gratitude for our Redeemer.

The memory of our previous miseries will be a matter of purely mental contemplation, with no renewal of any feelings connected with these experiences—much as learned doctors know by science many of those bodily maladies which, by suffering, they have no sensible experience. All ills, in fact, can be forgotten in the double way in which we learn them, namely, notionally and experientially. It is one thing to be a philosopher, learning by ethical analysis the nature of each and every vice, and another to be a scoundrel, learning his lessons from a dissolute life. So, too, the student who becomes a doctor forgets in a way different from that of a patient who has suffered disease. The one forgets by giving up his practice; the patient, by being freed from pains. Now, it is into this second kind of oblivion that the previous miseries of the saints will fall, for not a trace of any sensible experience of suffering will remain.

However, in virtue of the vigor of their minds, they will have not merely a notional remembrance of their own past but also a knowledge of the unending torments of the damned. For, if they had no kind of memory of past miseries, how could the Psalmist have said: 'The mercies of the Lord they will sing forever'? (cf. Ps. 88:2). And, surely, in all that City, nothing will be lovelier than this song in praise of the grace of Christ by whose Blood all there were saved.

Heaven, too, will be the fulfillment of that Sabbath rest foretold in the command: 'Be still and see that I am God.' (Ps. 45:11) This, indeed, will be that ultimate Sabbath that has no evening and which the Lord foreshadowed in the account of His creation: 'And God rested on the seventh day from all his work which he had done. And he blessed the seventh day and sanctified it: because in it he had rested from all his work which God created and made.' (Gen. 2:23) And we ourselves will be a 'seventh day' when we shall be filled with His blessing and remade by His sanctification. In the stillness of that rest we shall see that He is the God whose divinity we ambitioned for ourselves when we listened to the seducer's words, 'You shall be as Gods,' (Gen. 3:5), and so fell away from Him, the true God who would have given us a divinity by participation that could never be gained by desertion. For, where did the doing without God end but in the undoing of man through the anger of God?

Only when we are remade by God and perfected by a greater grace shall we have the eternal stillness of that rest in which we shall see that He is God. Then only shall we be filled with Him when He will be all in all. For, although our good works are, in reality, His, they will be put to our account as payment for this Sabbath peace, so long as we do not claim them as our own; but, if we do, they will be reckoned as servile and out of place on the Sabbath, as the text reminds us: 'The seventh day . . . is the rest of the Lord. . . . Thou shalt not do any work therein.' (Deut. 5:14) In this connection, too, God has reminded us, through the Prophet Ezechiel: 'I gave them my sabbaths, to be a sign between me and them, that they might know that I am the Lord that sanctifies them.' (Ezek. 20:12) It is this truth that we shall realize perfectly when we shall be perfectly at rest and shall perfectly see that it is He who is God.

There is a clear indication of this final Sabbath if we take the seven ages of world history as being 'days' and calculate in accordance with the data furnished by the Scriptures. The first age or day is that from Adam to the flood; the second, from the flood to Abraham. (These two 'days' were not identical in length of time, but in each there were ten generations.) Then follow the three ages, each consisting of fourteen generations, as recorded in the Gospel of St. Matthew: the first, from Abraham to David; the second, from David to the transmigration to Babylon; the third, from then to Christ's nativity in the flesh. Thus, we have five ages. The sixth is the one in which we now are. It is an age not to be measured by any precise number of generations, since we are told: 'It is not for you to know the times or dates which the Father has fixed by his own authority.' (Acts 1:7) After this 'day,' God will rest on the 'seventh day,' in the sense that God will make us, who are to be this seventh day, rest in Him.

There is no need here to speak in detail of each of these seven 'days.' Suffice it so say that this 'seventh day' will be our Sabbath and that it will end in no evening, but only in the Lord's day—that eighth and eternal day which dawned when Christ's resurrection heralded an eternal rest both for the spirit and for the body. On that day we shall rest and see, see and love, love and praise—for this is to be the end without the end of all our living, that Kingdom without end, the real goal of our present life.

I am done. With God's help, I have kept my promise. This, I think, is all that I promised to do when I began this huge work. From all who think that I have said either too little or too much, I beg pardon; and those who are satisfied I ask, not to thank me, but to join me in rejoicing and in thanking God. Amen.

Monasticism

---

16. The Rule of St. Benedict

The religious life, accompanied by renunciation and mortification, has always appealed to those especially devout souls who feel that religion demands a total dedication, and of course the ascetic life is not an exclusively Christian practice. But the fourth century witnessed an efflorescence of religious ascetism, no doubt partly because toleration removed the necessity of heroic sacrifice. Large numbers sought this kind of life in its secluded or solitary form as hermits, especially in the Egyptian desert near Alexandria. Most famous was St. Anthony, whose life became a model for others. But not all were successful, and the coenobitical or community form came to have greater appeal. The first rule for a community or monastic establishment was presumably that of Pachomius (d.c. 346), and the rule of life which won widest acceptance in the East was that of St. Basil the Great of Caesarea (329–379).

It was not long before monasticism made its appearance in the West. Various experiments were tried in Gaul, Italy, and even in faraway Ireland. But the monastic tradition which was eventually to predominate was that associated with the name of St. Benedict of Nursia, who lived in the first half of the sixth century. Like his eastern predecessor, St. Basil, Benedict had experimented with the eremitical life at Subiaco not far from Rome. Although not a scholar, he was an educated Roman and doubtless aware of the organizational achievements of the Roman popes. In fact, many have seen in his *Rule*—which was written sometime in the years 535 to 543—a "Roman" sense of order and moderation. Aware of the frailties of human nature, he directed, for example, that the entire psalter be recited in one week instead of one day as some of the eastern and less "tepid" monks were accustomed to do (cf. Chapter XVIII).

Benedict acknowledged his debt to earlier writers on the ascetic life, notably Basil and John Cassian. The latter had spent many years in the East and came to Marseilles early in the fifth century. Cassian's *Conferences*, in which he recorded his conversations with several leading abbots of the Egyptian desert, and his own treatise on monasticism, *The Institutes*, form a link between the eastern tradition and the new monasticism of the West. It is also probable, as many scholars now think, that Benedict used an earlier compilation known as the *Regula magistri* and that various sections of the *Rule* were composed at different times. At any rate, the early Benedictine years were those of the period following the destruction of Theodoric's Ostrogothic kingdom, the long wars of recovery under Justinian, and, shortly afterwards, the Lombard invasions of Italy. It was, therefore, a period of uncertainty and, above all, of the localization of all forms of political, economic, and social life. Monasticism was inevitably affected by such things. In fact, Cassinum (Montecassino), Benedict's original community in southern Italy, was destroyed in 577 and not re-established until 717.

Meanwhile, another form of monasticism had spread from Ireland into England and, under the influence of such founders as St. Columban (d. 615), to the continent. Finally, early in the ninth century, a namesake, St. Benedict of Aniane, reconstituted the *Rule*. It is largely owing to his efforts and the support of Carolingian rulers that the typical Benedictinism "of the *Rule*" came to predominate.

The chapters cited below give the principal part of the *Rule* as it applies to daily life in the monastery and the spiritual principles which are to govern such a life. The emphasis on the daily round of prayer according to a regular schedule of liturgical services or "hours" and on spiritual reading and meditation is evident throughout. Everything else is secondary. Though Benedictine monasticism did eventually influence western culture in many ways, it was not so conceived. According to St. Benedict, the monastic community was to be a self-sufficient spiritual family in which each monk persevered "until death." As he makes clear in his Prologue, the monastic life was to be a means of achieving personal sanctification, not a device to rejuvenate the world outside the monastery.

The passages are taken from the translation by Cardinal Gasquet, *The Rule of St. Benedict*, The Medieval Library (London, 1925), pp. 1–7, 11–50, 71–77, 84–88, 91–111, 123–124. Reprinted by permission of Chatto & Windus Ltd. The more familiar word "vespers" has been substituted for "evensong," and, in accordance with medieval usage, "vigils" and "matins" have been substituted for "matins" and "lauds."

The Prologue

Listen, my son, and turn the ear of thine heart to the precepts of thy Master. Receive readily, and faithfully carry out the advice of a loving Father, so that by the work of obedience you may return to Him, whom you have left by the sloth of disobedience. For thee, therefore, whosoever thou be, my words are intended, who, giving up thy own will, dost take the all-powerful and excellent arms of obedience to fight under the Lord Christ, the true King.

First, beg of Him with most earnest prayer to finish the good work begun; that He who now hath deigned to count us among His children may never be grieved by our evil deeds. For at all times we must so serve Him with the good things He has given us, that He may not, as an angry Father, disinherit His children, nor as a dread Lord, provoked by our evil deeds, deliver us to everlasting punishment as wicked servants who refuse to follow Him to glory.

Let us, therefore, arise at once, the Scripture stirring us up, saying, *It is now the hour for us to rise from sleep.* (I Rom. 13:2) And, our eyes now open to the divine light, let us with wondering ears hearken to the divine voice, daily calling to us and warning us, *To-day if you shall hear His voice, harden not your hearts* (Ps. 94:8); and again, *He that hath ears, let him hear what the Spirit saith to the Churches.* (Apoc. 2:7) And what does He say? *Come, ye children, and hearken unto Me: I will teach you the fear of the Lord.* (Ps. 33:12) *Run while ye have the light of life, that the darkness of death overtake ye not.* (John 12:35)

And our Lord, seeking His workman among the multitude of those to whom He thus speaks, says again, *Who is the man that will have life, and desireth to see good days?* (Ps. 33:13) And if thou, hearing this, reply, "I am he": God says to you, If thou desirest to possess true and everlasting life *restrain thy tongue from evil, and thy lips that they speak no guile. Decline from evil and do good; seek after peace and pursue it.* (Ps. 33:14-15) And when you have done this My eyes shall be on you, and My ears shall be open to your prayers. And before you can call upon Me, I will say to you, *Behold, I am present.* (Isa. 55:24) What can be more agreeable, dearest brethren, than this voice of our Lord inviting us? Behold how in His loving kindness He shows us the way of life!

Therefore, with our loins girt by faith, and by the practice of good works under the guidance of His Gospel, let us walk in the path He has marked out for us, that we may deserve to see Him who has called us in His kingdom. (Eph. 6:14-15)

If we would live in the shelter of this kingdom, we can reach it only by speeding on the way of good works (by this path alone is it to be attained). But let us, with the prophet, ask our Lord, and say to Him, *Lord, who shall dwell in Thy tabernacle? or who shall rest on Thy holy hill?* (Ps. 14:4) And when we have so asked, let us hear our Lord's answer, pointing out to us the way to this His dwelling, and saying, *He that walketh without spot and worketh justice: he that speaketh truth in his heart: that hath not forged*

guile with his tongue: he that hath not done evil to his neighbour,
and hath not taken up reproach against him. (Ps. 14:2–3) He that,
casting out of the inmost thoughts of his heart the suggestions of
the evil-minded devil trying to lead him astray, has brought them
all to naught: he that taking hold of his thoughts whilst in their
birth hath dashed them against the rock, which is Christ. They
who, fearing the Lord, are not lifted up by their good observance,
but knowing that all that is good in them comes not from themselves but from the Lord, extol His work in them, saying with the
prophet, *Not to us, O Lord, not to us, but to Thy Name give*
glory. (Ps. 113:1) Thus the Apostle Paul imputed nothing of his
preaching to himself, saying, *By the grace of God I am what I am.*
(I Cor. 15:10) And again he saith, *He that glorieth, let him glory*
in the Lord. (II Cor. 10:47)

Hence also our Lord in the Gospel says, *He that heareth these*
My words and doth them, I will liken him to a wise man that hath
built his house upon a rock. The floods came, the winds blew and
beat against that house, and it fell not, because it was founded upon
a rock. (Matt. 7:24f) In fulfilment whereof our Lord daily looketh
for deeds in us complying with His holy admonitions. Therefore
are the days of this our life lengthened for awhile for the mending
of our evil deeds, according to the words of the apostle, *Knowest*
thou not that the patience of God leadeth thee to repentance?
(Rom. 2:4) For our loving Lord says, *I will not the death of the*
sinner, but that he be converted and live. (Ezek. 18:23)

So questioning the Lord, brethren, we have heard on what
conditions we may dwell in His temple; and if we fulfil these we
shall be heirs of the kingdom of heaven. Therefore must our hearts
and bodies be prepared to fight under the holy obedience of His
commands, and we must beg our Lord to supply by the help of His
grace what by nature is not possible to us. And if, fleeing from the
pains of hell, we will to attain to life everlasting, we must, whilst
time yet serves and whilst we live in the flesh and the light is still on
our path, hasten to do now what will profit us for all eternity.

We are therefore now about to institute a school for the service
of God, in which we hope nothing harsh nor burdensome will be
ordained. But if we proceed in certain things with some little
severity, sound reason so advising for the amendment of vices or
the preserving of charity, do not for fear of this forthwith flee
from the way of salvation, which is always narrow in the begin-

ning. (cf. Matt. 7:13). In living our life, however, and by the growth of faith, when the heart has been enlarged, the path of God's commandments is run with unspeakable loving sweetness; so that never leaving His school, but persevering in the monastery until death in His teaching, we share by our patience in the sufferings of Christ, and so merit to be partakers of His kingdom (cf. II Cor. 1:7). . . .

Chapter II. What the Abbot Should Be

An abbot to be fit to rule a monastery should ever remember what he is called, and in his acts illustrate his high calling. For in a monastery he is considered to take the place of Christ, since he is called by His name as the apostle saith, *Ye have received the spirit of the adoption of sons, whereby we cry, Abba, Father.* (Rom. 8:15) Therefore the abbot should neither teach, ordain, nor require anything against the command of our Lord (God forbid!), but in the minds of his disciples let his orders and teaching be mingled with the leaven of divine justice. . . .

Let him make no distinction of persons in the monastery. Let not one be loved more than another, save such as be found to excel in obedience or good works. Let not the free-born be put before the serf-born in religion, unless there be other reasonable cause for it. If upon due consideration the abbot shall see such cause he may place him where he pleases; otherwise let all keep their own places, because *whether bond or free we are all one in Christ* (I Cor. 12:13), and bear an equal burden of service under one Lord: *for with God there is no accepting of persons.* (Eph. 6:9) For one thing only are we preferred by Him, if we are found better than others in good works and more humble. Let the abbot therefore have equal love for all, and let all, according to their deserts, be under the same discipline.

The abbot in his teaching should always observe that apostolic rule which saith, *Reprove, entreat, rebuke.* (II Tim. 4:2) That is to say, as occasions require he ought to mingle encouragement with reproofs. Let him manifest the sternness of a master and the loving affection of a father. He must reprove the undisciplined and restless severely, but he should exhort such as are obedient, quiet and patient, for their better profit. We charge him, however, to reprove and punish the stubborn and negligent. Let him not shut his eyes to the sins of offenders; but, directly they begin to show themselves and to grow, he must use every means to root them up utterly, remembering the fate of Heli, the priest of Silo. (I Kings 2:11–12) To the more virtuous and apprehensive, indeed, he may for the first or second time use words of warning; but in dealing with the stubborn, the hard-hearted, the proud and the disobedient, even at the very beginning of their sin, let him chastise them with stripes and with bodily punishment, knowing that it is written, *The fool is not corrected with words.* (Prov. 23:13) And again, *Strike thy son with a rod and thou shalt deliver his soul from death.* (Prov. 23:14) . . .

He should know that whoever undertakes the government of souls must prepare himself to account for them. And however great the number of the breathren under him may be, let him understand for certain that at the Day of Judgment he will have to give to our Lord an account of all their souls as well as of his own. In this way, by fearing the inquiry concerning his flock which the Shepherd will hold, he is solicitous on account of others' souls as well as of his own, and thus whilst reclaiming other men by his corrections, he frees himself also from all vice.

Chapter III. On Taking Counsel of the Brethren

Whenever any weighty matters have to be transacted in the monastery let the abbot call together all the community and himself propose the matter for discussion. After hearing the advice of the brethren let him consider it in his own mind, and then do what he shall judge most expedient. We ordain that all must be called to council, because the Lord often reveals to a younger member what is best. And let the brethren give their advice with all humble subjection, and presume not stiffly to defend their own opinion. Let them rather leave the matter to the abbot's discretion, so that all submit to what he shall deem best. As it becometh disciples to obey their master, so doth it behove the master to dispose of all things with forethought and justice.

In all things, therefore, every one shall follow the Rule as their master, and let no one rashly depart from it. In the monastery no one is to be led by the desires of his own heart, neither shall any one within or without the monastery presume to argue wantonly with his abbot. If he presume to do so let him be subjected to punishment according to the Rule.

The abbot, however, must himself do all things in the fear of

God and according to the Rule, knowing that he shall undoubtedly have to give an account of his whole government to God, the most just Judge.

If anything of less moment has to be done in the monastery let the abbot take advice of the seniors only, as it is written, *Do all things with counsel, and thou shalt not afterwards repent of it.* (Eccl. 32:24)

Chapter IV. The Instruments of Good Works

First of all, to love the Lord God with all our heart, with all our soul, with all our strength. (Deut. 6:5)

2. Then, to love our neighbour as ourself. (Luke 10:27)
3. Then, not to kill. (Luke 18:20)
4. Not to commit adultery. (Matt. 19:18)
5. Not to steal. (Exod. 20:15)
6. Not to be covetous. (Deut. 6:21)
7. Not to bear false witness. (Mark 10:19)
8. To respect all men. (I Pet. 2:17)
9. Not to do to another what one would not have done to oneself. (Tob. 4:16)
10. To deny oneself in order to follow Christ. (Luke 9:23)
11. To chastise the body. (I Cor. 9:27)
12. Not to be fond of pleasures. (II Pet. 2:13)
13. To love fasting. (Joel. 1:14)
14. To give refreshment to the poor. (Tob. 4:7)
15. To clothe the naked. (Isa. 58:7)
16. To visit the sick. (Matt. 25:36)
17. To bury the dead. (Tob. 1:21)
18. To come to the help of those in trouble. (Isa. 1:17)
19. To comfort those in sadness. (I Thes. 5:14)
20. To become a stranger to the ways of the world. (James 1:27)
21. To prefer nothing to the love of Christ. (Matt. 10:38)
22. Not to give way to wrath. (Matt. 5:22)
23. Not to harbour anger for any time. (Eph. 4:26)
24. Not to foster deceit in the heart. (Ps. 14:3)
25. Not to make a false peace. (Rom. 12:18)
26. Not to depart from charity. (I Pet. 4:8)
27. Not to swear at all, lest one forswears. (Matt. 5:33-37)

28. To speak the truth with heart and lips. (Ps. 14:3)

29. Not to return evil for evil. (I Thes. 5:15)

30. Not to do an injury, but patiently to suffer one when done. (I Cor. 6:7)

31. To love one's enemies. (Luke 6:27)

32. Not to speak ill of those who speak ill of one, but rather to speak well of them. (I Pet. 3:9)

33. To suffer persecution for justice sake. (Matt. 5:10)

34. Not to be proud. (Tob. 4:14)

35. Not to be a winebibber. (I Tim. 3:3)

36. Not to be a great eater. (Eccl. 31:17)

37. Not to be given to sleep. (Prov. 20:13)

38. Not to be slothful. (Rom. 12:11)

39. Not to be a murmurer. (I Cor. 10:10)

40. Not to be a detractor. (Wis. 1:11)

41. To put one's trust in God. (Ps. 72:28)

42. When one sees any good in oneself to attribute it to God, not to oneself. (I Cor. 4:7)

43. That a man recognize that it is he who does evil, and so let him attribute it to himself. (Hos. 12:9)

44. To fear the day of judgment. (Job 31:14)

45. To be afraid of hell. (Matt. 10:28)

46. To desire life everlasting with entire spiritual longing. (Phil. 1:23)

47. To have the vision of death before one's eyes daily. (Matt. 24:42)

48. To watch over the actions of one's life every hour of the day. (Deut. 4:9)

49. To know for certain that God sees one everywhere. (Prov. 5:21)

50. To dash at once against Christ (as against a rock) evil thoughts which rise up in the mind. (Ps. 136:9)

51. And to reveal all such to one's spiritual Father. (Eccl. 8:11)

52. To guard one's lips from uttering evil or wicked words. (Ps. 33:13)

53. Not to be fond of much talking. (Prov. 10:19)

54. Not to speak idle words, or such as move to laughter. (Matt. 12:36)

55. Not to love much or boisterous laughter. (Eccl. 21:23)

56. Willingly to hear holy reading. (Luke 11:28)

57. Often to devote oneself to prayer. (Col. 4:2)

58. Daily with tears and sighs to confess to God in prayer one's past offences, and to avoid them for the future. (Ps. 6:7)

59. Not to give way to the desires of the flesh: (Gal. 5:16) and to hate one's own will. (Eccl. 18:30)

60. In all things to obey the abbot's commands, even though he himself (which God forbid) should act otherwise, remembering our Lord's precept, *What they say, do ye, but what they do, do ye not.* (Matt. 23:30)

61. Not to wish to be called holy before one is so; but to be holy first so as to be called such with truth. (Matt. 6:1)

62. Daily in one's acts to keep God's commandments. (Eccl. 6:37)

63. To love chastity. (I Tim. 5:22)

64. To hate no man. (Levit. 19:17)

65. Not to be jealous or envious. (James 3:14–16)

66. Not to love wrangling. (II Tim. 2:24)

67. To show no arrogant spirit. (Ps. 130:1)

68. To reverence the old. (Levit. 19:32)

69. To love the young. (I Tim. 5:1)

70. To pray for one's enemies for the love of Christ. (Matt. 5:44)

71. To make peace with an adversary before the sun sets. (Eph. 4:26)

72. And, never to despair of God's mercy. (Ps. 51:10)

Behold these are the tools of our spiritual craft; when we shall have made use of them constantly day and night, and shall have proved them at the day of judgment, that reward shall be given us by our Lord, which He has promised, *Which eye hath not seen, nor ear heard, nor hath it entered into the heart of man to conceive what God hath prepared for those that love Him.* (I Cor. 2:9) Steadfastly abiding in the community, the workshop where all these instruments are made use of is the cloister of the monastery.

Chapter V. On Obedience

The first degree of humility is prompt obedience. This is required of all who, whether by reason of the holy servitude to which they are pledged, or through fear of hell, or to attain to the glory of eternal life, hold nothing more dear than Christ. Such disciples delay not in doing what is ordered by their superior, just as if the command had come from God. Of such our Lord says, *At the hearing of the ear he hath obeyed me.* (Ps. 17:45) And to the teachers He likewise says, *He that heareth you, heareth me.* (Luke 10:16)

For this reason such disciples, surrendering forthwith all they possess, and giving up their own will, leave unfinished what they were working at, and with the ready foot of obedience in their acts follow the word of command. Thus, as it were, at the same moment comes the order of the master and the finished work of the disciple: with the speed of the fear of God both go jointly forward and are quickly effected by such as ardently desire to walk in the way of eternal life. These take the narrow way, of which the Lord saith, *Narrow is the way which leads to life.* (Matt. 7:14) That is, they live not as they themselves will, neither do they obey their own desires and pleasures; but following the command and direction of another and abiding in their monasteries, their desire is to be ruled by an abbot. Without doubt such as these carry out that saying of our Lord, *I came not to do my own will, but the will of Him Who sent me.* (John 5:30)

This kind of obedience will be both acceptable to God and pleasing to men, when what is ordered is not done out of fear, or slowly and coldly, grudgingly, or with reluctant protest. Obedience shown to superiors is indeed given to God, Who Himself hath said, *He that heareth you, heareth Me.* (Luke 10:16) What is commanded should be done by those under obedience, with a good will, since *God loveth a cheerful giver.* (II Cor. 9:7) If the disciple obey unwillingly and murmur in word as well as in heart, it will not be accepted by God, Who considereth the heart of a murmurer, even if he do what was ordered. For a work done in this spirit shall have no reward; rather shall the doer incur the penalty appointed for murmurers if he amend not and make not satisfaction.

Chapter VI. On Silence

Let us do as the prophet says, *I have said, I will keep my ways, that I offend not with my tongue. I have been watchful over my mouth: I held my peace and humbled myself and was silent from speaking even good things.* (Ps. 38:2–3) Here the prophet shows that, for the sake of silence, we are at times to abstain even from good talk. If this be so, how much more needful is it that we refrain from evil words, on account of the penalty of the sin! Because of the importance of silence, therefore, let leave to speak be seldom given, even to perfect disciples, although their talk be of good and holy matters and tending to edification, since it is written, *In much speaking, thou shalt not escape sin.* (Prov. 18:21) The master, indeed, should speak and teach: the disciple should hold his peace and listen.

Whatever, therefore, has to be asked of the prior, let it be done with all humility and with reverent submission. But as to coarse, idle words, or such as move to laughter, we utterly condemn and ban them in all places. We do not allow any disciple to give mouth to them.

Chapter VII. On Humility

Brethren, Holy Scripture cries out to us, saying, *Every one who exalteth himself shall be humbled, and he who humbleth himself shall be exalted.* (Luke 14:11) In this it tells us that every form of self-exaltation is a kind of pride, which the prophet declares he carefully avoided, where he says, *Lord, my heart is not exalted, neither are my eyes lifted up; neither have I walked in great things, nor in wonders above myself.* And why? *If I did not think humbly, but exalted my soul: as a child weaned from his mother, so wilt Thou reward my soul.* (Ps. 130:1–2)

Wherefore, brethren, if we would scale the summit of humility, and swiftly gain the heavenly height which is reached by our lowliness in this present life, we must set up a ladder of climbing deeds like that which Jacob saw in his dream, whereon angels were descending and ascending. Without doubt that descending and ascending is to be understood by us as signifying that we descend by exalting ourselves and ascend by humbling ourselves. But the ladder itself thus set up is our life in this world, which by humility of heart is lifted by our Lord to heaven. Our body and soul we may indeed call the sides of the ladder in which our divine vocation has set the divers steps of humility and discipline we have to ascend.

The first step of humility, then, is reached when a man, with the fear of God always before his eyes, does not allow himself to forget, but is ever mindful of all God's commandments. He remembers, moreover, that such as contemn God fall into hell for their sins, and that life eternal awaits such as fear Him. And warding off at each moment all sin and defect in thought and word, of eye, hand or foot, of self-will, let such a one bestir himself to prune away the lusts of the flesh.

Let him think that he is seen at all times by God from heaven; and that wheresoever he may be, all his actions are visible to the eye of God and at all times are reported by the angels. The prophet shows us this when he says that God is ever present to our thoughts: *God searcheth the hearts and reins.* (Ps. 7:10) And again, *The Lord knoweth the thoughts of men that they are vain.* (Ps. 93:11) He also saith, *Thou hast understood my thoughts afar off;* and again, *The thought of man shall confess Thee.* (Ps. 138:3) In order, then, that the humble brother may be careful to avoid wrong thoughts let him always say in his heart, *Then shall I be without spot before Him, if I shall keep me from my iniquity.* (Ps. 75:11)

We are forbidden to do our own will, since Scripture tells us, *Leave thy own will and desire.* (Ps. 17:24) And again, *We beg of God in prayer that His will may be done in us.* (Matt. 6:10)

Rightly are we taught therefore not to do our own will, if we take heed of what the Scripture teaches: *There are ways which to men seem right, the end whereof plungeth even into the deep pit of hell.* (Prov. 16:25) And again, when we fear what is said about the negligent, *They are corrupted, and made abominable in their pleasures.* (Ps. 52:2) But in regard of the desires of the flesh we ought to believe that God is present with us; as the prophet says, speaking to the Lord, *O Lord, all my desire is before Thee.* (Ps. 37:10)

We have therefore to beware of evil desires, since death stands close at the door of pleasure. It is for this reason that Scripture bids us, *Follow not they concupiscences.* (Eccl. 18:30) If, therefore, the eyes of the Lord behold both the good and the bad; if He be ever looking down from heaven upon the sons of men to find one who thinks of God or seeks Him; and if day and night what we do is made known to Him—for these reasons, by the angels appointed to watch over us, we should always take heed, brethren, lest God may sometime or other see us, as the prophet says in the Psalm, *inclined to evil and become unprofitable servants.* (Ps. 52:4) Even though He spare us for a time, because He is loving and waits for our conversion to better ways, let us fear that He may say to us hereafter, *These things thou hast done and I held my peace.* (Ps. 49:21)

The second step of humility is reached when any one not loving self-will takes no heed to satisfy his own desires, but copies in his life what our Lord said, *I came not to do My own will, but the will of Him Who sent Me.* (John 6:3–8) Scripture likewise proclaims that self-will engendereth punishment, and necessity purchaseth a crown.

The third step of humility is reached when a man, for the love of God, submits himself with all obedience to a superior, imitating our Lord, of whom the apostle saith, *He was made obedient even unto death.* (Phil. 2:8)

The fourth step of humility is reached when any one in the exercise of his obedience patiently and with a quiet mind bears all that is inflicted on him, things contrary to nature, and even at times unjust, and in suffering all these he neither wearies nor gives over the work, since the Scripture says, *He only that persevereth to the end shall be saved* (Matt. 24:13); also *Let thy heart be comforted, and expect the Lord.* (Ps. 26:14) And in order to show that for our Lord's sake the faithful man ought to bear all things, no matter how contrary to nature they may be (the psalmist), in the person of the sufferers, says, *For thee we suffer death all the day long; we are esteemed as sheep for the slaughter.* (Ps. 43:22) Secure in the hope of divine reward they rejoice, saying, *But in all things we overcome by the help of Him Who hath loved us.* (Rom. 8:37)

Elsewhere also Scripture says, *Thou hast proved us, O Lord; Thou hast tried us, as silver is tried, with fire. Thou hast brought us into the snare; Thou hast laid tribulation upon our backs.* (Ps. 65:10–11) And to show that we ought to be subject to a prior (or superior) it goes on, *Thou hast placed men over our heads.* (Ps. 65:12) And, moreover, they fulfil the Lord's command by patience in adversity and injury, who, *when struck on one cheek, offer the other;* when one *taketh away their coat leave go their cloak also,* and who being compelled to carry a burden one mile, go two; who, with Paul the apostle, suffer false brethren, and bless those who speak ill of them. (II Cor. 11:26)

The fifth step of humility is reached when a monk manifests to his abbot, by humble confession, all the evil thoughts of his heart and his secret faults. The Scripture urges us to do this where it says, *Reveal thy way to the Lord and hope in Him.* (Ps. 36:5) It also says, *Confess to the Lord, because He is good, because His mercy endureth for ever.* (Ps. 105:1) And the prophet also says, *I have made known unto Thee mine offence, and mine injustices I have not hidden. I have said, I will declare openly against myself mine injustices to the Lord; and Thou hast pardoned the wickedness of my heart.* (Ps. 31:5)

The sixth step of humility is reached when a monk is content with all that is mean and vile; and in regard to everything enjoined him accounts himself a poor and worthless workman, saying with the prophet, *I have been brought to nothing, and knew it not. I have become as a beast before Thee, and I am always with Thee.* (Ps. 72:22–23)

The seventh step of humility is reached when a man not only confesses with his tongue that he is most lowly and inferior to others, but in his inmost heart believes so. Such a one, humbling himself, exclaims with the prophet, *I am a worm and no man, the reproach of men and the outcast of the people.* (Ps. 21:7) *I have been exalted and am humbled and confounded.* (Ps. 87:16) And again, *It is good for me that Thou hast humbled me, that I may learn Thy commandments.* (Ps. 118:7)

The eighth step of humility is reached when a monk does nothing but what the common rule of the monastery, or the example of his seniors, enforces.

The ninth step of humility is reached when a monk restrains his tongue from talking, and, practising silence, speaks not till a question be asked him, since Scripture says, *In many words thou shalt not avoid sin* (Prov. 10:19), and *a talkative man shall not be directed upon the earth.* (Ps. 139:12)

The tenth step of humility is attained to when one is not easily and quickly moved to laughter, for it is written, *The fool lifteth his voice in laughter.* (Eccl. 21–23)

The eleventh step of humility is reached when a monk, in speaking, do so quietly and without laughter, humbly, gravely and in a few words and not with a loud voice, for it is written, *A wise man is known by a few words.* (Eccl. 10:14)

The twelfth step of humility is reached when a monk not only has humility in his heart, but even shows it also exteriorly to all who behold him. Thus, whether he be in the oratory at the "Work of God," in the monastery, or in the garden, on a journey, or in the fields, or wheresoever he be, sitting, standing or walking, always let him, with head bent and eyes fixed on the ground, bethink himself of his sins and imagine that he is arraigned before the dread judgment of God. Let him be ever saying to himself, with the publican in the Gospel, *Lord, I a sinner am not worthy to lift mine eyes to heaven* (Luke 18:13); and with the prophet, *I am bowed down and humbled on every side.* (Ps. 118:107)

When all these steps of humility have been mounted the monk will presently attain to that love of God which is perfect and casteth out fear. By means of this love everything which before he had observed not without fear, he shall now begin to do by habit, without any trouble and, as it were, naturally. He acts now not through fear of hell, but for the love of Christ, out of a good habit and a delight in virtue. All this our Lord will vouchsafe to work by the Holy Ghost in His servant, now cleansed from vice and sin.

Chapter VIII. Of the Divine Office at Night Time

In the winter time—that is, from the first of November till Easter—the brethren shall get up at the eighth hour of the night[1] by reasonable calculation, so that having rested till a little after midnight they may rise refreshed. Let the time that remains after Vigils be used, by those brethren who need it, for the study of the Psalter or lessons. From Easter to the foresaid first of November let the hour for saying Vigils be so arranged that after a brief interval, during which the brethren may go forth for the necessities of nature, Matins, which are to be said at daybreak, may presently follow.

Chapter IX. How Many Psalms Are to Be Said in the Night Hours

In the winter season, having first said the verse, *O God, incline unto mine aid; O Lord, make haste to help me* (Ps. 69:2), the words, *O Lord, Thou shalt open my lips and my mouth shall declare Thy praise* (Ps. 50:17) are then to be said thrice. After this the third Psalm is to be said with a *Gloria;* after which the ninety-fourth Psalm, with an antiphon, is to be recited or sung, followed by a hymn, and then six psalms with their antiphons. When these

1. Ca. 2 to 2:30 A.M.

are ended and a versicle said, let the abbot give a blessing; and then, all being seated, let three lessons from the book placed on the lectern be read by the brethren in turns. Between these lessons three responsories are to be sung, two without a *Gloria*. After the third lesson, however, let the cantor add the *Gloria* to the responsory, and as soon as he begins it let all rise from their seats out of honour and reverence to the Holy Trinity.

Let the divinely inspired books of the Old and New Testament be read at Vigils, together with their expositions from the best known, orthodox and Catholic Fathers.

After these three lessons, with their responsories, let six other psalms be sung with the *Alleluia*. A lesson from the Apostle is then to be said by heart, and a verse with the petition of the Litany—that is, *Kyrie eleison*—and so let the night watches (or vigils) end.

Chapter X. How Vigils, or the Night Praises Are to Be Said in the Summer Season

From Easter to the first day of November the same number of psalms as above appointed are to be said. On account of the short nights, however, the lessons are not to be read from the book, but in place of the three lessons let one out of the Old Testament be said by heart and followed by a short responsory. Let all the rest be done as we have arranged above, so that, without counting the third and ninety-fourth Psalm, there may never be less than twelve psalms at Vigils.

Chapter XI. How Vigils, or the Night Watches, Are to Be Celebrated on Sundays

On Sunday let the brethren rise earlier for Vigils, in which the following order is to be observed: when six psalms and the versicle have been sung, as we have before arranged, let all sit down in proper order and let four lessons be read from the book with their responsories, in the manner before prescribed. To the fourth responsory only let the cantor add the *Gloria*, and when he begins it let all rise at once out of reverence. After these lessons six other psalms follow in order with their antiphons and a versicle as before. Then let four other lessons be read with their responsories in the same way as the former, and then three canticles out of the Prophets, appointed by the abbot: these canticles are to be sung with *Alleluia*.

When the versicle has been said, and the abbot has given the blessing, four more lessons from the New Testament are to be read, in the same order as before. After the fourth responsory let the abbot begin the hymn *Te Deum laudamus*, and when that is finished he shall read a lesson from the Gospel, with reverence and fear, whilst all stand. At the conclusion of this let all answer Amen, and let the abbot immediately go on with the hymn *Te decet laus;* after the blessing let them begin Matins.

This method of singing Vigils on Sundays is to be observed always, as well in summer as in winter, unless perchance (which God forbid) they get up late, and the lessons or responsories have to be somewhat shortened. Let great care be taken that this shall not happen; but if it does, let him to whose carelessness it is due make full satisfaction to God in the oratory.

Chapter XII. How Matins Are to Be Solemnized

At Matins on Sunday let the sixty-sixth Psalm be first said straight on and without an antiphon. After this the fiftieth is to be said with *Alleluia*, with the hundred and seventeenth and the sixty-second. Then follow the "Blessings" (or *Benedicite*) and the "Praises" (or *Laudate* psalms), a lesson from the Apoclypse, said by heart, a responsory and hymn, the versicle and the canticle from the Gospel (or *Benedictus*) with the litanies (or *Kyrie*), and so conclude.

Chapter XIII. How Matins Are to Be Celebrated on Ordinary Days

On ordinary week-days let Matins be celebrated as follows: the sixty-sixth Psalm is to be said, as on Sunday, straight on without any antiphon, and somewhat slowly, to allow of all being in their places for the fiftieth Psalm, which is to be said with an antiphon. After this come two other psalms according to custom: that is, on Monday, the fifth and thirty-fifth; on Tuesday, the forty-second and fifty-sixth; on Wednesday, the sixty-third and sixty-fourth; on Thursday, the eighty-seventh and eighty-ninth; on Friday, the seventy-fifth and ninety-first; on Saturday, the hundred and forty-second and the Canticle of Deuteronomy, which must be divided into two *Glorias*. But on other days let a canticle out of the Prophets be said, each on its proper day, according to the custom of the Roman Church. After these let the *Praises* (or *Laudate* Psalms) follow, then a lesson of the Apostle, said by heart, the responsory, hymn and versicle, the canticle from the Gospel (or *Benedictus*), the litanies (or *Kyrie eleison*), and the office is completed.

Matins and Vespers are never to be finished without the Lord's prayer at the end. This is said by the prior (that is, the superior) aloud, so that all may hear, because of the thorns of scandal which are always cropping up: that the community, by reason of the pledge given in this prayer, in the words, *Forgive us our trespasses as we forgive them that trespass against us*, may purge themselves from this kind of vice. In saying the other Hours, however, the last part of the prayer only is said aloud that all may answer, *But deliver us from evil*.

Chapter XIV. How Vigils Are to Be Said on the Feast Days of Saints

On Saints' feast days and on all solemnities let Vigils be said in the manner we have ordered for Sunday, except that the psalms, antiphons and lessons are said which are proper to the day itself. The method of saying them, however, shall remain as before prescribed.

Chapter XV. At What Seasons Alleluia Is to Be Said

From the holy feast of Easter until Whitsuntide *Alleluia* is to be always said both with the psalms and in the responsories. From Whitsuntide till the beginning of Lent let it be said every night at Vigils only with the last six psalms. On every Sunday out of Lent let the Canticles, Matins, Prime, Tierce, Sext and None be said with *Alleluia*, but Evensong with antiphons. Responsories, however, except from Easter till Pentecost, are never to be said with *Alleluia*.

Chapter XVI. How the Day Divine Office Is to Be Said

The prophet says, *Seven times I have sung Thy praises*. (Ps. 118:164) This sacred number of seven will be kept by us if we perform the duties of our service in the Hours of Matins, Prime, Tierce, Sext, None, Evensong and Compline. It was of these day Hours the prophet said, *Seven times a day I have sung Thy praises*, for of the night watches the same prophet says, *At midnight I arose to confess to Thee.* (Ps. 118:62) At these times, therefore, let us give praise to our Creator for His just judgments, that is, at Matins, Prime, Tierce, Sext, None, Vespers and Compline, and at night let us rise to confess to Him.

Chapter XVII. How Many Psalms Are to Be Said in These Hours

We have already settled the order of the psalmody for the Nocturns[1] and for Matins, let us now arrange for the Hours which follow. At Prime three psalms are to be said separately, that is, not under one *Gloria*. After the verse, *O God, incline unto mine aid*, and before the psalms are begun, the hymn of each Hour is to be said. At the end of the three psalms a lesson is recited, then with the versicle and *Kyrie eleison* the Hour is concluded. The Hours of Tierce, Sext and None are to be said in the same way, that is, the verse (*O God, incline, etc.*), the hymns of these Hours, three psalms, the lesson and versicle, and with *Kyrie eleison* they are concluded.

If the community be large the Hours shall be sung with antiphons, but if it be small they are to be without. Vespers shall be said with four psalms and antiphons, after which a lesson is to be recited, then a responsory, hymn, versicle, anticle from the Gospel (i.e. *Magnificat*), and it is concluded by the litanies (or *Kyrie*) and the Lord's Prayer. Compline shall consist in the saying of three psalms straight through and without antiphons, followed by the hymn of the Hour, a lesson, versicle, *Kyrie eleison*, and shall conclude with the blessing.

Chapter XVIII. The Order in Which the Psalms Are to Be Said

Let the verse, *O God, incline unto mine aid; O Lord, make haste to help me*, with a *Gloria*, always come first, followed by the hymn of each Hour. Then, on Sundays, at Prime, four divisions of the

---

1. Vigils. (Ed.)

hundred and eighteenth Psalm are to be said; and at the other
Hours of Tierce, Sext and None three divisions of the same. On
Monday, at Prime, psalms first, second and third are recited, and so
on each day till Sunday, three other psalms in order up to the
nineteenth Pslam: the ninth and seventeenth Psalm being each
divided in two by a *Gloria*. In this way the Sunday Vigils may
always begin with the twentieth Pslam.

On Mondays, at Tierce, Sext and None let the remaining nine
divisions of the hundred and eighteenth Psalm be said, three at each
Hour. The hundred and eighteenth Psalm being finished on the
two days, Sunday and Monday, therefore on Tuesday, at Tierce,
Sext and None the three psalms at each Hour shall be the nine
from the hundred and nineteenth to the hundred and twenty-
seventh. And these same psalms are to be repeated at the Hours till
the Sunday. A uniform order of the hymns, lessons and versicles is
to be likewise observed, so that the hundred and eighteenth Psalm
is always begun on the Sunday.

Four psalms are to be sung each day at Vespers. These begin
with the hundred and ninth Psalm and conclude with the hundred
and forty-seventh, omitting those already set apart for the various
other Hours, that is to say, from the hundred and seventeenth
Psalm to the hundred and twenty-seventh; the hundred and thirty-
third and the hundred and forty-second. All the rest are to be said
at Vespers, and because this leaves three psalms short the longest of
them, namely, the hundred and thirty-eighth, the hundred and
forty-third, and the hundred and forty-fourth, are to be divided.
The hundred and sixteenth, however, since it is brief, is to be
joined to the hundred and fifteenth.

The order of the psalms for Vespers being thus arranged, let the
other parts, such as the lessons, responsories, hymns, versicles and
canticles, be used as before directed. At Compline the same psalms
are repeated every day, namely, the fourth, the ninetieth and the
hundred and thirty-third.

The order of the psalmody for the day office being thus settled,
all the rest of the psalms are to be equally portioned to the seven
night watches (or Vigils). Those that are too long are to be
divided into two; and twelve psalms are to be arranged for each
night. If this distribution of the psalms displease any one we specially desire him to arrange otherwise, if he think something else
better, provided that care be taken that every week the whole

Psalter of a hundred and fifty psalms be sung, and that at Vigils on Sunday it be begun again. Monks, indeed, show themselves in their service too negligent and indevout who sing less than the Psalter, with the usual canticles, once in the week, when we read that our holy Fathers courageously performed in one day what I would that we who are tepid may do in a whole week.

Chapter XXXVIII. The Weekly Reader

There ought always to be reading whilst the brethren eat at table. Yet no one shall presume to read there from any book taken up at haphazard; but whoever is appointed to read for the whole week is to enter on his office on the Sunday. Let the brother when beginning his service after Mass and Communion ask all to pray for him, that God may preserve him from the spirit of pride. And let the following verse be thrice repeated by all in the oratory, he, the reader, first beginning: *O Lord, Thou wilt open my lips, and my mouth shall declare Thy praise* (Ps. 50:17), then, having received a blessing, let the reader enter upon his office. The greatest silence shall be kept, so that no whispering, nor noise, save the voice of the reader alone, be heard there.

Whatever is required for eating and drinking the brethren shall minister to each other so that no one need ask for anything. Yet should anything be wanted it ought to be demanded by sign rather than by word. Let no one ask any question there about what is being read or about anything else, lest occasion be given to the evil one; unless, perhaps, the prior shall wish to say something briefly for the purpose of edification. The brother who is reader for the week may take a mess of potage before beginning to read, on account of Holy Communion, and lest perchance it may be too long for him to fast. He shall eat afterwards with the weekly servers and kitchen helpers. The brethren, however, are not all to read or sing in course, but only such as may edify the hearers.

Chapter XXXIX. Of the Amount of Food

We believe that it is enough to satisfy just requirement if in the daily meals, at both the sixth and ninth hours, there be at all seasons of the year two cooked dishes, so that he who cannot eat of the one may make his meal of the other. Therefore two dishes of cooked food must suffice for all the brethren, and if there be any fruit or young vegetables these may be added to the meal as a third dish. Let a pound weight of bread suffice for each day, whether there be one meal or two, that is, for both dinner and supper. If there is to be supper a third of the pound is to be kept back by the cellarer and given to the brethren at that meal.

If, however, the community has been occupied in any great labour it shall be at the will, and in the power of the abbot, if he think fit, to increase the allowance, so long as every care be taken to guard against excess, and that no monk be incapacitated by surfeiting. For nothing is more contrary to the Christian spirit than gluttony, as our Lord declares, *Take heed to yourselves lest perhaps your hearts be overcharged with surfeiting.* (Luke 21:34) And the same quantity shall not be given to young children, but a lesser amount than to those older; frugality being maintained in everything. All, save the very weak and sick, are to abstain wholly from eating the flesh of quadrupeds.

Chapter XL. Of the Measure of Drink

Every one hath his proper gift from God, one thus, another thus. (I Cor. 7:7) For this reason the amount of other people's food cannot be determined without some misgiving. Still, having regard to the weak state of the sick, we think that a pint of wine a day is sufficient for any one. But let those to whom God gives the gift of abstinence know that they shall receive their proper reward. If either local circumstances, the amount of labour, or the heat of summer require more, it can be allowed at the will of the prior, care being taken in all things that gluttony and drunkenness creep not in.

Although we read that "wine is not the drink of monks at all," yet, since in our days they cannot be persuaded of this, let us at least agree not to drink to satiety, but sparingly, *Because wine maketh even the wise to fall away* (Eccl. 19:2).

XLII. That No One Shall Speak After Compline

Monks should practise silence at all times, but especially during the night hours. On all days, therefore, whether it be a fast day or otherwise (this shall be the practice). If it be not a fast day, as soon as they shall have risen from supper let all sit together whilst one of them read the *Collations*,[1] or *Lives of the Fathers*, or some other book to edify the hearers. He shall not, however, read the *Heptateuch*, or *Books of Kings*, for at that hour it will not profit weak understandings to listen to this part of Scripture; at other times, however, they may be read. If it be a fast day let the brethren, when Vespers is over, and after a brief interval, come to the reading of the *Collations*, as we have said. Four or five pages are to be read, or as many as time will allow, that during the reading all may come together, even such as have had some work given them to do. When all, therefore, are gathered together let them say Compline, and on coming out from Compline no one shall be permitted to speak at all. If any one shall be found breaking this rule of silence he shall be punished severely, unless the needs of a guest require it, or the abbot shall order something of some one. But even this shall be done with the greatest gravity and moderation.

Chapter XLVIII. Of Daily Manual Labour

Idleness is an enemy of the soul. Because this is so the brethren ought to be occupied at specified times in manual labour, and at other fixed hours in holy reading. We therefore think that both these may be arranged for as follows: from Easter to the first of October, on coming out from Prime, let the brethren labour till about the fourth hour. From the fourth till close upon the sixth hour[1a] let them employ themselves in reading. On rising from table after the sixth hour let them rest on their beds in strict silence; but if any one shall wish to read, let him do so in such a way as not to disturb any one else.

Let None be said somewhat before the time, about the middle of the eighth hour, and after this all shall work at what they have to do till evening. If, however, the nature of the place or poverty require them to labour at gathering in the harvest, let them not grieve at that, for then are they truly monks when they live by the labour of their hands, as our Fathers and the Apostles did. Let everything, however, be done with moderation for the sake of the faint-hearted.

From the first of October till the beginning of Lent let the

1. John Cassian.
1*a*. The sixth hour was about noon. (Ed.)

brethren be occupied in reading till the end of the second hour.[2] At that time Tierce shall be said, after which they shall labour at the work enjoined them till None. At the first signal for the Hour of None all shall cease to work, so as to be ready when the second signal is given. After their meal they shall be employed in reading or on the psalms.

On the days of Lent, from the morning till the end of the third hour, the brethren are to have time for reading, after which let them work at what is set them to do till the close of the tenth hour. During these Lenten days let each one have some book from the library which he shall read through carefully. These books are to be given out at the beginning of Lent.

It is of much import that one or two seniors be appointed to go about the monastery at such times as the brethren are free to read, in order to see that no one is slothful, given to idleness or foolish talking instead of reading, and so not only makes no profit himself but also distracts others. If any such be found (which God forbid) let him be corrected once or twice, and if he amend not let him be subjected to regular discipline of such a character that the rest may take warning. Moreover one brother shall not associate with another at unsuitable hours.

On Sunday also, all, save those who are assigned to various offices, shall have time for reading. If, however, any one be so negligent and slothful as to be unwilling or unable to read or meditate, he must have some work given him, so as not to be idle. For weak brethren, or those of delicate constitutions, some work or craft shall be found to keep them from idleness, and yet not such as to crush them by the heavy labour or to drive them away. The weakness of such brethren must be taken into consideration by the abbot.

Chapter XLIX. The Observance of Lent

The mode of a monk's life ought at all times to favour that of Lenten observance. Since few, however, are capable of this we exhort every one in these days of Lent to guard their lives in all purity, and during this holy season to wash away every negligence of other times. This we shall worthily accomplish if we restrain ourselves from every vice, and give ourselves to tearful prayer, to

2. About 9 A.M. (Ed.)

reading, to heartfelt sorrow and to abstinence. In these days of Lent, therefore, let us of our own accord add something to our usual yoke of service, such as private prayer, abstinence from food and drink. Let every one of his own will with joy of the Holy Ghost offer to God something above the allotted measure, that is, let him deny his body in food, drink, sleep, talking or laughter, and with spiritual joy await the holy feast of Easter. On this condition, however, that each one inform his abbot what it is that he is offering, for what is done without leave of the spiritual Father will be reckoned presumption and vain-glory, and merit no reward. All things, therefore, must be done with the approval of the abbot.

Chapter LIII. On the Reception of Guests

Let all guests who come be received as Christ would be, because He will say, *I was a stranger, and ye took Me in.* (Matt. 25:35) And let due honour be shown to all, especially to those who are of the household of the Faith, and to pilgrims. As soon, therefore, as a guest is announced let him be met by the prior or the brethren, with all marks of charity. And let them first pray together, that so they may associate in peace. The kiss of peace, however, is not to be given till after prayer, on account of the deceptions practised by the devil. And in the salutation itself let true humility be shown to all guests coming and going. By bowed head, or body prostrate on the ground, all shall adore Christ in them, Who, indeed, is received in their persons.

Let guest, after their reception, be conducted to prayer, and then the prior, or any one he may order, shall sit with them. Let the Divine Law be read in the presence of the guest for his edification, and after this let all courtesy be shown to him. For the guest's sake the prior may break his fast, unless it be a strict day when the fast may not be broken. The brethren, however, shall keep the accustomed fasts. Let the abbot pour water on the hands of the guests, and let him and all the community wash their feet. After this let them say the verse, *We have received Thy mercy, O God, in the midst of Thy temple.* (Ps. 47:10) Let special care be taken of the poor and pilgrims, because in them Christ is more truly received, for the very awe of the rich secures respect for them.

. . .

No one, unless ordered, may associate with or speak to the

guests. If any one shall meet or see them, after such humble salutation as we have above enjoined, having asked their blessing, let him
pass on, saying he is not permitted to talk with any guest.

Chapter LV. Of the Clothes and Shoes of the Brethren

Let clothing suitable to the locality and the temperature be given
to the brethren, for in cold regions more is needed, and less in
warm. The determination of all these things is in the hands of the
abbot. We believe, however, that in ordinary places it will be
enough for each monk to have a cowl and tunic; in winter the cowl
being of thicker stuff, in summer of finer or old cloth. He should
have also a scapular for working purposes, and shoes and stockings
for the feet.

Monks must not grumble at the colour or coarseness of these
things; they shall be such as can be procured in the district where
they live, or such as can be bought at the cheapest price.

Let the abbot see to their dimensions, that they be not too short,
but of the proper length for those who use them. When receiving
new clothes the monks shall always give back the old ones at the
same time, to be put away in the clothes-room for the poor. For it
is sufficient that a monk have two tunics and two cowls, as well for
night wear as for the convenience of washing. Anything beyond
this is superfluous, and must be cut off. Their shoes also, and
whatever is worn out, they shall return on getting new things.
Those who are sent on a journey shall get hosen from the wardrobe, which, on their return, when washed, they shall restore. Let
their cowls and tunics on such occasions be somewhat better than
those in ordinary use. These they shall receive from the wardrobe
when starting and restore on their return.

A mattress, blanket, coverlet and pillow are to suffice for bed-
ding. The beds shall be frequently searched by the abbot to guard
against the vice of hoarding. And if any one be found in possession
of something not allowed by the abbot let him be subjected to the
severest punishment. And to uproot this vice of appropriation let
all that is necessary be furnished by the abbot, that is, cowl, tunic,
shoes, stockings, girdle, knife, pen, needle, handkerchief and tab-
lets. By this every pretext of necessity will be taken away. The
abbot, however, should always bear in mind that sentence in the
Acts of the Apostles, *And distribution was made to every one*

according as he had need. (Acts 4:35) He should, therefore, consider the infirmities of such as need something, and not regard the ill-will of the envious. In all his decisions let him ponder upon the retribution of God.

Chapter LXIII. The Order of the Community

The brethren shall take their places according to the date of their conversion, the merit of their lives, or the appointment of their abbot. And the abbot must not disturb the flock committed to him, nor, as it were, by any arbitrary use of his power, ordain anything unjustly. But let him always remember that he will have to render an account to God of all his judgments and of all his works.

Wherefore in the order he shall appoint, or in that which they hold amongst themselves, let the brethren receive the Pax, approach Communion, intone a psalm and stand in choir. In all places, without exception, order shall not be decided by age, for this shall not be a prejudice to any one, since Samuel and Daniel, though children, were judges of the priests. With the exception therefore of those who, as we have said, for some weighty reason, the abbot shall advance, or for certain causes shall put in a lower place, let all the rest remain in the order of their conversion. For example, one who shall come to the monastery at the second hour of the day shall know that he is junior to him who has come at the first hour, no matter what his age or dignity may be. In regard to children, let them be kept by all under discipline in every way.

Let the juniors, therefore, honour their seniors, and the seniors love the juniors. In addressing each other in person no one shall call another by his mere name, but let the senior call the junior, *Brother,* and the junior call the senior, *Father.* But, because the abbot is held to take the place of Christ, he shall be called *Sir* and *Abbot,* not out of consideration for himself, but for the honour and love of Christ. He, however, should remember and so conduct himself as to be worthy of such an honour.

Wherever the brethren meet each other the junior shall ask a blessing from the senior. When a senior passes by let the junior rise and make place for him to sit down; neither shall the junior presume to sit unless the senior bid him so to do, in order to fulfil what is written, *In honour preventing one another.* (Rom. 12:10)

Little children or youths shall keep their respective places in the oratory and at table, under discipline. Outside watch shall be kept over them, everywhere indeed, till they come to an age of understanding.

Chapter LXXIII. That All Perfection Is Not Contained in This Rule

We have written this Rule, that, by its observance in monasteries, we may show that we have in some measure uprightness of manners or the beginning of religious life. But for such as hasten onward to the perfection of holy life there are the teachings of the Holy Fathers, the observance whereof leads a man to the heights of perfection. For what page or what passage of the divinely inspired books of the Old and the New Testament is not a most perfect rule for man's life? Or what book is there of the Holy Catholic Fathers that doth not proclaim this, that by a direct course we may come to our Creator? Also, what else are the *Collations* of the Fathers, their Institutes, their *Lives*, and the Rule of our Holy Father St. Basil, but examples of the virtues, of the good living and obedience of monks? But to us who are slothful, and lead bad and negligent lives, they are matter for shame and confusion.

Do thou, therefore, whosoever thou art who hasteneth forward to the heavenly country, accomplish first, by the help of Christ, this little Rule written for beginners, and then at length shalt thou come, under God's guidance, to the lofty heights of doctrine and virtue, which we have spoken of above.

The Bishop as Pastor

---

17. Gregory the Great, The Pastoral Rule

Gregory the Great (540–604), was born of a Roman patrician family somewhat before the middle of the sixth century. His early life, therefore, was passed during a period of exceptional turbulence in the Italian peninsula. Nevertheless, Gregory seems to have received a good education according to the standards of the day. Although he was certainly not a classical scholar in the old sense, and he knew no Greek, he was literate and well versed in Scripture. In all his manifold activities he showed a remarkable common sense.

After serving for a time as pretorian prefect of Rome, Gregory was drawn to the monastic life. But Pope Pelagius II (579–90) persuaded him to resume for several years an active, though now ecclesiastical, life as *apocrisarius*, or representative, of the pope in Constantinople. Not long after his return to Rome, catastrophe struck the ancient city. The Tiber overflowed in 589 causing, besides much material damage, a plague which cost the life of Pope Pelagius. Despite his evident reluctance, Gregory was chosen as his successor.

As pope (590–604), Gregory was constantly beset by diplomatic and political concerns. For the pope had not only to see to the administration of the papal patrimonies in Italy and Sicily; Rome and its material needs and food also came under his care. Neither the imperial government at Constantinople nor its representative, the exarch, in Ravenna was able to handle these problems or to meet the repeated challenges of the Lombards to the city itself.

Notwithstanding his manifold duties and chronic ill health, Gregory found time to write religious treatises, compose sermons, and dispatch letters both official and personal to every corner of the Christian world. His *Register*, a remarkable collection of over 800 extant letters, is by far the most extensive up to that time. In addition to all this, he sent a mission to far-off Britain.

Gregory's most famous work was the *Pastoral Rule*, which he addressed to Bishop John of Ravenna. The pastor here is the bishop, not the parish priest, for in the early Middle Ages, as in the primitive Church, it was the bishop who preached and who was the ruler of his people, the pastor or shepherd of his flock. In portraying what sort of man the ideal pastor should be and in suggesting how he should conduct himself, Gregory displayed a remarkable wisdom and understanding of human nature. There are, as indeed in all his writings, many references to Scripture. For although Gregory was somewhat fanciful in his interpretations and not a profound theologian, he knew the Bible thoroughly. And, as he acknowledges in the Preface to Part III, he was influenced by the fourth-century treatise of Gregory of Nazianzen.

Part III opens with a list of the kinds of human temperaments with which the pastor must deal. Only a few explanations have been cited here, but they may serve to illustrate Gregory's method.

The *Pastoral Rule* quickly achieved the wide circulation it was to maintain throughout the Middle Ages. Anastasius, patriarch of Antioch, translated it into Greek at the request of the emperor Maurice. Licinius, bishop of Cartagena, commended it, and two centuries later, Alfred the Great of England translated, or paraphrased, it into Anglo-Saxon. The translation is by J. Barmby, *The Book of Pastoral Rule and Selected Epistles of Gregory the Great*, Nicene and Post-Nicene Fathers, vol. XII (New York, 1895), pp. 1–2, 9–14, 20–25, 29, 71–72.

Part I

CHAPTER I

No one presumes to teach an art till he has first, with intent meditation, learnt it. What rashness is it, then, for the unskillful to assume pastoral authority, since the government of souls is the art of arts! For who can be ignorant that the sores of the thoughts of men are more occult than the sores of the bowels? And yet how often do men who have no knowledge whatever of spiritual precepts fearlessly profess themselves physicians of the heart, though those who are ignorant of the effect of drugs blush to appear as physicians of the flesh! But because, through the ordering of God, all the highest in rank of this present age are inclined to reverence religion, there are some who, through the outward show of rule within the holy Church, affect the glory of distinction. They desire to appear as teachers, they covet superiority to others, and, as the Truth attests, they seek the first salutations in the market-place, the first rooms at feasts, the first seats in assemblies (Matt. xxiii. 6,7), being all the less able to administer worthily the office they have undertaken of pastoral care, as they have reached the magisterial position of humility out of elation only. For, indeed, in a magisterial position language itself is confounded when one thing is learnt and another taught. Against such the Lord complains by the prophet, saying, "They have reigned, and not by Me; they have been set up as princes, and I knew it not" (Hos. viii, 4). For those reign of themselves, and not by the Will of the Supreme Ruler, who, supported by no virtues, and in no way divinely called, but inflamed by their own desire, seize rather than attain supreme rule. . . . And therefore the Truth complains of not being known of them, and protests that He knows not the principality of those who know not Him; because in truth these who know not the things of the Lord are unknown to the Lord; as Paul attests, who says, "But if any man knoweth not, he shall not be known" (I Cor. xiv. 38). Yet this unskillfulness of the shepherds doubtless suits often the deserts of those who are subject to them, because, though it is their own fault that they have not the light of knowledge, yet it is in the dealing of strict jugment that through their ignorance those also who follow them should stumble. Hence it is that, in the Gospel, the Truth in person says, "If the blind lead the blind, both fall into the ditch" (Matt. xv. 14). Hence the Psalmist (not expressing his own desire, but in his ministry as a prophet) denounces such, when he says, "Let their eyes be blinded that they see not, and ever bow thou down their back" (Ps. lxviii. 24). For, indeed, those persons are eyes who, placed in the very face of the highest dignity, have undertaken the office of spying out the road; while those who are attached to them and follow them are denominated backs. And so, when the eyes are blinded, the back is bent, because, when those who go before lose the light of knowledge, those who follow are bowed down to carry the burden of their sins. . . .

Part II. Of the Life of the Pastor

CHAPTER I

The conduct of a prelate ought so far to transcend the conduct of the people as the life of a shepherd is wont to exalt him above the flock. For one whose estimation is such that the people are called his flock is bound anxiously to consider what great necessity is laid upon him to maintain rectitude. It is necessary, then, that in thought he should be pure, in action chief; discreet in keeping silence, profitable in speech; a near neighbour to every one in sympathy, exalted above all in contemplation; a familiar friend of good livers through humility, unbending against the vices of evil-doers through zeal for righteousness; not relaxing in his care for what is inward from being occupied in outward things, nor neglecting to provide for outward things in his solicitude for what is inward. But the things which we have thus briefly touched on let us now unfold and discuss more at length.

CHAPTER II

The ruler should always be pure in thought, inasmuch as no impurity ought to pollute him who has undertaken the office of wiping away the stains of pollution in the hearts of others also; for the hand that would cleanse from dirt must needs be clean, lest, being itself sordid with clinging mire, it soil whatever it touches all the more. For on this account it is said through the prophet, "Be ye clean that bear the vessels of the Lord" (Isai. lii. 11). For they bear the vessels of the Lord who undertake, on the surety of their own conversation, to conduct the souls of their neighbours to the eternal sanctuary. Let them therefore perceive within themselves how purified they ought to be who carry in the bosom of their own personal responsibility living vessels to the temple of eternity. . . .

CHAPTER III

The ruler should always be chief in action, that by his living he may point out the way of life to those that are put under him, and that the flock, which follows the voice and manners of the shepherd, may learn how to walk better through example than through words. For he who is required by the necessity of his position to speak the highest things is compelled by the same necessity to exhibit the highest things. For that voice more readily penetrates the hearer's heart, which the speaker's life commends, since what he commands by speaking he helps the doing of by shewing. Hence it is said through the prophet, "Get thee up into the high mountain, thou that bringest good tidings to Sion" (Isai. xl. 9): which means that he who is engaged in heavenly preaching should already have forsaken the low level of earthly works, and appear as standing on the summit of things, and by so much the more easily should draw those who are under him to better things as by the merit of his life he cries aloud from heights above. . . .

CHAPTER IV

The ruler should be discreet in keeping silence, profitable in speech; lest he either utter what ought to be suppressed or suppress what he ought to utter. For, as incautious speaking leads into error, so indiscreet silence leaves in error those who might have been instructed. For often improvident rulers, fearing to lose human favour, shrink timidly from speaking freely the things that are right; and, according to the voice of the Truth (John x. 12) serve unto the custody of the flock by no means with the zeal of shepherds, but in the way of hirelings; since they fly when the wolf cometh if they hide themselves under silence. For hence it is that the Lord through the prophet upbraids them, saying, "Dumb dogs, that cannot bark" (Isai. lvi. 10). Hence again He complains, saying, "Ye have not gone up against the enemy, neither opposed a wall for the house of Israel, to stand in the battle in the day of the Lord" (Ezek. xiii. 5). Now to go up against the enemy is to go with free voice against the powers of this world for defence of the flock; and to stand in the battle in the day of the Lord is out of love of justice to resist bad men when they contend against us. For, for a shepherd to have feared to say what is right, what else is it but to have turned his back in keeping silence? But surely, if he puts himself in front for the flock, he opposes a wall against the enemy for the house of Israel. . . .

But, when the ruler prepares himself for speaking, let him bear in mind with what studious caution he ought to speak, lest, if he be hurried inordinately into speaking, the hearts of hearers be smitten with the wound of error, and, while he perchance desires to seem wise, he unwisely sever the bond of unity. For on this account the Truth says, "Have salt in yourselves, and have peace one with another" (Mark ix. 49). Now by salt is denoted the word of wisdom. Let him, therefore, who strives to speak wisely fear greatly, lest by his eloquence the unity of his hearers be disturbed. Hence Paul says, "Not to be more wise than behoveth to be wise, but to be wise unto sobriety" (Rom. xii. 3). . . .

Chapter V

The ruler should be a near neighbour to every one in sympathy, and exalted above all in contemplation, so that through the bowels of loving-kindness he may transfer the infirmities of others to himself, and by loftiness of speculation transcend even himself in his aspiration after the invisible; lest either in seeking high things he despise the weak things of his neighbours, or in suiting himself to the weak things of his neighbours he relinquish his aspiration after high things. . . . And for the most part it comes to pass that, while the ruler's mind becomes aware, through condescension, of the trials of others, it is itself also attacked by the temptations whereof it hears; since the same water of the laver in which a multitude of people is cleansed is undoubtedly itself defiled. For, in receiving the pollutions of those who wash, it loses, as it were, the calmness of its own purity. But of this the pastor ought by no means to be afraid, since, under God, who nicely balances all things, he is the more easily rescued from his own temptations as he is more compassionately distressed by those of others. . . .

Chapter X

It should be known too that the vices of subjects ought sometimes to be prudently connived at; but indicated in that they are connived at; that things, even though openly known, ought sometimes to be seasonably tolerated, but sometimes, though hidden, be closely investigated; that they ought sometimes to be gently reproved, but sometimes vehemently censured. For, indeed, some things, as we have said, ought to be prudently connived at, but indicated in that they are connived at, so that, when the delinquent is aware that he is discovered and borne with, he may blush to augment those faults which he considers in himself are tolerated in silence, and may punish himself in his own judgment as being one whom the patience of his ruler in his own mind mercifully excuses. By such connivance the Lord well reproves Judah, when He says through the prophet, "Thou hast lied, and hast not remembered Me, nor laid it to thy heart, because I have held My peace and been as one that saw not" (Isai. lvii. 11). Thus He both connived at faults and made them known, since He both held His peace against the sinner, and nevertheless declared this very thing, that He had held His peace. But some things, even though openly known, ought to be seasonably tolerated; that is, when circumstances afford no suitable opportunity for openly correcting them. For sores by being reasonably cut are the worse inflamed; and, if medicaments suit not the time, it is undoubtedly evident that they lose their medicinal function. But, while a fitting time for the correction of subordinates is being sought, the patience of the prelate is exercised under the very weight of their offences. Whence it is well said by the Psalmist, "Sinners have built upon my back" (Ps. cxxviii. 3). For on the back we support burdens; and therefore he complains that sinners had built upon his back, as if to say plainly, Those whom I am unable to correct I carry as a burden laid upon me.

Some hidden things, however, ought to be closely investigated, that, by the breaking out of certain symptoms, the ruler may discover all that lies closely hidden in the minds of his subordinates, and, by reproof intervening at the nick of time, from very small things become aware of greater ones. . . .

Some things, however, ought to be gently reproved: for, when fault is committed, not of malice, but only from ignorance or infirmity, it is certainly necessary that the very censure of it be tempered with great moderation. For it is true that all of us, so long as we subsist in this mortal flesh, are subject to the infirmities of our corruption. Every one, therefore, ought to gather from himself how it behoves him to pity another's weakness, lest, if he be too fervently hurried to words of reprehension against a neighbour's infirmity, he should seem to be forgetful of his own. Whence Paul admonishes well, when he says, "If a man be overtaken in any fault, ye which are spiritual restore such an one in the spirit of meekness, considering thyself, lest thou also be tempted" (Galat. vi. 1); as if to say plainly, When what thou seest of the infirmity of another displeases thee, consider what thou art; that so the spirit may moderate itself in the zeal of reprehension, while for itself also it fears what it reprehends.

Some things, however, ought to be vehemently reproved, that, when a fault is not recognized by him who has committed it, he may be made sensible of its gravity from the mouth of the reprover; and that, when any one smooths over to himself the evil that he has perpetrated, he may be led by the asperity of his censurer to entertain grave fears of its effects against himself. For indeed it is the duty of a ruler to shew by the voice of preaching the glory of the supernal country, to disclose what great temptations of the old enemy are lurking in this life's journey, and to correct with great asperity of zeal such evils among those who are under his sway as ought not to be gently borne with; lest, in being too little incensed against faults, of all faults he be himself held guilty. . . .

CHAPTER XI

But all this is duly excuted by a ruler, if inspired by the spirit of heavenly fear and love, he meditate daily on the precepts of Sacred Writ, that the words of Divine admonition may restore in him the power of solicitude and of provident circumspection with regard to the celestial life, which familiar intercourse with men continually destroys; and that one who is drawn to oldness of life by secular society may by the aspiration of compunction be ever renewed to love of the spiritual country. For the heart runs greatly to waste in the midst of human talk; and, since it is undoubtedly evident that, when driven by the tumults of external occupations, it loses its balance and falls, one ought incessantly to take care that through keen pursuit of instruction it may rise again. For hence it is that Paul admonishes his disciple who had been put over the flock, saying, "Till I come, give attendance to reading" (1 Tim. iv. 13). Hence David says, "How have I loved Thy Law, O Lord! It is my meditation all the day" (Ps. cix. 97). . . .

Part III. How the Ruler, While Living Well, Ought to Teach and Admonish Those That Are Put Under Him

PROLOGUE

Since, then, we have shewn what manner of man the pastor ought to be, let us now set forth after what manner he should teach. For as long before us Gregory Nazianzen of reverend memory has taught, one and the same exhortation does not suit all, inasmuch as neither are all bound together by similarity of character. For the things that profit some often hurt others; seeing that also for the most part herbs which nourish some animals are fatal to others; and the gentle hissing that quiets horses incites whelps; and the medicine which abates one disease aggravates another; and the bread which invigorates the life of the strong kills little children. Therefore according to the quality of the hearers ought the discourse of teachers to be fashioned, so as to suit all and each for their several needs, and yet never deviate from the art of common edification. For what are the intent minds of hearers but, so to speak, a kind of tight tensions of strings in a harp, which the skilful player, that he may produce a tune not at variance with itself, strikes variously? And for this reason the strings render back a consonant modulation, that they are struck indeed with one quill, but not with one kind of stroke. Whence every teacher also, that he may edify all in the one virtue of charity, ought to touch the hearts of his hearers out of one doctrine, but not with one and the same exhortation.

CHAPTER I

Differently to be admonished are these that follow:—
Men and women.

The poor and the rich.

The joyful and the sad.

Prelates and subordinates.

Servants and masters.

The wise of this world and the dull.

The impudent and the bashful.

The forward and the fainthearted.

The impatient and the patient.

The kindly disposed and the envious.

The simple and the insincere.

The whole and the sick.

Those who fear scourges, and therefore live innocently; and those who have grown so hard in iniquity as not to be corrected even by scourges.

The too silent, and those who spend time in much speaking.

The slothful and the hasty.

The meek and the passionate.

The humble and the haughty.

The obstinate and the fickle.

The gluttonous and the abstinent.

Those who mercifully give of their own, and those who would fain seize what belongs to others.

Those who neither seize the things of others nor are bountiful with their own; and those who both give away the things they have, and yet cease not to seize what belongs to others.

Those that are at variance, and those that are at peace.

Lovers of strifes and peacemakers.

Those that understand not aright the words of sacred law; and those who understand them indeed aright, but speak them without humility.

Those who, though able to preach worthily, are afraid through excessive humility; and those whom imperfection or age debars from preaching, and yet rashness impels to it.

Those who prosper in what they desire in temporal matters; and those who covet indeed the things that are of the world, and yet are wearied with the toils of adversity.

Those who are bound by wedlock, and those who are free from the ties of wedlock.

Those who have had experience of carnal intercouse, and those who are ignorant of it.

Those who deplore sins of deed, and those who deplore sins of thought.

Those who bewail misdeeds, yet forsake them not; and those who forsake them, yet bewail them not.

Those who even praise the unlawful things they do; and those who censure what is wrong, yet avoid it not.

Those who are overcome by sudden passion, and those who are bound in guilt of set purpose.

Those who, though their unlawful deeds are trivial, yet do them frequently; and those who keep themselves from small sins, but are occasionally whelmed in graver ones.

Those who do not even begin what is good, and those who fail entirely to complete the good begun.

Those who do evil secretly and good publicly; and those who conceal the good they do, and yet in some things done publicly allow evil to be thought of them.

But of what profit is it for us to run through all these things collected together in a list, unless we also set forth, with all possible brevity, the modes of admonition for each?

(Admonition 1.) Differently, then, to be admonished are men and women; because on the former heavier injunctions, on the latter lighter are to be laid, that those may be exercised by great things, but these winningly converted by light ones.

(Admonition 2.) Differently to be admonished are young men and old; because for the most part severity of admonition directs the former to improvement, while kind remonstrance disposes the latter to better deeds. For it is written, "Rebuke not an elder, but entreat him as a father" (1 Tim. v. 1). . . .

CHAPTER VIII

(Admonition 9.) Differently to be admonished are the forward and the faint-hearted. For the former, presuming on themselves too much, disdain all others when reproved by them; but the latter, while too conscious of their own infirmity, for the most part fall into despondency. Those count all they do to be singularly eminent; these think what they do to be exceedingly despised, and so are broken down to despondency. Therefore the works of the forward are to be finely sifted by the reprover, that wherein they please themselves they may be shewn to displease God.

For we then best correct the forward, when what they believe themselves to have done well we shew to have been ill done; that whence glory is believed to have been gained, thence wholesome confusion may ensue. . . .

But on the other hand we more fitly bring back the faint-hearted to the way of well-doing, if we search collaterally for some good points about them, so that, while some things in them we attack with our reproof, others we may embrace with our praise; to the end that the hearing of praise may nourish their tenderness, which the rebuking of their fault chastises. And for the most part we make more way with them for their profit, if we also make mention of their good deeds; and, in case of some wrong things having been done by them, if we find not fault with them as though they were already perpetrated, but, as it were, prohibit them as what ought not to be perpetrated; that so both the favour shewn may increase the things which we approve, and our modest exhortation avail more with the faint-hearted against the things which we blame. Whence the same Paul, when he came to know that the Thessalonians, who stood fast in the preaching which they had received, were troubled with a certain faint-heartedness as though the end of the world were nigh at hand, first praises that wherein he sees them to be strong, and afterwards, with cautious admonition, strengthens what was weak. For he says, "We are bound to thank God always for you, brethren, as it is meet, because that your faith groweth exceedingly, and the charity of every one of you all toward each other aboundeth; so that we ourselves too glory in you in the churches of God for your patience and faith" (2 Thess. i. 3,4). But, having premised these flattering encomiums of their life, a little while after he subjoined, "Now we beseech you, brethren, by the coming of our Lord Jesus Christ, and our gathering together unto Him, that ye be not soon shaken in mind, or be troubled, neither by spirit, nor by word, nor by letter as sent by us, as that the day of the Lord is at hand" (Ibid. ii. 1). For the true teacher so proceeded that they should first hear, in being praised, what they might thankfully acknowledge, and afterwards, in being exhorted, what they should follow; to the end that the precedent praise should settle their mind, lest the subjoined admonition should shake it; and, though he knew that they had been disquieted by suspicion of the end being near, he did not yet reprove them as having been so, but, as if ignorant of the past,

forbade them to be disquieted in future; so that, while they believed themselves to be unknown to their preacher with respect
even to the levity of their disquietude, they might be as much afraid
of being open to blame as they were of being known by him
to be so.

Part IV. How the Preacher, When He Has Accomplished All Aright, Should Return to Himself, Lest Either His Life or His Preaching Lift Him Up.

But since often, when preaching is abundantly poured forth in
fitting ways, the mind of the speaker is elevated in itself by a
hidden delight in self-display, great care is needed that he may
gnaw himself with the laceration of fear, lest he who recalls the
diseases of others to health by remedies should himself swell
through neglect of his own health; lest in helping others he desert
himself, lest in lifting up others he fall. For to some the greatness of
their virtue has often been the occasion of their perdition; causing
them, while inordinately secure in confidence of strength, to die
unexpectedly through negligence. For virtue strives with vices; the
mind flatters itself with a certain delight in it; and it comes to pass
that the soul of a well-doer casts aside the fear of its circumspection, and rests secure in self-confidence; and to it, now torpid, the
cunning seducer enumerates all things that it has done well, and
exalts it in swelling throughts as though superexcellent beyond all
beside. Whence it is brought about, that before the eyes of the just
judge the memory of virtue is a pitfall of the soul; because, in
calling to mind what it has done well, while it lifts itself up in its
own eyes, it falls before the author of humility. . . . Whence it is
needful that, when abundance of virtues flatters us, the eye of the
soul should return to its own weaknesses, and salubriously depress
itself; that it should look, not at the right things that it has done,
but those that it has left undone; so that, while the heart is bruised
by recollection of infirmity, it may be the more strongly confirmed
in virtue before the author of humility. For it is generally for this
purpose that Almighty God, though perfecting in great part the
minds of rulers, still in some small part leaves them imperfect; in
order that, when they shine with wonderful virtues, they may pine
with disgust at their own imperfection, and by no means lift
themselves up for great things, while still labouring in their

struggle against the least; but that, since they are not strong enough to overcome in what is last and lowest, they may not dare to glory in their chief performances.

See now, good man, how, compelled by the necessity laid upon me by thy reproof, being intent on shewing what a Pastor ought to be, I have been as an ill-favoured painter portraying a handsome man; and how I direct others to the shore of perfection, while myself still tossed among the waves of transgressions. But in the shipwreck of this present life sustain me, I beseech thee, by the plank of thy prayer, that, since my own weight sinks me down, the hand of thy merit may raise me up.

II

The Carolingian Age

If the age of Gregory the Great represents a transition from the Greco-Roman to a new stage in European civilization, Byzantine in the East and Romano-German in the West, the rise of Islam in the seventh century, followed by the reformation of the Frankish kingdom in the eighth and ninth centuries, produced a more complete severance from the old order. With the Moslem conquests, all North Africa was lost to Christendom, and the Christians of Egypt, Palestine, and Syria were forced, as were those of most of Spain, to live under Moslem rule. Despite its losses, the eastern Roman or Byzantine empire remained a power to be reckoned with in the eastern Mediterranean and managed to retain for a while longer its lands in southern Italy; but it was no longer able to exercise a preponderant influence in the West.

Meanwhile, regions formerly considered to lie beyond the frontiers of the Roman world were acquiring importance. A significant new area of western Christendom, for example, developed in the British Isles. The successors of St. Augustine of Canterbury whom Pope Gregory had sent to Saxon England, pushed northward, while Irish missionaries and monks (*Scoti*, as they were called) traveled to a land already colonized by their kindred and later named Scotland. They also penetrated Saxon England. Iona and Lindisfarne are among their most celebrated foundations. Thus it was that as St. Augustine and his successors were introducing Christianity and Latin culture to the Saxons of southern and central Britain, Irish monks were bringing religious learning to the north. By the seventh and eighth centuries, England was developing a vigorous as well as a varied Christian culture which was to contribute notably, with the help of such outstanding missionaries as St. Boniface (d. 755), to the reorganization of Christianity on the continent.

By the mid-eighth century the Frankish kingdom was developing political institutions of some stability. In 732 the Frankish mayor of the palace, Charles Martel, stopped the Arab advance at Tours. In subsequent decades he and his successor, Pippin (741–68), who with papal blessing assumed the title of king, brought the kingdom of the Franks to a new unity, following more than a century of division and disorder.

Frankish civilization reached its climax during the reign of Charlemagne (768–814). The frontiers were extended to include the Saxons beyond the Rhine, marches along the eastern borders, a march in northeastern Spain, and the northern half of Italy, an area of many diverse customs and languages. Such unity as the Frankish empire possessed resulted from Charlemagne's administrative skill and unflagging energy as well as from his ability to maintain the loyalty of a relatively small number of great magnates. For with the passing of Roman institutions and the decline in commercial life, western society, especially that newer part of it to the north and west, had become decentralized and predominantly agrarian.

To assist him in guiding the destinies of his kingdom, Charlemagne gathered around him a remarkable group of men, among them Alcuin of York; Theodulf, a Spaniard who became bishop of Orléans; Paul the Deacon; and Einhard, his biographer. These and others constituted a kind of learned elite and in their respective backgrounds represented those areas of Europe where Christian-classical culture had flourished. In fact, their searching in the classical past produced what has been called the Carolingian renaissance, a significant if limited achievement.

Although Charlemagne, after the manner of the Franks, planned to divide his kingdom, he was in fact succeeded by his oldest son, Louis the Pious (814–40). Throughout his reign Louis was beset by many difficulties—attacks on the frontiers, rebellions by his own sons, and his own hesitations. Once considered a relatively weak ruler, Louis nevertheless accomplished a number of things and did much to carry on the political and religious traditions of his father.

Following Louis's death the Frankish empire was divided, and after one or two ineffectual attempts to reconstitute it in its original form, it so remained. Norse, Slav, Magyar, and Saracen attacks on the frontiers ushered in a new period of political disorder, which scarcely ended before the mid-tenth century. Nevertheless, although the political creations of the Carolingians were not destined to survive, the entire era, from the first Carolingian rulers to the later ninth century, was a period of fundamental importance in the history of western Christianity, one in which certain basic elements of western religious life were formed.

One such element was the concept of a *respublica christiana*, a total Christian society in which the religious and the secular were merged and in which the ruler's religious role was on a par with his political one. This had been true to some extent in earlier times, but as the bonds of society in this emerging feudal age became more personal, linking man to man rather than man to government, the ruler's religious function took on a new importance. What is especially relevant here is the fact that Charlemagne, even more fully than his predecessors, regarded his royal responsibility as including ecclesiastical administration. For Charlemagne named bishops and summoned councils which dealt not only with administrative matters but with questions of doctrine and religious practice. His ordinances went out to Church dignitaries as well as to lay magnates. They were concerned with the life of the clergy, monastic as well as secular, and they dealt with the religious life of the laity. To his associates at court Charles was known as "David." Like the ancient Hebrew rulers, he was the anointed leader of the "People of God," responsible for their eternal as well as for their temporal welfare.

Einhard tells us that Charlemagne was familiar with St. Augustine's *City of God*. Indeed, some have characterized Carolingian society as "political Augustinianism," a sort of merger or confusion of the two cities, the earthly and heavenly, an identification of the city of God with Christian society. At any rate, the first great effort in the West to create a total Christian society was made under the leadership of the king. Further, this was no less true under Charlemagne's successors. Louis the Pious, educated by the men his father had brought to the royal court, had an even more profound sense of the sacred character of kingship than his father.

Among the things upon which the advisers of both Charlemagne and Louis were particularly insistent was the need for uniformity. Accordingly, they sought, though not always correctly, to reproduce the traditions of the fathers. Moreover, although they were not unwilling, if circumstances so indicated, to innovate, their norm was always what they believed to be Roman usage. The importance of this is clear. In a critical formative period in western Christian history, the customs of what was referred to as "the Roman church" came to be a standard for all.

In canon law, for example, the sources available to the Carolingians left much to be desired, so that there remained confusion and room for disagreement, and usages tended to vary according to regional tradition. Three collections of decrees of popes and councils were then in fairly wide, though local, use. In the East a council of the year 692 (Trullo-Quinisext) sanctioned a collection to which later additions were made—notably the canons of the Second Council of Nicea (787). In the West, the collection known as the *Hispana*, compiled in Visigothic Spain and sometimes referred to as *Isidoriana* because of an attribution to Isidore of Seville, was accepted in Spain.

Because there was no established canonical tradition in Gaul, the Frankish rulers turned to Rome. Meanwhile, in the sixth century a collection of Latin translations of Greek canons—to which were added 39 decretals of popes from Siricius (d. 398) to Anastasius (d. 498)— was made by the Scythian monk, Dionysius Exiguus. This was adopted in Rome and other papal decrees were subsequently added. It was this collection which was sent by Pope Hadrian I to Charlemagne and which, as a result, became known as the *Dionysio-Hadriana*.

Toward the middle of the ninth century certain impatient canonists, apparently alarmed at what they regarded as the anarchical state of the Frankish churches, drew up, probably at Rome, a new collection of canons. This was based largely on the *Isidoriana-Hispana,* but included a number of additions, notably 70 letters allegedly written by pre-Nicene popes but in fact invented to support positions felt to be sound. The famous Donation of Constantine was also added.

Later known as *Pseudo-Isidorian,* these forged decretals have occasioned a vast literature. There seems, however, to be general agreement that the modern connotation of the word "forged" is inappropriate to the situation in the mid-ninth century. The purpose appears to have been to strengthen and systematize canonical procedure; moreover, as the new material gradually found its way into later collections, the centralizing tendencies of the papacy were strengthened. But in this as in other matters, the process might perhaps better be described as a short cut than as a fundamental juridical innovation.

In the second half of the ninth century, and especially under the auspices of Nicholas I (858–67), the papacy emerged from the eclipse it had suffered during the days of the great Carolingians. Although Nicholas I made some use of the spurious canons, certain of his most important letters contain no such references. His many letters to prelates and rulers both eastern and western left no doubt about his insistence on the Roman primacy, and his words were frequently cited by the popes of the later eleventh century.

Charlemagne had intended to institute a thoroughgoing monastic reform, and he had secured from Montecassino an authentic copy of the *Rule of St. Benedict.* He was not, however, able to achieve this, and it remained for a second Benedict, Benedict of Aniane, under the patronage of Charlemagne's son, Louis, to make the *Rule* the universal norm for western monasticism. Certain additions were made to the monastic *horarium,* and monastic schools were reserved exclusively for boys who intended to become monks. Detailed rules were also drawn up to regulate the life of nuns, and a series of decrees on canons was designed to implement and extend an earlier rule of St. Chrodegang of Metz.

In seeking to achieve liturgical uniformity according to Roman usage, the Carolingian ecclesiastics ran into difficulties. By the early eighth century, western liturgical practices had become exceedingly confused. In the Carolingian lands and in Spain, for example, many local variations had been added to form what may loosely be called the "Gallican rite." In actual fact, the Gallican rite had remained intact only in Spain where it later came to be known as Mozarabic. As in many other matters, the impetus toward reform on the Roman model came from England. Influenced presumably by St. Boniface, Pepin decided to abolish Gallican usages and inaugurate a program of liturgical uniformity. And it was Alcuin, another Englishman, to whom Charlemagne entrusted the task of carrying the work further.

Carolingian churchmen also made important contributions to liturgical interpretation and embellishment. Not long after Charlemagne's death, Amalar of Metz produced an elaborate allegorical interpretation of the mass which, though adversely criticized by many, set a style that was to continue. Later in the ninth century, cantors commonly elaborated the final *a* of the word *Alleluia* into a melody known as a "sequence." Eventually the sequence became virtually a new hymn. Thus the Carolingians continued the ancient tradition of liturgical hymnody.

Carolingian Christianity was molded by a relatively small elite of distinguished ecclesiastics. They were confronted with an uneducated and still largely undisciplined public, of whom the vast majority were peasants isolated in rural parishes. Inevitably there resulted a separation between a clergy, in theory though not always in practice educated, and an ignorant laity—a separation which was to remain characteristic of medieval Christianity. Even in the liturgy this separation is evident. For it was during this period that the priest began to stand before the altar with his back to the congregation instead of behind it facing the people, according to the custom of the primitive church.[1] Latin was the exclusive liturgical language, and the Slavonic liturgy devised by Constantine-Cyril and Methodius along the eastern frontiers was strenuously resisted. The faithful no longer understood the language of the service, and the celebrant recited the canon of the mass with the prayers of consecration silently. The custom whereby the faithful brought the offering of bread and wine in procession to the altar also began to be abandoned.

Doubtless these things were necessary in a civilization not yet fully formed. Yet it remains true that there was formalism in Carolingian religious life. It was religion according to precept and law. This is evident in the royal and conciliar decrees. It is evident in instructions to priests. However, despite such weaknesses, the Carolingian religious achievement is impressive. Its influence was to endure long after the political structure had passed away.

Suggested Readings

Bainton, R. S., *The Medieval Church* (New York, 1962).

Baldwin, M. W., *The Mediaeval Church* (Ithaca, N.Y., 1953).

Cannon, W. R., *History of Christianity in the Middle Ages* (Nashville, Tenn., 1960).

Daly, L. J. (see under Part I).

Dawson, C., *Religion and the Rise of Western Culture* (London, 1950).

Deanesley, M., *A History of the Medieval Church* (new ed., London, 1965).

1. Apparently because the accumulation of relics on or behind the altar made the celebrant's former position impossible.

————, *A History of Early Medieval Europe, 476–911* (London, 1956).

Duckett, E., *Alcuin, Friend of Charlemagne* (new ed., Hamden, Conn., 1965).

————, *Anglo-Saxon Saints and Scholars* (London, 1947).

————, *Carolingian Portraits* (Ann Arbor, Mich., 1962).

Hughes, P., *A History of the Church*, vol. II (New York, 1935).

Knowles, Dom D. (see under Part I).

Russell, J. B., *A History of Medieval Christianity* (New York, 1968).

Schnurer, G., *Christianity and Culture in the Middle Ages*, vol. I, trans. G. J. Undreiner (Paterson, N.J., 1956).

Ecclesiastical Organization Under Royal Authority

18. Charlemagne

Admonitio generalis

The following selection (including parts of the Preface and certain chapters) from Charlemagne's general instructions, issued in 789, illustrates the Carolingian conception of theocratic monarchy and the king's own view of his responsibility for the spiritual as well as the temporal welfare of his people. The "canonical ordinances" which he mentions constituted a collection of canons (the *Dionysio-Hadriana*) which the king had received from Pope Hadrian I. Some 80 prescriptions on various aspects of religious life followed. A dozen or so years later (802), these were further implemented in detailed instructions to the *missi*.

In this selection and in the letter to Pope Leo which follows, it is likely that the language is that of one or more of the ecclesiastics at the royal court, most probably Alcuin. The selections are translated from *Monumenta Germaniæ historica, Leges* II (*Capitularia regum Francorum* I), pp. 533 ff.

Our Lord Jesus Christ ruling forever.

I, Charles by the grace of God and the gift of His mercy, king and ruler of the kingdom of the Franks, devout defender and humble supporter of holy church, give greetings of lasting peace and beatitude to all grades of the ecclesiastical order and to all ranks of the secular power, in Christ our Lord, eternal God.

Reflecting with dutiful and calm consideration, along with our priests and councilors, on the abundant mercy of Christ the King toward us and our people, we have considered how necessary it is not only with our whole heart and voice to offer thanks for His goodness unceasingly, but also to persist in the continuous exercise of good works in His praise so that He who has given our kingdom such honors may deign to preserve and protect us and our kingdom forever. Accordingly it has pleased us to solicit your efforts, O pastors of the churches of Christ and leaders of His flock and distinguished luminaries of the world, to strive to lead the people of God to the pastures of eternal life by watchful care and urgent advice and stir yourselves to bring back the wandering sheep within the walls of ecclesiastical constancy on the shoulders of good example or exhortation, lest the wolf, plotting against anyone who transgresses the canonical laws or evades the fatherly traditions of the ecumenical councils—which God forbid!—find him and devour him. Thus they must be admonished, urged, and even forced by the great zeal of piety, to restrain themselves within the bonds of paternal sanctions with staunch faith and unrelenting constancy. Therefore, we have sent our *missi* who by the authority of our name are to correct along with you what should be corrected. And we append herewith certain chapters from canonical ordinances which seem to us to be particularly necessary.

Let no one judge this admonition to piety, by which we endeavor to correct errors, remove superfluous matter, and condense those things which are right, to be presumptuous. I entreat him rather to accept it with a benevolent spirit of charity. For we read in the book of Kings how the holy Josias, traveling around the kingdom bestowed on him by God, correcting and admonishing, labored to recall it to the worship of the true God: not that I hold myself equal to his holiness, but because the examples of the saints are always to be followed by us, and we must bring together whomsoever we can to a devotion to the good life in the praise and glory of our Lord Jesus Christ. . . .

Chapter 70, To the Clergy

Bishops should carefully see to it that throughout their dioceses (*parochiae*) the priests observe their Catholic faith and baptism and understand well the prayers of the mass; and that the psalms are chanted properly according to the divisions of the verses and that they undertand the Lord's Prayer and preach that it is to be understood by all, so that each person may know what he is asking of God; and that the "Glory be to the Father" be sung with all dignity by everyone and that the priest himself with the holy angels and all the people of God with one voice intone the "Holy, Holy, Holy." And it should in every way be made clear to priests and deacons that they should not bear arms but trust in the protection of God rather than in arms.

CHAPTER 71, SOMETHING TO PRIEST, SOMETHING TO PEOPLE

It is likewise our will to urge your reverences that each through-out his diocese see that the church of God is held in His honor and the altars venerated with suitable dignity, and that the house of God is not used as a pathway for dogs and that the vessels conse-crated to God are kept with great care or used with honor; and that secular or mundane affairs are not transacted in churches because the house of God must be a house of prayer and not a den of thieves (Matt. 21:13); and that the people when they come to the solemnities of the mass are attentive and do not leave before the completion of the priest's blessing.

CHAPTER 72, TO THE CLERGY*

And we also demand of your holiness that the ministers of the altar of God shall adorn their ministry by good manners, and likewise the other orders who observe a rule and the congregations of monks. We implore them to lead a just and fitting life, just as God himself commanded in the Gospel. "Let your light so shine before men that they may see your good works and glorify your Father which is in heaven" (Matt. 5:16), so that by their example many may be led to serve God; and let them join and associate to themselves not only children of servile condition, but also sons of free men. And let schools be established in which boys may learn to read. Correct carefully the Psalms, the signs in writing (*notas*), the songs, the calendar, the grammar in each monastery or bishop-ric, and the catholic books; because often some desire to pray to God properly, but they pray badly because of the incorrect books. And do not permit your boys to corrupt them in reading or writing. If there is need of writing the Gospel, Psalter, and Missal, let men of mature age do the writing with all diligence.

CHAPTER 73, TO THE CLERGY

We have likewise taken pains to ask that all, wherever they are, who have bound themselves by the vow of a monastic life live in every way regularly in a monastic manner according to that vow.

* This chapter is translated by D. C. Munro, *University of Pennsylvania Translations and Reprints*, vol. VI (Philadelphia, 1899), no. V, p. 15.

For it is written, "Render your vows to the Lord God" (Deut. 23:21); and again, "it is better not to vow than not to fulfil" (Eccles. 5:4). And let those coming to monasteries according to the regular manner be first tested in the examination room and so accepted. And let those who come to the monastery from the secular life not be sent immediately on monastic tasks outside before they are well educated within. And monks are not to seek worldly pleasures. Likewise, those who are admitted to that clerical state which we call the canonical life, we desire that they live such a life canonically and in every way according to its rule; and the bishop should govern their life as the abbot does the monks.

CHAPTER 74, TO ALL

Let all have equal and correct weights and just and equal measures, whether in the towns or in the monasteries, whether in giving in them or in receiving, as we have the command in the law of the Lord (cf. Levit. 19:35–36), and likewise in Solomon, when the Lord says, "[Different] weight and [different] measure, my soul abhors." (cf. Prov. 20:10)

CHAPTER 80, TO ALL THE CLERGY

Let them teach fully the Roman chant and let the office be followed according to the direction of the nocturnal or gradual as our father Pepin, of blessed memory, ordered done when he suppressed the Gallican use for the sake of unity with the apostolic see and the peaceful harmony of the holy church of God.

CHAPTER 81, TO ALL

And we also decree, according to what the Lord ordained in the law (cf. Exod. 20:8–10), that there be no servile work on Sundays, as my father, of good memory, ordered in the edicts of his synods, that is: that men do no farm work, either in plowing fields or in tending vineyards, in sowing grain or planting hedges, in clearing in the woods[1] or in cutting trees, in working with stone or in building houses, or in working in the garden; nor are they to gather for games or go hunting. Three tasks with wagons may be

---

1. *Stirpare*, to "staddle," i.e., to leave saplings standing in a forest clearing. On the terminology here, see R. Latouche, *The Birth of Western Economy*, trans. E. M. Wilkinson (London, 1961), 176.

performed on Sunday, the arms' cart or the food wagon, or if it is necessary to bear someone's body to the grave.

Likewise, women are not to work with cloth nor cut out clothes, nor sew or embroider; nor is it permissible to comb wool or crush flax or wash clothes in public, or shear sheep, to the end that the honor and quiet of the Lord's day be kept. But let people come together from all places to the church for the solemnities of the mass and praise God on that day for all the good things He has done for us.

Chapter 82, To All

And you are to see to it, O chosen and venerable pastors and rulers of the church of God, that the priests whom you send through your dioceses (*parochiae*) for ruling and preaching in the churches to the people serving God, that they rightly and justly preach; and you are not to allow any of them to invent and preach to the people new and unlawful things according to their own judgment and not according to Holy Scripture. And you too are to preach those things which are just and right and lead to eternal life, and instruct others that they are to preach these same things.

Letter from Charlemagne to Pope Leo III

This letter was written in 796 after the death of Hadrian I and the accession of Leo. The paragraphs quoted illustrate Charlemagne's ideas about the duties of kings and popes. Evidently he had no hesitation in reading the pope a lesson on pontifical behavior. The text is translated from the Latin text in *MGH, Epistolae,* vol. IV, 137–138.

. . . Just as we entered into an agreement with the most blessed father, your predecessor Hadrian, so we desire to establish with your beatitude the same inviolable bond of faith and charity; to the end that with divine grace invoked by the prayers of your apostolic holiness, the apostolic blessing may follow us everywhere and the see of the most holy Roman church, God willing, always be defended by our devotion. For it is our task, with the aid of divine goodness, to defend the holy church of Christ everywhere from the attacks of pagans without and to strengthen it within through the knowledge of the Catholic faith. And it is your duty, O Holy Father, with your hands raised high to God, after the manner of Moses, to aid our armies so that by your intercession with God, our leader and benefactor, the Christian people may always and everywhere be victorious over the enemies of His Holy Name, and the name of Our Lord Jesus Christ be proclaimed throughout the world.

Let the wisdom of your authority adhere everywhere to the canonical laws and follow always the statutes of the holy fathers, in order that examples of perfect holiness in your discourse may shine clearly to all and the exhortations of holy counsel be heard from your mouth. Thus may your light shine before men that they may see your good works and glorify your Father who is in heaven (Matt. 5:6).

Letter from Alcuin to Charlemagne

This letter was written in 799 after an attack on Pope Leo III by certain factions of Romans and refers also to the deposition of the emperor Constantine V in Constantinople. Although allowance must be made for the customary language of flattery, it is noticeable that in the passage cited here Alcuin exalts the royal dignity over the papal and the imperial and emphasizes its religious character. The text is translated from *Ibid.,* p. 288.

. . . For there were three persons most high in this world. There is the apostolic sublimity which customarily governs by the authority of vicar the see of Blessed Peter the Apostle. . . . Another is the imperial dignity, the secular power of the second Rome. . . . The third is the royal dignity, in which the ordering of our Lord Jesus Christ has placed you, the ruler of the Christian people, in power more excellent than the other dignities mentioned, more clear in wisdom, more sublime in the authority of government. For lo! in you rests the entire safety of the churches of Christ. You are the avenger of evil, the guide of those who wander, the consoler of the afflicted, and the exaltation of the good. . . .

19. Theodulf of Orléans

Precepts to the Priests of His Diocese

Royal letters and capitularies give evidence only of a policy, not of what was actually accomplished. The following selection from the writings of a prominent bishop is, therefore, highly significant. Theodulf of Orléans, a Spaniard of Visigothic background, stands out among Charlemagne's bishops as a scholar, builder, and composer of hymns. The churches erected under his auspices (for example, Germigny des Près) are archeologically important. And his hymn, *All Glory Laud and Honor*, has found a permanent place in the liturgy of Palm Sunday. His direction to his clergy on their pastoral responsibilities is one of the few documents of its kind to survive from the period. Moreover, although this document tells us nothing of what was subsequently done by the parish clergy, it does bring us one step closer to the religion of the people. The translation is by G. E. McCracken, *Early Medieval Theology*, The Library of Christian Classics, vol. IX (Philadelphia, 1957), pp. 382 ff. Reprinted by permission of The Westminster Press, Philadelphia, and SCM Press Ltd., London. Certain chapters and all notes except for scriptural citations have been omitted.

1. I beg you, my most beloved brothers, to labor with the most watchful care with regard to the progress and improvement of the people subject to you, so that, by showing them the way of salvation and instructing them by word and example, we shall bring back fruitful harvests to our Lord Jesus Christ with his aid, you from their progress, and ourselves from yours. I beg your brotherhood, also, that you read carefully these chapters which I have briefly laid down for the improvement of life, and commit them to memory, and that by reading them and the Holy Scriptures you may regulate the morals and improve the life of the people put under you, and with them, the Lord being your helper, you may strive to reach the heavenly Kingdom. You ought to know truly and always to remember that we, to whom the care of governing souls has been entrusted, will render an accounting in regard to those who perish through our neglect, but in regard to those whom by word and example we shall have gained, we shall receive the reward of eternal life. For to us the Lord has said, "You are the salt of the earth." (Matt. 5:13) Because if a faithful people is God's food, we are the spice of his food. Know that your rank is second to our rank and is almost joined to it. For as the bishops hold in the church the place of the apostles, so the presbyters hold the place of the other disciples of the Lord. The former hold the rank of the chief priest Aaron, but the latter the rank of his sons. For this reason you ought to be mindful always of so great authority, mindful of your consecration, mindful of the holy unction which you have received in your hands, that you do not lower this authority, nor nullify your consecration, nor defile with sin the

hands besmeared with holy oil, but preserving purity of heart and body, offering to the people an example of proper living, you may offer to those over whom you are in charge guidance to the heavenly kingdoms.

2. You ought to be continually reading and constantly at prayer, because the life of the righteous man is taught and equipped by reading, and by constantly reading a person is fortified against sin, according to him who said, "In my heart have I hidden thy word that I might not sin against thee." (Ps. 119:11) For these are the arms, namely, reading and prayer, by which the devil is defeated; these are the means by which eternal blessedness is obtained; with these arms vices are suppressed; upon these foods virtues are nourished.

3. But, also, if there be any interruption in reading, the hands should then be used, because "idleness is the enemy to the soul" and the ancient enemy easily carries off to vices the one whom he finds free from reading or praying. By the use of reading you will learn how you should live and how to teach others; by the use of prayer you will be able to be of value both to yourselves and to those united with you in love. By the operation of the hands and the chastisement of the body, you will both deny nourishment to the vices and will supply your own needs and have something to offer for the needs of sufferers.

6. Let women never approach the altar when the priest is celebrating Mass, but let them stand in their own places and there let the priest receive their offerings as he will offer them to God. For women ought to be mindful of their weakness and of the infirmity of their sex, and therefore fear to touch anything holy in the ministry of the church. These even laymen ought to fear, lest they undergo the punishment of Uzzah, who was willing to touch in an unusual fashion the Ark of the Lord but, struck by the Lord, died.

7. Let a priest never celebrate Mass alone, because as it cannot be celebrated without the salutation of a priest, the response of the people, the admonition of the priest, and again the response of the people, thus it ought never to be celebrated by one man alone. For there should be people to stand around him, to receive his salutation, to give responses to him, and to recall to him that saying of the Lord: "Wherever two or three shall be gathered in my name, there also am I in their midst." (Matt. 18:20)

10. You ought not to gather in the church for any other cause except for praise of the Lord and for carrying on his service. Controversies, however, and tumults, and vain speaking, and other proceedings should be entirely forbidden in that holy place. For where the name of God is invoked, sacrifice is offered to God, and as without doubt angels congregate there in great numbers, it is dangerous to say anything or do anything there which is not fitting to the place. For if the Lord cast out from the Temple those who bought and sold the victims which were to be offered to himself, with how much greater anger will he cast out thence those who defile with lies, vain speaking, jokes, and trifles of this sort, the place set for divine worship?

11. The celebrations of Masses ought never to take place elsewhere than in a church, not in just any houses or in mean places, but in a place which the Lord shall choose, according to the passage of Scripture: "See that you do not offer your burnt offerings in any place which you see, but in a place which the Lord sha l choose to place his name there." (Deut. 12:13)

12. Let no woman live with a presbyter in a single house. Although the canons permit a priest's mother and sister to live with him, and persons of this kind in whom there is no suspicion, we abolish this privilege for the reason that there may come, out of courtesy to them or to trade with them, other women not at all related to him and offer an enticement for sin to him.

13. You should take care to refrain from drunkenness, and to preach that the people under your care should refrain, and that you should never go through the taverns eating and drinking, nor travel around through houses and villages out of curiosity, nor attend feasts with women or with any impure persons, unless some head of a household, perhaps, shall invite you to his home and, with his wife and children, wishes to rejoice with you in spiritual joy, and to receive the refreshment of your words and to offer you carnal refreshments in the duty of love, for it is fitting that, if at any time any of the faithful gives you the refreshment of carnal foods, he should be given spiritual refreshment by you.

20. Let the presbyters keep schools in the villages and hamlets, and if any of the faithful desires to entrust his small children to them to be taught their letters, let them not refuse to receive and teach them, but let them teach them with the greatest love, noticing what is written: "They, however, who shall be learned shall

shine as the splendor of the firmament, and they who instruct many to righteousness shall shine as the stars forever and ever." (Dan. 12:13) When, therefore, they teach them, let them demand no fee for this instruction, nor take anything from them, except what the parents shall offer them freely through zeal for love.

22. The faithful must be reminded that all of them together, from the least to the greatest, should learn the Lord's Prayer and the Creed, and they must be told that upon these two propositions the whole foundation of the Christian faith rests and unless anyone shall remember these two propositions and believe them with his whole heart, and repeat them very often in prayer, he cannot be catholic. For it has been established that none shall be anointed, nor baptized, nor be lifted up from the water of that fountain, nor can he hold anyone before the bishop to be confirmed, unless he has committed to memory the Creed and the Lord's Prayer, save only those whose age has not yet taught them to speak.

23. They must be told that every day he who cannot pray more often should at least pray twice, that is, in the morning and evening, saying the Creed or the Lord's Prayer or the "O Thou who hast fashioned me," or even, "God, be merciful to me a sinner," and, "Thanks be to God," in return for the provisions of daily life and because He has deigned to create him after his own image and distinguish him from the beasts. When this has been done and God the sole Creator has been adored, let him call upon the saints that they may deign to intercede on his behalf with the divine Majesty. Let those near a church do this in a church; he who, however, is on a journey or for some reason is in the forests or the fields, wherever the morning or evening hour itself finds him, let him do so, knowing that God is present everywhere, as the psalmist says: "In every place of his dominion" (Ps. 103:22) and "If I should ascend into heaven, thou art there" (Ps. 139:8), etc.

24. On the Lord's Day, however, because on it God established light, on it rained manna in the desert, on it the Redeemer of the human race voluntarily for our salvation rose again from the dead, on it he poured forth the Holy Spirit upon his disciples, there should be so great an observance that besides prayers and the solemnization of the Masses, and those things which pertain to eating, nothing else should be done. For if there should also be need of sailing, or traveling, permission is given provided that on these

occasions the Mass and prayers are not passed by. Each Christian must come on the Sabbath Day to church with lights; he must come to the night vigils or to the morning office. He must come also with offerings for the solemnization of Masses. And while they come to church, no case should be pleaded or heard, no lawsuits may be held, but the time must be free for God alone, namely, in the celebration of the holy offices, and in the offering of alms, and in feasting spiritually on praise of God with friends, neighbors, and strangers.

25. They must be exhorted to love hospitality and to refuse to furnish shelter to no one, and if by chance they should supply shelter to anyone, not to take pay from him, unless perhaps the recipient gives something of his own accord. They must be told how many have pleased God through the duty of hospitality, as the apostle says: "For by this some have pleased God, having received angels under their roof" (cf. Heb. 13:2). And again, "Hospitable without grumbling." (I Pet. 4:9) And the Lord himself will say at the Judgment, "I was a stranger and you made me your guest." (Matt. 25:35) Let them know also that whoever loves hospitality receives Christ in the guests. For that limitation of hospitality is not only inhuman but even cruel, in which a guest is never received unless the one who gives the hospitality is first paid, and what the Lord has bidden to do in regard to receiving the Heavenly Kingdom, let this be done in regard to receiving earthly possessions.

26. You must preach also that the faithful beware of perjury and to refrain from it absolutely, knowing that this is a great crime both in the Law and the Prophets, and prohibited in the Gospels. For we have heard that some people think this crime of no importance and somehow place upon perjurers a small measure of penance. They ought to know that the same penance should be imposed for perjury as for adultery, for fornication, for homicide, and for other criminal vices. If anyone, however, who has committed perjury or any criminal sin, and, being afraid of the pain of long penance, is unwilling to come to confession, he ought to be expelled from the church, from both Communion and association with the faithful, so that no one eats with him, nor drinks, nor speaks, nor takes him into his house.

27. They must be told to abstain from false testimony, knowing that this also is a very serious crime, and forbidden by the Lord

himself on Mt. Sinai, when the same Lord said : "Thou shalt not give false testimony" (Exod. 20:16), and, "A false witness will not be unpunished." (Prov. 19:5) Let whoever has done this know that he must be purified by such penance as was stated above concerning perjury, or he must be condemned by the same condemnation and excommunications as was stated. They must be told that it is the highest—I shall not say stupidity but—wickedness, to incur guilt for so great a crime on account of a desire for silver and gold, or clothing, or any other thing, or, as very frequently happens, because of drunkenness, so that he be kept in close confinement for seven years, or be expelled from the church, as the Lord says, "What does it profit a man if he shall gain the whole world and cause the loss of his soul?" (Matt. 16:26) Although he may seem more cruel to others, let him really be cruel to himself.

28. We exhort you to be ready to teach the people. He who knows the Scriptures, let him preach the Scriptures, but he who does not know them, let him at least say to the people what is very familiar, that they "turn from evil and do good, seek peace and pursue it, because the eyes of the Lord are upon the righteous and his ears are turned to their prayers," etc. No one can therefore excuse himself because he does not have a tongue which he can use to edify someone. For when he shall see anyone in error, he can at once, to the best of his ability and powers, by arguing, pleading, reproving, withdraw him from his error and exhort him to do good works. But when, with the Lord's help, we assemble together for a synod, let each man know how to tell us how much he has accomplished with help from the Lord, or what fruit he has accomplished. And if any man perhaps needs our aid, let him tell us this in love, and we with no less love will not postpone bringing aid to him as we are able.

31. Confessions should be made concerning all sins committed in either deed or thought. There are eight chief vices, from which hardly anyone can be found free. The first is gluttony, that is, voracity of the belly; second, fornication; third, languor or sadness; fourth, avarice; fifth, vainglory; sixth, envy; seventh, anger; eighth, pride.[1] When, therefore, anyone comes to confession, he should be diligently asked how or when he has committed the sin which he confesses he has done, and according to the measure of

1. More commonly seven in the Middle Ages. (Ed.)

the deed ought the penance to be indicated to him. He ought to be persuaded that he should even make confession of wicked thoughts. He ought also to be directed to make his confession of the eight principal vices, and the priest ought to mention each one of them by name and to receive confession about it.

36. One week before the beginning of Lent confessions should be given to the priests, penance received, quarrels reconciled, and all disputes settled, and from their hearts they ought to forgive debts, so that they may freely say, "Forgive us our debts as we also forgive our debtors." (Matt. 6:12) And so, entering upon the blessed Lenten season, they may, with clear and purified minds, approach the holy Easter, and through penitence may renew themselves, which is a second baptism. For as Baptism cleanses sins, so does penitence. And because after Baptism the sinner cannot be baptized again, this remedy of penitence has been given by the Lord that through it in place of Baptism sins committed after Baptism may be washed away. For the Holy Scriptures show that sins can be forgiven in seven ways: First, in Baptism, which has been given on account of the forgiveness of sins. Secondly, by martyrdom, according to the words of the psalmist: "Blessed is he to whom the Lord imputes no sin" (Ps. 32:2), because, according to what the same David says, "Blessed are those whose iniquities are forgiven and whose sins are covered." (Ps. 32:1) Sins are forgiven through Baptism; they are covered through penitence; they are imputed not through martyrdom. Thirdly, by alms, according to Daniel, who says to the heathen king Nebuchadnezzar, "Redeem thy sins with alms in mercies to the poor" (Dan. 4:27), and this: "Water quenches burning fire and alms quench sin." (Eccl. 3:33) And the Lord in the Gospel: "But give alms and behold, all things pure are yours." (Luke 11:41) Fourthly, if anyone forgives the sins of the one who sins against him, according to this: "Forgive and it will be forgiven to you" (Luke 6:37), and this: "So also your Father will forgive you your sins, if you forgive anyone from your hearts" (cf. Matt. 6:14). Fifthly, if through his preaching anyone should, by the exercise of good works, convert others from their error, in accordance with what the apostle says: "If anyone should make a sinner to turn from the error of his way, he will save his soul from death, and will cover a multitude of sins." Sixthly, through love, according to this: "The love of God covers

a multitude of sins" (James 5:20) through Jesus Christ our Lord. Seventhly, through penitence, according to what David says: "I turned in my affliction, while it is transfixed with a thorn." (I Pet. 4:8)

37. Lent itself, however, ought to be kept with highest observance, so that in it the fast never be broken except on the Lord's Days, which are excepted from fasting, because those days are the tithes of our year, which we ought to pass through with all devotion and sanctity. Let there be in them no occasion for breaking the fast because at another time it is customary to dispense with the fasting for the sake of love, but this should not be then. Because at another time, whether to fast or not is based on the wish and judgment of the individual, but at this time a failure to fast is to transcend the will of God. And to fast at another time is to get a reward for the one who fasts, but at this time, except for the sick and the little children, whoever does not fast shall gain punishment for himself because these same days the Lord has consecrated to holy fasting through Moses and through Elijah and through himself.

38. On the days of the fast, alms should be given, so that anyone, if he does not fast as he ought, may distribute food and drink to the poor, because to fast and to keep the food for lunch until dinner is an increase, not of recompense, but of foods.

39. Many who think they are fasting have the habit of eating as soon as they hear the bell for nones, but they should not believe that they are fasting if they should eat before the office of vespers. For one must go to Masses, and hear the solemnization of Masses and office of vespers, and also give alms, before approaching food. If anyone should be so limited of necessity that he cannot attend Mass, he should break his fast having shown respect to the vesper hour and having completed his prayer.

40. On those days there should be abstention from every pleasure and they must live soberly and chastely. He who can abstain from eggs, cheese, fish, and wine, gains great credit for virtue; he, however, who cannot abstain from them, either because some illness comes or some sort of work, may make use of them. Only let the fasting continue until the celebration of vespers; and let him take wine, not to get drunk, but to restore his body. To abstain, however, from cheese, milk, butter, and eggs, and not to fast [on wine], is foolishness to the highest degree, and bereft entirely of

rationality. For getting drunk on wine and profligacy are forbidden, not milk and eggs. The apostle does not say, "Do not take milk and eggs," but "Do not get drunk on wine in which there is profligacy." (Eph. 5:18)

41. On each Lord's Day in Lent the sacraments of the body and blood of Christ should be taken by all except those who are excommunicated, and on the Lord's Supper, and on the day of preparation, on the eve of the Passover, and on the day of the Lord's resurrection, should be communicated to absolutely all, and all those days of the Passover week should be kept with equal sanctity.

42. On these days of fasting there should be no lawsuits, no quarrels, but one should continue in the praise of God and doing necessary work. For the Lord reproves those who engage in quarrels and lawsuits in the time of Lent and who demand debts from debtors, speaking through the prophet: "Behold, on the day of your fasting your pleasures are to be found, and you keep looking for all your debtors. Behold, you fast for lawsuits and for quarrels, and you strike wickedly with your fist." (Isa. 58:3)

43. One should abstain from wives on these most consecrated days, and live chastely and piously, so that these holy days be passed with heart and body made holy, and so arrive at the holy day of Pascha because fasting is of little value if defiled by the marital act, and what prayers, vigils, and alms do not recommend.

44. The people must be admonished to approach the most sacred and holy sacrament of the Lord's body and blood with no delay and never to refrain from it, but with all diligence to choose a time when for a little they abstain from the marital act and cleanse themselves from vices, adorn themselves with virtues, be continually in almsgiving and prayers, and so approach so great a sacrament. Because, as it is dangerous for an impure person to approach so great a sacrament, so also it is dangerous to abstain from it for a long time. Except for the list of those who are excommunicated, let them take Communion, not when they please but at specified times, and for those who live devoutly and in holy fashion let them do this almost every day.

45. Let it be ordained that when special Masses are celebrated by priests on Lord's Days, they should not take place in public in such a way that the people can hear them and particularly so that they do not draw themselves away from the public solemnization

of Masses according to the canon at the third hour. For some people have a very bad practice in that when, on Lord's Days or on other holy days, they look to hear Masses—they may be Masses for the dead or for other purposes, which are privately celebrated by priests—and then from early morning through the whole day they give themselves to drunkenness and feasting and vain speaking, rather than to serving God.

46. On account of which care must be taken that all come together in public to holy mother church to hear the solemnization of Masses and preaching. Likewise, it is decreed that in a city in which a bishop has been established, all the presbyters and people, both of the city and of its environs, in vestments, should stand with devout heart at that Mass itself until the benediction of the bishop and Communion, and afterward, if they wish, they may with permission revert to their own rank, after the benediction and Communion have been received. And the priests should diligently watch out that neither in the oratories nor the monasteries in the countryside, nor in churches in the countryside, should they presume to celebrate Masses before the second hour except with great caution, and with the doors locked, so that the people may not at all be able to take occasion to absent themselves from the public solemnities, from the Mass or preaching of the bishop, but all of them, the priests of the suburbs as well as those assigned to the city, and all the people, as we said above, may come together with them for the public celebration of Masses, and nobody except little children and the sick, though they may have heard a Mass, both in the cities and in the parish churches, may presume to eat and drink before the completion of the public office.

If anyone should try to transgress these statutes, let him be brought before the canonical judges until he give satisfaction.

Hymn for Palm Sunday

The translation is by J.M. Neale, *op. cit.*, No. 98. Latin version from F. J. E. Raby, *op. cit.*, No. 81, verses 1, 2, 4, 5.

> *Gloria, laus et honor tibi sit, rex Christe, redemptor,*
> *cui puerile decus promptsit hosana pium.*

> All glory, laud, and honor
> To Thee, Redeemer, King,
> To Whom the lips of children
> Made sweet Hosannas ring.

Israel es tu rex, Davidis et inclita proles,
nomine qui in Domini, rex benedicte, venis.

Thou art the King of Israel,
Thou David's Royal Son,
Who in the Lord's Name comest,
The King and Blessed One.

Plebs Hebraea tibi cum palmis obvia venit;
cum prece, voto, hymnis adsumus ecce tibi.

The people of the Hebrews
With palms before Thee went;
Our praise and prayer and anthems
Before Thee we present.

Hi tibi passuro solvebant munia laudis
nos tibi regnanti pangimus ecce melos.

To Thee before Thy Passion
They sang their hymns of praise;
To Thee now high exalted
Our melody we raise.

20. *Ardo Smaragdus*, Life of Benedict of Aniane and Inda

The agent of Louis the Pious's monastic reforms was St. Benedict of Aniane (d. 821), whom the emperor brought from Aquitaine and installed in a monastery at Inda not far from the royal residence at Aachen. A life of Benedict was written by Ardo (Smaragdus), and from him we learn how this devoted follower of the original St. Benedict studied the *Rule* and adapted it to the conditions prevailing in Frankland. Two innovations are to be attributed to Benedict of Aniane: extra prayers and a visit to the altars three times a day, later called the "*trina oratio*," and regular prayers for the dead.

Louis's enthusiastic support for Benedict is evident throughout Ardo's work. In fact, in 817 a capitulary on monasticism was promulgated which specified the universal observance of the *Rule of St. Benedict*. Thus with royal support and under the influence of the second St. Benedict was inaugurated a movement which firmly established Benedictine monasticism in the West.

The passages are translated from the Latin text in *MGH Scriptores*, XV, 261 ff.

. . . The emperor [Louis] placed him over all the monasteries in his kingdom so that as he had instructed Aquitaine and Gothia in the ways of salvation he might also by salutary example teach Francia. There were many monasteries which had at one time been regularly instituted, but gradually, with discipline slackening, the regular routine had almost disappeared. Moreover, after he had assembled the fathers of the abbeys and many monks, he remained several days, so that just as there was one [monastic] profession for all, there might by the emperor's command be one saving rule for all the monasteries. Accordingly, to all so placed he discussed the rule anew and elucidated obscure matters for everyone, resolved doubts, rooted out former errors, and confirmed useful customs and usages. When opinions regarding the *Rule* and all doubts were resolved, with the consent of all, he explained those usages which the *Rule* does not present clearly. He presented a capitulary on these things to the emperor for his confirmation and so that he might order it observed in all monasteries in the kingdom. To this we refer the reader desirous of more information.[1] The emperor immediately assented to this and appointed inspectors for each monastery who were to see to it that all things which he had ordered were observed and to explain the proper procedures to those who were not informed. And so the work was carried out and speeded with the aid of divine mercy; and one established rule is universally observed by everyone and all monasteries brought to a standard of unity, as though they were instructed by one master in one place. A norm to be observed in drink, in food, in the office, and in all matters was handed down. And since he [Benedict] laid down that the *Rule* should be observed for other monasteries, he expounded it in all its significance to his own at Inda, so that monks coming from various regions might see a clearly depicted pattern of discipline in the customs, and the manner and bearing of everyone, and not need to be instructed in, so to speak, superfluous words. . . .

. . . After the brothers have risen quickly as the *Rule* prescribes, they must bless themselves with holy water and make the rounds of all the altars humbly and reverently. Thus they must finally reach their appointed places and be ready so that when the bell for Tierce rings they may rise without delay and attentively await the priest who has come out to begin the office.

1. *Capitulary on Monasticism* (817).

. . . He commanded that five psalms be sung for all the living faithful in the entire world and also five for all the faithful departed. And also for those recently deceased, because it does not come immediately to the attention of each one, he ordered, nevertheless, five psalms always to be sung. In the course of the five psalms each one is to devote his attention to prayer, commending to God those for whom he chants; and then finally he is to begin the petitions for others . . .

. . . But in the summer season when the office of Matins is finished, he next ordered all to leave the church on account of sleepiness. When they had put on their sandals and washed their faces, they were to return quickly to the church and, according to the manner mentioned above, visit the altars after blessing themselves with holy water and then finally take their appointed places to chant properly the day office.

. . . Even after compline he directed that no one go out on his own accord, or remain in the oratory. But in winter they were first to sing ten psalms, in summer five. Then when the bell rang, all, according to the manner described, were to visit the altars and proceed to bed for rest. He ordered them to visit all the altars thus three times a day and on the first of these to say the Lord's Prayer and the Creed; and on the others, to recite the Lord's Prayer or confess their sins.

. . . He established these three times of prayer a day so that those who were slothful and reluctant to pray would at least do by compulsion what they did not want to do freely and not presume to neglect the constituted hours, and those who were moved by over much zeal be restrained lest they indiscreetly seek extraneous things.

. . . And he also gave the emperor in writing the explanation for those things which the *Rule* orders and which for certain reasons are to remain untouched, and for those about which the *Rule* is silent but might usefully be added. He had bent his entire will toward the observance of the *Rule* and it was his greatest desire that nothing take precedence over its intent. For this reason he had found out who were the experts and inquired diligently of them far and near, even those in these regions who were travelling to

Montecassino and would be able to take notice not only of what they heard but of what they saw.

. . . Finally, he prepared a book compiled from the rules of various fathers which he ordered read at all seasons at morning collation so that the *Rule* of St. Benedict took precedence over all. Further, to demonstrate from this to the contentious that nothing frivolous or empty had been put forth by St. Benedict, but rather that the *Rule* found support from others, after collecting opinions, he composed another book of rules which he called the *Concordia regularum*, so that although the opinions of St. Benedict took precedence, these rules might reasonably and in conscience be adjoined. The other book, no less taken from the sermons of the holy doctors delivered for the exhortation of monks, he added and ordered it read in all seasons at evening collation.[2]

21. *Halitgar's* Roman Penitential

As the ancient practice of public penance died out, systems of private confession to a priest gradually developed. This is mentioned, for example, in the instructions of Theodulf of Orléans. To guide priests in assigning suitable penances, books called penitentials were compiled. The Celtic churches were among the leaders in this, and Archbishop Theodore, a distinguished prelate of Greek ancestry and one of St. Augustine's successors at Canterbury, was instrumental in furthering their use. But apparently, in the course of time, various inadequate penitentials came into use and in 816 the Council of Aachen condemned them.

In 830 Bishop Ebbo of Rheims, presumably with the idea of ending the confusion, requested Halitgar of Cambrai to prepare a new penitential. Halitgar's compilation is clearly derived from northern and Celtic sources. But, no doubt because its author wanted to give it that stamp of Roman authority which Carolingian churchmen generally sought to maintain, he claimed for it a Roman origin.

Halitgar's so-called *Roman Penitential*, therefore, provides an illustration of the penitential practices of the Frankish church of his day. Moreover, there were no major changes in the West until the great reform of the eleventh and twelfth centuries. There is, for example, as yet little evidence of any attempt to distinguish motives underlying acts or the extent to which the will is involved.

2. Evidently the first book mentioned, known as the *Codex regularum*.

Halitgar's penitential also reveals much about the character of Carolingian lay society. Its level of civilization was still primitive and many pagan superstitions remained. In fact, later penitentials indicate that such practices persisted throughout the Middle Ages. Yet lists of misdeeds with appropriate penalties, however revealing, must be studied with caution. Perhaps no more than in a sophisticated society was the majority of the population involved in the spectacular human failings.

The translation is by J. T. McNeill and H. M. Gamer, *Medieval Handbooks of Penance*, Columbia Records of Civilization, vol. XXIX (New York, 1938), pp. 295 ff. Reprinted by permission of Columbia University Press.

. . . We [Halitgar] have also added to this work of our selection another, a Roman penitential, which we have taken from a book repository of the Roman Church, although we do not know by whom it was produced. We have determined that it should be joined to the foregoing decisions of the canons for this reason, that if perchance those decisions presented seem to anyone superfluous, or if he is entirely unable to find there what he requires respecting the offenses of individuals, he may perhaps find explained, in this final summary, at least the misdeeds of all.

Prologue

How Bishops or Presbyters Ought to Receive Penitents

As often as Christians come to penance, we assign fasts; and we ourselves ought to unite with them in fasting for one or two weeks, or as long as we are able; that there be not said to us that which was said to the priests of the Jews by our Lord and Savior: "Woe unto you scribes, who oppress men, and lay upon their shoulders heavy loads, but ye yourselves do not touch these burdens with one of your fingers." For no one can raise up one who is falling beneath a weight unless he bends himself that he may reach out to him his hand; and no physician can treat the wounds of the sick, unless he comes in contact with their foulness. So also no priest or pontiff can treat the wounds of sinners or take away the sins from their souls, except by intense solicitude and the prayer of tears. Therefore it is needful for us, beloved brethren, to be solicitous on behalf of sinners, since we are "members one of another" and "if one member suffers anything, all the members suffer with it." And therefore, if we see anyone fallen in sin, let us also make haste to call him to penance by our teaching. And as often as thou givest advice to a sinner, give him likewise at once a penance and tell him to what extent he ought to fast and expiate his sins; lest perchance thou forget how much it behooves him to fast for his sins and it become necessary to thee to inquire of him regarding his sins a second time. . . .

Moreover, he who on coming to penance sees the priest sad and weeping for his evil deeds, being himself the more moved by the fear of God, will be the more grieved and abhor his sins. And any man who is approaching for penance, if thou seest him in a state of ardent and constant penitence, receive him forthwith. Him who is able to keep a fast which is imposed upon him, do not forbid, but allow him to do it. For they are rather to be praised who make haste quickly to discharge the obligation due, since fasting is an obligation. And so give commandment to those who do penance, since if one fasts and completes what is commanded him by the priest, he will be cleansed from his sins. But if he turns back a second time to his former habit or sin, he is like a dog that returns to his own vomit. Therefore, every penitent ought not only to perform the fast that is commanded him by the priest but also, after he has completed those things that were commanded him, he ought, as long as he is commanded, to fast either on Wednesdays or on Fridays. If he does those things which the priest has enjoined upon him, his sins shall be remitted; if, however, he afterward fasts of his own volition, he shall obtain to himself mercy and the kingdom of Heaven. Therefore, he who fasts a whole week for his sins shall eat on Saturday and on the Lord's day and drink whatever is agreeable to him. Nevertheless, let him guard himself against excess and drunkenness, since luxury is born of drunkenness. Therefore the Blessed Paul forbids it, saying: "Be not drunk with wine, wherein is luxury" (Eph. 5:8); not that there is luxury in wine, but in drunkenness.

Here ends the Prologue.

Directions to Confessors

If anyone perchance is not able to fast and has the means to redeem himself, if he is rich, for seven weeks [penance] he shall give twenty solidi. But if he has not sufficient means, he shall give

ten solidi. But if he is very poor, he shall give three solidi. Now let
no one be startled because we have commanded to give twenty
solidi or a smaller amount; since if he is rich it is easier for him to
give twenty solidi than for a poor man to give three solidi. But let
everyone give attention to the cause to which he is under obligation to give, whether it is to be spent for the redemption of
captives, or upon the sacred altar, or for poor Christians. And
know this, my brethren, that when men or women slaves come to
you seeking penance, you are not to be hard on them nor to
compel them to fast as much as the rich, since men or women slaves
are not in their own power; therefore lay upon them a moderate
penance.

Here begins the form for the administration of Penance.

In the first place the priest says, Psalm XXXVII, "Rebuke me
not O Lord in thy indignation." And after this he says, "Let us
pray," and Psalm CII, "Bless the Lord O my soul" as far as "shall
be renewed." And again he says: "Let us pray," and Psalm L,
"Have mercy," as far as "Blot out my iniquities." After these he
says, Psalm LXIII, "O God, by thy name," and he says, "Let us
pray," and says, Psalm LI, "Why dost thou glory," as far as "the
just shall see and fear." And he says, "Let us pray:"

> O God of whose favor none is without need, remember, O
> Lord, this Thy servant who is laid bare in the weakness of a
> transient and earthly body. We seek that Thou give pardon to
> the confessant, spare the suppliant, and that we who according to
> our own merit are to blame may be saved by thy compassion
> through our Lord Jesus Christ.

[Several other similar prayers are suggested]

Prescriptions of Penance

OF HOMICIDE

1. If any bishop or other ordained person commits homicide. If
any cleric commits homicide, he shall do penance for ten years,
three of these on bread and water.

2. If [the offender is] a layman, he shall do penance for three
years, one of these on bread and water; a subdeacon, six years; a
deacon, seven; a presbyter, ten; a bishop, twelve.

3. If anyone consents to an act of homicide that is to be committed, he shall do penance for seven years, three of these on bread and water.

4. If any layman intentionally commits homicide he shall do penance for seven years, three of these on bread and water.

5. If anyone overlays an infant, he shall do penance for three years, one of these on bread and water. A cleric also shall observe the same rule.

OF FORNICATION

6. If anyone commits fornication as [did] the Sodomites, he shall do penance for ten years, three of these on bread and water.

7. If any cleric commits adultery, that is, if he begets a child with the wife or the betrothed of another, he shall do penance for seven years; however, if he does not beget a child and the act does not come to the notice of men, if he is a cleric he shall do penance for three years, one of these on bread and water; if a deacon or a monk, he shall do penance for seven years, three of these on bread and water; a bishop, twelve years, five on bread and water.

8. If after his conversion or advancement any cleric of superior rank who has a wife has relations with her again, let him know that he has committed adultery; therefore, that he shall do penance as stated above.

9. If anyone commits fornication with a nun or one who is vowed to God, let him be aware that he has committed adultery. He shall do penance in accordance with the foregoing decision, each according to his order.

10. If anyone commits fornication by himself or with a beast of burden or with any quadruped, he shall do penance for three years; if [he has] clerical rank or a monastic vow, he shall do penance for seven years.

11. If any cleric lusts after a woman and is not able to commit the act because the woman will not comply, he shall do penance for half a year on bread and water and for a whole year abstain from wine and meat.

12. If after he has vowed himself to God any cleric returns to a secular habit, as a dog to his vomit, or takes a wife, he shall do penance for six years, three of these on bread and water, and thereafter not be joined in marriage. But if he refuses, a holy synod or

the Apostolic See shall separate them from the communion of the Catholics. Likewise also, if a woman commits a like crime after she has vowed herself to God, she shall be subject to an equal penalty.

13. If any layman commits fornication as the Sodomites did, he shall do penance for seven years.

14. If anyone begets a child of the wife of another, that is, commits adultery and violates his neighbor's bed, he shall do penance for three years and abstain from juicy foods and from his own wife, giving in addition to the husband the price of his wife's violated honor.

15. If anyone wishes to commit adultery and cannot, that is, is not accepted, he shall do penance for forty days.

16. If anyone commits fornication with women that is, with widows and girls, if with a widow, he shall do penance for a year; if with a girl, he shall do penance for two years.

17. If any unstained youth is joined to a virgin, if the parents are willing, she shall become his wife; nevertheless they shall do penance for one year and [then] become man and wife.

18. If anyone commits fornication with a beast he shall do penance for one year. If he has not a wife, he shall do penance for half a year.

19. If anyone violates a virgin or a widow, he shall do penance for three years.

20. If any man who is betrothed defiles the sister of his betrothed, and clings to her as if she were his own, yet marries the former, that is, his betrothed, but she who has suffered defilement commits suicide—all who have consented to the deed shall be sentenced to ten years on bread and water, according to the provisions of the canons.

21. If anyone of the women who have committed fornication slays those who are born or attempts to commit abortion, the original regulation forbids communion to the end of life. What is actually laid down they may mitigate somewhat in practice. We determine that they shall do penance for a period of ten years, according to rank, as the regulations state.

OF PERJURY

22. If any cleric commits perjury, he shall do penance for seven years, three of these on bread and water.

23. A layman, three years; a subdeacon, six; a deacon, seven; a presbyter, ten; a bishop, twelve.

24. If compelled by any necessity, anyone unknowingly commits perjury, he shall do penance for three years, one year on bread and water, and shall render a life for himself, that is, he shall release a man or woman slave from servitude and give alms liberally.

25. If anyone commits perjury through cupidity, he shall sell all his goods and give to the poor and be shaven and enter a monastery, and there he shall serve faithfully until death.

Of Theft

26. If any cleric is guilty of a capital theft, that is, if he steals an animal or breaks into a house, or robs a somewhat well-protected place, he shall do penance for seven years.

27. A layman shall do penance for five years; a subdeacon, for six; a deacon, for seven; a presbyter, for ten; a bishop, for twelve.

28. If anyone in minor orders commits theft once or twice, he shall make restitution to his neighbor and do penance for a year on bread and water; and if he is not able to make restitution he shall do penance for three years.

29. If anyone violates a tomb, he shall do penance for seven years, three years on bread and water.

30. If any layman commits theft he shall restore to his neighbor what he has stolen [and] do penance for the three forty-day periods on bread and water; if he is not able to make restitution, he shall do penance for one year, and the three forty-day periods on bread and water, and [he shall give] alms to the poor from the product of his labor, and at the decision of the priest he shall be joined to the altar.

Of Magic

31. If one by his magic causes the death of anyone, he shall do penance for seven years, three years on bread and water.

32. If anyone acts as a magician for the sake of love but does not cause anybody's death, if he is a layman he shall do penance for half a year; if a cleric, he shall do penance for a year on bread and water; if a deacon, for three years, one year on bread and water; if a priest, for five years, two years on bread and water. But if by this means anyone deceives a woman with respect to the birth of a

child, each one shall add to the above six forty-day periods, lest he be accused of homicide.

33. If anyone is a conjurer-up of storms he shall do penance for seven years, three years on bread and water.

Of Sacrilege

34. If anyone commits sacrilege—(that is, those who are called augurs, who pay respect to omens), if he has taken auguries or [does it] by any evil device, he shall do penance for three years on bread and water.

35. If anyone is a soothsayer (those whom they call diviners) and makes divinations of any kind, since this is a demonic thing he shall do penance for five years, three years on bread and water.

36. If on the Kalends of January, anyone does as many do, calling it "in a stag," or goes about in [the guise of] a calf, he shall do penance for three years.

37. If anyone has the oracles which against reason they call "Sortes Sanctorum," or any other "sortes," or with evil device draws lots from anything else, or practices divination he shall do penance for three years, one year on bread and water.

38. If anyone makes, or releases from, a vow beside trees or springs or by a lattice, or anywhere except in a church, he shall do penance for three years on bread and water, since this is sacrilege or a demonic thing. Whoever eats or drinks in such a place, shall do penance for one year on bread and water.

39. If anyone is a wizard, that is, if he takes away the mind of a man by the invocation of demons, he shall do penance for five years, one year on bread and water.

40. If anyone makes amulets, which is a detestable thing, he shall do penance for three years, one year on bread and water.

41. It is ordered that persons who both eat of a feast in the abominable places of the pagans and carry food back [to their homes] and eat it subject themselves to a penance of two years, and so undertake what they must carry out; and [it is ordered] to try the spirit after each oblation and to examine the life of everyone.

42. If anyone eats or drinks beside a [pagan] sacred place, if it is through ignorance, he shall thereupon promise that he will never repeat it, and he shall do penance for forty days on bread and water. But if he does this through contempt, that is, after the priest

has warned him that it is sacrilege, he has communicated at the table of demons, if he did this only through the vice of gluttony, he shall do penance for the three forty-day periods on bread and water. If he did this really for the worship of demons and in honor of an image, he shall do penance for three years.

43. If anyone has sacrificed under compulsion [in demon worship] a second or third time, he shall be in subjection for three years, and for two years he shall partake of the communion without the oblation, in the third year he shall be received to full [communion].

44. If anyone eats blood or a dead body or what has been offered to idols and was not under necessity of doing this, he shall fast for twelve weeks.

OF VARIOUS TOPICS

45. If anyone intentionally cuts off any of his own members, he shall do penance for three years, one year on bread and water.

46. If anyone intentionally brings about abortion, he shall do penance for three years, one year on bread and water.

47. If anyone exacts usury from anybody, he shall do penance for three years, one year on bread and water.

48. If by power or by any device anyone in evil fashion breaks into or carries off another's goods, he shall do penance as in the above provision and give liberal alms.

49. If by any device anyone brings a slave or any man into captivity or conveys him away, he shall do penance as stated above.

50. If anyone intentionally burns the courtyard or house of anybody, he shall do penance as stated above.

51. If anyone strikes another through anger and sheds blood or incapacitates him, he shall first pay him compensation and secure a physician. If he is a layman [he shall do penance] for forty days; a cleric, two forty-day periods; a deacon, six months; a presbyter, one year.

52. If anyone engages in hunting, if he is a cleric he shall do penance for one year; a deacon shall do penance for two years; a presbyter, for three years.

53. If anyone belonging to the ministry of holy Church is dishonest in respect to any task or neglects it, he shall do penance for seven years, three years on bread and water.

Of Things Offered to Idols

86. If while he is an infant anyone through ignorance tastes of those things which were offered to idols or of a dead body or of anything abominable, let that person fast for three weeks.

87. On account of fornication, moreover, many men do not know the number of the women with whom they have committed fornication: these shall fast for fifty weeks.

88. But if he ate without knowing it what was offered to idols or a dead thing, pardon shall be given him, since he did this unaware; nevertheless, he shall fast three weeks.

Of Things Strangled

98. If any dog or fox or hawk dies for any cause, whether he is killed by a cudgel or by a stone or by an arrow which has no iron, these are all "things strangled." They are not to be eaten, and he who eats of them shall fast for six weeks.

99. If anyone strikes with an arrow a stag or another animal, and if it is found after three days, and if perchance a wolf, a bear, a dog, or a fox has tasted of it, no one shall eat it; and he who does eat of it shall fast for four weeks.

100. If a hen dies in a well, the well is to be emptied. If one drinks knowingly of it, he shall fast for a week.

101. If any mouse or hen or anything falls into wine or water, no one shall drink of this. If it falls into oil or honey, the oil shall be used in a lamp; the honey, in medicine or in something else needful.

102. If a fish has died in the fishpond, it shall not be eaten; he who eats of it shall fast for four days.

103. If a pig or a hen has eaten of the body of a man, it shall not be eaten nor be used for breeding purposes, but it shall be killed and given to the dogs. If a wolf tears an animal, and if it dies, no one shall eat it. And if it lives and a man afterward kills it, it may be eaten.

Of Polluted Animals

104. If a man has sinned with a goat or with a sheep or with any animal, no one shall eat its flesh or milk, but it shall be killed and given to the dogs.

105. If anyone wishes to give alms for his soul of wealth which was the product of booty, if he has already done penance, he has the right to give it. Here endeth.

Carolingian Liturgical Documents

---

22. *Charlemagne*, Epistola generalis

In Chapter 80 of the *Admonitio generalis,* cited above (p. 118), Charlemagne indicated his solicitude for the correct Roman usage in the liturgy which was thenceforth to replace any remaining Gallican forms. Although, in the selection given here, he mentions the desirability of further study on the part of the clergy, it is evident that, with the aid of Paul the Deacon's collections, they will still rely on the fathers for sermon material. The translation is by D. C. Munro, *Pennsylvania Translations and Reprints,* vol. VI, no. 5, pp. 14–15.

. . . Incited, moreover, by the example of our father Pippin, of venerated memory, who by his zeal decorated all the churches of the Gauls with the songs of the Roman church, we are careful by our skill to make these churches illustrious by a series of excellent lectionaries. Finally, because we have found the lectionaries for the nocturnal offices, compiled by the fruitless labor of certain ones, in spite of their correct intention, unsuitable because they were written without the words of their authors and were full of an infinite number of errors, we cannot suffer in our days discordant solecisms to glide into the sacred lessons among the holy offices, and we purpose to improve these lessons. And we have entrusted this work to Paul the Deacon, our friend and client. We have directed him to peruse carefully the sayings of the catholic fathers and to choose, so to speak, from the most broad meadows of their writings certain flowers, and from the most useful to form, as it were, a single garland. He, desiring to obey devoutly our highness, has read through the treatises and sermons of the different catholic fathers, has chosen from each the best, and has presented to us in two volumes lessons suitable for the whole year and for each separate festival, and free from error. We have examined the text of all these with our wisdom, we have established these volumes by our authority, and we deliver them to your religion to be read in the churches of Christ.

23. *Alcuin,* Preface *and Additions to the Roman Mass*

Preface *to the Sacramentary Sent by Hadrian I*

One of the most important, in fact, one of the most enduring of Charlemagne's liturgical reforms was the establishment of a uniform mass rite according to Roman usage. When he decided to push further the reforms inaugurated by Pippin, he requested of Pope Hadrian I an official book of sacraments, the so-called Gregorian *Sacramentary*. Alcuin of York, who has been called the king's master liturgist, proceeded to prepare a *Lectionary*, that is, a book of scriptural readings, epistles, and gospels, to go with it.

When Hadrian's book finally arrived, however, it proved to be a somewhat embarrassing disappointment. Its language seemed overly rigid and it lacked many elements. Moreover, as has been noted, what Pope Gregory I had done was to compile for his own use a sacramentary incorporating material from various earlier books, notably those of Popes Leo and Gelasius. Apparently it did not enjoy the wide circulation it was once thought to have had. Thus it became the task of Alcuin to revise and supplement this "Roman" book of Hadrian.

To explain what he had done, Alcuin composed what became a rather celebrated *Preface*, which he placed between the part received from Rome and the *Supplement* he then added. In later times the *Preface* was moved back, thus giving what was held to be a more "Gregorian" character to the whole. It was also reduced—and finally dropped. Nevertheless, although Alcuin's mass book was subsequently re-edited, it has remained in its essentials the source of western liturgical practice. The selection cited here is followed in the original by 144 titles forming a sort of table of contents and indicating the masses for Sundays and other occasions, special devotions, etc. The translation is by G. Ellard, S.J., *Master Alcuin Liturgist* (Chicago, 1956), pp. 111–118. Father Ellard used the translation of Edmund Bishop (1894) with corrections from a new edition by R. Amiet then in preparation (*Scriptorium*, VII, 1953). Ellard's translation is reprinted by permission of Loyola University Press.

The foregoing sacramentary up to this point is known to have been put forth by the Blessed Pope Gregory, except for those items which the reader will find marked at the beginning with a dagger, the Nativity and Assumption of the Blessed Virgin, but chiefly [the Thursdays] in Lent. For as we have often had it by hearsay, the pope on such days holds no station at all, but, wearied from the stational Masses on all the other days, he gives himself to rest, so that, free from the tumultuous thronging of people, he may distribute alms to the poor, and more freely dispatch other external affairs. But that Mass entitled "For the Feast" of the same Blessed Gregory is also marked (as an interpolation), for it was doubtless added to his Sacramentary out of love, and even veneration for him.

The aforesaid Sacramentary, although marred by many a copyist's error, could not be reckoned to be in the condition in which it had left its author's hands, [so] it was our task to correct and restore it, for the benefit of all. Let a careful reader examine it, and he will promptly agree with this judgement, unless the work be again corrupted by scribes.

But since there are other materials which Holy Church necessarily uses, and which the aforesaid Father [Gregory], seeing that they had been already put forth by others, left aside, we have thought it worth while to gather them like spring flowers of the meadows, and collect them together, and place them in this book apart, but corrected and amended and headed with their [own] titles, so that the reader may find in this work all things which we have thought necessary for our times, although we had found a great many also embodied in other sacramentaries.

But for the purpose of separation we have placed this little preface in the middle, so that it may form the close of one book [Gregory's], and the beginning of the other [Alcuin's]; to the intent that, one book being before the preface and the other after it, every one may know what was put forth by Blessed Gregory and what by other Fathers.

And as we thought it was not at all decent or possible to pay no regard to the wishes of those who look to find these so excellent and varied holy observances, we would at any rate satisfy the most worthy desires of all these persons by the present abundant collection. [And] if it please any one to accept what, without any desire of imposing ourselves on others, we have collected with pious affection and the greatest care, we beg him not to be of [a] mind ungrateful for our toil, but with us to render thanks to the Giver of all good things.

But if he consider our collection a superfluity and not necessary for himself, let him use the work of the aforesaid Father alone, which in not a tittle may he reject without peril to himself; and let him also tolerate those who demand [our supplement] and wish piously to use it. For, not for the thankless and the scornful, but for the zealous and the devout have we brought together this collection in which he to whom these prayers are dear and familiar may find wherewith he may worthily and with a mind unruffled pay to our Lord his due vows, and perform the service of divine worship.

Let the reader be assured that we have inserted nothing but what has been written with great accuracy and care by men of excellent learning and the highest repute; we have collected many things from many sources, that we might look to the service of many.

Moreover, we entreat those to whom they are acceptable, to receive with charity the collection of prefaces added at the end of the volume, and sing them; but we beg they be neither adopted nor sung by those who, understanding, do not like them, or who, willing to receive, do not understand them.

We also add blessings imparted by the bishop over the people, and also—what was not contained in the aforesaid volume of the Blessed Gregory—the ordination forms for the minor orders.

We therefore beg of you, whoever take this book to read or to transcribe, that you offer a prayer to the Lord on our behalf, who labored in collecting and correcting this, for the common welfare.

We also entreat that you transcribe with care, so that the text may both please the ears of the learned, and not suffer the unschooled to err; for, as Blessed Jerome saith, the correcting of a book availeth naught, unless the emendation be preserved by the care of the scribes.

[A table of Sundays and major feasts follows]

These things carefully tabulated are followed by Prefaces to be sung on Sundays, feasts and ferias, on the festivals of the saints, or for other ecclesiastical offices. And if the prudent user will look with care, diligence, and curiosity, he will readily find them all corrected and set out in their proper places.

Additions to the Roman Mass

Alcuin also compiled a book of votive masses. These were masses designed to be used on special occasions for purposes of entreaty, thanksgiving, and the like. Some of this material he garnered from local usage, some of it he composed himself. It soon gained immense popularity and much of it, as, for example, the Mass of the Blessed Virgin on Saturdays (parts of which are cited below) is still in use today.

Alcuin's handiwork is also evident in the prayers of the mass itself, for it was he who composed the prayers which immediately precede the communion. When all of Alcuin's liturgical contributions are considered, it is clear that he played a major role in establishing the Roman rite as it continued into modern times. Translation is from the Roman missal.

PRAYERS FROM THE MASS OF THE BLESSED VIRGIN FOR SATURDAY

Collect. Grant, O Lord God, that we your servants may ever enjoy health of mind and body; and through the glorious intercession of Blessed Mary ever-virgin be freed from present sorrow and attain to eternal happiness . . .

Secret. Through your mercy, O Lord, and by the intercession of Blessed Mary ever-virgin may this oblation secure for us well-being and peace now and forever . . .

Postcommunion. Grant, O Lord, that we who have received these aids to our salvation may always and everywhere be protected by the suffrages of Blessed Mary ever-virgin, in whose honor we have offered these things to Your Majesty . . .

PRAYERS BEFORE COMMUNION RECITED BY THE PRIEST

Lord Jesus Christ, Son of the Living God, You who by the will of the Father and with the cooperation of the Holy Spirit have by Your death restored life to the world, free me through this Your holy Body and Blood from all my sins and from all evils; make me always adhere to Your commandments and never let me be separated from You . . .

May the receiving of Your Body, O Lord Jesus Christ, which I, though unworthy, presume to do, not result in my judgment and condemnation, but because of Your goodness serve me as safeguard and healing remedy of mind and body . . .

24. Latin the Exclusive Liturgical Language of the West

Frankish efforts to achieve liturgical uniformity extended to the frontier regions of the East where, especially under Louis the German (843–76), Germans were penetrating the Slavonic areas. Partly to offset Frankish pressure, Rastislav, prince of Moravia (846–69), sought assistance from the Byzantine emperor, Michael III. Photius, the Greek patriarch whose election Pope Nicholas I had protested (cf. Document 26, p. 163), responded by sending a mission headed by two brothers, Constantine and Methodius. They were Greeks, natives of Thessalonica, but familiar with the old Slavonic language.

Constantine devised an alphabet (Glagolitic) for the Moravian language and prepared a Slavonic liturgy which was apparently a combination of the Greek and Roman rites. This soon had great success, but aroused the opposition and jealousy of the east Franks. Moreover, since neither missionary was a bishop, they could not establish a local hierarchy. Journeying first to Venice, apparently with the intention of returning to Constantinople, they received there, according to one account, an invitation from Nicholas I to visit Rome. Constantine brought with him relics of St. Clement, the first-century pope whose letter was cited above (Document 1). The two missionaries were well received by Hadrian II, Nicholas I's successor, and mass was celebrated in St. Peter's in the Slavonic liturgy. In 869 Constantine, having taken the monastic habit and the name Cyril, died in Rome. Methodius, who was subsequently named archbishop with jurisdiction over the old Roman Pannonia and lands north and east, returned alone.

On his return, Methodius encountered persistent German opposition. He was twice denounced to Rome and once put in confinement. Eventually he was set at liberty and firmly supported by Rome. Pope John VIII, who temporarily yielding to German pressure, had formerly forbidden the Slavonic liturgy, now authorized it. The closing sentences of the pertinent letter, however, seem to reveal a disposition on the pope's part to make some concessions to the Latin (Frankish) element, whose pressure continued. Thus, though not free from further molestation, Methodius continued his work, often under great difficulties, until he died in 884.

After Methodius's death the Germans triumphed both politically and religiously in Old Moravia. The kingdom fell and the Latin liturgy gradually replaced the Slavonic throughout most of the area, although traces of the latter remained until the eleventh century and later popes in fact had to forbid its use. As Methodius's disciples fled among the Bulgars, the Slavonic liturgy was adopted in that region and later by the Russians. Since both these peoples were associated ecclesiastically with Constantinople, the Slavonic liturgy in its turn came to be identified with the New rather than the Old Rome.

The following selections are taken from contemporary chronicles of Constantine and Methodius and from papal correspondence.

Life of Constantine (Cyril)

From the French translation by F. Dvornik, *Les Légendes de Constantin et de méthode* (Prague, 1933), pp. 378–379. Reprinted by permission of F. Dvornik.

CHAPTER XVII

The pope of Rome was informed about him [Constantine] and sent for him. When he arrived at Rome, the "apostolicus" Hadrian went in person to meet him accompanied by all the citizens, all carrying candles, for he was also carrying the relics of St. Clement, martyr and Roman pope. God then accomplished three famous miracles. A paralytic was entirely cured and many others were delivered of different ailments. Even prisoners who had invoked Christ and St. Clement were liberated by those who had captured them.

The pope took the Slavonic books, blessed them and placed them in the church of the Blessed Virgin which is called Platna. And they chanted over them the sacred liturgy. Then the pope designated two bishops, Formosa and Gundricus, to ordain the Slavic disciples. And after their ordination they chanted the liturgy in the Slavic tongue in the church of the apostle Peter. On the next day they chanted in the church of St. Petronilla and on the day following in the church of St. Andrew, then in the church of the great catholic doctor, the apostle Paul. They chanted all night glorifying God in Slavic. And the next day they sang the liturgy once again over his tomb, assisted by bishop Arsenius who was one of the seven bishops, and by Anastasius, the Bibliotecarius. And the Philosopher never ceased worthily rendering thanks to God with his disciples . . .

Letter of Pope John VIII to Svatopluk of Moravia (880)

Translated from *MGH, Epistolae,* vol. VII, 223 ff.

. . . Finally we justly approve the Slavonic letters devised by Constantine the Philosopher, and may the praise of God duly resound in them, and we direct that the words and deeds of Christ our Lord be expounded in that same language. For we are not admonished to praise in only three languages,[1] but in all tongues, by the sacred authority which commanded and said, "O praise the Lord, all ye nations, praise Him all you peoples!" (Ps. 117) And the apostles, filled with the Holy Spirit, spoke the praises of God in all tongues. And Paul, too, sounds as a heavenly trumpet, warning, " . . . that every tongue should confess that Jesus Christ our Lord is in the glory of God the Father." (Phil. ii, 11) Moreover, concerning these languages he clearly and sufficiently advises us in the first epistle to the Corinthians that we honor the church of God in whatever tongue we speak. Nor, surely, is it in any way contrary to faith or doctrine either to sing masses in the Slavonic language or to read the Holy Gospel or other sacred readings of the New and Old Testament, well translated and interpreted, or to chant all other offices of the hours. For He who created the three principal languages, namely, Hebrew, Greek, and Latin, created all the others for His praise and glory. For the doing of greater honor, we direct that in all the churches of your land the Gospel be read in Latin and then proclaimed in the Slavic language for those hearers who do not understand Latin, as apparently is done in certain churches. And if it is preferable to you and your councillors to hear masses in the Latin language, we order that the solemnities of the mass be celebrated for you in Latin.

Letter of Pope Stephen V to Svatopluk (885)

In this passage Pope Stephen V, after commending Bishop Wiching, rejects the "superstition" of Methodius. Wiching was one of the principal opponents and betrayers of Methodius during the pontificate of John VIII. He was presumably the author of the report that Methodius had sworn not to use the Slavonic liturgy, as mentioned in the pope's letter. Translated from *Ibid.*, pp. 355 ff.

. . . As to the divine offices and sacred mysteries and rites of the mass which the same Methodius presumed to celebrate in the language of the Slavs, and which, horrified by the accusation of perjury, he had confirmed by an oath over the sacred body of St. Peter he was no longer doing, let this henceforth be not presumed by anyone in any way. By our apostolic authority from God we forbid

1. One of the arguments of the opponents of the Slavonic liturgy was that only three languages, Hebrew, Greek, and Latin, were of divine sanction.

it under pain of anathema. If, however, for the instruction of simple
and uneducated folk the gospel and epistle are read in that language
by learned persons, this we grant and urge and admonish that it
be done very frequently so that all may praise and acknowledge
God. . . .

25. Liturgical Interpretation: Symbolism and Allegory

As Alcuin's name is associated with establishing a form of liturgy to be
used everywhere in the West, so the name of Amalar of Metz is linked
with liturgical interpretation. Amalar, who for a time held the see of
Lyons where Bishop Leidrad had furthered training in the chant, had
between 831 and 835 compiled an antiphonary from materials he had
searched out at the monastery of Corbie. In 833 he produced his *Liber
officialis*,[1] a detailed work on the symbolism of the liturgy. Throughout the entire ecclesiastical year he finds meaning not only in the
episodes of the life of Christ, but in the various attitudes of uncertainty, sorrow, and rejoicing among God's people. In his discussion of
the ritual of the mass, Amalar finds meaning in the acolytes, deacons,
cantors, their every movement and gesture, and in the vestments.

The *Liber officialis* was at first severely criticized by Carolingian
ecclesiastics, notably by Agobard, who replaced Amalar at Lyons.
Some found fault with Amalar's interpretations, especially with the
phrases he had used in describing the consecrated Host. In fact,
Amalar was condemned and forced to vacate his see and retire. There
is no reason to believe, however, that Amalar had heretical ideas. As
Eleanor Duckett has put it, "His imagination may at times have lacked
dignity; but neither in his thought nor in his interpretation was he ever
heretic, fool, or knave."[2] More important, Amalar's work stimulated
others to ponder the meaning of the liturgy. In spite of the critics—
and not all were unfavorable—allegorical interpretation of the liturgy
continued.

The first selection presented here is the schema of a shorter work,
the *Eclogae de officio missae*, which is a sort of synopsis of the entire
mass. The second selection contains a number of passages from
Book III of the *Liber officialis* which deal with the entrance of the

1. This is the title used by J. M. Hanssens, *Amalarii episcopi opera liturgica
omnia* (3 vols., Vatican City, 1948–50). The work is also found in J. P.
Migne, *Patrologia latina* (cited hereafter as *MPL*) 105, under the title
De ecclesiasticis oficiis libri IV.
2. *Carolingian Portraits* (Ann Arbor, 1962), p. 117. Cf. also A. Cabaniss,
Amalarius of Metz (Amsterdam, 1954).

bishop, the Introit. It is evident that Amalar had in mind a basilica church with the celebrant—the bishop—still facing the congregation, a practice which changed during the Carolingian period. In a brief section describing the *Alleluia*, there is an early reference to the sequence which was to give rise to considerable musical and liturgical invention in later times. The passages describing the offertory indicate that bread and wine to be used in the canon of the mass, and even other gifts, were still offered publicly. This custom was also soon to die out.

Both selections were translated from *MPL*, 105. *Eclogae de officio missae* can be found in cols. 1315–1316; *Liber officialis* in cols. 1108–1132.

Amalar of Metz, Eclogae de officio missae

I   It should be made known that the things that we solemnize in the service of the Mass before the reading of the Gospel are reflections upon Christ's first coming up to the time when he was hastening toward Jerusalem to suffer.

II   The *Introit* refers to the company of prophets; and indeed, we rightly mention this, since, as Augustine said, Moses was the minister of the Old Testament.

III   The *Kyrie eleison* looks back upon those prophets who were there at the time of our Lord's coming, among whom were Zacharias and his son, John.

IV   The *Gloria in excelsis Deo* reminds us of the choir of angels who announced to the shepherds the good news of the birth of Christ.

V   The first Collect recalls what Our Lord was doing when he went up to Jerusalem at about his twelfth year and sat in the temple in the midst of the doctors and listened to them and asked them questions.

VI   The Epistle refers to the prophecy of John.

VII   The Response refers to the goodwill of the apostles when they were called by the Lord and followed Him.

VIII   The *Alleluia* reflects the joy they had in their minds because of his promises or on account of the miracles which they saw performed by him or in his name.

IX   The Gospel recalls His preaching up to the time mentioned above.

X   What occurs afterwards in the service of the Mass reflects that time from the Sunday when the children came out to meet Him to his Ascension or Pentecost.

XI   The prayer which the priest says from the Secret (Prayer) to the *Nobis quoque peccatoribus*, signifies that prayer which Jesus uttered on the Mount of Olives.

XII   That which follows signifies that time when the Lord lay in the sepulcher.

XIII   When the bread is dipped into the wine, it demonstrates that the soul of the Lord returned to the body.

XIV   And what is observed afterward, signifies those visits which Christ made to his disciples.

XV   The breaking of the oblations signifies the breaking (of bread) which the Lord did for his two disciples at Emmaus.

Amalar of Metz, Liber officialis, *Book III*

CHAPTER V. ON THE ENTRANCE OF THE BISHOP TO MASS

The office which we call the Introit of the mass begins with the first antiphon which is called the Introit, and ends with the prayer which is said by the priest before the *Lectio* (Epistle). The entrance of the bishop, who is the vicar of Christ, to mass recalls to mind His coming to us and the uniting of the people to Him, either through His preaching or that of His own preachers. The entrance of the bishop is observed until his seating. It symbolizes, in a measure, the service which Christ or his disciples performed corporally on earth until He ascended to the paternal seat. . . .

. . . Christ, the Son of God, "Who chose his own before the foundation of the world, so that they might be holy and unspotted" (cf. Ephes. I, 4), sent heralds in the Old Testament, not to mention others, to gather His own people to the worship of the one God, by the charm and melody of their call. Their leader was David concerning whom we cited Augustine above saying (City of God, XVII, 14). "For David was a man skilled in song who did not love harmonious music because of common pleasure, but because of a faithful will . . ." After him Eman, Asaph, Ethan, and Idithun whom we have already mentioned, as also what their psaltery, cithara, tympanum, strings, organ, etc. mean. All these things are in deed and in song. Hence it has become the custom not to sit in church as long as this particular office lasts, since those are accounted workmen and laborers of Christ or of his heralds who are predestined and called to the worship of the one God. . . .

The deacons represent the prophets who announce the life to come in accordance with the Gospel. The subdeacons represent the wise men who knew how to arrange the vessels of the Lord properly and what must be done first and what later. The acolytes represent the scribes who inflame the hearts of the faithful in accordance with Holy Scripture. Incense is placed in the thurible because it signifies the body of Christ, full of sweet odor. First of all this body must be proclaimed to all the people. Wherefore, Paul spoke to the unlearned Corinthians (I Cor. II, 2) "For I judged not myself to know anything among you, but Jesus Christ, and Him crucified."

The bishop should have before his eyes most often what he should always keep in mind. Seven prophets, or deacons, are in the ministry because Scripture is divided in a sevenfold manner into New Testament and Old which minister to the Gospel. Because the vicar of Christ is a mediator, the bishop, as though he were the Gospel, has in the New Testament the ministers of history, for example, Luke in the *Acts of the Apostles*. He has ministers in the seven canonical *Epistles;* the ministers in the fourteen *Epistles* of Paul. He has ministers in the *Apocalypse*, in the Old Testament, and in the [Books of] Law, in the Prophets, and in the Psalms . . .

. . . When the time has been fulfilled, the one proclaimed by the prophets, Christ makes His way to Jerusalem where is the altar which he kisses in the middle, since it is He of whom it is spoken in the Song of Songs, "The midst he covered with charity for the daughters of Jerusalem" (Cant. III, 10). The vicar of Christ does all these things in remembrance of the first advent of Christ. He kisses the altar to show that Christ's coming was in Jerusalem; he kisses the Gospel, in which the two peoples are united at the end so that we may even love those who were separated from us. The kisses of the vicar of Christ correspond to the kiss of Christ. Just as Christ first bestowed his kiss on those who believed at first, so also the bishop to his first ministers [deacons]. Just as Christ freely offered Himself to those to whom He said, I was sent to the sheep which were lost of the House of Israel, (Matt. XV, 24) so also the bishop at the altar through which we recall Jerusalem where, according to John, the Lord loved his own to the end. And just as Christ afterwards adopted the people of the gentiles who are reconciled to God in the New Testament, so the bishop does with the Gospel which is the New Testament. The Gospel remains on the altar from the beginning of the office until it is taken by the minister to be read; because from the first coming of Christ the Gospel teaching resounded in Jerusalem (Matt. XV) and thence went forth abroad as it is written (Isaiah, II, 3), "For the law shall come forth from Sion, and the word of the Lord from Jerusalem." . . .

CHAPTER XVI. DE TABULIS

. . . Likewise again in the 149th psalm, "when they take up the timbrel and psaltery, their hands harmonize with their voice." So also you, if when you sing *Alleluia* you offer bread to the hungry, clothe the naked, take a stranger under your protection, not only does your voice sound, but your hand "sounds" with it because the deeds are in accord with the words. The versicle, *Alleluia*, touches the cantor inwardly so that he thinks about how he should praise the Lord or how he should rejoice. This rejoicing which the cantors call *sequence* brings that state to our minds when words will not be necessary, but [one] mind will show to [another] mind by thought alone what it retains within. Here is finished the second summary of preaching. The word of preaching runs to the state mentioned above; what lies beyond is veiled by the wings of the Seraphim. . . .

CHAPTER XIX. ON THE OFFICE WHICH IS CALLED THE OFFERTORY

When the previous ceremonies, mentioned above, have been completed, an office is begun in which is solemnized the offering of those who fulfill their vows to the Lord. First to be remembered is the offering according to the Law and finally ours of Christ [There follows a description of sacrifices in the Old Testament]
. . . The office which we call the offertory begins at the place where the priest says, "the Lord be with you," and ends when with his voice raised he says, "world without end." And so the last part is proffered in a high voice so that it may be heard by the people and the message be confirmed by the response of the people.
For Christ deigned to come to Jerusalem on Palm Sunday and

await there the day of his immolation. Each previous sacrifice prefigures that one. On that day He came down from the Mount of Olives, and a great crowd came out to meet Him (Matt. II). There is no doubt but that He greeted the crowd according to a good custom of ancient tradition, which in fact not only the learned church, but even the crowd holds to. It is usual, on meeting someone, to wish him some good as a greeting. And especially for this reason we say that the Lord saluted the crowd coming to meet Him since that was the custom among the Jews . . .

No one passed by and saw something being done in the field or the vineyard or the harvest or anything of the kind, and was permitted to pass by without a blessing. This custom remains to-day in our church, when we make the transition from one ceremony to another, as though we were going among the workmen we salute them with words full of benediction. Afterwards, the priest says, "Let us pray." Unless the power of Christ filled the hearts of the people for prayer, they would not sing to Him such glorious praises. By prayer, the heart is made clear for understanding the Lord. The purity of the linen which is placed on the altar, signifies the purity of the minds of those who used to sing to the Lord. That same purity with which He filled the hearts of the singers He found lacking in the temple when He cast out the buyers and sellers, saying, "It is written, My house shall be called the house of prayer" (Matt. XXI, 13). For while the priest receives the offerings the cantors sing. So long as the crowd was singing *Hosanna in excelsis*, Christ received their prayers. When the oblation has been received, the priest returns to the altar, so that on it either he or the deacon may place the oblations in the presence of the Lord which he will sacrifice to Him in the following part of the mass. For Christ, after he accepted the offerings of the singers, went into Jerusalem and the temple of the Lord, in which there was an altar and there presented Himself to God the Father for his sacrifice to come . . .

. . . Afterwards he [the bishop] says *Let us pray* and warns each one of those offering to look into his conscience. If he has anything to sacrifice, let him sacrifice, that is, if anyone is conscious of his own sin, let him ask that it be smitten by an invisible sword.

If anyone has a voluntary or free will sacrifice, or for whatever reason it be, before it leaves his hand, let him pray that he be acceptable to the Lord and not despised as was Cain because he did not offer justly (Gen. IV). Meanwhile, a cloth is placed on the altar. By this cloth, which we usually call the corporal, everyone is admonished, that is, the people and ministers at the altar and also the priest, that as the linen is cleansed of all natural freshness and moisture, so may the minds of those offering be free from all carnal desire; and just as it shines in its splendor so may the intention of those offering shine in purity before God. Then the priest crosses to receive the oblations. Meanwhile, the singers chant after the manner of the ancients, as we have said, or of the crowds which sang to Christ as he entered Jerusalem. The people give their oblations, that is, bread and wine according to the order of Melchisedech. The bread which they offer and the wine express all the pious wishes lying hidden within whether they are for the sacrifice or for the living victim. What is done outwardly is a sign of that which lies within. . . .

. . . Therefore, the priest . . . prepares the minds of the brethren, saying *Lift up your hearts:* so that as the people respond, *We have lifted them up unto the Lord,* they may be admonished that it behooves them to think of nothing save God. Let the heart be closed against the enemy and open to God alone. Let it not permit God's enemy to approach it in time of prayer. . . .

When this has been done, the priest turns to the people and beseeches them to pray for him, that he may be worthy to offer to the Lord the sacrifice of all the people.

The Re-emergence of the Papacy

26. Pope Nicholas I, Letters

Nicholas to the Bishops of Gaul (865)

Although the popes seemed somewhat overshadowed during the reign of Charlemagne, such was not the case in the mid-ninth century. This is especially well illustrated by the career of Nicholas I (858–67). For, as the following excerpts from two of Nicholas's letters show, he insisted on the primacy of jurisdiction of the Roman see over any metropolitan or bishop, East or West. It is true that a century after Nicholas I papal authority had seriously deteriorated. Nevertheless, Nicholas's pontificate is important in the history of the Roman see. His letters were cited in the papal reform of the eleventh century, and thus contributed to the growth of canon law. Extended sections of the first letter cited here, for example, were included by Gratian in the twelfth century in his compilation, the *Decretum*.[1]

The first selection, written to the bishops of Gaul, concerns the excommunication and deposition of Bishop Rothad of Soissons. Rothad (apparently a particularly exasperating person), determined to protect his own episcopal rights against those of his metropolitan, Hincmar of Rheims, had deprived a priest of his powers. His action was condemned by Hincmar, who proceeded to excommunicate Rothad. Rothad refused the sentence, talked of appeal to Rome, and, somewhat contradictorily, demanded another judgment locally. He was finally judged by a synod at Soissons and deposed. Nicholas reversed the decision and ordered Rothad's reinstatement in letters to both Hincmar and the other bishops.

In this letter—translated from *MGH Epistolae*, vol. VI, no. 71, Nicholas refers to the Pseudo-Isidorian decretals, partly to justify the citation of papal letters and partly to condemn the misuse of them by others.

. . . Even if he [Rothad] had not appealed at all to the apostolic see, you should not, in the face of so many decretals and statutes of such importance, have deposed a bishop without consulting us. . . .

For if by a decree of these same [papal] decretals the works of other writers are approved or condemned so that what the apostolic see has approved be held accepted today and what it has formerly rejected be held invalid, how much more should what it has at different times written for the catholic faith, for correct doctrines, for the various and manifold necessities of the church and the conduct of the faithful be preferred with due honor and reverently be received by all on whatever occasions with discernment or as the charge of a superior.

Although certain of you have written that these decrees of former pontiffs are not to be found mentioned in the entire body of the code of canons, the same persons, when they see that they support their contentions, use them indiscriminately, and only now for the purpose of diminishing the authority of the apostolic see

1. See below, Part III, Document 31.

and the enhancing of their own privileges do they maintain that they have not been accepted. For many of these writings we have in our possession which are known to present in their causes the decrees not only of various Roman pontiffs, but even of their predecessors. But now when it becomes evident to them that the privileges of the Roman see are thereby defended, they hasten to repudiate them. In order that they may be preserved undiminished, we do not cease to proclaim these privileges, in so far as they are proved to have been, or are, or always will be for the benefit of the entire church, for it is fitting when the entire weight rests on a structure that there be everywhere a firm and stable foudation.

Furthermore, if they say that the decretals of the earliest Roman pontiffs are not to be admitted because they are not included in the book of canons, then no decree or writing of St. Gregory nor any other who came before or after is to be admitted because it is not included in the code of canons. Therefore, because they are not considered to be written in the book of canons, they erase from their book the teaching and ordinances of these men which are venerated by every tongue. How, then, do they find a place in the documents and are not afterwards accepted? But why do we dwell longer on this, since if we concluded that these persons should be heeded, we would not have the sacred scriptures of the Old and New Testaments. For neither of these is included in the corpus of ecclesiastical canons. But those who are always more ready to resist than obey would answer, saying that among the canons there is found a chapter of Blessed Pope Innocent by whose authority it is taught that each testament is to be received by us, although in these same canons of the fathers nothing at all from them is included. It should further be made clear, that if the Old and New Testaments are to be included, they are not to be considered as added to the corpus of canons in entirety, but that concerning their reception the opinion of Pope Innocent be understood as preferred. Whence it follows: that the decretals of the Roman pontiffs are to be received even if they are not joined to the book of canons, since it is established that among these same canons one chapter of Blessed Leo is included by which all the established decretals of the apostolic see are ordered to be observed. Thus if anyone is guilty of a fault in this matter he will know that pardon is denied him. For he says in the fifth chapter of his decretals: "In order that nothing be omitted by us which should be strongly held, all the decretals established that among these same canons one chapter of Blessed cessors which have been promulgated concerning ecclesiastical orders and the teachings of the canons we decree should be observed by your grace so that if anyone is guilty of fault in this matter he will know that pardon is denied him."

Indeed, in saying "all the decretals established," he omitted no one of the established decretals, which he did not order to be observed. And again in saying, "of all our predecessors," he excepted none of the Roman pontiffs who were before him, none whose decretals he did not order all to observe, so that if anyone should be guilty in this matter he would know that pardon would be denied him. Therefore, it makes no difference whether all the decretals issued by the apostolic see are included among the canons of the councils, since they cannot all be joined together in one corpus and those are inserted which may lend strength and their own vigor to those which are omitted; especially since conciliar proceedings in which these same canons were enacted are not considered to be in the corpus of canons, yet are venerated by us with all due reverence. Moreover, Pope Gelasius, holy and most fruitful in his ordinances, agrees with blessed Pope Leo, speaking thus: "The decretal letters which blessed popes have at different times given from the city of Rome in consultation with various fathers, are to be reverently acknowledged." It is to be noted here that he did not say decretal letters which are included among the canons, nor only those which modern popes have issued, but "those which blessed popes have at different times given from the city of Rome." In saying "different times," moreover, the holy man understood those which, owing to the frequent persecutions of the pagans, permitted cases of bishops to be referred to the apostolic see with difficulty.

And so with the help of divine grace we have demonstrated by these things that there is no difference between those decrees of the bishops of the apostolic see which are included in the book of canon law and those which owing to the great number are scarcely found throughout each body of volumes, since we have proved that the celebrated popes Leo and Gelasius ordered all decretals and the decretals established by their predecessors, as well as the decretal letters which blessed popes at different times issued from the city of Rome to be reverently acknowledged and observed. . . .

Nicholas to the Emperor Michael (860)

The second selection from the correspondence of Nicholas I illustrates his determination not to permit any challenge to the jurisdiction of the Roman see over the entire Church, East as well as West. A council at Constantinople had deposed the incumbent patriarch, Ignatius, and elected Photius, a prominent theologian, though he was only a layman. After some delay, Nicholas upheld Ignatius and condemned the synod's action. The Photius affair continued some time after Nicholas's death, and the Byzantine church was for a few years (867–70) in formal schism with the West. Moreover, the controversy became further complicated by other factors such as the jurisdiction over the Illyrian provinces, which originally belonged to the Roman patriarchate, and which the emperor Leo III (717–41) had transferred to the patriarchate of Constantinople. Translated from *Ibid.*, no. 82.

In establishing the pre-eminence of that divine power which the Creator of all bestowed on his chosen apostles, on the solid faith of the chief of the apostles, to wit, Peter, He determined his as an especial or, indeed, a first see. For it was said to him by the same Lord's voice (Matt., XVI, 18), "You are Peter and on this rock I will build my church. And the gates of Hell will not prevail against it." Peter, therefore, from the firmness of the rock which is Christ did not cease to fortify by his prayers the unshaken structure of the universal church which was made so firm by the strength of faith that it might speedily bring back to the norms of true faith the madness of those who stray and fearlessly take care to reward those who make that faith firm, to the end that the gates of Hell, the promptings of malign spirits, and the attacks of heretics should not avail to shatter the unity of this same church.

Wherefore, we give great thanks to God omnipotent who deemed it worthy to infuse in your heart that as supporter of the church of God you desire to uphold that very concord which God accomplished lest it be consumed by any shame of error and the understanding of the apostolic tradition be torn from the comeliness of faith.

For the integrity of this care, there has, as you yourself know, many times been held an assembly of the Holy fathers by whom it was determined as [something] to be considered and looked after that no final conclusion must be given to any deliberation which arises without the consent of the Roman see and the Roman pontiff. Therefore, the council assembled by you at Constantinople, as it has been communicated to us, in your letter, has not feared to divert its considerations away from such ordinances, holding of no account traditions of this nature. Accordingly, assembling there without consulting the Roman pontiff, it deprived of his proper honor Ignatius, patriarch of the aforesaid city. That this is deserving of rebuke, even those who were opposed to him bear witness. For such persons of whom we read in your letter canon law censures and clearly shows them to have been hostile, since neither did he say with his own voice, as your letters assert, those things which were held against him, nor did his accusers investigate [them]. Further, after these things had been carried through so unjustly, the above-mentioned group of persons, directing the choice of their recklessness to more reprehensible things, elected a pastor to preside over them from the ranks of the laity. O! what presumptuous temerity! . . .

III

The Central Middle Ages (900–1150)

During the one hundred years or so following the death of Louis the Pious, Europe was badly battered by invasions of Norsemen, Slavs, Magyars, and Saracens. Many of the institutions established by the Carolingians, notably the single Frankish empire-kingdom, failed to survive the storm. Life became more and more localized, and the new western Europe which began to emerge in the mid-tenth century was a Europe of several kingdoms.

Gradually, though not without numerous setbacks, many erstwhile invaders became Christian and new Christian states were formed on the northern and eastern peripheries of the older empires. Other signs of progress were evident. In short, there began in the tenth century a remarkable religious, political, social, and economic revival. This in turn led to a period of growth, one of the longest in Europe's history, which was to last until toward the end of the thirteenth century.

Inevitably, ecclesiastical administration suffered during the invasions and was markedly affected by the fragmentation of political life which followed. An effective papal jurisdiction such as Nicholas I might have envisaged was out of the question. Churches and monasteries, or the lands which they possessed, tended to become feudalized, and abbots and bishops liable to various secular obligations. The rural parish became virtually the property of the local seigneur. There were grave lapses in normal ecclesiastical discipline. Clerical celibacy, for example, was widely disregarded. Largely because ecclesiastical positions often carried with them secular emoluments and property as well as responsibilities, simony—the buying and selling of Church offices—appears to have been all too common.

Nevertheless, the Church too was to enter into its era of renewal and to share in the general European revival. The first stages of this renewal were carried forward with the cooperation, often the initiative, of the secular authorities. For the traditional association of religion and government which the Carolingians had established continued at least through the middle years of the eleventh century.

In the religious reorganization of the tenth and eleventh centuries, two areas of activity predominate: one affected monastic life, the other concerned itself with the reform of the secular clergy. The two are related in many ways. Certain prominent persons figured in both. Each came to depend increasingly on papal direction or support. Nevertheless, the two are distinct in purpose and character.

To a few devoted persons, monastic renewal meant a return to a strict eremitical or quasi-eremitical life. In general, however, the monastic revival presupposed the normal community life revitalized under the Benedictine *Rule*. Such, for example, was the purpose of the reforms centering at Gorze in northwestern Germany and Cluny in French Burgundy. Each of these, and somewhat later Cîteaux, while following the *Rule* scrupulously, developed its own peculiar emphasis.

During the second half of the eleventh century, the initiative in revivifying and reforming the secular clergy was at length taken by the papacy. This movement, once called the "Gregorian reform" after its most illustrious proponent, Gregory VII, but now more commonly designated "papal reform," began toward the middle of the century, and its impetus carried it well into the following century. In essence it was to be a thorough overhauling of the body ecclesiastic, a purging of its major abuses, notably simony, clerical marriage, immorality, and over-much involvement with things secular. This was to be done by means of various improvements in the machinery of ecclesiastical government, in particular its more effective centralization in Rome. As a consequence, the papal office gradually assumed a new character. Under the influence of contemporary canonists, Rome came to be regarded as something more than the see of the Apostle Peter and the place of his tomb, a holy object of pilgrimage, and possessing a spiritual predominance over all other churches. It became in fact the center of an effective system of jurisdiction, sometimes referred to as the papal monarchy.

As the reform gained momentum, it seemed evident to some ardent spirits that a complete rupture with the existing conditions of lay interference in religion was necessary. The practice whereby lay rulers invested bishops with the symbols of their office was above all the target of such reformers. Thus it came about that, although moderate opinions persisted and there even remained a few champions of the traditional union of throne and altar, the secular ruler's predominant position in the Church, established by the Carolingians and revived by later German emperors, was seriously challenged by a revitalized papacy.

This challenge reached a climax during the pontificate of Gregory VII (1073–85). At first Gregory seems to have hoped for imperial cooperation in implementing further reforms. But Henry IV's resistance to his decree banning lay investiture prompted the pope to excommunicate the emperor in 1075 and again in 1080 and to justify his action on the basis of the superior character before God of the ecclesiastical power. It must be emphasized, however, that although a profoundly significant and potentially revolutionary confrontation with lay authorities did in fact take place throughout Europe, this was not the purpose of the papal action. To Gregory and to his successors this confrontation seemed necessary to the achievement of their religious aims. Its ultimate consequence, a papal interference in lay affairs rather than the opposite, was scarcely foreseen at the time.

Gregory did not live to see the fruition of his labors. In fact, the settlement by compromise of the long investiture controversy did not come until 1106 in England and 1122 in the empire. But it soon became evident that what Gregory and his predecessors had started was a continuing operation which was to last into the next century. Especially important in this context is the fact that Gregory's successors relied more successfully than he had been able to do on better integrated and more rationally articulated studies in both canon law and theology. For this was the period of the flowering of the famous cathedral schools of Chartres, Rheims, Paris, and others, and the first systematic analysis of Roman and canon law at such places as Ravenna and Bologna. All this was characteristic of the broadening intellectual climate of the age which produced what has been called the renaissance of the twelfth century.

Two significant examples of such studies, each illustrative of the new analytic method of juxtaposing and commenting on conflicting authorities, are the *Concord of Discordant Canons* (commonly called the *Decretum*) by the canonist Gratian, which appeared around 1140, and the *Quatuor libri sententiarum* (*Four Books of Sentences*) of Peter Lombard, a theological treatise which appeared about a decade later.

We have been concerned so far with the Church as an institution. Little has been said about lay persons who, after all, constituted the vast majority of Christians. This subject is at once important and difficult. Indeed, the nature of popular religion is one of the most elusive aspects of medieval history. Sources are scarce and all too often describe the unusual rather than the normal. More is said about saints and heretics than about the average Christian, and what is said about the saints tends more often than not to be stereotyped.

Those sources that do exist give the impression that popular religion in this period was not profound. In short, the intellectual revival may have influenced some rulers, nobles, or bourgeois, but did not penetrate to the mass of the population. As a result, lay religious life continued to be external, the fulfillment of obligations set down by the authorities from the time of the Carolingians. There was a proliferation of the cults of local saints with whose shrines and relics miracles were associated. That religion also continued to be mixed with superstition is evident in the persistence of ordeals as forms of judicial procedure; despite occasional condemnation by ecclesiastical authorities, these continued to receive the blessing of local clerics.

Such practices do, however, reveal a popular urge to associate religion with the affairs of life, and there is significant evidence of a popular desire to participate in the great religious movements of the day. There was, for example, considerable support, not always orthodox but nonetheless real, for the reform of clerical behavior. In the tenth century is found the first evidence of a paraliturgical ceremony, which, though monastic in origin, presumably attracted a wider audience. This, the remote origin of religious drama, was the addition or interpolation of words and action into a part of the formal liturgy for seasons such as Easter which lent themselves to such practices.

The tenth and eleventh centuries also witnessed the growth of a "peace movement." Following the invasions and before a certain amount of order was restored by kings and greater feudatories, violence and banditry caused considerable suffering. With a great deal of popular support and participation, the peace movement came ultimately to be directed by the Church, itself often a victim of violence. Legislation was enacted first by local councils and finally by the Council of Clermont under Urban II (1095). Such measures as the Peace or Truce of God forbade fighting on certain days and decreed an immunity for certain categories of persons.

Another significant manifestation of popular religion was the custom of pilgrimage to a hallowed shrine. The greatest of all pilgrimage centers were Rome, Compostela, and Jerusalem. Rome was associated in the popular mind with the tombs of the Apostles Peter and Paul and thus a place of especial sanctity. At Compostela in northwestern Spain there was a shrine dedicated to St. James the Apostle, whose body was believed to have been brought there sometime in the eighth century. The Compostela pilgrimage was associated with the *Reconquista* and is reflected in contemporary vernacular literature, notably in the *Song of Roland*.

During the eleventh century, pilgrimages to Jerusalem grew in number and size. Moreover, the earthly city was often spoken of as the image or symbol of the heavenly Jerusalem. Many, even humble folk, wanted to go and die in the city hallowed by the suffering and death of their Savior. Toward the end of the eleventh century a sense of urgency seems to have developed, and more than one writer spoke of the coming of Antichrist and the imminent end of the world.

It was in such an atmosphere that Pope Urban II preached the crusade at the Council of Clermont in 1095. In fact, it has been aptly said that the First Crusade occurred at a "unique moment in history." For the forces of popular religion were channeled, as it were, in this undertaking and were made something perhaps entirely different from what was originally intended. It is striking, for example, that chroniclers, reporting these events many years after Clermont, reflect the prevailing mood of the "way to Jerusalem" as expiation for sin. Thus there developed a "theology" of the crusade. Jerusalem, the holy city, must be rescued from the hands of the infidel. War against the infidel (in Spain, as well as in the East) is a holy act, deserving of spiritual reward, the remission of sin.

In many of the manifestations of popular religion there appears a growing sense of solidarity, a consciousness of Christianity as a company of believers on earth as well as of pilgrims to eternity. To the educated cleric these ideas might have an essentially spiritual meaning. They appear, for example, in much of the symbolic interpretation of the liturgy. But by many lay persons, and especially the nobles, the admonition to be a "soldier of Christ" was taken quite literally.

Eventually a sense of Christian community which, to some degree at least, transcended local loyalties developed. Unfortunately, this further engendered a xenophobia, a fear of "others," whoever they might be, Moslems, Jews, heretics, or schismatic Greeks. Nor were such feelings confined to the warrior class. There was a Peoples' Crusade as well as a barons', and it was the populace which massacred the Jews. This was Christianity's heroic age. Only at such a time could a phenomenon such as the crusades have taken place.

The final decades before 1150 have sometimes been called "the age of St. Bernard," and there is much to be said for such a designation. For during the first half of the twelfth century a great deal of the political as well as the religious life of western Europe was dominated by the towering figure of one man, St. Bernard of Clairvaux (1090–1153).

Bernard was first and last a monk, and the growth and success of the Cistercian order may be attributed in considerable measure to his efforts. He would undoubtedly have preferred to pass his days entirely in the beloved monastery of Clairvaux, which he founded. But the exigencies of the times frequently required his services. Thus it was St. Bernard who spoke out against the Roman reformer Arnold of Brescia, who opposed the scholar Abelard, who traveled about Europe in the cause of Pope Innocent II against a rival antipope, who, at the urgent request of Pope Eugenius III, preached the Second Crusade. Yet St. Bernard was one of the greatest of contemplatives, whom no less a person than Dante placed in the highest sphere of heaven. All these varied aspects of his career are apparent in an extraordinary output of treatises, letters, sermons, and hymns, written in a fluent Latin style.

St. Bernard's view of the world was traditional and monastic, grounded on biblical and patristic literature. Some have called him "the last of the fathers," and many have seen him with all his manifest strength as the representative of an age that was passing. It would be incorrect, however, simply to classify Bernard as a conservative opponent of all things new. He was an educated, highly intelligent man, one of the founders of speculative mysticism. He gave to medieval religion an element of love, human love of the highest order, which was often lacking. He was in large measure responsible for the devotion to the Virgin Mary and to the human, suffering Christ which developed in subsequent decades and is so evident in late twelfth- and thirteenth-century art.

Although he was primarily a monk, Bernard understood the problems of the secular clergy and was fully aware of contemporary clerical shortcomings. In his famous treatise, *De consideratione*, he anticipated later critics of the papal curia, while at the same time epitomizing the spirit of the entire reform movement.

The pope to whom Bernard addressed the *De consideratione*, Eugenius III, was a fellow Cistercian and former protégé. He was the last of a line of monastic popes who had left their impression on the period in which they lived. They were to be followed by men of a different stamp, men trained in the schools in law and theology. These too were to leave their imprint, but it was to be a different one, for a new age was dawning in the middle years of the twelfth century.

Suggested Readings

(In addition to the works of Bainton, Baldwin, Cannon, Daly, Dawson, Deanesley, Hughes, Knowles, and Russell mentioned above under Part II.)

Daniel-Rops, H., *Cathedral and Crusade*, trans. J. Warrrington (London and New York, 1957).

James, B., *St. Bernard of Clairvaux* (New York, 1957).

Knowles, Dom D., *The Evolution of Medieval Thought* (New York, 1962).

Kuttner, S., *Harmony from Dissonance* (Latrobe, Pa., 1960); [canon law].

Latourette, K. S., *A History of the Expansion of Christianity*, vol. II (New York, 1938).

Leff, G., *Medieval Thought* (New York, 1958).

Mortimer, R. C., *Western Canon Law* (Berkeley, 1953).

Tellenbach, G., *Church, State, and Christian Society at the Time of the Investiture Controversy*, trans. R. F. Bennett (London, 1940).

Tierney, B., *The Crisis of Church and State, 1050–1300* (Englewood Cliffs, N.J., 1964).

Ullmann, W., *Medieval Papalism* (London, 1950).

———, *The Growth of Papal Government in the Middle Ages* (London, 1955).

Williams, S., *The Gregorian Epoch: Reformation, Revolution, Reaction?* (Boston, 1964).

Williams, W., *St. Bernard of Clairvaux* (2nd ed., Manchester, 1953).

Monastic Reform

---

27. Ulrich, Customs of Cluny

Two collections of Cluniac customs have come down to us from the days of Abbot Hugh: that of Bernard, which first appeared around 1074, and that of Ulrich, around 1183. Ulrich wrote, therefore, before the building of Cluny III, the final and greatest abbey church. A second edition of Bernard's work was published two or three years later. Ulrich's *Consuetudines*, which borrowed heavily from Bernard, were apparently compiled for Abbot William from the German abbey of Hirschau and are presented in a question-answer form. Although both works reflect personal and occasionally even critical attitudes, each is the contribution of a dedicated monk and the two gradually acquired a quasi-official status.

The sections cited below from Ulrich's *Consuetudines* have been chosen to show how, as a consequence of additions to the number of psalms and prayers indicated by St. Benedict, the Cluny *horarium* had become so lengthy as to be found at times burdensome. It even exceeded the 150 psalms a day of the desert fathers that St. Benedict had abandoned. Moreover, the chant was more elaborate. Thus, with two solemn masses each day, little time was left for any other activity. And, as Ulrich points out, since the number of monks had increased, processions took longer and remembrances for the dead were necessarily lengthened.

Care must be taken, however, in judging the Cluniac observance. A recent study has suggested that in actual fact it may not have been as overweighted as Ulrich seems to indicate.[1] Many of the additions were for Lent only and, therefore, not typical of the entire year, and Ulrich noted how on certain occasions reductions were made. Accordingly, reading, manual labor, services to the poor, etc., may have been diminished, but they did not disappear. In fact, Cluny was noted for its charity toward the poor.

Nevertheless, the elaborateness of Cluny evoked criticism from other monastic reformers, notably St. Peter Damiani and later St. Bernard of Clairvaux. But Damiani accepted the invitation—almost a

---

1. Noreen Hunt, *Cluny Under St. Hugh* (London, 1967).

challenge—of Abbot Hugh to visit Cluny to see for himself. He came away convinced that his original judgment had been mistaken and that Cluny was in reality a great center of spiritual life. It is also significant that he especially solicited the monks' prayers for his soul after his death. For, following the precepts of Abbot Odilo (994–1049), Cluny made much of the office for the dead.

Modern studies on the architecture of the great abbey church and on the development of medieval music have made it possible for us to visualize in some degree the grandeur and sublimity of the liturgy as the Cluny monks observed it. Perhaps at no other time in history has so large a religious community been so exclusively dedicated to the task of rendering the public worship of God as perfect as possible.

The text is translated from Udalrici, *Consuetudines Cluniacences*, *MPL*, 149, cols. 645 ff.

Book I

CHAPTER II

Q. Do you ordinarily add to nocturns [vigils] or the other hours more than what St. Benedict directed?

A. How much it is, if I remember well, I will tell you. First, there is no antiphon so short that we do not complete it with the full ending of its tone. We do not know what kind of prayers St. Benedict said after the Lord's Prayer because it has not been found in writing, but those we say at nocturns, matins, tierce, sext, nones, and vespers are included in fourteen versicles. If it is a week day, and neither an octave nor in Paschal season, the fiftieth psalm is added. At matins and vespers, four other psalms are added and two at compline. Why the change was made by our superior I do not know. S¨nce, beginning with nocturns four psalms should be said for the household after each hour except compline, they are said at matins and vespers between the prayers before the last versicle, before the brothers rise from their pews and the collect is said. Therefore, I mention these psalms once and for all without delaying to designate them by name. . . .

[A number of specific psalms are then designated]

But to return to what I was saying a moment ago, and also to mention the prayers of prime and compline, when the Lord's Prayer and Apostles Creed have been said first, at prime there are prayers of thirty-one versicles and the confession must be inserted in its proper place. At compline there are seventeen. On the week days of Advent and Lent, at matins and vespers there may be as many as twenty versicles. Actually the diversity of prayers and other things of this kind can be noted for you individually on one chart so that there would be no need now to dwell on this longer. For I do not recall anything else which is incorporated in any canonical hour of an ordinary day which may not in some way be included for a feast day.

CHAPTER III

Q. Please explain what psalms you say in the convent in addition to the regular hours.

A. These are considerably more extensive and varied in Lent than at any other time . . .

. . . It is found also in the rule that St. Benedict directed that in Lent something should be added to the burden of our customary service, and this is not ignored by us. At matins and vespers, after the suffrage of the saints, and at other hours after the four psalms, the supplements of the hours, so to speak, we prostrate ourselves completely to say two psalms, the first from the seven penitential psalms, the other from the canticles of fifteen verses. . . . The declaration of faith [Creed], that is the *Quicunque* written by St. Athanasius[1] (which many churches do not recite except on Sunday) is on no day omitted so that we do not say it, but on week days it is said together with the other psalms and on Sunday after the prayers. . . .

After regular vespers, and after the psalms, which are said by those prostrate, there is again a procession to the church of St. Mary, with the same canticle. And as at matins, there is again said vespers of All Saints and for the faithful departed. After supper we return to the church with Psalm 50, as always after food. The office which is popularly called vigils by our people is also said by the servants who wait until we get up from the table because sometimes when there are not so many deceased it is usual to do with only three readings and responses, unless the anniversary of some brother supervenes. But now, when there is no day without many departed, this office is never said at all without the nine readings and responses and collects which follow it. Two psalms precede, that is 119 and 3, as also at vespers, 143 and 123. At matins the *De*

---

1. This is the long form of the Creed written by Athanasius in the fourth century.

profundis and *Usquequo*. Therefore, as far as I can recall there is no greater psalmody than in our usage. . . .

CHAPTER VI

Q. How many masses will you generally celebrate each day in the monastery?

A. Two: the first of the day, the other if it is an ordinary week day, for the dead. To add something more about this, since you do not fail to ask, the litany again customarily precedes the major mass on ordinary week days. This, however, is not very lengthy since only three saints of each rank have to be named. When the first collect has been said, these customarily follow: [seven are then named, plus one each for Easter and the feast of St. Michael]. Although it is well enough known why some are said, it is not clear concerning the others. The fourth is for the kings and other princes; the fifth is for our bishops and abbots, the sixth is for the members of our household, the seventh is for the kings of Spain in turn.[1] And other collects are added if there is a cause for which there is a special need as words of grace on behalf of those making a journey, on behalf of the sick, or on account of any tribulation which may occur. Moreover, the entire chant is sung simply and in the same way in which it is sung in other churches. Only the Introit, as is the custom with others, following the *Gloria Patri*, is repeated three times. I know nothing else to bring up about the verses which are to be offered except that the precentor according as he sees fit sometimes adds one, sometimes adds all, especially because of those who are making the oblation. For on three days a week the offering is made and the [kiss of] peace given and received by those of the choir on the left side. And for those who deem it good to receive the Body of Our Lord, accordingly, three hosts are consecrated. On the other three days, those on the right in their turn receive the peace and communicate if they desire. . . .

CHAPTER XXX

Tell us some more about the *opus manuum* (manual labor) which you mentioned briefly, that is, what this *opus manuum* is and how it is done.

1. This is interesting evidence of the special connections of Cluny with Spain.

Certainly, although I do not falsify what I have often seen, it is nothing other than shelling new beans not yet fully ripe, or pulling out weeds which were suffocating the good plants, and sometimes preparing loaves in the bakery. Let me now explain just how it is done on the appointed day. When the brothers have gotten up and said prayers, the signal is given for prime which, with certain psalms omitted, is followed by the litany alone and the morning mass. The chapter, also, is shorter than on other days. And there is not the customary psalmody as they go to St. Mary's, but when the altar is struck and the *Benedicite* has preceded, the lord abbot says: "Let us go out for the *opus manuum*." The psalms omitted after prime are placed here; they move in procession in such a way that the boys are first and the priors last. When they reach the place of work, all turn toward the east and stand in a row. At the end of each individual psalm they face forward and backward[1] and, with the abbot leading, they then say this verse, *Deus in adjutorium*, etc., followed by the *Kyrie eleison*, *Pater noster*, and the verse, *Adjutorium nostrum*. After they have once again bowed, they begin work. These are the psalms which are sung while working: first what remained after prime and after the chapter; then all the regular hours according to canonical custom beginning with prime. To the prayers of prime is also added the fifth psalm and seven psalms divided among the other hours. The remaining three are all said among the prayers at compline. Compline is preceded by vespers for the faithful departed, and the psalms normally said for the community after tierce and the two following hours are added. If it seems to the lord abbot that they should work more, there are also added the psalms beginning with *Ad Dominum cum tribuler*, to the end of the psalter, and then even from the beginning the *Gloria Patri*, etc., is inserted after each three psalms. When these psalms for the community have been finished, as soon as the lord abbot wishes, he signals to the brothers to stop working and come closer to him. He orders something to be read, although to be finished quickly, since he is about to give a homily. He discourses on something, especially the lives of the fathers, calculated to edify his hearers. When this is finished, and psalms again are added, they return. As soon as the boys have reached the threshold of the cloister, they raise [sing] the psalms in a higher key,[2] and do not

1. "*Faciunt ante et retro . . .*"
2. "*Altiore voce levant . . .*"

stand in the chapter until after the assembly just preceding. While the lord abbot leads the verse, *Adjutorium*, they all turn forward and backward. Again, after the *Benedicite*, they are given license to talk. Therefore, nones is said more rapidly than on other days. After an hour of talking they are again required to go out for manual labor. . . .

If it seems proper to the lord abbot that they should drink after work is done, after the bell is rung when they have finished vespers, a cymbal is struck and they go into the refectory, and a drink made of honey, wine, and absinthe is served.[3] And it should be noted, because this takes place many times, that never again, as once was the custom, do they drink during a meal. Whenever they do not work, then the place for the sermon is in the cloister, and the verse is not changed, so that the *Benedictus es, Domine*, is not said immediately. And if there are twelve readings on the following night, they do not work twice. . . .

CHAPTER XVIII [LAST SECTION]

Q. The permission and time for conversation, ordinarily how long is it?

A. At the time when I first came to the monastery, a priest who wanted to celebrate a private mass could finish it during that time. This now rarely happens because the number of brothers has greatly increased. While the oblation is made by these at each mass, while [the kiss of] peace is given and received, while this and that is talked about by one or another in chapter, while so many are served in the refectory, a large part of the day is spent. All of these things cannot, however, remain without upsetting our entire schedule. As a consequence, the hour for conversation is necessarily very short. And if we speak somewhat less, no one, indeed, feels that there is any loss in this arrangement. When the bell has rung for tierce and the prayer said, they sit in choir reading until the priest and the other servers are vested for mass. After mass they sit in the cloister again reading with great attention and in silence until the boys who have received their share [of food] leave the refectory. Then they begin to read aloud. As soon as the guardian of the church hears them he immediately without delay rings the bell for sext. And so that you do not think that we are overbur-

3. A spiced wine-honey drink later much criticized by St. Bernard.

dened beyond measure with vigils because the night begins to be so short and, all the same, the customary psalmody is not diminished, the principal guardian of the church is enjoined, as though by permanent regulation, that during the entire summer he shall arrange for this to take place after lunch, as soon as it is noon. At that moment also, the brothers generally gather for a break, although many are more intent on reading than relaxing. Moreover, nones, for which they are about to rise, will be so late that after they have something to drink in the refectory and again have permission to talk, that hour for conversation and the interval before vespers, I shall add not without justice, is nothing if not brief. For often before all sit down in the cloister and before some brother has spoken even one word, the bell is rung for vespers and there is the end of talking. . . .

Chapter XLI [last section]

Q. After vespers, when you have neither eaten nor sung the office of the dead, what else is done?

A. We go into the dormitory, put down our knives, take off our day sandals and put on our night ones. We sit in the cloister for reading. The bell is rung for us to wash our hands and come into the refectory to drink. We sit again for reading and the bell is sounded for collation. Likewise, you can be sure that if it happens in spite of ourselves and never on purpose that it is still partially daylight when we fall asleep,[1] we can, therefore, stand among other things very long readings which for some of our fellow monks,[2] who want to change the customs of the fathers as well as the institution itself, are certainly no less burdensome to listen to than it would be to carry a lump of lead. No wonder they are not eager to sleep with us if they are not eager to watch with us. . . .

If you were to see also at what hour we try our best to go to sleep in Lent, you would admit that we get up early enough for nocturns. These somewhat extraordinary things are to be said so that you will know that we have no desire to spend the night in revelry.

1. *"Ut lux diei adhuc clare non appareat . . ."* The meaning is not clear. Presumably, the monks fell asleep after vespers while it was still daylight. 2. Postulants, according to Dom David Knowles, "The Monastic Horarium," *Downside Review,* LI (1933), 715.

28. *The Cistercian* Exordium

Exordium coenobii et ordinis Cisterciensis

The *Exordium* is a brief chronicle of the foundation and early days of the Cistercian monks. It describes first the original establishment under Robert of a small community at Molesme in Burgundy and his departure along with Alberic, the Englishman Stephen Harding, and others to form a new community at Cîteaux. After Robert had been instructed by Pope Urban II to return to Molesme, Alberic was chosen to succeed him, and he in turn was succeeded by Stephen in 1109.

Under Stephen the characteristic usages were clarified. Many of the liturgical additions to the original Benedictine *Rule* were abandoned, and more time was left for religious reading and manual labor. Manorial possessions were not received and lay brothers, called *conversi*, did most of the heavy farm work, often in remote and newly established communities. The constitution of the order, the Charter of Love (*Carta caritatis*)—ratified by Pope Calixtus II in 1119 for Cîteaux and its associated houses—contained two important features which the Fourth Lateran Council in 1215 ordered adopted by all monastic orders: a yearly visitation of all the houses by the abbot of Cîteaux and an annual meeting of all the abbots at Cîteaux. These measures effected a compromise between the original isolation of the Benedictine system and the centralization of Cluny.

In a sense, Cîteaux with its extreme simplicity of life represented a reaction against the elaborateness of Cluny. Moreover, as the following passages show, its rigorous life was such as to deter prospective members. The arrival of a band of young nobles in the company of Bernard, later to become celebrated as abbot of Clairvaux, gave the new community a great stimulus. In fact, the order attained in the twelfth century an influence in the Church comparable to that of Cluny in the eleventh.

The following passages are translated from *MPL*, 166, cols. 1501 ff.

PROLOGUE

We Cistercians, first founders of this church, formally notify our successors with the present writing by what authority, by what persons, and at what time their monastery and way of life had its beginnings, so that when the real truth of this matter is manifest they may love most earnestly both the place and the observance of the holy *Rule* whenever, by the grace of God, it was instituted therein by us; and also that they may pray for us who have untiringly borne the burden and heat of the day; that they may exert themselves in the straight and narrow way which the *Rule* prescribes until the last breath; so that when the burden of the flesh is laid down they may joyfully repose in everlasting rest.

Chapter XV. The Rules of the Cistercian Monks Coming from Molesme

Therefore, that abbot[1] and his brethren, not unmindful of their promise to institute the *Rule of St. Benedict* in that place, unanimously decided to stay. They rejected anything opposed to the *Rule*, frocks, fur tunics, linsey-woolsey shirts and cowls, straw for beds and various dishes of food in the refectory, as well as lard and all other things which ran counter to the letter of the *Rule*. And so, holding to the strictness of the *Rule* over the entire tenor of their life, in ecclesiastical as well as in other observances, they were adjusted or conformed to the pattern of the *Rule*. They rejoiced that the old man had been cast off and that they had put on the new. Neither in the *Rule* nor in the life of St. Benedict did they read that that doctor possessed churches or altars, or oblations or burials, or tithes from any persons, or ovens, or mills, or villages or peasants, or that women entered his monastery or dead were buried there, except his sister. Therefore, they gave up all these things saying that when the holy father Benedict teaches that "a monk should hold himself away from worldly concerns," it is there clearly demonstrated that such things ought not to remain in the deeds or hearts of monks who, fleeing them, should follow regularly the full intent of the name.

They also said that the holy fathers, who were the mouthpiece of the Holy Spirit and whose statutes it is a sacrilege to transgress, divided the tithes into four parts: one for the bishop, another for the priest, a third for the guests coming to the church, whether widows, orphans or poor who have no sustenance elsewhere, and finally a fourth for the upkeep of the church. Because they did not find in this reckoning the person of a monk who possessed fields

1. Presumably Alberic, since he is mentioned in the following chapter.

from which he might live laboring by himself and with his cattle, for this reason they refused to usurp for themselves these things which belong of right to others.

Thus when the new soldiers of Christ had spurned the riches of this world, poor with the poor Christ, they began to manage among themselves with whatever skill, whatever artifice, or whatever device to sustain in this life themselves, guests, rich and poor who came, whom the *Rule* prescribed that they should receive as Christ. And they decided that with the permission of the bishop they would receive lay brothers with beards, *conversi*, and that when they had taken up the monastic life they would treat them in their life and death as they would treat themselves, both as men and as hired servants. For they did not see how without their assistance they could fully preserve by day or by night the commandments of the *Rule*. They were also to receive lands remote from the dwellings of men, and vineyards, and fields, and woods, and streams for setting up mills and for their own exclusive use and for fishing, and horses, and various cattle useful for men's needs. When they had established farming centers anywhere, they decreed that the aforementioned *conversi* should administer such dwellings because the abode of monks ought, according to the *Rule*, to be in the cloister.

Since these holy men knew that St. Benedict had not built his monasteries in cities or in castles or in villas, but in places removed from the concourse of people, they promised to emulate this. And as he established monasteries for twelve monks associated with an abbot, they decided to do likewise.

Chapter XVI. Concerning Their Sadness

That man of God, mentioned above, the abbot [Alberic], and his monks were somewhat saddened because it was rare in those days for anyone to come there to imitate them. For these holy men, having found the treasure of the virtues from heaven, were eager to hand it on to their successors for the salvation of men to come. But almost all, on seeing and hearing about the unusual and, as it were, unheard of severity of their life, hastened mentally and physically to remain aloof rather than to approach them, and did not cease to falter in their perseverance. But the mercy of God which instilled this marshal spirit in His followers did not cease to enlarge and perfect it notably for the growth of many, as what follows will explain.

CHAPTER XVII. CONCERNING THE DEATH OF THE FIRST ABBOT AND THE ELECTION OF SECOND, AND CONCERNING HIS ORDINANCES

The man of God, Alberic, who for nine and a half years labored fruitfully in regular discipline and in the school of Christ, passed on to the Lord, glorious in faith and virtues and worthy to be blessed in life eternal with God. A certain brother, Stephen by name and of the English nation, succeeded him. He had come there with the others from Molesme and loved the *Rule* and the place. During his time, the brothers along with the abbot forbade the duke of that land or any other prince to hold court at any time in that church, as was formerly done on solemn occasions. Then, in order that nothing should remain in the house of God where they desired to serve Him day and night which smacked of pride or superfluity, or which might even corrupt the poverty which they had freely chosen as the guardian of virtue, they also declared that they would not keep gold or silver crosses, but only just painted wooden ones, or candelabra, except one of iron, or thuribles, unless made of copper or iron, or chasubles, unless of fustian or linen without cloth of gold or silver, or albs or amices except of linen and also without cloth of gold or silver. In fact, they abandoned entirely mantles and dalmatics, caps and tunics. But they kept chalices of silver, not of gold but gilded if it could be done, and the silver stem gilded if possible. They kept only stoles and maniples of fine cloth without gold and silver. They ruled that the altar cloths should be made of linen and entirely without designs, and that the wine cruets should be made without gold or silver.

In those days, in the lands, vineyards, fields, and hamlets the church [i.e., monastic community] flourished and did not diminish in worship. Therefore, the Lord visited the place in those days pouring out the very heart of His mercy on those who besought Him, crying to Him, weeping in His presence, day and night bringing forth deep sighs, and approaching Him as though through the door of desperation because they were almost without followers. For the grace of God at one time committed to that church so many learned and noble clerics, who in the secular world had been as powerful as they were noble, that thirty eagerly entered the house of novices, and struggling manfully against their own weaknesses and the temptings of malign spirits finished their course. Inspired by their example, old and young, men of different ages and different parts of the world, seeing in them what they had formerly feared as impossible in keeping the *Rule* to be, in fact, possible, began to hasten there to subject their necks to the sweet yoke of Christ, to love ardently the hard and severe precepts of the *Rule*, and wonderfully to invigorate and gladden the community.

Papal Reform

---

29. Pope Gregory VII, Dictatus papae

This remarkable series of pronouncements on the prerogatives of the Roman see was issued in 1075, just as the struggle with Emperor Henry IV was beginning. Somewhat resembling a table of contents for a collection of canons, the statements evidently required further explanation, and it is possible that the pope planned an allocution at the council of 1075 which for some reason he abandoned. At any rate, an entire theory of ecclesiastical administration under the pope is outlined here. His sovereign power permits him to legislate for the entire Church and to judge cases either of especial gravity or which local ecclesiastical courts have been unable to resolve. It is also the pope's prerogative to modify old or create new dioceses, to transfer or depose incumbents for cause. Local councils have only local jurisdiction. Papal legates, regardless of rank, take precedence over all local clergy.

It must be remembered that the decrees assembled in the *Dictatus* represent no fundamentally new provision. Each was based on some previous canon; some were derived from the false decretals, many from the canons of previous popes.

The translation is from O. J. Thatcher and E. H. McNeal, *A Source Book of Medieval History* (New York, 1905), pp. 136–137.

1. That the Roman church was established by God alone.
2. That the Roman pontiff alone is rightly called universal.
3. That he alone has the power to depose and reinstate bishops.
4. That his legate, even if he be of lower ecclesiastical rank, presides over bishops in council, and has the power to give sentence of deposition against them.

5. That the pope has the power to depose those who are absent [*i.e.,* without giving them a hearing].

6. That, among other things, we ought not to remain in the same house with those whom he has excommunicated.

7. That he alone has the right, according to the necessity of the occasion, to make new laws, to create new bishoprics, to make a monastery of a chapter of canons, and *vice versa*, and either to divide a rich bisophric or to unite several poor ones.

8. That he alone may use the imperial insignia.

9. That all princes shall kiss the foot of the pope alone.

10. That his name alone is to be recited in the churches.

11. That the name applied to him belongs to him alone.

12. That he has the power to depose emperors.

13. That he has the right to transfer bishops from one see to another when it becomes necessary.

14. That he has the right to ordain as a cleric anyone from any part of the church whatsoever.

15. That anyone ordained by him may rule [as bishop] over another church, but cannot serve [as priest] in it, and that such a cleric may not receive a higher rank from any other bishop.

16. That no general synod may be called without his order.

17. That no action of a synod and no book shall be regarded as canonical without his authority.

18. That his decree can be annulled by no one, and that he can annul the decrees of anyone.

19. That he can be judged by no one.

20. That no one shall dare to condemn a person who has appealed to the apostolic seat.

21. That the important cases of any church whatsoever shall be referred to the Roman church [that is, to the pope].

22. That the Roman church has never erred and will never err to all eternity, according to the testimony of the holy scriptures.

23. That the Roman pontiff who has been canonically ordained is made holy by the merits of St. Peter, according to the testimony of St. Ennodius, bishop of Pavia, which is confirmed by many of the holy fathers, as is shown by the decrees of the blessed pope Symmachus.

24. That by his command or permission subjects may accuse their rulers.

25. That he can depose and reinstate bishops without the calling of a synod.

26. That no one can be regarded as catholic who does not agree with the Roman church.

27. That he has the power to absolve subjects from their oath of fidelity to wicked rulers.

30. Pope Gregory VII, Letters

A glance at the titles in Gregory's *Register* of letters and decrees reveals that he corresponded with many persons, both clerical and lay, on a wide variety of subjects. It is noticeable too that the controversy with Henry IV, which certainly occupied the center of the stage in his pontificate, is only one of many concerns. Several letters are purely personal. Throughout Gregory's correspondence a sense of urgency is always evident. He seems almost to have thought of himself as a sort of prophet, one called by God to root out the evils which were afflicting Christian society. In short, Gregory's contribution to religious renewal was not so much accomplishment as the example of personal dedication. So distinguished a successor as Urban II could claim no better credentials than to be a follower in his footsteps.

Gregory's uncompromising championship of papal supremacy has led some to view him not as a humble man, but as a proud seeker after power. Most historians today would acquit Gregory of such a charge, however much they might question the wisdom of his policies. Later generations were to number him among the saints of the Church.

The first letter cited here illustrates the pope's manner in dealing with a recalcitrant bishop. The second is especially revealing of the man himself. It was written toward the end of his life when the course of the investiture controversy was going against him. It is a moving document which might well be taken as a sort of last will and testament.

The translations are by E. Emerton, *The Correspondence of Pope Gregory VII*, Columbia University Records of Civilization (New York, 1932), pp. 52-53, 193-195. Reprinted by permission of Columbia University Press.

To Bishop Otto of Constance, Summoning Him to the Lenten Synod at Rome

Gregory . . . to Otto, bishop of Constance, greeting . . .

A report has come to us with regard to Your Fraternity, which I have heard with grief and regret—a report which, if it had been made to us of the lowest member of the Christian community, would undoubtedly have called for a severe disciplinary sentence. While we were zealously striving to wipe out the heresy of Simony and to enforce the chastity of the clergy, inspired by apostolic authority and the authentic opinions of holy fathers, we enjoined upon our colleague, the venerable archbishop of Mainz, whose suffragans are numerous and widely scattered, that he should diligently impress this decree upon his whole clergy, in person and through his assistants, and should see that it was carried out without exception.

To you also, who preside over the numerous clergy and the widespread population of the church of Constance, it has, for the same reason, seemed good to us to send a special letter under our own seal. With this as your authority you can more safely and more boldly carry out our orders and expel from the Lord's holy place the heresy of Simony and the foul plague of carnal contagion. The apostolic authority of St. Paul is here of especial force, where, counting in fornicators and adulterers with other vicious persons, he gives this plain decision: "With such a one, no, not to eat."

Furthermore the whole body of the Catholic Church consists of virgins or married persons or those holding themselves in restraint. Whoever, therefore, is outside those three classes is not to be counted among the sons of the Church or within the bounds of the Christian religion. Wherefore we also, if we should know for certain that even the lowest layman was involved in concubinage, would cut him off completely from the body and blood of the Lord until he should perform due penance. How then shall one be the distributor or server of the holy sacraments who cannot in any wise be partaker of them? Further, we are urged to this by the authority of the blessed Pope Leo [I] who deprived subdeacons of the right to marry, a decree to which his successors in the Holy Roman Church, especially that famous doctor Gregory [I], gave such force of law that henceforth the marriage bond has been absolutely forbidden to the three orders of priests, levites and subdeacons.

But when we, in our pastoral forethought, sent word to you that these orders were to be carried out you, not setting your mind on the things that are above, but on the things that are upon the earth, loosed the reins of lust within the aforesaid orders so that, as we have heard, those who had taken concubines [*mulierculis*] persisted in their crime, while those who had not yet done so had no fear of your prohibitions. Oh, what insolence! Oh, what audacity, that a bishop should despise the decrees of the Apostolic See, should uproot the precepts of holy fathers—nay more, by orders from his high place and his priestly office should impose upon his subjects things contrary and repugnant to the Christian faith.

Wherefore we command you to present yourself before us at the approaching synod in the first week of Lent to give answer according to canon law as well for this disobedience and contempt of the Apostolic See as for all the other offenses charged against you.

A Call to the Faithful to Protect the Church from Her Enemies

Gregory . . . to all the faithful in Christ who truly love the Apostolic See, greeting . . .

You are aware, beloved brethren, that in our day the question arises which was asked in the Psalm: "Why do the nations rage and the peoples imagine a vain thing? The kings of the earth set themselves and the rulers take counsel together against the Lord and against his anointed."

The rulers of the people and the rulers of the priests have taken counsel together against Christ, son of Almighty God, and against Peter, his Apostle, to crush the Christian faith and to spread abroad the iniquity of heresy. But, by the grace of God, they have not been able to turn those who trust in the Lord to their impious ways by any fear or cruelty or by any promise of earthly glory. These evil conspirators have lifted up their hands against us for no other reason except that we would not let the peril of Holy Church pass in silence and those . . .[1] who are not ashamed to reduce the bride of Christ to slavery. In every country even the poorest of women is permitted to take a lawful husband according to the law of the land and by her own choice; but, through the desires and evil practices of the wicked, Holy Church, the bride of God and mother of us all, is not permitted lawfully to cling to her spouse on earth in accordance with divine law and her own will. We ought not to suffer the sons of the Church to be subjected to heretical adulterers and usurpers as to their fathers and to be branded by these with the mark of adultery.

1. Hiatus in the text.

How many evils, what diverse perils and unheard-of criminal cruelties have arisen from this cause you may see as plain as day from the true reports of our legates. If you are truly grieved at the ruinous confusions of the Christian faith and desire to lend a helping hand, you may receive ample instruction from them. For they are most loyal to St. Peter and are numbered, each in his own order, among the chief members of his House. No promises and no earthly rewards have been able to turn them from their loyal defense of him or to separate them from the bosom of Holy Mother Church. But because, as you my brethren know, the divine voice speaks to the unworthy and the sinful by the Prophet: "Upon a high and lofty mountain . . .," and again, "Cry aloud, spare not!" therefore, setting aside all false shame or fear or any earthly affection, I preach the Gospel, whether I will or no. I cry aloud again and again, and I declare to you that the true Christian faith, as taught to us by our fathers through the son of God descending from Heaven, is turned over to the evil fashions of this world and is alas! alas! almost annihilated. Its ancient colors are changed, and it has become the laughingstock, not only of the Devil, but of Jews, Saracens and pagans.

For these obey their own laws, though they are now of no avail for the salvation of souls and are not, like our law, set forth and sanctioned by repeated declarations of the Eternal King. Whereas we, intoxicated by worldly desire and setting greed and pride above all religion and honor, appear like outlaws and simpletons. We do not regard our welfare and dignity in this life or in the future as our fathers did, nor have we their hope as we ought to have. Or if there be some—and very few they are—who fear God, they are willing enough to fight for themselves but not for the common welfare of their brethren. Who is there, or how many are there who, in the fear and love of Almighty God in whom we live and move and have our being, strive and labor even unto death as do soldiers of this world for their masters or even for their subordinates? Behold thousands of these rushing into death daily for their masters, but for the true God of Heaven and for our Redeemer they will not only not meet death, but will not even brave the enmity of a few men.

And if there be those—for by God's mercy there are some, though few indeed—who stand up and face the wicked even unto death for love of the Christian law, not only are they not supported by their brethren as they should be, but they are looked upon as weak and reckless madmen. But now, since these and other evils are threatening us, that we may be able, by God's grace, to root out vice from the hearts of our brethren and plant virtue in its place, we beg and beseech you in the name of our Lord Jesus, who redeemed us by his death, to inform yourselves by careful inquiry what trials and oppressions we suffer from the enemies of the Christian faith and why we suffer them. From the moment when by divine inspiration Mother Church raised me, unworthy and God knows unwilling, to the apostolic throne, I have labored with all my power that Holy Church, the bride of God, our Lady Mother, might come again to her own splendor and might remain free, pure, and Catholic. But because this was not pleasing to our ancient enemy, he stirred up his members against us to bring it to nought. Thus he accomplished against us—nay, against the Apostolic See—what he had not been able to do since the time of Constantine the Great. And no wonder! for the nearer the day of Antichrist approaches, the harder he fights to crush out the Christian faith.

And now, beloved brethren, give attentive ear to what I say. Throughout the world all who own the Christian name and truly understand the Christian faith know and confess: that St. Peter, chief of the Apostles, is the father of all Christians and, under Christ, their chief pastor; and that the Holy Roman Church is the mother and mistress of all churches. If, therefore, you believe and hold this without a doubt, I ask and command you, by Almighty God, to aid and rescue these your father and mother if you wish to gain through them absolution for all your sins and grace and blessing in this world and the world to come.

May Almighty God, from whom all good things do proceed, enlighten your minds forever and fill them with love for him and for your neighbor. So that you may be worthy to have your father and your mother as your debtors and may enter without shame into their fellowship. Amen.

Canon Law

---

31. Gratian, The Concord of Discordant Canons

Gratian's *Concord of Discordant Canons* (commonly known as the *Decretum*), which appeared around 1140, marked the culmination of a stage in the renaissance of legal studies, canon and civil, which had begun in the eleventh century. During this preliminary period a whole procedure of comment and analysis was elaborated. Glosses, originally marginal notations, could be combined into an *apparatus*. For purposes of exposition, material was presented in the form of *quaestiones, distinctiones*, causes, etc. Although canon law was not found in one *corpus* or treatise, such as the *Code* or *Digest*—in fact, canon law in the early twelfth century was still in its "classical" period—most of the procedures of the civilians were taken over by the canonists. Much of the spirit of Roman jurisprudence is evident in canon law, and Roman jurists are often cited. In dealing with personal acts, for example, there is conscious effort to determine degrees of guilt by exploring motives for an act or conditions under which an act is committed.

In compiling his work, Gratian included no less than 3,458 texts from conciliar decrees, papal decretals, citations from the fathers, etc., which he classified according to subject matter and to which he added his own comments[1] and attempted to resolve contradictions. The first part was subdivided by a pupil, Paucapalea, into categories called "Distinctions." The second part consists of 36 Causes, that is, kinds of cases, in turn subdivided into questions and chapters.

Despite the title, there remained much that was discordant and contradictory in Gratian's work. There was also considerable overlapping into the field of theology. Nevertheless, the *Decretum* is a landmark in the history of canon law and set the stage for future development. In fact, it became customary to refer to what was done previously as the *ius antiquum* in contrast to the *ius novum* which was thereby inaugurated.

The first selection cited here is taken from Part I, Distinction III. Gratian opens his treatise with a discussion of the nature of law, the distinction between divine and human law, what the law of nature is, etc. He proceeds in the first two distinctions to analyze the species or kinds of law. In Distinction III he considers the nature of canon law.

---

1. Indicated in the passages cited below by Gratian's name in parentheses.

Isidore of Seville (d. 636), to whom Gratian refers here and in preceding passages, was a native of Visigothic Spain, a noted scholar, and bishop of Seville. His work entitled the *Etymologies* was a kind of encyclopedic compendium of various fields of learning. Although it contained many errors, it was useful in the early Middle Ages as a source of information not found elsewhere. Such, it will be recalled, was Isidore's reputation that the false decretals were attributed to him in the ninth century.

The selections are translated from A. Friedberg (ed.), *Corpus Juris Canonici*, Part I, *Decretum magistri Gratiani* (Leipzig, 1879; reprinted Graz, 1959), cols. 4–758 *passim*, unless otherwise stated.

Part I, Distinction III

Part I. All these species are parts of the secular law. But because, in fact, a civil decree is one thing, an ecclesiastical decree another, [and] the civil law (*ius*) is called public or civil, we must see by what name an ecclesiastical decree is called. An ecclesiastical decree is denoted by the term canon. And what a canon is Isidore declared in his *Etymologies*, Book VI, as follows:
Ch. I. What a canon is.
It is called canon in Greek, rule in Latin.
Ch. II. Why it is called a rule (*ibid.*).
It is called a rule because it leads rightly and leads no one astray. Others have said it is a rule either because it governs, or provides the norm for right living, or corrects what is crooked and evil.
Part II. (Gratian) Further, some of the canons are decrees of the pontiffs, others the statutes of councils. Some councils are universal, some are provincial. Some provincial councils are held by the authority of the Roman pontiff, namely, in the presence of a legate of the Holy Roman Church; others, in fact, by the authority of patriarchs, or primates, or the metropolitan of the province. These things must be understood about the general rules. There are also certain private laws, ecclesiastical as well as secular, which are called privileges. Concerning these, Isidore says in Book V:
Ch. III. What a privilege is.
Privileges are laws for individual persons, in a sense, private laws. For it is called a privilege because it is held privately. . . .

Part I, Distinctions XIX, XX (*Selected Chapters*)

In the second selection presented here, taken from Part I, Distinctions XIX and XX, Gratian addresses himself to one of the problems which confronted canonists in the formative period of canon law, namely, the weight to be given papal decretals. In Distinction XIX he cites ten passages which support the validity of papal decretals as part of the regular apparatus of canon law. The problem had been raised before, notably, it will be recalled, during the ninth century at the time the Pseudo-Isidorian decretals were issued.

In Distinction XX he distinguishes between the personal or religious prestige of an individual writer and the character of the papal office, and concludes that in law the latter has the greater weight. The importance of this is clear, for papal decretals were increasingly cited and, in the period following Gratian, were to become a major source of canonical precedent. In fact, these selections illustrate the extent to which Gratian supported the Roman primacy, a characteristic of his entire work.

DISTINCTION XIX

Part I. It is inquired concerning the decretal letters, whether they have authoritative force when they are not found in the corpus of canons.

Concerning these Pope Nicholas I wrote thus to the archbishops and bishops in Gaul.

Ch. I. Decretal letters have authoritative sanction.

[Here Gratian quotes from the letter of Nicholas I given above, Document 9.

Chapters II–X contain statements from various popes regarding the primacy of the Roman see. A typical letter is that of Pope Leo I.] Leo I to the bishops of Vienne.[1]

Ch. VII. Let anyone who departs from the solid foundation of Peter understand that he is banished from the sacred ministry.

Our Lord Jesus Christ, Savior of mankind, ordained that . . . the truth, which before was confined to the announcements of the law and the prophets, might through the apostles' trumpet blast go out for the salvation of all men, as it is written: "Their sound has gone out into every land, and their words into the ends of the world" (Ps. 19:4). But this mysterious function the Lord wished to be indeed the concern of all the apostles, but in such a way that He has placed the principal charge on the Blessed Peter, chief of all the apostles; and from him as from the head wishes His gifts to flow to all the body so that anyone who dares to secede from

---

1. On Leo see above, p. 25. The translation of Leo's letter is from C. L. Feltoe, *The Letters and Sermons of Leo the Great*, Nicene and Post-Nicene Fathers, vol. XII (New York, 1895), p. 110.

Peter's solid rock may understand that he has no part or lot in the divine mystery. For He wished him who had been received into partnership in His undivided unity to be named what He Himself was, when he said: "Thou art Peter, and upon this rock I will build My church," that the building of the eternal temple by the wondrous gift of God's grace might rest on Peter's solid rock; strengthening His church so surely that neither could human rashness assail it nor the gates of hell prevail against it. But this most holy firmness of the rock, reared, as we have said, by the building hand of God, a man must wish to destroy in over-weening wickedness when he tries, by favoring his own desires and not following what he receives from men of old, to break down its power.

(Gratian) This, therefore, is to be understood concerning those rulings or decretal letters in which nothing is found contrary to the decrees of earlier fathers or to the precepts of the gospels . . .

DISTINCTION XX (GRATIAN)

Part I. Therefore, decretal letters are to be carried out with an authority equal to that of the canons of councils. Now there is an inquiry concerning those who interpret sacred scripture. Are they to be followed, or to be subject to these [letters]? For the more a man depends on reason, the more his words seem to be of greater authority. Indeed, many writers of treatises, excelling others in a greater knowledge, as if by a more ample grace of the Holy Spirit, are shown to have adhered more to reason. Therefore, it seems that to the decrees of many of the pontiffs must be preferred the opinions of Augustine, Jerome and other writers of treatises.

Part II. It is, however, one thing to terminate cases, another to expound sacred scripture correctly. In settling litigations not only is wisdom necessary, but also authority. Christ, in order to say to Peter, "Whatever you bind on earth, shall be bound in heaven, etc.," first gave him the keys of the kingdom of heaven. In one case he gave him wisdom to discern between one leprosy and another, in another giving him the power of casting out some from the church or of receiving them. Since, therefore, any causes whatever are terminated either in the absolution of the innocent or in the condemnation of the guilty, absolution, indeed, or condemnation require not only the wisdom but also the power of those presiding. It appears that the commentators on the sacred scripture, even if they

excel the pontiffs in wisdom and are placed before them in interpretation of holy scripture, nevertheless, because they have not
attained to their peak of dignity, merit, in defining legal cases, a
place after them in rank.

Wherefore Leo IV wrote to the bishops of Britain (c.850):
Ch. I. The writings of others must not be preferred to the decrees
of the Roman pontiffs.

It is not proper for anyone to pass judgment on the books and
commentaries of others or to depart from the canons of the sacred
councils or the rules of the decretals which are observed with us
along with the canons. We use these in all ecclesiastical adjudica-
tions, namely: the councils of the Apostles, of Nicea, Ancyra,
Neocaesarea, Gangra, Sardica, Carthage, Africa, and with these the
regulations of the Roman primates, Sylvester, Siricius, Innocent,
Zosimus, Celestine, Leo, Hilary, Gelasius, Hormisdas, and Gregory
the Younger. These are the men, certainly, by reason of whom the
bishops judge and by whom both bishops and clerics are judged.
But if a matter of such an unusual nature should arise that it can in
no way be terminated by these, then the opinions of those whom
you have mentioned, Jerome, Augustine, Isidore or, similarly, the
opinions of other comparable doctors, if they can be found, should
be generously retained and promulgated, or such cases should be
referred to the Holy See. Accordingly, I am not afraid to deliver
the verdict eloquently and with loud voice: whoever, whether he
be bishop, cleric or layman, is convicted of not having received
those statutes of the holy fathers which we have spoken of and
which we entitle canons with impartiality is proved not to believe
or retain effectually for his own benefit either the catholic and
apostolic faith or the [teachings] of the four evangelists.
Ch. II. Those who do not have or do not observe the decretals of
the Roman pontiffs are to be rebuked.

Pope Nicholas I to the clergy of Constantinople:
If you do not have the decretals of the Roman pontiffs, you
must be charged with neglect and carelessness. If, indeed, you have
them and do not observe them you must be rebuked and reproved
for your temerity.

Part I, Distinctions XXXI, XXXII (Selected Chapters)

The third selection from Distinctions XXXI and XXXII provides a
review of most of the papal and conciliar decisions on clerical celibacy.

Distinction XXXI considers the patristic period when the discipline had not yet been universally adopted. In general, men baptized as adults and already married were permitted to live with their wives after ordination. In the West, those baptized early in life were usually permitted marriage as far as the subdiaconate. The eastern Church permitted priests to marry but not bishops.

From the fourth century, canon law in the West further established the practice of celibacy from the subdiaconate on. Those already married at the time of their ordination were not, according to Leo I, to put away their wives. Rather, they were to abstain from carnal relations. The marriage, therefore, became a spiritual one.

During the early Middle Ages the rule of celibacy was widely disregarded in the West. Hence strenuous efforts were made by the reformers of the eleventh century to enforce the ancient discipline. These efforts included decrees forbidding the faithful from frequenting the sacraments of noncelibate priests.

A final step was to declare such clerical marriages not merely illicit, but in themselves invalid. Holy Orders, it was argued, constituted a diriment impediment[1] to marriage. A decree of the Second Lateran Council (1139) and a decretal of Boniface VIII (1294–1303) are added here to complete this explanation of the medieval Church's teaching on clerical celibacy.

DISTINCTION XXXI

Part I. The time when it was not yet established that priests should observe continence.

Whence Gregory (I) wrote to Peter, subdeacon of Sicily.*

Ch. I. Whoever did not promise chastity must not be forced to separate himself from his wife.

Three years ago the subdeacons of all the churches in Sicily, in accordance with the custom of the Roman Church, were forbidden all conjugal intercourse with their wives. But it appears to me hard and improper that one who has not been accustomed to such continency, and has not previously promised chastity, should be compelled to separate himself from his wife, and thereby (which God forbid) fall into what is worse. Hence it seems good to me that from the present day all bishops should be told not to presume to make any one a subdeacon who does not promise to live chastely; that so what was not of set purpose desired in the past may not be forcibly required, but that cautious provision may be made for the

1. Absolutely nullifying.
* From the translation by Barmby, *op. cit.*, p. 91, col. 2.

future. But those who since the prohibition of three years ago have lived continently with their wives are to be praised and rewarded, and exhorted to continue in their good way. But, as for those who since the prohibition have been unwilling to abstain from intercourse with their wives, we desire them not to be advanced to a sacred order; since no one ought to approach the ministry of the altar but one who has been of approved chastity before undertaking the ministry.

Part II. (Gratian) The reason for this decree was priestly purity, that they [the priests] could freely devote all their days to prayer. For if (as the Apostle says) we abstain from our wives that we may be more ready for prayer, it is never permitted the minister of the altar on whom falls the daily obligation to prayer, to fulfill the duties of marriage.

Whence Bede on Luke:

Ch. II. Priests are admonished always to observe chastity.

It is commanded that priests must always abstain from their wives and observe chastity, in order that they may be always able to serve the altar.

Ch. IV. Priests and Levites [deacons] should not have carnal intercourse with their wives.

Innocent I (401-17) to Victricius, bishop of Rouen.

The church ought in every way to insist that priests and Levites do not have carnal intercourse with their wives because as ordinary ministers they are occupied with obligations. For it is written, "Be holy, as I your Lord God am holy" (Lev. 11:44). For in former times (as we read about Zacharias) they did not try to leave the temple during the year of their own office, nor did they try to go to their homes at all. Therefore, the custom was relaxed for them for the good issue of children, because it was decreed that no one should be raised to the priesthood from another tribe other than the seed of Aaron; how much more ought these priests and Levites to observe chastity from the day of their ordination, for whom the priesthood or ministry is without succession and a day does not pass by in which they should not be occupied with the divine sacrifice or the office of baptism?

Ch. V. The same. For as Paul wrote to the Corinthians and said, "Hold yourselves back for a time, that you may give yourselves to prayer" (I Cor. 7:5), and this, indeed, he commanded to laymen:

so much the more priests, for whom praying and offering sacrifice is a perpetual oblation, shall always be obligated to abstain from partnership of this kind.

Ch. IX.[1] If anyone shall remain a virgin, or observe continence, abstaining from marriage because he abhors it, and not on account of the beauty and holiness of virginity itself, let him be anathema. Part III. (Gratian) This can be understood otherwise, as it is read in the canons of the apostles, so that the chapter, "If anyone teaches a priest to despise his wife," does not refer to the wife the priest received as a priest, but the one he had married while still a layman or established in minor orders [and] with whom he vowed continence when he was raised to holy orders. No one ought to despise her, that is to cast her out of his mind and care, but ought rather to provide for her the necessities [of life]. This interpretation is proved also by the authority of Pope Leo [I] who in writing to Rusticius bishop of Narbonne, says:

Ch. X. The law of continence is the same for ministers of the altar as for bishops and priests.   The law of continence is the same for the ministers of the altar as for the bishops and priests, who when they were laymen or readers, could lawfully marry and have offspring. But when they reached to the said ranks, what was before lawful ceased to be so. And hence, in order that their wedlock may become spiritual instead of carnal, it behooves them not to put away their wives but to "have them as though they had them not" (I Cor. 7:9), whereby both the affection of their wives may be retained and the marriage functions cease.*

Ch. XI. A bishop or priest should not deprive his own wife of his care.

Leo IX against the letter of Abbot Nicetas.[2]

We acknowledge entirely that it is not allowed a bishop, priest or deacon to reject his own wife from his care for the sake of religion, but that he should provide food and clothing, though not

1. This chapter and those immediately preceding were concerned with sects in the early period of Christianity—Manichaean and the like—which condemned marriage in general.

* Letter translated by C. L. Feltoe, *op. cit.*, p. 110.

2. Although ascribed here to Pope Leo IX, this is a paragraph from the treatise of his legate, Cardinal Humbert of Moyenmoutier, *Contra Nicetam*. This treatise was an important element in the Greek-Roman controversy of the months preceding the mutual excommunications of 1054 [Friedberg].

remain with her in a carnal manner. We read that the holy apostles acted thus when St. Paul says, "Have we not power to carry about a woman, a sister, as well as the rest of the apostles, and the brethren of the Lord and Cephas?" (I Cor. 9:5). See, O stupid one, that he did not say, "have we not power of 'embracing' a woman as sister, but of 'carrying about'" obviously so that she might be supported by them from the stipends of preaching. After that, however, there would be no further carnal intercourse.

(Gratian) Hence even thus in the Dialogues of Gregory [I]:

(1) As, therefore, it appears from these authorities, priests who legitimately married wives as laymen or in minor orders can provide the necessaries [of life], but not fulfill the marriage debt.

Part IV. (2) But there is objection to this in the Tripartite Histories.*

Ch. XII. Dissuaded by Pahfnucius the Nicene Council did not order priests not to have intercourse with their wives.

Since it wished to reform the life of those who were engaged about the churches, the Nicene synod enacted laws which we call canons. In consideration of which, some thought it best that a law should be passed enacting that bishops and presbyters, deacons and subdeacons should hold no intercourse with the wife they had espoused before they entered the priesthood. But Pahfnucius, the confessor, stood up and testified against this proposition; he said that marriage was honorable and that cohabitation with one's own wife was chaste, and advised the synod not to frame such a law, for, he declared, it was a grievous situation which would serve as a pretext for incontinence for them or their wives. Such was the advice of Pahfnucius, although he himself was unmarried. The synod approved his counsel and enacted no law about the matter but left it to the decision of individual judgement, and not to compulsion.

Ch. XIII. Not continually, but at the time of offering [the sacrifice] priests are to abstain from the embrace of their wives. Sixth Council (Quinisext, 692, can. xiii).†

Since we know it to be handed down as a rule of the Roman Church that those who are deemed worthy to be advanced to the

---

* Adapted in part from the translation of C. D. Hartranft, *History of Sozomen*, Nicene and Post-Nicene Fathers (New York, 1890), p. 256, col. 2.
† Translated by H. R. Percival, *op. cit.*, p. 371. Reprinted by permission of Charles Scribner's Sons, New York, and T. & T. Clark, London.

diaconate or presbyterate should promise no longer to cohabit with their wives, we, preserving the ancient rule and apostolic perfection and order, will that the lawful marriages of men who are in holy orders be from this time forward firm, by no means dissolving their union with their wives nor depriving them of their mutual intercourse at a convenient time. Wherefore, if anyone shall have been found worthy to be ordained subdeacon, or deacon, or presbyter, [they are] by no means to be prohibited from admittance to such a rank, even if they shall live with a lawful wife. Nor shall it be demanded of [them] at the time of ordination that they promise to abstain from lawful intercourse with a wife. For it is meet that they who assist at the divine altar should be absolutely continent when they are handling holy things, in order that they may be able to obtain from God what they ask in sincerity. . . .

(Gratian) This also is to be understood here. The oriental church, for which the Sixth Council prescribed a rule of life, did not take upon itself the vow of chastity for the ministers of the altar.

DISTINCTION XXXII

Part I. (Gratian) Therefore continence must be observed by all ordained in holy orders.

Wherefore, Pope Leo I to the bishop of Thessalonica (Anastasius).*

Ch. I. Marriage is not permitted to subdeacons.

For the choosing of priests is of such surpassing importance that things which in other members of the church are not blameworthy, are yet held unlawful in them. For although they who are not within the ranks of the clergy are free to take pleasure in the companionship of wedlock and the procreation of children, yet for the exhibiting of the purity of complete continence, even subdeacons are not allowed carnal marriage: so that "both those that have may be as though they had not" (I Cor. 7:29), and those who have not may remain single. But if in this order, which is the fourth from the head, this is worthy to be observed, how much more is it to be kept in the first, or second, or third, lest anyone be reckoned fit for the deacon's or presbyter's honorable position, or the

* Trans. C. L. Feltoe, *op. cit.*, p. 18.

bishop's preeminence, who is discovered not yet to have bridled his uxorious desires?

Ch. II. (likewise)

Gregory I to the bishop of Catana.*

We have found from the report of many that a custom has of old obtained among you for subdeacons to be allowed to have intercourse with their wives. That anyone who should any more presume to do this was prohibited by the servant of God, the deacon of our see, under the authority of our predecessor in this way: so that those who at that time had been coupled to wives should choose one of two things, that is, either to abstain from their wives, or on no account whatever to presume to exercise their ministry. And, according to the report, Speciosus, then a sub-deacon, did for this reason suspend himself from the office of administration, and up to the time of his death, bore indeed the office of notary, but ceased from the ministry which a subdeacon should have exercised. . . .

But for the future let thy Fraternity be exceedingly careful in the case of any who may be promoted to this office, to look to this with the utmost diligence, this, if they have wives, they shall enjoy no license to have intercourse with them: but you must strictly order them to observe all things after the pattern of the Apostolic See.

Ch. IV. It is not permitted a subdeacon to marry.

Nicholas I to Adonus, archbishop of Vienne.

Concerning the cleric, Alwic by name, who, you say, has lived in holy orders as far as subdeacon, we wonder why he has married by your authority, because we have given permission to no one to marry (except to those whom ecclesiastical regulation permits).

CANON 7, SECOND LATERAN COUNCIL (1139)†

Following in the footsteps of our predecessors, the Roman pontiffs Gregory VII, Urban, and Paschal, we command that no one attend the masses of those who are known to have wives or concubines. But that the law of continence and purity, so pleasing

* Trans. J. Barmby, *op. cit.*, pp. 158-159.
† This paragraph is translated by H. J. Schroeder, *The Disciplinary Decrees of the Ecumenical Councils* (St. Louis, 1937). Reprinted by permission of B. Herder Book Co., St. Louis, Mo.

to God, may become more general among persons constituted in sacred orders, we decree that bishops, priests, deacons, subdeacons, canons regular, monks, and professed clerics (*conversi*) who, transgressing the holy precepts, have dared to contract marriage, shall be separated. For a union of this kind which has been contracted in violation of the ecclesiastical law, we do not regard as matrimony. Those who have been separated from each other, shall do penance commensurate with such excesses.

BONIFACE VIII TO THE BISHOP OF BOURGES*

You have been pleased to seek our advice as to what vow should be called solemn and effective toward dissolving a marriage. Therefore, considering that the binding character of a vow is found in the law of the church alone, whereas the bond of matrimony received its union and indissolubility from the Head of the church, Himself, the Creator of all things, Who instituted it in paradise and in the state of innocence: we have decided to declare as an authoritative statement of the law now in use that for dissolving a previously contracted marriage only that vow should be called solemn which has been solemnized through the reception of holy orders or through a profession, expressed or tacit, made to any religious [order] approved by the Holy See. Other vows, indeed, although they prevent the contract of marriage, and the more openly they have been made, the harsher the penance is due because of the great scandal and example, cannot, however, abrogate marriages contracted afterward.

Part II, Cause XV, Selected Chapters from Questions I, II, III, V, VI, VII

The fourth selection is taken from Part II, Cause XV. The second part of Gratian's *Decretum* includes specific cases at law in which he assembles the arguments pro and con and attempts to reach a solution. In the cause cited here he poses an hypothetical case and raises eight specific questions concerning procedures for determining the guilt or innocence of an accused person which he considers in detail. The entire discussion is significant in that it illustrates the tendency in Gratian's day, noticeable in theology as well as in law, to probe into such matters as the motives behind a particular act and all the conditions surrounding it, rather than simply to attach a preassigned penalty.

* This paragraph is translated from Friedberg (ed.), *op. cit.*, Part II, col. 1053.

Here, too, the citations from Roman civil law, apparently added subsequently by Gratian's pupils, indicate its influence on canonist thinking. It is worth noting that in Question VI Gratian presents the view that a confession may not be extorted by torture.

PART II, CAUSE XV

(Gratian) A certain cleric is said to have fallen into a sin of the flesh before he obtained priestly blessing (i.e., ordination). After, in fact, he was received into the priesthood, he killed a man in a fit of madness. When he recovered his sanity, he was accused before the bishop by the woman with whom he was said to have sinned. Moreover, the bishop heard the case on Sunday. The priest was informed of the crime charged against him; he sought the advocacy of certain clerics. They agreed to defend him but not without a price. At length the bishop through his questions extorted a confession; finally he alone sentenced him and without a hearing before a synod.

Question I. It is inquired whether those things done with unsound mind should be charged.

Part I. That those things done with unsound mind should not be charged it seems can easily be proven. For some sins appear to belong to the will of the soul, others to the infirmity of nature. Moreover, the will, as Augustine says in Book I of his *Retractions*, is the mover of the soul. . . . (1) From the will, therefore, sins proceed which are committed by the free judgment of the mind with the intent of so doing. (2) Further, there is one infirmity of the soul, another of the flesh. The infirmity of the soul is ignorance; that of the flesh is concupiscence. What proceeds from each infirmity is ascribed to sin. . . .

[Citations from Scripture and St. Augustine follow]

Ch. II. *Digest*, Tit. *De iniuriis*, I. 3.

. . . Clearly there are those who can not act—whether mad or too young—who are not capable of fraud. These can suffer injury but not inflict it. Since, therefore, injury arises from the disposition of the one doing, it will be logical to say that these [persons], whether they accuse or speak insults, are not regarded as having inflicted injury. Therefore, a man can suffer injury even if he does not perceive it; but no one can do injury unless he knows he is doing it, even if he does not know to whom he does it. Wherefore, if anyone strikes in jest, or during a contest, he is not held for injuries. If anyone kills a free man, thinking him a slave, in that case he is not to be held for injuries.

(Gratian) As it appears from the above, whether sins proceed from will or weakness, it is clear that they are to be reckoned. But infirmity of the flesh is understood in two ways. For it is a weakness of nature which is called concupiscence of the flesh which can truly be called an infirmity of the soul. But it is called an infirmity of the flesh because it happens to the soul from a corruption of the flesh which is joined to it. Futher, there is another infirmity which is properly called of the flesh in which (the harmony of elements or humors being disturbed) the flesh itself is affected and is finally destroyed. (1) Similarly, the infirmity of the soul is twofold: one which is called vice by which the soul is separated from God, such as anger, hatred and other things of the kind; another infirmity of the soul which, although not itself a sin, is nevertheless a penalty and cause of sin, such as forgetfulness and ignorance. On the other hand, madness, although it is not a sin, is nonetheless the penalty of sin, as are fevers and other ills which we say pertain particularly to the flesh, whose effects, that is what is done through their disturbances, are regarded as sin by no one. . . .

Ch. VI. A defendant is bound over because of the [exercise of free] will, not necessity. Thus Ambrose in the *Exameron,* in the tractate on the first day.

Those faults of youth and the irrational passions of the body which proceed from our will are to be avoided. Accordingly, we are masters of those [faults] whose beginnings we neither seek from without, nor attribute to others, but recognize as things which are properly our own. We should ascribe the choice of that evil which we are able not to do, if we so will, to ourselves rather than to others. Therefore, in judgments of this kind guilt binds over and punishment condemns those who are charged with willful acts not compelled by necessity. For if someone destroys an innocent person in madness he is not liable to death, but actually by the oracle of divine law if anyone causes death through ignorance, he has the hope of impunity, the chance of refuge, so that he may escape. Let this be said of that which is properly evil. Those things are not evil which do not implicate the mind in crime nor bind the conscience. Whence no wise man will call poverty, humble birth, sickness, death evil nor number them in the lot of evils.

Question II. The Council of Tarragona forbade clerics to exact charges for defense given, and so decreed.

We declare that care must be taken lest anyone of the priests or clerics dare to accept payments for defense given, after the manner of secular jurors, unless they are offered freely in the church and do not seem to be accepted by way of payment, but presented as a contribution of devotion. But if it is proven that anyone has accepted profits he should know that he must be degraded according to the statutes of the fathers as a collector of interest or possessor of usurious [funds].

(Gratian) This, however, must be understood as concerning those who professed and declared that they would live the canonical life regularly. For it is accepted in the general custom of the church and approved by usage that clerics after the manner of advocates may give defense and require payments for defense given.

Question III. Is he to be condemned by the confession of a woman?

(Gratian) Thirdly, it is asked whether this man must be condemned as a result of the confession of a woman. In this, it must first be considered whether a woman may validly accuse a priest. This seems to be prohibited entirely by sacred canons. For it is generally laid down in the decrees of Pope Fabian (236–50) that those persons may not accuse priests of the Lord, nor testify against them who are not of their order, nor can be. Moreover, women cannot be raised either to the priesthood or even to the diaconate, whence they are not able to accuse priests nor testify against them. The laws (*Digest*) also stipulate that on account of the modesty of her sex a woman may not intercede in behalf of another man before the praetor unless perhaps she wishes to take action against injuries to her or to hers. But she who neither proceeds against injuries to her or hers should not be admitted to this accusation. . . .

Ch. I. Whence in the *Code* (IX, Tit. I, 1.12) Emperor Diocletian (284–305) wrote and said: A woman is not allowed to make accusation about a crime which comes under the province of the public judges except under the following circumstances, namely, if she is prosecuting an injury to her or hers, according to the statutes of the old law, to the extent that it is specially conceded concerning these, but not in precise written form. Therefore, the presiding officer of the province will first inquire into the possibilities as to whether the crime is such as not to exclude the woman from supporting an accusation.

Ch. IV. (Gratian) . . . (1) But (as was stated at the beginning of this work) the laws of the emperors are to be used in ecclesiastical affairs only as often as they are found not to go against the sacred canons . . .

Since, contrary to the general rules, certain crimes are especially excepted in which it is permitted a woman to accuse, among which fornication is not included, it is clear that the accusation of this woman is doubly weakened, both because she averred the sin of fornication and because, as she confessed it she should not be believed concerning the crime of another.

Question V. An opportunity to clear himself[1] must be offered to one who denies [guilt]; Stephen [VI (885–891)] to Bishop Leo.
Ch. I. Let the deacon whom it has not been possible to convict of crime clear himself privately in the presence of the bishop.

Your deacon claimed to be free of the crime imputed to him. Nevertheless, if he is held in suspicion and proper accusers are found and such witnesses as the sacred canons sanction, when you have summoned the definitive number of bishops, let the accusers come and let the deacon, Alderic, himself be called; and if he refuses, let the case be discussed canonically. If he shall have confessed of his own will or shall have been convicted by legitimate witnesses, let him be punished with the canonical sentence. But if he neither confesses of his own will nor have legitimate accusers and witnesses been found, and evil rumor has increased, let him clear himself, not by public examination, but by a private oath in your presence and with a certain number of reverend priests and deacons. And thereafter, make it known that he is of good repute and constrain and warn the sons of your church not to defame further a priest of God, fearing, as Cham was accursed because he derided the nakedness of his father (cf. Gen. 9:22 ff.).

Question VI. (Gratian) Part I. Pope Alexander I (106–15) testifies writing to all orthodox that a confession must not be extorted by torture.[2]

1. *Purgatio* [*canonica*]: a proving of innocence.
2. The letter of Alexander I is taken from the Pseudo-Isidorian decretals (ed. Friedberg).

Ch. I. The confession of ministers should not be forced but voluntary.

If certain writings are extorted from priests or other authorities of the church in some way through fear or fraud, or have been composed and supported by any kind of ingenuity, so that they can free themselves, we decree that they have no validity as a prejudice or injury to them, nor do we permit them to sustain any disgrace or calumny or any sequestration of their goods, by the authority of God and the holy apostles and their successors. In such cases a confession should not be compelled, but freely given. For every confession which is made by necessity is not in good faith. Therefore, a confession in such cases ought not to be extorted but offered freely. For it is most reprehensible to judge anyone on suspicion or forced confession, since the Lord looks into the heart rather than to the deed. . . .

Question VII. Part I. That a priest be condemned without a hearing before a synod is prohibited by the Council of Seville at which Isidore [of Seville] was present, as follows:
Ch. I. In the sixth case we learned that Fragitanus, a priest of the church of Cordova, at one time was unjustly degraded by his bishop and condemned innocent to exile, and was again restored to his order. We have finally decreed this against your presumption, that according to the conciliar opinion of the holy fathers no one is to consider degrading any priest or deacon whatever without examination before a council. For there are many who condemn persons unheard by tyrannical power, and not by canonical authority. And just as they promote some by special favor they humble others by hatred and envy; and they condemn on the basis of fickle opinion or rumor those whose misdeeds they do not prove. The bishop who alone can show honor to the priests and ministers, cannot alone remove it. For if those who in secular life attain to the favor of liberty from their masters, are not returned to the yoke of slavery unless they are publicly accused in open court before the praetors, how much more [so] those persons consecrated at sacred altars who are endowed with ecclesiastical honor? In fact, they can neither be condemned by one [judge] nor deprived of the privilege of honor by one judge, but by the judgment of a council. It should be made clear that on these things the law so decrees entirely.

Ch. II. The bishop should not hear cases of clergy except with the elders of the church.
Gregory I to John, bishop of Palermo.

If anything comes to your ears concerning any cleric which can justly offend you, do not believe it easily nor let an unknown affair arouse you to vindictiveness. Rather the truth must be carefully sought out with the elders of your church and then, if the nature of the affair demands, let canonical rigor be brought to bear on the fault.
Ch. III. By how many bishops must priests and deacons be heard.
Council of Carthage I (348).

Whoever is puffed up with pride or insulting to one of greater age, or has some case, if the accused is a deacon let him be heard by three neighboring bishops; if it is a priest by six, if a bishop by twelve fellow priests. All bishops have said: obstinacy and pride should be destroyed and crushed in all men. Therefore, let cases concerning persons be heard by these in the number specified.

The Theology of the Sacraments

---

32. *Peter Lombard*, Four Books of Sentences

Peter Lombard had been educated first at Bologna and then at Rheims. Evidently he was a brilliant student, and he was recommended around 1139 by no less a person than St. Bernard to the abbey school of St. Victor at Paris. This was the period when the schools at Paris were rapidly becoming famous, and in all probability the Lombard, as he is often called, was a student of Abelard. Later he himself taught at the cathedral school of Notre Dame, the nucleus of the future *studium generale* or university. In 1159, a year before his death, he became bishop of the city. His successor was the famous Maurice of Sully, builder of the great cathedral which still stands.

Peter Lombard's major work, *Four Books of Sentences*, completed around 1150–52, consists of four parts which deal respectively with (1) God, (2) creatures, the world before Christ, (3) the incarnation and redemption, and (4) the sacraments and the "last things," death and judgment, hell and heaven. Of the patristic writers, Augustine provided the vast majority of the Lombard's citations, but many other authorities were utilized and he was perhaps the first to use systematically the *On the Orthodox Faith* of St. John of Damascus, a seventh-century writer whose work had been translated recently by Burgundio of Pisa at the request of Eugenius III. Peter, it seems, was in Rome around 1148–50.

The Lombard's work may also be said to have summed up theological teaching as it had developed up to the mid-twelfth century, now beginning to show the influence of a greater knowledge of Aristotle's logical works. In his topical arrangement of subject matter there is a marked resemblance to Gratian's *Decretum*. He follows the current method which Abelard exploited so successfully of citing conflicting authorities, but whenever possible adds a resolution of the problem posed. Two contemporary works were especially influential, Hugh of St. Victor's *De sacramentis* and the *Summa sententiarum* by an author whose identity is unknown. From these, as also from the *Decretum*, many passages are lifted bodily. Scholarly opinion of that day did not regard such practices as plagiarism, but rather as a common quest for truth.

The selections cited here are taken from Book IV, *On the Sacraments*. The first section, on the nature of a sacrament, shows how medieval theological thinking was approaching some degree of consensus on this matter as well as on the number of the sacraments. The Lombard enumerates seven, as had some other writers, and that number came to be accepted in subsequent decades. Each of the seven sacraments is investigated thoroughly. The second part of the following selection is taken from the Lombard's chapters on penance. Penance was still under discussion, especially the question whether oral confession to a priest was necessary in all circumstances. The translation is by Elizabeth F. Rogers, *Peter Lombard and the Sacramental System* (New York, 1917), pp. 79–82, 85, 151, 171–174, 177–184, 219–220. Reprinted by permission of Elizabeth F. Rogers. Notes have been omitted except for scriptual references. A further elaboration of the same subject by Thomas Aquinas will be found below, Document 54.

Distinction I

Part I

I. Of Sacraments

The Samaritan who tended the wounded man, applied for his relief the dressings of the sacraments, just as God instituted the remedies of the sacraments against the wounds of original and actual sin. Concerning the sacraments, four questions first present themselves for consideration: what a sacrament is, why it was instituted; wherein it consists, and how it is performed; and what the difference is between the sacraments of the old and the new covenants.

II. What a Sacrament Is

"A sacrament is the sign of a sacred thing (res)." (Augustine) However, a *sacred mystery* is also called a sacrament, as the sacrament of divinity, so that a sacrament may be the *sign of something sacred*, and the *sacred thing signified;* but now we are considering a sacrament as a *sign.*—So, "A sacrament is the visible form of an invisible grace." (Berengar of Tours, d. 1088)

III. What a Sign Is

"But a sign, is the thing (res) behind the form which it wears to the senses, which brings by means of itself something else to our minds." (Augustine)

IV. How a Sign and a Sacrament Differ

"Furthermore, some signs are *natural,* as smoke which signifies fire; others *conventional;*" (Augustine) and of those which are *conventional,* some are sacraments, some not. For every sacrament is a sign, but the converse is not true. A sacrament bears a resemblance to the thing, of which it is a sign. "For if sacraments did not bear a resemblance to the things of which they are the sacraments, they could not *properly* be called sacraments." For a sacrament is properly so called, because it is a sign of the grace of God and the expression of invisible grace, so that it bears its image and is its cause. Sacraments, therefore, were not instituted merely in order to signify something, but also as a means of sanctification. For things which were instituted only to signify are signs only, and not sacraments; such as the sacrifices of flesh, and the ceremonial observances of the old law, which could never justify those who offered them; because, as the apostle says (Hebrews 9:13), "The blood of goats and of oxen and the ashes of an heifer, being sprinkled, sanctify such as are defiled, to the cleansing of the flesh," but not of the spirit. Now this uncleanness was the touching of a dead body. Wherefore Augustine: "By that defilement which the law cleanses I understand merely the touching of a dead body, since anyone who had touched one, *was unclean seven days;* but he was purified according to the law on the third day and on the seventh, and was cleansed," so that he might enter the temple.

These legal observances also cleansed sometimes from bodily leprosy; but no one was ever justified by the *works of the Law*, as
says the apostle (Romans 3:20; Gal. 2:16), even if he performed
them in faith and charity. Why? because God has ordained them
unto servitude, not unto justification, so that they might be *types
of something to come*, wishing that these offerings should be made
to him rather than to idols. They therefore were *signs*, yet also
sacraments, although they are often called so incorrectly in the
Scriptures, because they were rather signs of a sacred thing than
availing anything themselves. These moreover the apostle (Romans
3:20; Gal. 2:16) calls *works of the Law*, which were instituted
only to signify something, or as a yoke.

V. WHY THE SACRAMENTS WERE INSTITUTED

The sacraments were instituted for a three-fold reason: for
humility, instruction, and *exercise.* For *humility,* so that while man,
by order of the Creator, abases himself in worship before insensible
things, which by nature are beneath him, through this humility and
obedience, he may become more pleasing to God, and more meri-
torious in his sight, at whose command he seeks salvation in things
beneath him, yet not from them, but through them from God. For
instruction also were the sacraments instituted, so that the mind
might be taught by what it sees outside in visible form, to recognize the invisible virtue which is within. For man, who before sin
saw God without a mediator, through sin has became so dulled that
he is in no wise able to comprehend divine things, unless trained
thereto by human things.—Likewise, the sacraments were instituted for exercise, because since man cannot be idle, there is offered
him in the sacraments a useful and safe exercise by which he may
avoid vain and harmful occupation. For he who devotes himself to
good exercise is not easily caught by the tempter; wherefore
Jerome warns us: "Always do some sort of work, that the devil
may find you occupied." "There are, moreover, three kinds of
exercises: one aims at the *edification of the soul,* another aims at the
nourishment of the body, another at the *destruction of both.*"—
And inasmuch as without a sacrament, to which God has not
limited his power, he could have given grace to man, he has for the
aforesaid reasons instituted the sacraments. "There are two parts of
which a sacrament consists, namely *words* and *things: words,* as the
invocation of the Trinity; *things,* as water, oil, and the like."

VI. Of the Difference Between the Old and the New Sacraments

Now it remains to note the difference between the old and the new sacraments; as we call sacraments what anciently they called sacred things, such as sacrifices and oblations and the like. The difference between these Augustine indicated briefly when he said, "because the former only promised and signified salvation, while the latter give it." . . .

Distinction II

I. Of the Sacraments of the New Law

Let us now come to the sacraments of the new covenant; which are baptism, confirmation, the blessing of bread, that is the eucharist, penance, extreme unction, ordination, marriage. Of these some offer a remedy for sin, and confer helping grace, as baptism; others are merely a remedy, as marriage; others strengthen us with grace and virtue, as the eucharist and ordination.

If indeed we are asked why these sacraments were not instituted immediately after the fall of man, since in them are justification and salvation; we say that before the advent of Christ, who brought grace, the sacraments of grace could not be granted, for they have derived their virtue from his death and passion. Now Christ was unwilling to come before man was convinced that he could find help in neither natural nor written law.

Marriage, however was instituted before sin, "not at all as a remedy, but as a sacrament and a duty" (Hugh of St. Victor); after sin indeed it became a remedy against the corruption of carnal concupiscence; of which we will treat in its place. . . .

Distinction XIV

Part I

I. Of Penance, and Why It Is Called Penance

Next we must discuss penance. Penance is needful to those who are far from God, that they may come near. For it is, as Jerome says, "the second plank after shipwreck"; because if anyone by sinning sullies the robe of innocence received in baptism, he can restore it by the remedy of penance. The first plank is baptism, where the old man is laid aside and the new put on; the second, penance, by which after a fall we rise again, while the old state which had returned is disdained, and the new one which had been lost is resumed. Those who have lapsed after baptism can be restored by penance, but not by baptism. A man is allowed to do penance often, but not to be baptized often. Baptism is called only a sacrament, but penance is called both a sacrament and virtue of the mind. For there is an inner penance, and an outer: the outer is the sacrament, the inner is the virtue of the mind; and both are for the sake of salvation and justification.—But whether all outer penance is a sacrament, or if not all, what is to be classed under this name, we shall investigate later.—With penance began the preaching of John who said: "Do penance, for the kingdom of heaven is at hand. (Matt. 3:2)" "And what the herald taught, the Truth afterwards preached, beginning his discourse with penance (St. Ambrose, d. 397)" . . .

Distinction XVI

Part I

I. Of the Three Things Which Must Be Considered in Penance, That Is, Compunction, Confession, Satisfaction

Moreover in the perfection of penance three steps are to be observed, that is compunction of the heart, confession of the mouth, satisfaction in deed. Wherefore John the golden-mouthed (Chrysostom, d. 407): "Perfect penance compels the sinner to bear all things cheerfully; in his heart contrition, in his mouth, confession, in deed all humility. This is fruitful penance; that just as we offend God in three ways, that is, with the heart, the mouth, and the deed, so in three ways we make satisfaction." For there are three different sins, as Augustine says, "of the heart, and of deed, and of habit or word, as it were three deaths: one as if in the home; that is, when there is consent to lust in the heart; another as if carried next outside the door, when assent proceeds to deed; the third when the soul is oppressed by force of evil habit as by a weight, or armed with the shield of guilty defence, as if already decaying in the grave. These are the three kinds of dead men whom the Lord is said to have raised." To this triple death is supplied a triple remedy: contrition, confession, satisfaction. Compunction is commended to us here: "Rend your hearts, and not your garments (Joel 2:13)," confession here: "The just man is first accuser of himself (Prov. 18:17)"; for truly he confesses who accuses himself, who imputes evil to himself by execration. And here: "Pour out your hearts in his presence (Ps. 61:9)" And again: "Confess your sins one to another (James 5:16)."

II. What True Satisfaction Is

Satisfaction is commanded by John, where he says, "Bring forth fruits worthy of penance (Matt. 3:8; Luke 3:8)" that is, that according to the quality and quantity of the guilt should be the quality and quantity of the punishment. "For the fruit of good work ought not be the same for him who has sinned not at all, or to a slight degree, and for him who has fallen grievously."—Therefore discretion for the penitent is very necessary, that he may do what Augustine teaches, saying: "Let a man consider the quality of his offence, in place, in time, in persistence, or in change of the person, and under how much temptation he has done it, and how repeatedly he has committed the sin itself. . . . —From these passages we are shown what are the fruits worthy of penance, by which true satisfaction is procured, also that not all worthy fruits are fruits worthy of penance; which last is to be understood of that penance, which belongs to greater offences. For what suffices for men who sin not at all or little, does not suffice for the grievously delinquent. . . .

Distinction XVII

Part I

I. Whether Sins Are Forgiven Without Confession

Here arises a question that has many parts. For first we are asked whether without satisfaction and confession of the mouth, by contrition of the heart only, sin may be forgiven anyone. Secondly, whether it suffices for anyone to confess to God without a priest. Thirdly, whether confession made to a faithful layman would be valid.—On these points even the learned are found to think differently, because the doctors seem to have taught varied and almost contradictory views about them. For some say, that without confession of the mouth and satisfaction of deed no one is cleansed from sin if he has time for doing these things.—But others say, that before confession of the mouth and satisfaction through the contrition of the heart sin is forgiven by God, if however the sinner has the desire to confess. Wherefore the Prophet (Ps. 31:5): "I have said, I will confess against myself my injustice to the Lord, and thou hast remitted," etc. Which Cassiodorus (d. 583) explains saying: " 'I have said,' that is, I have determined within myself, that 'I would confess, and thou hast remitted it.' Great pity of God, who hast remitted the sin for the mere promise! For the promise is accepted for the deed." Also Augustine: "Not yet does he make it known, but he promises that he will make it known; and the Lord remits it, because to say just this is to make something known in the heart. Not yet is the voice in the mouth, so that a man may hear the confession, and God hears." Also: "The sacrifice of God is a troubled spirit, a contrite heart," etc. Elsewhere also we read: "At whatever hour a sinner turns and laments, he shall live in life and shall not die"; it does not say: he confesses with his mouth, but "turns, laments." "Wherefore we are given to understand, that even though the mouth be silent, we may sometimes obtain pardon. . . . From these and many other authorities it is proved that before confession or satisfaction sin is forgiven upon contrition alone; and those who deny it, find it hard to explain these authorities; and they introduce the testimony of other authors for the overthrow of this opinion and the support of their own. For the Lord says through Isaiah (Is. 43:26): "Tell thou thy iniquities that thou mayest be justified." Also Ambrose: "No man can be justified from sin unless he has first confessed the sin itself." He also says: "Confession frees the soul from death, confession opens paradise, confession gives the hope of salvation, because he does not deserve to be justified who is not willing to confess his sin in his life-time. Confession frees us, which is done with penance. But penance is the grief of the heart and the bitterness of the soul for the evils which each one has committed." Also John (Chrysostom): "No man can receive the grace of God unless he has been purified of all sin by the confession of penance and by baptism." Also Augustine: "Do penance, as it is done in the Church. Let no one say to himself: I do it secretly, because I do it before God; God knows, who has pardoned me, because I do it in my heart. Then without cause was it said: 'What thou loosest on earth, shall be loosed in heaven'? Then without cause 'were the keys given'? Then we make vain the word of Christ. Job says: 'If I have blushed to confess my sins in the sight of the people' (31:33)!" . . .

What therefore is to be thought about these things? What believed? It can certainly be said that without confession of the mouth and payment of the outward penalty sins are effaced by contrition and humility of heart. For from the moment anyone proposes to confess, being pricked in conscience, God forgives; because there is there the confession of the heart, though not of the mouth, by which the soul is cleansed within from the stain and contagion of committed sin, and the debt of eternal death is relaxed. Therefore that which was said above regarding confession and penance, should be referred either to the confession of the heart, or to inward punishment—just as this saying of Augustine, "that no one obtains pardon, unless first he has paid some small penalty for his sin"—must be understood of the external penalty, and applied to the scornful or negligent, just as this: "Let no one say, I do it secretly," etc. For some neglect to confess sins in their lifetime or are ashamed to do it, and therefore do not deserve to be justified. For just as inward penance is enjoined upon us, so also confession of the mouth, and outward satisfaction, if we have the opportunity. Wherefore he is not truly penitent who does not have the desire to confess. And just as remission of sin is the gift of God, so penance and confession by which sin is wiped out, cannot take place save from God, as Augustine says: "Now, he says, he has the gift of the holy Spirit, who confesses and repents, because there cannot be confession of sin and compunction in man of himself. For when anyone is angry at himself and dissatisfied with himself, it is not without the gift of the holy Spirit." Therefore a penitent ought to confess his sins, if he have time; and yet before confession of the mouth, if there is the promise in the heart, forgiveness is extended to him.

Part II

II. Whether It Suffices to Confess to God Alone

Now let us look into the second division of the question, that is, whether it suffices to confess sins to God alone, or whether it is necessary to confess to a priest.—To some it seems to suffice, if confession is made to God alone without the judgment of the priest and confession of the Church, because David said (Ps. 31:5): "I said, I will confess to the Lord, and thou hast remitted," etc.; he does not say "to the priest," and yet he says the sin is forgiven him. Also Ambrose: "Peter wept, because his guilt had come suddenly upon him; I do not find what he said, I find that he wept. I read of his tears, I do not read of his satisfaction. But what cannot be defended, can be washed away. Tears wash away a sin, which one is ashamed to confess with the voice. Weeping brings about both pardon and a natural feeling of shame." Bishop Maximus says the same also; likewise John Chrysostom: "I do not say to you that you should betray yourself in public, nor accuse yourself among others, but I wish that you would obey the Prophet when he says: 'Reveal thy life to God.' Before God therefore confess your sins, before a true judge with prayer, declare your guilt not with your tongue but in the memory of your conscience; and then at last hope that you may obtain pity. If you have your sins continually in mind, you will never harbor evil against your neighbor in your heart." . . .

On these authorities do they depend who maintain that it suffices to confess one's sins to God without a priest. For they say that if anyone fears to disclose his guilt among men, lest he be held in opprobrium therefor, or lest others might resort to sin by his example, and therefore is silent to man, and reveals everything to God; he will obtain pardon.

III. That It Does Not Suffice to Confess to God Alone, if Time Allows, Provided It Is Possible to Confess to a Man

But that it is necessary to confess to priests, is proved not only on the authority of James (James 5:16): "Confess your sins to one another," etc., but also by the testimonies of many others. For Augustine says: "Let a man of his own will judge himself while he is able, and let him change his ways to better, lest when he no longer is able, he be judged without his will by the Lord; and when he has pronounced upon himself a sentence of the severest but the most profitable medicine, let him come to the priests by whom the power of the keys of the Church is exercised. Just as one beginning to be a good son should observe the order of his mother's members, and accept the manner of his satisfaction from those placed in command of sacred things, offering the sacrifice of a contrite heart devoutly and humbly. Let him however do that which not only benefits him for salvation, but serves also for an example to others; so that if his sin is not only a grievous evil for him, but also a great stumbling-block for others, and it seems to the priest expedient for the Church, let him not refuse to do penance to the knowledge of many or of the whole people, lest through shame he inflame the deadly wound." "When the wound of sin and the power of the disease are so great, that the medicaments of the body and blood of the Lord must be postponed according to the authority of the priest, each one ought to withdraw from the altar to do penance, and then to be reconciled by the same authority." Also Pope Leo (440–61): "The manifold love of God succors human beings who have fallen, so that they regain their hope of life not only by baptism, but also by penance, since the helps of the divine will have been so ordained, that sinners cannot obtain the indulgence of God save through the supplications of priests. For Christ gave this power to those set over the Church, that they might give the satisfaction of penance to those who confessed, and when they had been purged by saving satisfaction, they might admit them to the communion of the sacraments through the door of reconciliation." Also Augustine: "Let him who repents, repent wholly, and let him show his grief with tears; let him present his life to God through the priest, let him anticipate the judgment of God by confession. For the Lord gave command to those who needed to be cleansed, that they show themselves to the priests, teaching thus that sins must be confessed by bodily presence, not set down in writing." . . . For the mind labors when it suffers shame; and since a feeling of shame is great punishment, he who is ashamed for the sake of Christ becomes worthy of mercy. Wherefore it is clear that to the more persons one confesses the baseness of his offence, the more easily does one gain the grace of remission. For the priests themselves are able to accomplish more and spare those who confess more." Also Pope Leo: "Although a fullness of faith seems to be laudable, which through fear of God does not fear to be ashamed before men; yet—because everyone's sins are not of such a kind that those which demand penance may be freely published,—let the unwise custom be abolished, lest many be kept from the remedies of penance, because they are either ashamed or afraid to reveal their deeds to their enemies, by whom they may be ruined through the provisions of the laws. For confession suffices, which is first offered to God, and then to the priest, who acts as intercessor for the sins of the penitents. For many can be incited to penance, if the conscience of the one who confesses is not published to the ears of the people."—By these and many other statements we are shown beyond a doubt that it is necessary that confession be offered first to God, and then to the priest; nor can the sinner otherwise approach the entrance of paradise, if he had an opportunity to confess. . . .

Distinction XXII

II. What the Sacrament Is, and What the Thing

After the foregoing, it remains to inquire what the sacrament is, and what the thing, in the act of penance. For a sacrament is the sign of a sacred thing; what therefore is the sign here?—Some say, as Grandulph, that the sacrament here is what is done outwardly only, that is, the outer penance, which is the sign of the inner penance, that is, of contrition of the heart and humility.—If this be so, not every sacrament of the gospel accomplishes that which it figures; for the outward penance does not effect the inward; rather the inward is the cause of the outward. But to this argument they reply that this rule must be understood of those sacraments which were instituted in the New Testament; that is, the sacraments of baptism, confirmation and of the body of Christ. But the sacrament of penance, as also that of marriage, existed before the time of grace, even from the beginning of the human race. For both were instituted for our first parents.—Also, if outer penance is the sacrament, and inner the thing of the sacrament, the thing more often precedes the sacrament, than the sacrament the thing.—But not even this is inconsistent. For it often happens also in other sacraments which accomplish what they figure.

But some say that both outer penance and inner are the sacrament, not two sacraments, but one, as the forms of bread and wine are not two sacraments, but one. And as in the sacrament of the body, so also in this sacrament they say that one is the sacrament only, that is, outer penance; another the sacrament and the thing, that is, inner penance; another the thing and not the sacrament, that is, the remission of sins. For inner penance is both the thing of the sacrament, namely, of outer penance, and the sacrament of the remission of sin, which it signifies and accomplishes. Outer penance is both the sign of the inner and of the remission of sins.

Popular Religion

---

33. *Rodulfus Glaber*, Five Books of Histories (Historarium libri quinque)

Many of the manifestations of popular religion are reflected in Rodulfus Glaber's *Histories,* a work which the author completed in the four or five years before 1050 and dedicated to St. Odilo, abbot of Cluny. Glaber, who was placed in a monastery by his uncle at the age of twelve, showed little aptitude for the monastic calling and, in fact, soon became one of those monks, not in those days uncommon, who wandered from monastery to monastery. Because William, abbot of St. Bénigne at Dijon, was sufficiently discerning to appreciate Glaber's flair for investigation and narrative, it was at Dijon that he commenced his history. On William's death he moved to Cluny, where he passed the rest of his life and finished the work.

The *Historiarum libri quinque,* planned to cover the years from 900 to 1044, is a rather poorly organized, rambling chronicle in which the eleventh-century taste for signs and wonders is evident. There are also historical and geographical errors, but Glaber through his association with William of St. Bénigne and his residence at Cluny had access to important sources of information. In short, though once discounted because of its inaccuracies, Glaber's work is now prized for the picture if affords of many of the most characteristic aspects of eleventh-century religious life: unsophisticated heresy, hatred of Jews, love of pilgrimage, the peace movement, the reverence for Jerusalem. Glaber also reflects the contemporary emotions regarding the imminent coming of Antichrist and the end of the world. It was once supposed that these events were popularly awaited in the year 1000, but it now seems clear that such ideas were not associated with a particular date—although Glaber does speak of 1033, the anniversary of the Redemption—but rather persisted throughout the century.

The text is translated from the Latin text in M. Prou (ed.), *Raoul*

Glaber, Les cinq livres de ses histoires (900–1044), (Paris, 1886), pp. 49–50, 71–75, 103–109.

Book II, Chapter XI

Concerning Leutard, the Insane Heretic

Toward the end of the year 1000 a peasant named Leutard was living in Gaul at a village called Vertus in the district of Châlons. As the outcome of the affair proved, it was possible to believe him to be the envoy of Satan, for his perverse insanity had this beginning. He was spending some time in a field to finish his farmwork when, worn out by his labor, he fell asleep. It seemed to him that a great swarm of bees entered his body, through nature's secrets and, noisily issuing from his mouth, stung him mercilessly. When he was much agitated by their goads they seemed to speak to him and to teach him to do many things impossible to men. Exhausted at last, he got up and returned home and dismissed his wife as if he were divorcing her by evangelical precept. Going out as though to pray he entered a church, seized the cross and ground to bits the image of Our Savior.

Those who saw this were frightened out of their wits, believing him to be insane, as indeed he was. But since they were impressionable rustics, he persuaded them that he accomplished these things by a wonderful revelation of God. Moreover, he spoke in discourses of no value and devoid of truth and, wishing to appear as a teacher, he tried to undo the teachings of the masters. For he kept saying that the giving of tithes was in every way superfluous and senseless. And as with other heresies which, in order to deceive cleverly, cloak themselves in Holy Writ, to which in fact they are opposed, so also this fellow maintained that the prophets had in part told useful things, but in part things not to be believed.

In a short time, by his reputation, as though by the intellect of a sane and devout person, he drew to himself a considerable part of the crowd. When Jebuin, the elderly and most learned bishop of Châlons in whose diocese, it seems, he was, ascertained this, he ordered the man to be brought to him. When he had questioned him about all he discovered that he had said and done, he [Leutard] decided to conceal the poison of his evil, and tried to obtain for himself evidence that he had not given instruction about the Holy Scriptures. When the most wise bishop heard these things

which were not in agreement, indeed more disgraceful than reprehensible, he showed that the man had become an insane heretic and
he recalled the partly deceived people from their madness and duly
restored them to the Catholic faith. But he [Leutard], seeing
himself defeated and no longer flattered by the crowd, drowned
himself in a well.

Book III, Chapter VII

Concerning the Overthrowing of the Temple of Jerusalem and the Slaughter of the Jews

At that same time, that is in the ninth year after the millennium
just mentioned, the church at Jerusalem which contained the
sepulcher of Our Lord and Savior was completely demolished by
order of the King of Babylon.[1] The reason for this destruction is
known to have had the origin we are about to describe. Since a
great multitude of people from all over the world was constantly
going to Jerusalem on account of this great memorial of the Lord,
the envious devil again began to pass on to the worshippers of the
true faith the poison of his iniquity through the race of the Jews
who were accustomed to him. There was at the royal city of Orléans in Gaul a considerable number of these people who were
found to be more puffed up and envious and audacious than others
of their race. And these, after they formed a plan, seduced by
bribery a certain good-for-nothing man, obviously a tramp in
pilgrim's garb, named Rotbert, a runaway serf from the monastery
of St. Mary Melerensis. After carefully taking him in, they directed him to the king of Babylon with letters written in Hebrew
characters on little leaves of parchment attached to an iron staff in
such a way that they could not by any chance be separated from it.

He set out and brought to the aforementioned prince the letters
full of deceit and wickedness [which said] that unless he destroyed
the venerable home of the Christians very quickly he would
discover that he was wholly without authority in the neighboring
kingdom with the Christians occupying it. When the prince heard
these things he was immediately seized with anger and sent his own

1. Glaber is evidently referring in this section to the eccentric Fatimid
Caliph al-Hakim, who ordered (c. 1009) the destruction of the Holy
Sepulcher and other churches, then later changed his mind and authorized
rebuilding.

men to Jerusalem to demolish completely the temple mentioned above. They went there and did as they were commanded; but they did not succeed in their attempt to shatter the vaulted tomb of the sepulcher with iron hammers. Then in like manner they did destroy the church of the holy martyr, St. George, in Ramla, whose spiritual strength had greatly terrified the Saracen people. Indeed, it was reported that those desiring to enter were often stricken with blindness.

When, therefore, as we said, the temple was destroyed, it became clear after a short time that this most impious deed had been perpetuated by the wickedness of the Jews. And so it was spread abroad throughout the entire world and decreed by the common consent of all Christians that all the Jews should be entirely expelled from their lands and cities. Thus, everywhere regarded with hatred, expelled from cities, some put to the sword, others drowned in rivers or destroyed by various kinds of death, many even took their own lives in various ways. Therefore, when an evidently deserved punishment had been inflicted upon them, only a few of them could be found in the Roman world. Then also it was decreed by the bishops and forbidden to any Christian to do any business with them. If, however, any of them desired to be converted to the grace of baptism and to reject all Jewish customs and practices, they ordained that such persons should so receive baptism. And many did this, more out of love of the present life and fear of death than for the sake of the joys of eternal life. For some of them who had dishonestly requested that they be made [Christian], shamelessly returned a little later to their former ways.

. . . About five years after the destruction of the temple, a few of the fugitive and wandering Jews, who had survived the slaughter mentioned above by hiding in out-of-the-way places, began to appear in cities. And inasmuch as it is fitting, although to their confusion, that some of them remain for the future either to confirm their own wickedness or as testimony to the shedding of Christ's blood, we verily believe that the animosity of the Christians toward them through the intervention of divine providence had for some time abated. Moreover, in that same year, with the aid of divine mercy, the mother of the same prince, that is the Emir of Babylon, a very devout Christian woman named Mary, began to rebuild with polished and squared stones the temple of Christ which her son had orderd destroyed. And her husband, in fact the father of him of whom we are speaking, as though another Nicodemus, is said to have been clothed secretly as a Christian. Then from all over the world an incredible number of persons exultantly journeying toward Jerusalem brought gifts to the restored house of God.

Book IV, Chapter V

Concerning Peace and Abundance in the One Thousandth Year of the Passion of Our Lord

In the one thousandth year from the passion of Our Lord, following the famine recounted above, and when the storm clouds obeying the divine mercy and goodness quieted, the smiling face of the skies began to clear and to blow with agreeable breezes, and by calm fair weather to show forth the magnanimity of the Creator. All the lands of the earth, flourishing in a friendly manner, began to portend an abundance of fruit by driving away famine. Then for the first time, in the region of Aquitaine, councils of bishops, abbots and other men devoted to holy religion from the entire people began to be assembled. Many bodies of saints and countless gifts of holy relics were brought before them. Thereafter, throughout the Arelate, Lyonnais, all of Burgundy as far as the remote areas of France, it was proclaimed throughout all dioceses that in certain places councils should be assembled by prelates and magnates of the entire country for the purpose of re-establishing peace and the teaching of holy faith. On hearing this, a great multitude of all the people, the great, the middle class, and the humble, eagerly came forth ready to obey whatever might be commanded by the pastors of the church. Indeed, it seemed almost as though a voice from heaven were speaking to men on earth. For the disasters of times past still worried everyone and they all feared lest they could not enjoy the good things to come.

A list was drawn up, both of those things which were prohibited and those actions to be offered freely pledged to Almighty God. And most important among the latter was the preservation of an inviolable peace so that men of every condition, whatever their previous perils, might now travel unarmed without fear. The brigand or robber of another's property was to be fined by giving up his possessions or be subject to severe bodily punishment to the extent of the law. Nevertheless, in holy places the honor and reverence due the churches was to be shown, so that if anyone guilty of sin in any form whatsoever sought refuge there he should go without injury, except someone who had violated the pact of peace just mentioned. When such a one was taken from the altar he was to suffer the prescribed punishment. Similarly, all clerics, monks and nuns [were to be respected] so that a person passing through the region with them should suffer no violence from anyone.

Many things were decided in these councils which we are disposed to refer to at length. It should be especially noted that it was unanimously agreed by a perpetual decree that there was to be abstinence from wine on the sixth day of each week and from flesh on the seventh, unless by chance serious illness prevented it or the observance of an important feast intervened. And if something caused this regime to be relaxed a little, three poor persons were then to be supplied with sustenance. Many were the healings of the sick brought about in these gatherings of holy men. But that it might not seem a trifling thing to anyone, there was in many broken skin and torn flesh, and much blood was shed as limbs, lately bent, were restored to their original state. All this, as in other cases where there had been doubt, restored faith. Everyone was ardently inspired by these things to raise a staff to heaven through the hands of the bishops, and with their palms extended cried to God with one voice, "Peace, peace, peace!" so that this might be a symbol of the perpetual pact on this between themselves and God to which they had agreed; and for the reason that, thanks to the confirmation of peace when five years had elapsed, this very wonder might be accomplished by all. For at length in the same year there was a greater abundance of grain and wine and other fruits than could have been hoped for in the ensuing five years. Except for meat or special breadstuffs, some food was inexpensive. In fact, there was the semblance of that great rejoicing of the Israelites. Nor did things prosper less in the third and fourth years following.

Book IV, Chapter VI

Concerning the Concourse of People from the Whole World to the Sepulcher of the Lord at Jerusalem

At that time an innumerable multitude from all over the world such as no man could have hoped for before began to flock together at the Sepulcher of Our Lord at Jerusalem. First came the lower order of people, then the middle, and following these the very great, kings and counts, margraves and governors, and last, what had never happened, many women, the noble with the poor went there. It was the desire of many to die before they returned home.

Now it so happened that from the vicinity of Autun in Burgundy there came with others going there a man named Lethbald. After he had seen all the holy places, he came to the Mount of Olives whence Our Lord ascending into heaven before the eyes of so many reliable witnesses promised that he would return to judge the living and the dead. There he threw himself down in the form of a cross, his body prostrate, and with tears exulted in the Lord with unutterable joy of spirit. Standing up again and again, with palms extended to heaven he thrust his body upward with every possible effort and revealed his heart's desire in a speech like this, for he said, "O Lord Jesus, who for us deigned to descend to earth from the seat of Your Majesty to save mankind and Who from the place which I behold with my eyes clothed in flesh returned to Heaven whence You had come, I beseech Your omnipotent bounty that if in this year my soul shall leave this body, I shall not depart from hence, but that this will happen in sight of the place of Your resurrection. For I believe that, as I have followed You in the body, so that I came to this place, so my soul unimpaired and rejoicing will follow You into Paradise."

When he had said these things he returned to the inn with his companions. It was meal time. When the others sat down, with an expression of joy he suddenly turned to his bed as though about to fall into a deep slumber for a little while. For, instantly falling asleep, he did not know what he saw. When he had fallen asleep he straightway cried out, "Glory to You, O Lord!" When his companions heard this they tried to persuade him to get up and eat. He did not want to, but turning to the other side complained of feeling ill. He lay down until evening; then he called together his traveling companions earnestly asked for the eucharist and received the viaticum; and when he had graciously wished them well he rendered up his spirit. This man, assuredly free from the false notions which prompted many to set out, that marvels only occur because of a journey to Jerusalem, faithfully besought the Father in the name of Our Lord Jesus that which he received. His companions on their return brought back those things we have described, which later were placed in the monastery of Bèze [near Dijon].

At the same time, Odolric, bishop of Orléans, traveling there, told us what seemed to be a noteworthy miracle. On Holy Saturday when the fire coming from the wonderful power of God is awaited by all the people, that same bishop was standing there with the others. Suddenly toward the hour when it was expected that the fire would appear, an impudent buffoon of a Saracen from among a crowd of others who each year are accustomed to come along with the Christians, exclaimed, as is the Christian custom as soon as the fire is seen, "Hail, *Kyrie eleison!*" Then he uttered a derisive laugh, stretched out his hand, seized a candle from the hands of a certain Christian and tried to escape. When he was caught on the spot he began to be most shamefully tormented by a demon; and a Christian following him took the candle away from him. Yet he was really terribly tormented and died forthwith in the company of the Saracens. This threw everyone into a panic. To the Christians, however, it gave great joy and exultation. Immediately, as usual, by the power of God the fire coming out of one of the seven lamps which are seen to hang there speedily blazed forth and ignited the others. And together with the oil he had bought for a gold pound from Jordan, who was then patriarch, the bishop took this back with him and deposited it in his own see, and it brought many benefits to the sick. He also brought to King Robert a rather large piece of the venerable cross of Our Savior, with a great number of silk mantles, sent by Constantine, the emperor of the Greeks,[1] to whom the same king had sent by the bishop a sword having a gold hilt and gold sheath with precious gems.

Furthermore, when certain of the more concerned people at that time were consulted by many as to what was the meaning of such a concourse of people going to Jerusalem, unheard of in earlier times, the answer was given, somewhat cautiously, that it portended nothing other than the coming of the accursed Anti-Christ who, according to the testimony of divine authority, is to come around the end of that very century. And then when the route of the oriental region whence he is to come has been revealed to all people, all nations are to proceed against him without delay; indeed, so that the prophecy of the Lord may be fulfilled, since even at that time

1. Presumably Glaber is referring here to the emperor Constantine VIII (1025–28). Robert was king of France (996–1031).

even the elect may fall into temptation, if that be possible. Here ends this discussion; for the rest, we do not deny that the devoted labor of the faithful receives reward and mercy from the just Judge.

34. *Reports of Urban II's Speech at Clermont*

The two selections cited here by Guibert of Nogent and Robert the Monk reflect the popular *élan* which had been generating in preceding decades and which was evident in the selections cited above. Neither was present at Clermont in 1095 when the pope spoke; each wrote some years after the event, Guibert around 1109 and Robert around 1122. Their reports, therefore, are valuable less as accounts of what Urban said than as evidence of contemporary religious feeling. It is possible, for example, that Urban did not actually mention Jerusalem. Yet the Holy City, "the navel of the world," and the Sepulcher of the Lord are central in both these chronicles. Guibert, too, mentions the coming of Antichrist. Robert appeals to the "Franks," the heirs of Roland and Charlemagne. The translation is by A. C. Krey, *The First Crusade* (Princeton, N.J., 1921), pp. 31–39. Reprinted by permission of Princeton University Press.

Guibert de Nogent

". . . If, when the Lord had but just been crucified and the city was still held by the Jews, it was called holy by the evangelist when he says, 'Many bodies of the saints that had fallen asleep were raised; and coming forth out of the tombs after His resurrection, they entered into the holy city and appeared unto many,' and by the prophet Isaiah when he says, 'It shall be His glorious sepulchre,' then, surely, with this sanctity placed upon it by God the Sanctifier Himself, no evil that may befall it can destroy it, and in the same way glory is indivisibly fixed to His Sepulchre. Most beloved brethren, if you reverence the source of that holiness and glory, if you cherish these shrines which are the marks of His foot-prints on earth, if you seek (the way), God leading you, God fighting in your behalf, you should strive with your utmost efforts to cleanse the Holy City and the glory of the Sepulchre, now polluted by the concourse of the Gentiles, as much as is in their power.

"If in olden times the Maccabees attained to the highest praise of piety because they fought for the ceremonies and the Temple, it is also justly granted you, Christian soldiers, to defend the liberty of your country by armed endeavor. If you, likewise, consider that the abode of the holy apostles and any other saints should be striven for with such effort, why do you refuse to rescue the Cross, the Blood, the Tomb? Why do you refuse to visit them, to spend the price of your lives in rescuing them? You have thus far waged unjust wars, at one time and another; you have brandished mad weapons to your mutual destruction, for no other reason than covetousness and pride, as a result of which you have deserved eternal death and sure damnation. We now hold out to you wars which contain the glorious reward of martyrdom, which will retain that title of praise now and forever. . . .

"And you ought, furthermore, to consider with the utmost deliberation, if by your labors, God working through you, it should occur that the Mother of churches should flourish anew to the worship of Christianity, whether, perchance, He may not wish other regions of the East to be restored to the faith against the approaching time of the Antichrist. For it is clear that Antichrist is to do battle not with the Jews, not with the Gentiles; but, according to the etymology of his name, he will attack Christians. And if Antichrist finds there are no Christians (just as at present when scarcely any dwell there), no one will be there to oppose him, or whom he may rightly overcome. According to Daniel and Jerome, the interpreter of Daniel, he is to fix his tents on the Mount of Olives; and it is certain, for the apostle teaches it, that he will sit at Jerusalem in the Temple of the Lord, as though he were God. And according to the same prophet, he will first kill three kings of Egypt, Africa, and Ethiopia, without doubt for their Christian faith. This, indeed, could not at all be done unless Christianity was established where now is paganism. If, therefore, you are zealous in the practice of holy battles, in order that, just as you have received the seed of knowledge of God from Jerusalem, you may in the same way restore the borrowed grace, so that through you the Catholic name may be advanced to oppose the perfidy of the Antichrist and the Antichristians—then, who can not conjecture that God, who has exceeded the hope of all, will consume, in the abundance of your courage and through you as the spark, such a thicket of paganism as to include within His law Egypt, Africa, and Ethiopia, which have withdrawn from the communion of our belief? And the man of sin, the son of perdition, will find some to oppose him. Behold, the Gospel cries out, 'Jerusalem shall be trodden down by the Gentiles until the times of the Gentiles be fulfilled.' 'Times of the Gentiles' can be understood in two ways: Either that they have ruled over the Christians at their pleasure, and have gladly frequented the sloughs of all baseness for the satisfaction of their lusts, and in all this have had no obstacle (for they who have everything according to their wish are said to have their time; there is that saying: 'My time is not yet come, but your time is always ready,' whence the lustful are wont to say 'you are having your time'). Or, again, 'the times of the Gentiles' are the fulness of time for those Gentiles who shall have entered secretly before Israel shall be saved. These times, most beloved brothers, will now, forsooth, be fulfilled, provided the might of the pagans be repulsed through you, with the co-operation of God. With the end of the world already near, even though the Gentiles fail to be converted to the Lord (since according to the apostle there must be a withdrawal from the faith), it is first necessary, according to the prophecy, that the Christian sway be renewed in those regions, either through you, or others, whom it shall please God to send before the coming of Antichrist, so that the head of all evil, who is to occupy there the throne of the kingdom, shall find some support of the faith to fight against him.

"Consider, therefore, that the Almighty has provided you, perhaps, for this purpose, that through you He may restore Jerusalem from such debasement. Ponder, I beg you, how full of joy and delight our hearts will be when we shall see the Holy City restored with your little help, and the prophet's, nay divine, words fulfilled in our times. Let your memory be moved by what the Lord Himself says to the Church: 'I will bring thy seed from the East and gather thee from the West.' God has already brought our seed from the East, since in a double way that region of the East has given the first beginnings of the Church to us. But from the West He will also gather it, provided He repairs the wrongs of Jerusalem through those who have begun the witness of the final faith, that is the people of the West. With God's assistance, we think this can be done through you." . . .

Robert the Monk

. . . "Oh, race of Franks, race from across the mountains, race chosen and beloved by God—as shines forth in very many of your works—set apart from all nations by the situation of your country, as well as by your Catholic faith and the honor of the Holy Church! To you our discourse is addressed . . .

"Let the deeds of your ancestors move you and incite your minds to manly achievements; likewise, the glory and greatness of King Charles the Great, and his son Louis, and of your other kings, who have destroyed the kingdoms of the pagans, and have extended in these lands the territory of the Holy Church. Let the Holy Sepulchre of the Lord, our Saviour, which is possessed by unclean nations, especially move you, and likewise the holy places, which are now treated with ignominy and irreverently polluted with filthiness. Oh, most valiant soldiers and descendants of invincible ancestors, be not degenerate, but recall the valor of your forefathers!

"However, if you are hindered by love of children, parents, and wives, remember what the Lord says in the Gospel, 'He that loveth father, or mother more than me, is not worthy of me.' 'Every one that hath forsaken houses, or brethren, or sisters, or father, or mother, or wife, or children, or lands for my name's sake shall receive an hundred-fold and shall inherit everlasting life.' Let none of your possessions detain you, no solicitude for your family affairs, since this land which you inhabit, shut in on all sides by the sea and surrounded by mountain peaks, is too narrow for your large population; nor does it abound in wealth; and it furnishes scarcely food enough for its cultivators. Hence it is that you murder and devour one another, that you wage war, and that frequently you perish by mutual wounds. Let therefore hatred depart from among you, let your quarrels end, let wars cease, and let all dissensions and controversies slumber. Enter upon the road to the Holy Sepulchre; wrest that land from the wicked race, and subject it to yourselves. That land which, as the Scripture says, 'floweth with milk and honey' was given by God into the possession of the children of Israel.

"Jerusalem is the navel of the world; the land is fruitful above others, like another paradise of delights. This the Redeemer of the human race has made illustrious by His advent, has beautified by His presence, has consecrated by suffering, has redeemed by death, has glorified by burial. This royal city, therefore, situated at the center of the world, is now held captive by His enemies, and is in subjection to those who do not know God, to the worship of the heathen. Therefore, she seeks and desires to be liberated and does not cease to implore you to come to her aid. From you, especially, she asks succor, because, as we have already said, God has conferred upon you, above all nations, great glory in arms. Accordingly, undertake this journey for the remission of your sins, with the assurance of the imperishable glory of the kingdom of heaven." . . .

35. The Book of the Pilgrim

The belief that the bones of St. James the Apostle had been brought from the East to Compostela in Spain dates from the early eighth century and was soon associated with that saint's patronage of the *Reconquista*. His grave soon became a favorite object of pilgrimage from all parts of the Christian world, and over his remains was finally erected a magnificent romanesque church which still stands.

Around 1120 a work in five parts, entitled *Liber sancti Jacobi*, appeared. Part V is a guide for pilgrims that indicates the main routes to be taken through France to the orders of Spain and thence to Compostela. In addition to directions concerning roads, mountains, towns, people, food, etc., it includes information about important shrines along each route and the relics which each possesses. Particularly interesting are the references to Charlemagne and Roland, who evidently had become in the popular mind actual saints and heroes who made war against the Moslems. A final section of the guide describing the church in considerable detail has been of great importance to archeologists.

The following selection includes a few sample chapters, some of them about saints whose shrines are outstanding examples of French romanesque architecture.

The translation is from the Latin text in *Le Guide du pèlerin de St. Jaques de Compostelle* (ed. Jeanne Vielliard, Macon, 1950), pp. 2–4, 24–26, 34–40, 46–54, 60–62, 78–80.

Chapter I. The Routes to St. James

There are four routes leading to St. James which join together at Puente la Reina in the land of Spain. One goes through St. Giles, Montpellier, Toulouse and Somport; another by St. Mary of Le Puy, St. Faith of Conques, and St. Peter of Moissac; another passes through St. Mary Magdelen of Vézelay and St. Leonard of Limoges and the town of Périgord; the other goes by St. Martin of

Tours and St. Hilary of Poitiers, St. John of Angély and St. Eutropius of Saintes, and the city of Bordeaux. The route which goes by St. Faith, that which goes by St. Leonard, and the one which goes via St. Martin all come together at Ostabat and after crossing the pass of Cize, join the road which crosses by Somport at Puente la Reina; thence they make a single route as far as St. James.

Chapter VII. The Names of the Countries Which the Road to St. James Traverses and the Kinds of People Who Live There

. . . In the land of the Basques, on the route to St. James there is a very imposing mountain which is called Port de Cize, either because the entrance to Spain is there or because necessary supplies are transported across it to that country. The ascent is eight miles, as is also the descent. The height is so great that it seems to reach the sky, and appears to the climber as though he could touch the sky with his own hand. From the summit one can see the sea of Brittany and the western ocean and the frontiers of three countries, Castile, Aragon, and Gaul. At the top of this mountain is a place called the Cross of Charles because once, when he crossed into Spain with his armies, he made a path with hatchets, pickaxes, shovels, and other implements. In that place he first set up the standard of the cross of our Lord. Then, on bended knee, facing Galicia, he poured out his prayer to God and St. James. Therefore, at that place pilgrims bend their knees toward the fatherland of St. James, pray, as is the custom, and each plants his own standard of Our Lord's cross. A thousand crosses can be found there. As a result, this is the first place of prayer to St. James. On the same mountain, before Christianity had reached its full strength within the frontiers of Spain, the impious Navarrese and Basques used not only to prey on the pilgrims journeying to St. James, but even used to ride at them as asses and destroy them. Close to the mountain, toward the north, that is, is a valley, called the Valley of Charles, where Charles stayed with his armies when the warriors were killed at Roncevaux.

Next, on the descent of the same mountain, is found a hospice and church wherein is the stone which that most mighty hero, Roland, split in the middle from top to bottom with three blows of his own sword. Then Roncevaux is reached, the very place where a great battle was once fought in which the King Marsile and Roland and Oliver and other warriors with forty thousand Christian and Saracen soldiers were killed . . .

Chapter VIII

On the Bodies of the Saints Which Repose on the Route to St. James Which Ought to Be Visited by Pilgrims

First of all, the body of St. Trophime, the confessor, at Arles must be visited by those who take the road to St. James by St. Giles. St. Paul mentioned him in his letter to Timothy. He was ordained bishop by that same apostle, and was the first sent to preach the gospel of Christ in the aforementioned city. From this most clear spring, as Pope Zosimus wrote, all Gaul received streams of faith. His feast is celebrated on the fourth day before the Kalends of January.

Likewise the body of St. Cesarius, bishop and martyr who instituted the monastic rule in that same city, and whose feast is kept on the Kalends of November, should be visited.

Likewise in the cemetery of the same city the relics of St. Honoratus, bishop, must be sought. His feast is celebrated on the seventeenth day before the Kalends of February. And in his splendid and venerable basilica rests the body of the most esteemed saint and martyr, Genesius. There is a village near Arles, between two arms of the Rhône, called Trenquetaille, where there is a certain marble column, unusually fine and raised high above the ground right behind his church. To this column the faitheless people, so it is said, bound blessed Genesius and beheaded him, and even to this day it is red with his blood. And he, indeed, as soon as he had been decapitated, took his head in his own hands, threw it into the Rhône, and brought his body through the middle of the river as far as the basilica of St. Honoratus where it lies in honor. Then the head, floating with angelic guidance down the Rhône and through the sea, came to Cartagena, a city of the Spaniards, where it now most excellently reposes and performs many miracles. His feast is celebrated on the eighth day before the Kalends of September.

The cemetery of the dead near the city of Arles in a place called Ailiscampis should be visited next to make intercession with prayers, psalms, and alms, as is the custom, for the dead. The cemetery is a mile in length and width. So many and such fine marble coffins laid on the ground can be found in no cemetery except this one. They are of varied workmanship and inscribed in Latin letters in an ancient and unintelligible tongue. As far as you cast your eye you will see sarcophagi. In the same cemetery there are seven churches. If any priest celebrates the eucharist for the dead in any one of them, or if a layman devoutly has some priest celebrate, or a cleric reads the psalter, surely he will have those pious dead who lie there as aids in his own salvation in the final resurrection before God. Many bodies of holy martyrs and confessors rest there whose souls rejoice in the abode of paradise. It is the custom for their commemoration to be observed on the second week day after the octave of Easter.

Likewise, the most worthy body of holy St. Giles, confessor and abbot, must above all be visited attentively. For the most blessed Giles, famous throughout every clime, should be invoked and petitioned most diligently by everyone. After the apostles and prophets, no one among the other saints is more deserving than he, no one holier, no one more glorious, no one swifter in aid. For he, more promptly than the other saints, is wont to assist the needy and the afflicted and anguished who call upon him. Oh what a wonderful and beautiful thing it is to visit his sepulcher! Indeed, on the day on which anyone beseeches him with all his heart, without a doubt he will be happily aided. Who will adore God in his most sacred basilica? Who, further, will embrace his sarcophagus? Who will kiss his venerable altar or who will tell the story of his most holy life? A sick man puts on his tunic and is healed; another, struck by a snake, is healed by his unfailing power; another, seized with a demon, is freed, a storm at sea is calmed. The daughter of Theocritus is restored to a health long desired. A sick man with no health in his entire body is brought back to a long desired strength; a deer which formerly was wild, is tamed and obeys his commands; a monastic order under the patronage of this abbot grows. A man possessed of a devil is freed. The sin of Charles, revealed to him by an angel, is forgiven the king. A dead man is restored to life. A cripple is restored to his former health.

[The following section is a description of the altar and tomb]

. . . So stands the burial place of blessed Giles, the confessor, in which his venerable body solemnly resposes. Therefore, let the

Hungarians blush who say they have his body, and all confusion to the Cammelarii who foolishly prate that they have his entire body. And may the Saint-Sequanais wither away who proclaim that they have his head. Likewise the Normans of Coutances who boast that they have his whole body, should be confounded since, as it is proved by many, his sacred bones can in no way be taken out of this very country. For at one time certain people attempted fraudulently to carry the confessor's arms to be venerated far outside of the St. Giles region, but they were in no way able to depart with it. As it is demonstrated by many there are four bodies of saints which, it is reported, can not be removed by anyone from their own sarcophagi: that is, St. James of Zebidee, St. Martin of Tours, St. Leonard of Limoges, and Blessed Giles, the confessor. It is said that Philip, king of the Gauls, tried to carry these same bodies to Gaul [France] but could in no way remove them from their own sarcophagi.

Then, those traveling to St. James by the Toulouse road must visit the body of Blessed William, the confessor. For the most holy William, a distinguished standard bearer, count under the great Charles, was no less outstanding a soldier, skilled in warfare. He, as it is reported, brought under the yoke of the Christian empire the city of Nîmes, and Orange and several other cities, by his mighty prowess. And he took with him the wood of the Holy Cross into the valley of Gellone. . . . In that valley, indeed, he led the life of a hermit and, after a holy death, the confessor of Christ reposes there in honor. His feast is celebrated on the fifth day before the Kalends of June.

Also on the same road the body of the most worthy St. Saturninus, bishop and martyr, should be visited. In the capitol of the city of Toulouse he was held by the pagans and tied to fierce untamed bulls and from the top of the arch of the capitol dragged headlong a distance of one mile over all the stone steps. His head bruised, his brains beaten out, and his entire body mangled, he gave up his worthy soul to Christ. He is buried in an attractive place near the city of Toulouse where the faithful erected a great basilica in his honor and where the canonical rule of St. Augustine is observed. Many favors are given by the Lord to those who ask. His solemnity is observed in the third day before the Kalends of December.

Likewise, the Burgundians and Germans journeying to St. James by the Le Puy road ought to visit the most holy body of St. Faith, virgin and martyr. After the executioners had beheaded her on the mountain of the town of Agen, a choir of angels in the likeness of doves carried away to heaven and adorned with the laurel of immortality her most holy soul. Blessed Caprasius, bishop of the city of Agen, avoiding the madness of persecution, was hiding in a certain cave. When he saw this, he was inspired to undergo his passion and hastened to the place where the holy virgin suffered, and struggling bravely merited the palm of martyrdom, and even denounced the slowness of his persecutors. Finally, the most precious body of St. Faith, virgin and martyr, was solemnly buried by the Christians in a valley popularly called Conques, and over it a beautiful basilica was built by Christians, in which even to this day the rule of St. Benedict is properly observed in honor of the Lord. Many favors are bestowed on sick and well. In front of the doors there is a lovely fountain, unspeakably marvelous. Her feast is on the second day before the nones of October.

Then on the road which goes to St. James by St. Leonard, first the body of the most worthy St. Mary Magdalen must be visited by pilgrims. For here is that glorious Mary who in the home of Simon the leper washed the feet of the Savior with her tears, and dried them with her hair, and kissing them, anointed them carefully with precious ointment. Therefore, many sins were forgiven her because she greatly loved Him who loved all, Jesus Christ, her redeemer. After the Lord's ascension, she along with blessed Maximus, a disciple of Christ, and other disciples of the Lord came from the region of Jerusalem by sea through the port of Marseilles to the land of Provence. There, indeed, for some years she led a life alone and finally was buried in the city of Aix by that same Maximus, then bishop of the city. After a considerable time, a saintly devotee of the monastic life, named Badilo, brought her precious corpse from that city to Vézelay where it reposes to this day in a much venerated tomb. Moreover, in that place a large and most beautiful basilica and abbey of monks is established. Through love of her, sins are remitted to sinners by the Lord, sight is restored to the blind, the tongues of the dumb are loosened, the lame walk, those seized by demons are freed, and ineffable favors are bestowed on many. Her feast is celebrated eleven days before the Kalends of August.

Also to be visited is the sacred body of St. Leonard, confessor,

who although he was a high noble among the race of the Franks
and brought up in the royal court, renouncing the wicked world
for love of the supreme God, led for a long time in the region of
Limoges at a place called Noblat the celibate life of a hermit, with
frequent fasts and many vigils, cold and nakedness, and indescrib-
able labors. At length in that same free property of his, he rested in
a holy passing. His sacred corpse was found to be immovable.

Therefore, may monks of Corbigny blush who say that they
possess the body of St. Leonard! For as we have said, in no way
can his smallest bone or bit of dust be moved. In fact the monks of
Corbigny and many others are enriched by his benefits and miracles; but they are deceived in his corporal presence. Since they
cannot possess his body, they venerate, instead of St. Leonard of
Limoges, the body of a certain man named Leotardus, which they
say was brought to them from the region of Anjou, placed in a
silver coffer. They even changed his name after his death, as
though he were again baptized, and gave him the name of St.
Leonard, so that owing to the repute of such a famous name, that
is, of St. Leonard of Limoges, pilgrims would come there and
enrich them with their offerings. . . . Whoever it is who accomplishes miracles at Corbigny, it nonetheless is St. Leonard of
Limoges, who although separated from the jurisdiction of their
church, delivers captives and leads them there. Therefore, the
people of Corbigny are doubly guilty since they do not recognize
him who liberally enriches them with his miracles, nor do they
celebrate his feast, but improperly venerate another instead. Divine
clemency has therefore spread the fame of blessed Leonard far and
wide throughout the entire world and his most potent virtue has
led innumerable thousands of captives from prisons. And their iron
chains, more barbarous than one can say, thousands upon thousands, in his basilica, all around to the right and the left, inside and
outside are hung in testimony of so many miracles . . .

Likewise on this route [via Tours] the venerable body of blessed
Martin of Tours, bishop and confessor, must be visited. It is said of
him that he gloriously raised three persons from the dead and
restored to their lost health lepers, those possessed of devils, those
who had left the accustomed paths, lunatics and those possessed by
demons and other infirm people. The sarcophagus wherein his most
holy remains are found in the city of Tours is resplendent with
much silver and gold and precious stones and made illustrious by

frequent miracles. Over this a large and venerable basilica similar, in fact, to that of St. James, is built with marvelous skill in his honor. To this the sick come and are healed, demons are cast out, the blind see, the lame rise up and every sort of illness is cured, and a full and worthy release is given to all who ask. Therefore, his glorious fame is properly spread abroad everywhere to the honor of Christ with appropriate praise.

Thence the most holy body of Blessed Hilary, bishop and confessor, is to be visited in the city of Poitiers. There among other miracles of God, filled with virtue and subduing the Arian heresy, he taught [men] to maintain the unity of faith. His tomb where his most sacred and venerable bones repose is exceptionally adorned with gold and silver and precious stones, and his great basilica is favored by frequent miracles. His sacred solemnities are observed on the Ides of January. . . .

Then at Blaye on the coast is to be sought the protection of St. Romanus. In his basilica reposes the body of blessed Roland the martyr, who, being of noble birth, in fact a count of King Charles, fired by zeal for the faith went into Spain one of twelve warriors to fight the infidels. He was endowed with such strength that, as it is reported, he split a certain stone at Roncevaux down the middle from top to bottom with a triple blow with his sword, and sounding his horn, he similarly split this in the middle by the wind from his mouth. The ivory horn, indeed split, is kept at Bordeaux in the church of St. Severinus, and over the stone at Roncevaux a certain church is erected. Indeed, after Roland has won many battles against kings and nobles, worn out by hunger, cold, and great heat, and by great blows and frequent lashings for the love of divine will, and wounded by arrows and spears, he is at length carried to the above-mentioned valley to die a worthy martyr of Christ. His sacred body was reverently buried by his companions in the basilica of St. Romanus at Blaye. . . .

The Liturgy: Sequence, Trope, and Drama

36. The Sequence

The origin and development of the sequence have for long been the subject of discussion among liturgical scholars and musicologists, and a great deal remains obscure. The chant *Alleluia*, like the *Kyrie eleison*, was a vestige of the Greek rite which had remained in the Latin rite of Rome, as Gregory the Great indicates in the letter cited above (p. 41). It had become the custom, especially in joyous seasons such as Easter, to prolong the final *a* of the *Alleluia* that commonly followed the antiphon and versicle (the gradual) between the Epistle and Gospel. This produced an additional melody which was called a *jubilus* or *jubilatio*. Sometimes the *jubilus* itself was divided into separate musical phrases called sequences (*sequentiae*). A further step was the addition of words to fit the melody, thus forming a new liturgical text.

The sequence as it developed in the West, including the use of the word "sequence" to describe the whole process, is a development of the ninth century. Amalar of Metz, it will be recalled, mentioned it in his *Liber officialis* (see Document 25), and a monk named Notker of St. Gall toward the end of the century states that another monk from Jumièges explained to him how the words were added, how he composed sequences himself, and how his master advised him. Eventually the sequence became a virtually independent liturgical element and elicited the talents of some of the finest medieval poets.

The Easter Sequence

This famous sequence, still in use, was composed by Wipo (d. 1050), chaplain to the Holy Roman emperor. The Latin text is that of F. J. E. Raby, *op. cit.*, no. 133.

> *Victimae paschali laudes*
> *immolent Christiani.*

Let Christians offer sacrifices of praise to the paschal victim.

> *Agnus redimit oves:*

> *Christus innocens patri reconciliavit*
> *peccatores.*

The lamb has redeemed the sheep: Christ, the blameless one, has reconciled sinners to the Father.

> *Mors et vita duello*
> *conflixere mirando, dux vitae mortuus*
> *regnat vivus.*

Death and life have met in wondrous conflict, the ruler of life, though he died, reigns living.

> *Dic nobis Maria*
> *"quid vidisti in via?" "Sepulcrum Christi viventis*
> *et gloriam vidi resurgentis: Angelicos testes*
>
> *sudarium vestes. Surrexit Christus spes mea,*
> *praecedet suos in Galilaea."*

Tell us Mary, "What did you see on the way?" "I saw the sepulcher of the living Christ and the glory of the risen one: the angelic witnesses, the napkin and the linen cloths. Christ, my hope has risen and will go before his own into Galilee."

> *Credendum est magis*
> *Mariae veraci soli[1] quam Iudaeorum turbae fallaci.*

The truthful Mary alone is more to be believed than the deceitful crowd of Jews.

> *Scimus Christum surexisse*
> *a mortuis vere; tu nobis, victor rex, miserere!*

We know Christ has really risen from the dead; O victor king, have mercy on us!

1. This verse was removed from the sequence in the sixteenth century.

Adam of St. Victor, Sequence for the Nativity of the Virgin Mary

The following verses illustrate the sequence fully developed into a hymn with meter and rhyme, a development in which the author, Adam of St. Victor (fl. c. 1140), was one of the most important figures. The community to which he belonged, the Augustinian abbey of St. Victor in Paris, was celebrated for its biblical studies as well as for its contributions to theological knowledge. Adam exploited the use of scriptural imagery, a practice which had become popular with the theologians and biblical scholars of his day and which figures so prominently in the sermons and writings of St. Bernard of Clairvaux. Passages in the Old Testament, especially in the *Canticle of Canticles,* were interpreted as prefiguring the characteristics of Mary, the pure virgin, mother of the Savior. The thorn and the thorn bush become the symbols of sin.

The story was told of Adam that one day when he was meditating before the virgin's altar she appeared to him and nodded her approval of his verses. The Latin version is that of F. J. E. Raby, *op. cit.,* no. 163, verses 1–3, 11.

> *Salve, mater salvatoris,*
> *vas electum, vas honoris,*
> *vas caelestis gratiae;*
> *ab aeterno vas provisum,*
> *vas insigne, vas excisum*
> *manu sapientiae!*

> Hail, mother of the Savior,
> Chosen vessel, vessel of honor,
> Vessel of heavenly grace;
> Vessel prepared from eternity,
> Vessel distinguished, vessel carved out
> By the hand of Wisdom!

> *Salve, verbi sacra parens,*
> *flos de spina, spina carens,*
> *flos, spineti gloria!*
> *nos spinetum, nos peccati*
> *spina sumus cruentati,*
> *sed tu spinae nescia.*

> Hail, holy mother of the Word,
> Flower made from the thorn, but without the thorn,
> Flower, glory of the thornbush.
> We, the thornbush, from the thorn
> Of sin are bleeding,
> But you know not the thorn.

> *Porta clausa, fons hortorum,*
> *cella custos unguentorum,*
> *cella pigmentaria;*
> *cinnamomi calamum,*

myrrham, tus et balsamum
superas fragrantia.

Closed portal, fountain of gardens,
Guardian of the storeroom of ointments,
The storeroom of sweet odors;
Reed of cinnamon,
Myrrh, incense, and balsam
You surpass in fragrance.

Tu convallis humilis,
terra non arabilis,
quae fructum parturiit;
flos campi, convallium
singulare lilium,
Christus ex te prodiit.

You the lowly valley,
The barren land,
Which bore fruit;
Flower of the field
One and only lily of the valley,
Christ came forth from you.

Salve mater pietatis,
et totius trinitatis
nobile triclinium.
verbi tamen incarnati
speciale maiestati
praeparans hospitium!

Hail, mother of holiness,
And of the whole Trinity
Noble sustenance.
Yet for the Incarnate Word
In special majesty
Preparing lodging!

37. *The* Quem quaeritis *Trope*

Another usage which originated in the liturgy but eventually became
an entirely independent element was the trope. The trope has been
defined as "a text which is employed (with the accompaniment of

music) as introduction, intercalation, or addition to a portion of the liturgy, such as the Introit, the Kyrie, the Gloria, etc."[1] A famous example is the *Quem quaeritis*, composed by an unknown author around 900, which later became associated with the origin of liturgical drama. The Latin text is from F. J. E. Raby, *op. cit.*, no. 99.

> *Quem quaeritis in sepulchro,*
> *O christicolae?*
> *Iesum Nazarenum crucifixum,*
> *O caelicolae.*

Whom are you seeking in the sepulcher, O worshippers of Christ? Jesus of Nazareth, the crucified, O heavenly dwellers.

> *Non est hic;*
> *surrexit, sicut praedixerat.*
> *ite, nuntiate,*
> *quia surrexit.*

He is not here; He has risen as he had foretold. Go, make it known, that he has risen.

> *Alleluia, resurrexit Dominus,*
> *hodie resurrexit leo fortis*
> *filius Dei.*
> *Deo gratias: dicite, eia.*

> *Resurrexi et adhuc tecum*, etc. (the Introit for Easter).

Alleluia, the Lord has risen; today the strong lion has risen, the Son of God: speak, thanks be to God.

I have risen and even now am with you, etc.

38. The Quem quaeritis *"Play"*

Medieval drama grew out of the liturgy and resulted from the addition of action to the text in certain especially striking passages in the Gospel narrative. The earliest example of this procedure is the *Quem quaeritis* "play," so named because it utilizes the text just cited: members of the clergy act out the episode of the three women finding the empty tomb

1. F. J. E. Raby, *Christian Latin Poetry* (2nd. ed., Oxford, 1953), p. 219.

on Easter morning. It is described in the *Regularis concordia* or *Monastic Agreement*, a compilation of monastic usages drawn up in England around 970. The translation is by T. Symons, *The Monastic Agreement of the Monks and Nuns of the English Nation* (London, 1953), pp. 49–50.[1] Reprinted by permission of Thomas Nelson & Sons Ltd., Publishers.

51. While the third lesson [of nocturns] is being read, four of the brethren shall vest, one of whom, wearing an alb as though for some different purpose, shall enter and go stealthily to the place of the 'sepulchre' and sit there quietly, holding a palm in his hand. Then, while the third respond is being sung, the other three brethren, vested in copes and holding thuribles in their hands, shall enter in their turn and go to the place of the 'sepulchre,' step by step, as though searching for something. Now these things are done in imitation of the angel seated on the tomb and of the women coming with perfumes to anoint the body of Jesus. When, therefore, he that is seated shall see these three draw nigh, wandering about as it were and seeking something, he shall begin to sing softly and sweetly, *Quem quaeritis*. As soon as this has been sung right through, the three shall answer together, *Ihesum Nazarenum*. Then he that is seated shall say *Non est hic. Surrexit sicut praedixerat. Ite, nuntiate quia surrexit a mortuis*. At this command the three shall turn to the choir saying *Alleluia. Resurrexit Dominus*. When this has been sung he that is seated, as though calling them back, shall say the antiphon *Venite et videte locum*, and then, rising and lifting up the veil, he shall show them the place void of the Cross and with only the linen in which the Cross had been wrapped. Seeing this the three shall lay down their thuribles in the same 'sepulchre' and, taking the linen, shall hold it up before the clergy; and, as though showing that the Lord was risen and was no longer wrapped in it, they shall sing this antiphon: *Surrexit Dominus de sepulchro*. They shall then lay the linen on the altar.

52. When the antiphon is finished the prior, rejoicing in the triumph of our King in that He had conquered death and was risen, shall give out the hymn *Te Deum laudamus*, and thereupon all the bells shall peal. After this a priest shall say the verse *Surrexit Dominus de sepulchro* right through and shall begin Matins. . . .

1. For the significance of this passage in the history of the drama, see K. Young, *The Drama of the Medieval Church* (Oxford, 1933) and, more recently, O. B. Hardison, Jr., *Christian Rite and Drama in the Middle Ages* (Baltimore, 1965).

St. Bernard of Clairvaux

39. Sermons on the Virgin Mary

Although there are occasional references which suggest a wider audience, St. Bernard's sermons were usually delivered to monks. He spoke, therefore, to presumably religiously educated listeners who would have been familiar with his biblical allusions and able to understand his imagery. They would also have appreciated the strong emphasis on humility, for humility was the monastic virtue par excellence. In fact, St. Bernard wrote a commentary, *The Steps of Humility*, on the twelve degrees of humility mentioned in the *Rule of St. Benedict*.

The selections cited here consist of excerpts from Homilies I, II, and III on the text *Missus est:* ". . . The angel Gabriel was sent from God . . . to a virgin . . . and the virgin's name was Mary" (Luke i, 26–27). These sermons, delivered on the Vigil of Our Lady's Nativity, contain some of the most famous passages of St. Bernard's concerning the Virgin Mary. It is interesting that despite his great reverence for the virginal purity of Mary, "full of grace," Bernard did not share the belief in her immaculate conception. This doctrine was much discussed in the Middle Ages, but not officially defined as dogma until 1854. The translation is by S. J. Eales, from Dom J. Mabillon (ed.)., *The Life and Works of St. Bernard of Clairvaux* (London, 1896), vol. III, pp. 293–299, 315–316. For another sermon of St. Bernard, see below, Document 62.

5. To that city then was sent the Angel Gabriel by God; but to whom was he sent? *To a Virgin, espoused to a man whose name was Joseph.* Who is this virgin so worthy of reverence as to be saluted by an Angel: yet so humble, as to be betrothed to a carpenter? A beautiful combination is that of virginity with humility: and that soul singularly pleases God in which humility gives worth to virginity, and virginity throws a new lustre on humility. But of how great respect must she not be thought worthy, in whom maternity consecrates virginity, and the splendour of a Birth exalts humility? You hear her, a virgin, and humble: if you are not able to imitate the virginity of that humble soul, imitate at least her

humility; Virginity is a praiseworthy virtue; but humility is more necessary. . .

6. What say you to this O virgin who art proud? Mary forgets her virginity and dwells only upon her humility: And you think only of flattering yourself about your virginity, while neglecting humility. *The Lord,* she said, *has had regard to the humility of His handmaid.* Who was she who speaks this? A virgin holy, prudent and pious. Would you claim to be more chaste, more pious than she? Or do you think that your modesty is more acceptable than the purity of Mary, since you think that you are able by it to please God without humility, whilst she was not able? The more honourable you are by the singular gift of chastity, the greater is the injury you do to yourself, by staining it with an admixture of pride. It were better for you not to be a virgin, than to grow haughty about virginity. It is not granted to all to live in virginity; but to much fewer to do so with humility. . . .

7. There is something still more admirable in Mary: namely, her maternity joined with virginity. For from the beginning was never such a thing heard, as that one should be at the same time Mother and Virgin. If you consider also of whom she is Mother, to what degree will not your admiration of such a marvellous advancement soar? Will you not feel that you can hardly admire it enough? Will not your judgment or rather that of the Truth, be, that she whose Son is God, is exalted even above the choirs of Angels? Is it not Mary who says boldly to God, the Lord of Angels, *Son, why hast thou thus dealt with us?* Who of the Angels would dare to speak thus? It is sufficient for them, and they count it for a great thing, that they are spirits by nature, that they were made and called Angels by His grace, as David testifies: *Who makes His Angels Spirits* (Ps. civ. 4). But Mary, knowing herself to be Mother, with confidence names Him Son, whom they obey with reverence. Nor does God disdain to be called by the name which He has deigned to assume. For a little after the Evangelist adds: *And He was subject unto them* (S. Luke ii. 51). Who, and to whom? God, to human beings; God, I say, to whom the Angels are subject, whom Principaltities and Powers obey, was subject unto Mary; and to Joseph also for her sake. Admire then both the benign condescension of the Son and the most excellent dignity of the Mother; and choose whether of the two is the more admirable. Each is a wonder, each a miracle. God is obedient to a woman, an unexampled humility! a woman is in the place of ancestor to God, a

distinction without a sharer! When the praises of virgins are sung, it is said, that they follow the Lamb whithersoever He goeth (Apoc. xiv. 4), of what praise shall she be thought worthy, who even goes before Him?

8. Learn, O man, to obey; learn, O dust and ashes, to abase thyself and submit. The Evangelist, speaking of thy Creator, says: *He was obedient to them*, that is, to Mary and Joseph. Blush then, O ashes, that darest to be proud! God humbles Himself, and dost thou raise thyself up? God submits Himself unto men, and dost thou lord it over thy fellow creatures, and prefer thyself to thy Creator? Would that God, if ever I should nourish such an inclination, would deign to reply to me as He once reproached His Apostle: *Get thee behind Me, Satan, for thou savourest not the things which be of God* (S. Matt. xvi. 23). . . .

9. But happy was Mary: to her neither humility was wanting, nor virginity. And what a virginity was that, which Maternity did not violate, but honoured. And what an incomparable maternity, which both virginity and humility accompanied. Is there anything here, which is not admirable, incomparable and unique? Will not anyone hesitate in deciding which is the more worthy of admiration, which is the more wonderful, the Birth from a Virgin or Virginity in a Mother: the exalted rank of the Son, or the great humility in exaltation: except that, without doubt, the whole is to be preferred to any of its parts, and that it is incomparably more excellent and more happy to obtain the whole, than any part of it. And what wonder is there, if God, Who is *wonderful in His saints* (Ps. lxviii. 35. VULG.), has shown Himself still more wonderful in His Mother? Reverence then, O you who are married, the purity of the flesh in corruptible flesh: you also, holy virgins, admire the Motherhood in a Virgin: and all ye who are men, imitate the humility of the Mother of God. Holy angels, honour the Mother of your King, ye who adore the Son of a Virgin of our race, Who is at once our King and yours, the Restorer of our race and the founder of your State. To Him, among you so exalted, among us so humble, be given equally by you and by us, the reverence which is His due, the honour and glory for His great condescension for ever and ever. Amen. . . .

17. The verse of the Evangelist ends thus: *And the Virgin's name was Mary*. Let us say a few words upon this name also. The word Mary means *Star of the Sea*, which seems to have a wonder-

ful fitness to the Virgin Mother. For she is fitly compared to a star; for just as a star sends forth its ray without injury to itself, so the Virgin, remaining a virgin, brought forth her Son. The ray does not diminish the clearness of the star, nor the Son of the Virgin her Virginity. She is even that noble star risen out of Jacob, whose ray enlightens the whole world, whose splendour both shines in the Heavens and penetrates into Hell: and as it traverses the lands, it causes minds to glow with virtues more than bodies with heat, while vices it burns up and consumes. She, I say, is that beautiful and admirable star, raised of necessity above this great and spacious sea of life, shining with virtues and affording an illustrious example. Whosoever thou art who knowest thyself to be tossed about among the storms and tempests of this troubled world rather than to be walking peacefully upon the shore, turn not thine eyes away from the shining of this star, if thou wouldst not be overwhelmed with the tempest. If the winds of temptation arise, if you are driving upon the rocks of tribulation, look to the star, invoke Mary. If you are tossed upon the waves of pride, of ambition, of envy, of rivalry, look to the star, invoke Mary. If wrath, avarice, temptations of the flesh assail the frail skiff of your mind, look to Mary. If you are troubled by the greatness of your crimes, confused by the foulness of your conscience, and desperate with the horror of judgment, you feel yourself drawn into the depth of sorrow and into the abyss of despair; in dangers, in difficulties, in perplexities: invoke and think of Mary. Let not the name depart from heart and from lips; and that you may obtain a part in the petitions of her prayer, do not desert the example of her life. If you think of and follow her you will not go wrong, nor despair if you beg of her. With her help you will not fall or be fatigued; if she is favourable you will be sure to arrive; and thus you will learn by your own experience how rightly it is said: *The Virgin's name was Mary*. But now let us stop for a little, that we may not have merely a passing glance at the lustre of the great light. For to use the words of the Apostles *It is good for us to be here;* it is a happiness to be able to contemplate in silence what a laboured discourse could not sufficiently explain. But in the meantime the pious contemplation of that brilliant star will give us new ardour for what remains to be said.

40. On Consideration

Toward the end of his life, during the years 1149 to 1153, Bernard composed a treatise which in many ways summarized the thoughts of a lifetime, certainly his views on the state of the Church in general and the position and duties of the supreme pontiff in particular. Few men have more eloquently expressed their loyalty to and veneration for the Holy See, but few, also, have been more outspoken in criticism of its shortcomings. The *De consideratione* was written for Pope Eugenius III, the former Bernard of Pisa, abbot of St. Vincent and Anastasius in Rome. He had long been a disciple and dear friend of his namesake of Clairvaux. In fact, his elevation to the papacy at first shocked St. Bernard, who evidently mourned the loss of a good monk. Yet the two men remained close, and it is not surprising that Eugenius should have urgently requested his former spiritual adviser to write these words of counsel.

St. Bernard had known Rome and its turbulence and had denounced Arnold of Brescia and the Roman republican movement. At the time he was writing the republic had in fact been established and had come to terms with Eugenius. More trouble lay ahead, but Eugenius had been able to return to the city in 1152 after a third absence. Although the temporal responsibilities of the papacy concerned Bernard, he was more interested in the problems created by the increasing centralization of ecclesiastical administration. He shows a remarkable awareness of both the advantages and dangers inherent in the manifold demands placed on the curia. Such matters as the excessive number of appeals did not escape his attention. He understood that a more numerous curial personnel was necessary, but he warned his protégé to see that only worthy men be chosen lest corruption be condoned.

Underlying the entire discussion is the principal theme of Bernard's treatise: consideration or deliberation, something akin to but not the same as contemplation, must be applied to the various duties confronting a pope. He must, in short, "consider" the people with whom he deals, his household, the cardinals, the church of Rome, the Church universal, the world outside. But he must not neglect himself and his own spiritual welfare. In the final section, the longest of all, he turns to that which must underlie any and every action of a pope, the highest consideration of all, the contemplation of God. And here Bernard the mystic rises to the heights.

In developing his theme in relation to all these concerns, St. Bernard produced a treatise on papal government which was at once a blueprint for the ideal, a frank criticism of the actual, and a remarkable summary of the principles of religious renewal as they had developed in his time. In fact, the *De consideratione* has been called a papal examination of conscience, a manual and guide not only for Eugenius but for all of his successors. Not many, it would seem, have attained the goal which Bernard set.

The translation is by a priest of Mount St. Melleray, *St. Bernard's Treatise on Consideration* (Dublin, 1921), pp. 1–144 *passim*. Reprinted by permission of Browne and Nolan Limited, Dublin.

Preface

. . . What matters it that thou hast ascended the papal throne? Even if thou were to "walk upon the wings of the winds" (Ps. xvii. 11) thou shalt not withdraw thyself from my affection. . . . Though thou shouldst mount up to heaven, though thou shouldst descend into the abyss, thou canst not escape from me: I will follow thee whithersoever thou goest. I have loved thee poor and I will love thee now that thou art become the father both of rich and poor. For unless I am grievously mistaken in thee, even as the father of the poor thou wilt not cease to be poor in spirit. It is my hope and confidence that this change of rank has not been accompanied by any change of sentiment: that the old disposition has not yielded place but only a support to the new dignity. Therefore shall I admonish thee now, not as a master, but as a mother, yea, as a most loving mother. Some, as I perceive, will think me beside myself, but only such as know not what it is to love, only such as have never experienced in themselves the violence of a mother's affection.

Book I

[In Book I the author discusses the "multitudinous cares" of the papal office and emphasizes the necessity for consideration. The selections are taken from Chapters I, III, IV, VII, VIII, X, and XI.]

With what therefore had I best begin? Doubtless, with thy occupations, because it is especially with regard to them that I condole with thee. I say I *condole with* thee, but that is only true on condition that thou art grieving for thyself. . . . Yes, this is what I am most afraid of, that despairing of ever seeing the end of the multitudinous cares which distract thee, thou shouldst begin at last to stifle thy conscience, and thus little by little to deaden this sense of good and salutary discomfort. How much more prudent would it not be to withdraw thyself from thy occupations occasionally, even for a short time, instead of allowing them to overwhelm thee and to lead thee gradually "whither thou wouldst not" (John xxi. 18)! Wither is that, dost thou inquire? To hardness of heart. Ask me not what this means. For if thou art without fear for thyself, it is something which is already thine. It is only the heart which is hardened that abhors not itself, as not sensible of its evil. . . .

Tell me, I pray thee, what kind of life is it to be daily occupied from dawn to dusk in pleading causes or listening to pleaders? And would to God the day were sufficient for the evil thereof! But alas! the litigations even encroach upon the night. Hardly enough time is left free to satisfy the poor body's natural need of rest, and then up again to resume the wrangling! . . .

What slavery can be more degrading and more unworthy of the Sovereign Pontiff than to be kept thus busily employed, I do not say every day, but every hour of every day, in furthering the sordid designs of greed and ambition? What leisure hast thou left for prayer? What time remains over to thee for instructing the people, for edifying the Church, for meditating on the law? True, thy palace is made to resound daily with noisy discussions relating to law, but it is not the law of the Lord, but the law of Justinian. Is this as it ought to be? Let thy conscience answer. "The law of the Lord is unspotted, converting souls," as the Psalmist sings (Ps. xviii. 8): but as to these other laws, they seem to serve no better purpose than to furnish occasions for quarrels and quibbling, which tend to subvert rather than to enlighten the judgment. Then tell me, I pray thee, with what conscience canst thou, the supreme "Shepherd and Bishop of souls" (I Peter ii. 25), permit the former to be condemned to perpetual silence in thy court, whilst allowing the latter to deafen thee with an uninterrupted clamour? I am greatly mistaken if thou canst contemplate so shocking an abuse with an easy mind. I suspect that thou art sometimes constrained to cry out to the Lord in the words of the Prophet, "The wicked have told me fables, but not as Thy law" (Ps. cxviii. 85). . . .

. . . I am asking nothing hard of thee, nothing thou canst not easily do. I do not require of thee to renounce the judicial office altogether. . . .

But it is one thing to adjudge civil questions occasionally when necessity requires, and quite another to devote thyself freely and exclusively to this office, as if it were something great and worthy to engross the attention of the Vicar of Christ. This, therefore, and a great deal besides to the same purpose, should I say to thee, if I desired to speak of what relates to fortitude, to fittingness, and to truth. But "because the days are evil" (Ephes. v. 16), let it suffice to have admonished thee not to give thyself up completely or uninterruptedly to action, but to reserve for consideration something of thyself, of thy heart, and of thy time. . . .

The first effect of consideration is to purify the mind which has given it birth. Then it regulates the affections, directs the actions, cuts away all excesses, forms the character, orders and ennobles the life, and lastly, it endows the understanding with a knowledge of things divine and human. It is consideration which distinguishes what is confused, unites what is divided, collects what is scattered, discovers what is concealed, searches out what is true, examines what is probable, exposes what is false and deceptive. It is consideration which preordains what we have to do, and passes in review what has been accomplished, so that nothing disordered may remain in the mind, nor anything requiring correction. It is consideration, finally, which in prosperity makes provision for adversity, and thus endures misfortune, as it were, without feeling it, of which the former is the part of prudence, and the latter the function of fortitude.

Consideration will also show thee the beautiful concord and connection which exists between the virtues, and how they depend one upon the other. . . .

However, I have no intention to treat here of the virtues in particular. The foregoing remarks have been made merely for the purpose of exciting thee to apply thyself to consideration, which leads us to the knowledge of such truths as those I have been discussing. For wasted surely will thy life have been, if no part thereof be devoted to so useful and sacred a study. . . . I would have thee to decide after a brief and careful hearing those suits which it is necessary thou shouldst adjudge in person—this necessity will not extend to all—and to exclude all those unnecessary delays which are designed for the purpose either of defeating justice or of multiplying fees. Let the cause of the widow have free access to thy tribunal, and the cause of the poor, and of him from whom thou hast nothing to hope for. There will be many other suits, the decision of which thou canst entrust to subordinates, and a large number may be dismissed at once as unworthy of any hearing at all. For what is the use of granting a hearing to those whose "sins are manifest, going before them to judgment" (I Tim. v. 24)? Yet so brazen is the impudence of some that, although the whole face of their cause bears the manifest stamp of ambition, they still have the effrontery to ask for a hearing, thus proclaiming their guilt to the knowledge of many, whereas, in truth, their own conscience should suffice to confound them. Hitherto there has been no one to repress the audacity of such persons, and consequently they have increased both in numbers and in shamelessness. . . .

If thou wouldst be a true disciple of Christ, let thy zeal be enkindled and thy authority exerted against this impudence, this universal plague. Look at the example which the Master has given thee, and remember His words, "If any man minister to Me, let him follow Me" (John xii. 26). He, so far from granting a hearing to the sacrilegious traffickers, made a whip to scourge them out of the temple. . . . For thou also art armed with a scourge. Let the money-changers tremble; let their money be to them a source, not of confidence, but of fear; let them be anxious to hide their gold from thee, as knowing that thou art more ready to pour it out than to accept it. By acting in this manner with constancy and zeal, thou shalt gain many, converting the hunters after filthy lucre to more honourable occupations; and thou shalt also preserve many from the temptation to this vice, for they will not dare to attempt what they behold thee so much opposed to. A further advantage from this mode of acting is, that it will enable thee to secure those intervals of leisure which I have so earnestly recommended. For thou shalt have many a vacant hour to devote to consideration, if, according to my counsel, thou wilt dismiss some causes unheard, refer others to subordinates, and decide such as are worthy to come before thine own tribunal after as brief an investigation as is consistent with thoroughness. . . .

Book II

[Book II defines consideration and explains its objectives.]

SELECTIONS FROM CHAPTER II, III, IV

In the first place, then, observe what I mean by consideration. I would not have thee to understand it as identical in all respects with contemplation, because, whereas this latter occupies itself with truths already known, the former is concerned with the investigation of truth. According to this sense, contemplation may be defined as the true and certain intuition of any object by the intellect, or as the certain apprehension of truth; and consideration as an intense exercise of thought in inquiry, or as an intense application of the mind to the investigation of truth. Nevertheless the two terms are commonly used without distinction. . . .

Now, with respect to the matter of consideration, there are four objects which, as I think, ought particularly to engage thy attention, and in the order in which they are here set down: thou thyself, things beneath thee, things about thee, things above thee. Let thy consideration begin with thyself, for if thine own self be neglected, attention to other things can be of little avail. "What doth it profit a man if he gain the whole world, and suffer the loss of his own soul?" . . .

The consideration of thyself may be divided into three points. Thou mayest consider what thou art, who thou art, and what kind thou art: what thou art by nature, who thou art in rank and dignity, what kind thou are in character and disposition. Thus, it would be an answer to the first question to say that thou art a man; to the second, that thou art Pope or Sovereign Pontiff; to the third, that thou art gentle, kind, and so forth. And although the investigation of the first of these points belongs more to the disciple of Aristotle than to the successor of St. Peter, there is something nevertheless in the definition usually given of man, viz., a mortal rational animal, which, if it seems good to thee, thou mayest with profit consider more attentively. Such a study has nothing in it which would be out of keeping either with thy dignity as Pontiff or with thy profession as a monk, whereas it might contribute importantly to thy spiritual progress. . . .

SELECTIONS FROM CHAPTER V, VI

Consider in the next place who thou art now and who thou wert formerly. . . . Thou hast not yet forgotten thy first profession; although thou hast been torn from its protection, the love and the recollection of it remain with thee still. It will be very profitable for thee to keep the thought of it before thy mind in all thy injunctions, in all thy judgments, and in all thy undertakings, for it will make thee a despiser of honour even in the height of honour—and that is no small benefit. Never suffer it to leave thy memory: it will be as a shield to protect thee from even this fatal arrow: "And man when he was in honour did not understand" (Ps. xlviii. 13).

Therefore, speak thus to thyself: " 'Formerly I was an abject in the house of my God' (Ps. lxxxiii. 11). How then has it come to pass that I am lifted up out of poverty and abjection and set over peoples and kingdoms? Who am I and what is my father's house (I Par. xvii. 16) that I should be placed above princes? Undoubtedly, He Who said to me, 'Friend, go up higher' (Luke xiv. 10) expects that I shall prove His friend. It is not expedient for me, therefore, to disappoint His expectation. . . .

That thou hast been raised to the pinnacle of honour and power is a fact undeniable. But for what purpose hast thou been thus elevated? Here is a question that calls for the most serious consideration. It was not, as I suppose, merely that thou mightest enjoy the glory of lordship.

. . . Always bear this in mind, that a duty of service has been imposed on us, and not a dominion conferred. . . . Does the Pontifical See which thou art occupying flatter thy pride? Regard it as a watch-tower. Thou art placed there for no other purpose than to exercise surveillance over the Church. For even the name of bishop (*episcopus*) expresses rather the duty of superintendence than the power of ruling. And why shouldst not thou, who art the universal supervisor, be placed on an eminence whence thou canst oversee all the world? Yet this superintendence has little leisure in it and incessant toil. How, then, canst thou glory in an office which never allows thee a moment's rest? Surely repose is impossible where "solicitude for all the churches" (I Cor. xi. 28) is constantly pressing. And what else but this has the holy Apostle Peter bequeathed thee? . . .

CHAPTER VIII

Well, then, let us examine with still greater diligence who thou art, that is to say, what role thou fulfillest, according to the time, in the Church of God. Who art thou? Thou art the High Priest and the Sovereign Pontiff. Thou art the Prince of pastors and the Heir of the apostles. By thy primacy thou art an Abel; by thy office of pilot (in Peter's barque), a Noe; by thy patriarchate, an Abraham; by thy orders, a Melchisedech; by thy dignity, an Aaron; by thy

authority, a Moses; by thy judicial power, a Samuel; by thy jurisdiction, a Peter; and by thy unction, a Christ. Thou art he to
whom the keys have been delivered (Matt. xvi. 19) and the sheep
entrusted (John xxi. 17). There are indeed other gate-keepers of
heaven, and there are other shepherds of the flock; but thou art in
both respects more glorious than they in proportion as thou hast
"inherited a more excellent name" (Heb. i. 4). They have assigned
to them particular portions of the flock, his own to each; whereas
thou art given charge of all the sheep, as the one Chief Shepherd of
the whole flock. Yea, not only of the sheep, but of the other
pastors also art thou the sole supreme Shepherd. Wouldst thou
know how I prove this? I prove it from the words of Christ. "If
thou lovest Me," He said to Peter, "feed My sheep" (John xxi.
17). . . .

Therefore, according to thine own canons, whilst the other
bishops are called to a share of the solicitudes of government, thou
art invested with the plentitude of power. Their authority is confined within certain limits, but thine extends itself even to them
that have received power over others. Hast not thou the power to
shut the kingdom of heaven even to a bishop, when necessity
demands it, and to deprive him of his see, yea, and to deliver him
over to Satan (I Cor. v. 5)? Thy prerogative, therefore, remains
secure and inviolable, both by reason of the keys entrusted to thy
keeping and by reason of the flock committed to thy care. . . .

CHAPTER IX

Now thou knowest *who* thou art. But remember also *what* thou
art. . . . Thinkest thou that thou didst enter this world wearing
the tiara? or glittering with jewels? or clothed in silk? or adorned
with plumes? or bespangled with gold? No. If, then, from before
the face of thy consideration thou wilt with a breath, so to speak,
blow away these things, as morning mists that quickly pass and
disappear: thou shalt behold a man, naked and poor, and wretched
and miserable. . . . Justly, then, is he described as "filled with
many miseries," since to the infirmity of his flesh and the fatuity of
his spirit there is added the heritage of guilt and the doom of
dissolution. I will now recommend to thee a wholesome combination. Whenever thou rememberest thy dignity as Sovereign Pontiff, reflect also that not only wert thou once, but that thou art still

nothing better than the vilest slime of the earth. Let not thy consideration imitate nature, let it rather imitate a worthier model, the Author of nature, by uniting what is highest with what is lowest. For does not nature unite in the human person an immortal soul with the slime of the earth. And has not the Author of nature in His own Person wedded the Word Divine to our common clay? Do thou, therefore, take to thyself an example as well from the primitive constitution of our nature as from the mystery of our redemption; so that, although seated on high, thou mayest not be high-minded, but humble in thy conceit of thyself, and "consenting to the humble" (Rom. xii. 16).

Selections from Chapter X, XI

But after considering how great thou art in rank and dignity, thou shouldst consider likewise and especially what kind thou art in disposition and character. This consideration will confine thee to thyself, it will not suffer thee to fly far away from thy centre, neither will it allow thee to "walk in great matters or in wonderful things above thee" (Ps. cxxx. 2). For thou oughtest to be content with thyself and thine own measure, not going beyond thy limits either in height or in depth, either in length or in breadth. If thou wouldst not lose the mean of virtue, keep thyself in the middle place. Here shalt thou find security, here is the seat of the golden mean, and the golden mean is virtue. . . .

Thou must proceed with great caution, therefore, in this consideration of thyself, and act with the most perfect honesty, so that thou mayest neither attribute to thyself more than is due to thee, nor spare thyself more than is right. But thou mayest attribute to thyself overmuch, not only by pretending to the good which thou hast not but also by appropriating the good which thou hast. So be careful to distinguish what thou art of thyself from what thou art by the grace of God, and let there be no guile in thy spirit (Ps. xxxi. 2). But guile there will be, unless, making a faithful division, thou renderest to God without fraud the things that are God's (Matt. xxii. 21) and to thyself what is thine. Thou art persuaded, I doubt not, that whatever thou hast of evil is thine own produce, and that all thy good is from the Lord.

But whilst considering what manner of man thou art now, it will evidently be of advantage to recall to mind what thy dispositions were formerly. Thy present state of soul ought to be compared with thy past. Thou must examine and see whether thou hast made progress in virtue, in wisdom, in understanding, in sweetness of manners, or whether (which God forbid!) there has been some falling off in any of these respects. . . . It is necessary that thou shouldst ascertain what thy zeal is, and what thy clemency, what thy discretion also, which is the regulator of these two other virtues; that is to say, thou must reflect upon thy manner of condoning and upon thy manner of avenging injuries, and find out how far thou dost observe propriety in both, with regard to measure, place, and time. It is absolutely essential to take account of these three circumstances in the exercise of clemency and zeal, which without them, or any one of them, would cease to be virtues at all. . . . Thou shalt not be guiltless, if either thou punishest him who ought to be spared, or if thou sparest him who deserves to be punished. . . .

Let thy consideration apply itself now to the things beneath thee. But perhaps it will be wiser to reserve this subject for another book, as a short discourse will better fall in with the multiplicity of thy occupations.

Book III

[The papal office is a stewardship and its functioning should not be impeded by excessive appeals, dispensations, etc.]

CHAPTER I

This third book begins at the point where the second concluded; for in accordance with the promise made at the close of the latter, I will now propose for thy consideration the things that are beneath thee. O Eugenius, best of priests, do not imagine there is any necessity to ask me what these are. Perhaps it would be more reasonable to inquire what they are not. For he who wishes to discover something which does not appertain to thy charge, will have to go outside the world. Thy predecessors, the holy apostles, were sent forth to conquer for Christ, not this or that particular nation, but the whole universe. "Go ye into the whole world and preach the Gospel to every creature" (Mark xvi. 15)—such was their commission. . . . Thou hast succeeded them in their inheritance. Consequently, thou art the heir of the apostles, and thy inheritance is the whole world. But in what respect this portion has fallen to thee, or in what respect it fell to them, is a matter which calls for thy most serious consideration. For not in all respects, as I think, but only in some, has it been made thine or thy predecessors': thou hast been charged with its administration, not endowed with it as a possession. . . . Consequently, I should like to impress upon thee that, however great and exalted thou mayest consider the prerogatives of thy pontifical office, thou art under a grievous delusion, if thou thinkest thou hast inherited anything more from the great apostles than the administration of the Church. Remember now the words of St. Paul, "To the wise and to the unwise I am a debtor" (Rom. i. 14). And if thou deemest it a duty to make them thine own, remember this also, that the unattractive name of debtor more properly designates a servant than a master. . . . Therefore thou art a debtor to the infidels also, whether Jews, Greeks, or Gentiles.

From this it follows that thou art obliged to do all in thy power that unbelievers may be converted to the faith, that they may not fall away after conversion, and that they who have lapsed may return. Let them that have gone astray be brought back to the right road; let them that have been perverted be restored to truth; and let the seducers be confounded with invincible arguments, so that they may correct themselves—if that is possible: otherwise let them be deprived of all authority, and therewith of the power to lead others astray. Thy zeal must by no means refuse to occupy itself even with that class of the unwise which is the worst of all: I mean heretics and schismatics, who are perverted themselves and the perverters of others, who rend and tear like dogs, and deceive like foxes. These, I say, ought particularly to engage thy attention, so that they may either be converted and saved, or at least prevented from propagating their errors. With regard to the Jews, I allow that the time excuses thine inactivity: they have "appointed for them their bounds which cannot be passed" (Job xiv. 5). "The fulness of the gentiles must come in" before the blindness is taken away that hath happened in Israel (Rom. xi. 25). But concerning the Gentiles, what excuse canst thou make? . . .

Reflect thus with thyself on these matters. I should also like to direct thy attention to the obstinacy of the Greeks, who are with us in a sense and in a sense are not with us: united with us in faith, divided from us in communion. Although even in matters of faith they have not continued to walk in the right way but "have halted from their paths" (Ps. xvii. 46). . . .

CHAPTER II

Since I have happened on the subject of appeals, perhaps I had better go into it a little further. In matters of this nature thou hast need of much pious vigilance, lest abuse should render unprofitable what has been established to meet a crying necessity. Nay, it seems to me that appeals may become the source of great and manifold mischief unless they are conducted with the utmost caution. Men appeal to the Sovereign Pontiff from every part of the world. That in itself is testimony to thy supreme and singular authority. . . . Could anything be more fitting than that the invocation of thy name should bring deliverance to the oppressed and leave no escape to the crafty? On the other hand, what could be more perverse, more repugnant to one's sense of right and justice, than that the evildoer should have cause to rejoice at the result of the appeal, whilst he who has suffered the wrong should have wearied himself in vain? It would certainly be most cruel of thee not to feel compassion for a man who, in addition to the pain of the original wrong, has had to endure the labour of a long journey, to say nothing about the costs of the case; but thou wouldst show thyself not less apathetic and cowardly, wert thou not moved to indignation against him who has been in part the cause and in part the occasion of so many misfortunes to his brother. Arouse thyself, thou man of God, whenever such things occur. Let thy compassion be stirred, and stirred too thy anger. The first is due to him who has suffered the wrong; the second to him who has done it. Let the injured party be consoled by the repayment of his expenses, by the redress of his grievances, and by a speedy deliverance from legal chicanery. As for the other, deal with him in such a manner that he may repent of having done what he was not afraid to do, and that he may have no reason to mock at the misery of his victim.

But I think that he who makes an unnecessary appeal should suffer the same punishment as the convicted oppressor. This is the form of justice prescribed to thee, both by the immutable law of divine equity and, unless I mistake, even by the ecclesiastical law of appeals, so that an unjust resort to these shall neither injure the appellees nor profit the appellants. For why should an innocent man be subjected to annoyance and obliged without any necessity to undertake a wearisome journey? And what could be more just than that he who designed to injure his neighbour should rather injure himself? Therefore to appeal unnecessarily is a manifest injustice; and to allow unnecessary appeals to go unpunished is to encourage their multiplication. Hence we must regard as unjust every appeal to which the appellant is not constrained by the impossibility of otherwise obtaining justice. The right of appeal is granted us, not to be used as a means of oppression, but as a means of deliverance from oppression. Appeals should only be made from the sentence of an inferior judge. They are unlawful whenever they anticipate this sentence, except in the case where such anticipation is rendered necessary by manifest injustice. He therefore who makes an appeal whilst suffering no wrong, betrays an intention either to oppress his neighbour or simply to gain time. As if, forsooth, appeals had been instituted rather to serve as a subterfuge for guilt, than as a refuge for innocence. . . . For they are now made without justice or right, without either order or the sanction of usage. There is no observance of propriety with regard either to place, or time, or manner, or cause, or person. . . .

The wicked appeal against the righteous to prevent them from doing good; and these, terrified by the thunders of Rome, abstain from speaking in their own justification. . . . What mystery of iniquity have we here? It is more thy duty to ponder it than mine to discuss it. But perhaps thou wilt ask me why those who are unjustly appealed against do not come forward to establish their innocence and to confound their malicious accusers? I will tell thee what answer they are wont to make to this. "We do not want," they say, "to weary ourselves to no purpose. For the judges who preside in the papal court are accustomed to favour appellants and to encourage appeals. Consequently, as we should certainly lose our case there, we prefer to yield at home and so save ourselves the expense and trouble of a useless journey."

For myself, I cannot say that my own opinion of the papal court is altogether different. For out of all the numberless appellants who come for a hearing at the present time, canst thou point to a single one that has been obliged to repay the travelling expenses of his appellee? Now surely it is a very extraordinary thing that before thy tribunal all appellants have been found to be in the right and all appellees in the wrong! . . . I acknowledge, therefore, that the right of appeal is a great boon to mankind in general; I even consider it not less necessary for mortals than the sun which enlightens the world. For in truth it may be regarded as a sun of justice, since by its means the works of darkness are exposed and reproved. Obviously, then, appeals have a claim to thy attention and protection, yet only such as necessity demands, not also those which cunning has recourse to. These latter are but so many abuses, designed rather to foster iniquity than to relieve distress. . . .

Let me now offer thee some examples of the abuse whereof I have been speaking. A young man and a young woman have been publicly espoused to each other. The day appointed for the marriage is come. A great number of guests have been invited, and now all is in readiness. But lo! one who covets his neighbour's affianced suddenly interrupts with an appeal, affirming that the maiden had been first espoused to himself, and is under an obligation to marry him. The fiancé is bewildered; there is general consternation; the sacred minister dares not proceed further with the ceremony; the expenses incurred in the preparation are gone for nothing; every man descends to his own house to eat his own supper; and the bride that was to be is excluded from the table and the society of her intended husband pending the arrival of a verdict from Rome! This happened in Paris, the metropolis of France and the residence of her royalty. Take a second instance. In the same city of Paris another young couple were engaged to each other and had fixed upon the day for the nuptials. But in the meantime a groundless objection was made by certain individuals, who pretended that it was not lawful for the parties to marry. The matter was referred to the eccesiastical court of the diocese. But without awaiting the decision of this tribunal, without reason or necessity, solely with the intention of causing delay and disappointment, the plaintiffs appealed to Rome. The fiancé, however, either because he was unwilling to lose the expenses incurred in his preparations, or because he would not submit to be any longer separated from his betrothed, whatever the reason, despised or disregarded the appeal, and had the marriage celebrated on the day appointed. What shall I say of the presumptuous attempt made by a young man recently in the church of Auxerre? The former holy bishop having died, the clergy assembled according to custom and were proceeding to elect a successor, when this youth interposed with an appeal, and forbade them to go on with the election until he had come back from Rome! Yet he himself refused to submit to the authority of the court to which he had appealed. For, when he saw himself despised there as an unreasonable appellant, he gathered about him as many sympathisers as he could, and held an election of his own, three days after the other election had taken place. . . .

. . . Wouldst thou repress more thoroughly the contempt for appeals? Kill the evil germ in its evil root. And the best way to accomplish this is by visiting the abuse of appeals with severe penalties. Put a stop to the abuse. . . .

CHAPTER IV

Let us come now to another question, if yet it is indeed another; for, in some respects at any rate, it may be viewed not unreasonably as identical with the last. I will leave this, however, for thy consideration to decide. . . . To what do I allude? Listen: abbots are exempted from the jurisdiction of bishops, bishops from the jurisdiction of archbishops, archbishops from the jurisdiction of patriarchs or primates. Has not this at least the semblance of evil? I shall be very much surprised if the thing itself can be shown to be other than evil. By acting in this arbitrary way thou provest clearly enough that thou hast the plenitude of power, but not so clearly that thou hast also the plenitude of justice. Thou dost these things because thou hast the power: but whether thou hast the right as well is a matter open to question. For thou hast been appointed Head of the Church to preserve to the various orders in the hierarchy their respective degrees of honour and dignity, not surely to confound them out of envy. Hence one of thy predecessors tells thee to "render honour to whom honour is due" (Rom. xiii. 7).

Do not try to excuse these exemptions by telling me of their fruit. I deny that there is any fruit—except indeed that they have made bishops more arrogant and religious more lax, to say nothing of increasing their poverty. Examine carefully the resources and the conduct of the communities thus exempted from episcopal authority—they are everywhere to be found—and tell me if thou dost not find in the former extreme scantiness, in the latter serious disorder. . . . Dispensations are excusable when necessity demands them; they are even praiseworthy when utility suggests them—I speak of *public*, not of *private* utility. But where there is neither necessity nor utility to justify them, they are no longer faithful exercises of administrative power, but rather acts of criminal dissipation. Nevertheless, who does not know that there are many monasteries, situated in different dioceses, which, in accordance with the will of their founders, have been always immediately subject to the Apostolic See? But there is a great difference between his case who out of devotion desires to be directly dependent on the Vicar of Christ, and the case of him who wants this relation with Rome from a motive of ambition and as a means of escape from episcopal authority. Let so much suffice on this subject.

<h2 style="text-align:center">CHAPTER V</h2>

It remains for thee now to direct thy attention to the general state of the whole Church, to see if the people are submissive to the clergy, with all due humility, the clergy to the bishops, and the bishops to God; to see if good order and strict discipline are maintained in monasteries and other religious establishments; to see if evil deeds and false doctrines are sternly repressed by ecclesiastical censures; to see if the mystical vines are flourishing by reason of the virtues and good morals of the priests, and if the flowers are yielding fruit in the obedience of a faithful people; to see if thine own apostolical decrees and the constitutions of thy predecessors are observed with becoming solicitude; to see finally lest there should be anything growing wild through neglect in the field of thy Lord, or anything surreptitiously removed therefrom. Doubt not that something needing correction can still be discovered. To say nothing of the many, yea innumerable, vines which everywhere lie prostrate and uncared for, I could show thee not a few, even of those which thine own right hand hath planted, already plucked up by the roots. At the late Council of Rheims [1148] did not thine own mouth promulgate the subjoined canons? But who now observes them? Who has ever observed them? If thou believest that they are obeyed, thou art labouring under a grave delusion. If thou dost not so believe, thou hast sinned by making laws which no one was obliged to obey, or by conniving at the general disregard of thy authority. . . .

. . . It is now four years since the promulgation of these ordinances, and during that period not once have we been excited to

sorrow by the spectacle of a cleric deprived of his benefice, or of a
bishop suspended from episcopal functions. But the only real
consequence of this legislation is something worthy to be wept
with bitterest tears. Dost thou ask me what that is? It is impunity,
the daughter of indifference, the mother of arrogance, the root of
impudence, the nurse of transgression. Blessed art thou if with all
assiduity thou endeavourest to guard against this indifference,
which is the first parent of all our evils. But I think I have said
enough to make thee solicitous on this point. And now lift up thine
eyes and see if to-day no less than formerly the clerical state is not
dishonoured by the use of particoloured garments, and by the
affectation of a fashion which outrages modesty. Those that transgress in this manner are accustomed to say when reproved "Hath
God care of garments and not rather of morals?" But this fashion
of dress indicates a depravity of mind and a corruption of morals.
Wherefore should clerics desire to be one thing and to appear
another, offending thereby against both modesty and truth?
Judged by their dress they appear to be soldiers, but in the way
they get their living they are more like churchmen, whilst their
manner of life proclaims them to be neither the one nor the
other. . . . Oh, what a misfortune for the Spouse of Christ to
have been entrusted to the care of such paranymphs, who are not
ashamed to keep for their own use and profit what was intended
for her adornment! Surely they are no friends but rather the rivals
of the heavenly Bridegroom.

Book IV

[The pope and his own household, the cardinals, the Roman people.]

CHAPTER I

 . . . Having therefore examined the first objects of consideration in the preceding books, I shall occupy myself in this with a
discussion of the things which are about thee. As a matter of fact,
these things also are beneath thee, yet they are closer to thee than
the objects last treated of, and because of their greater vicinity may
give thee greater trouble; for inasmuch as they are placed before
thine eyes, thou canst neither disregard them, nor forget them, nor
pretend not to see them. They press upon thee more violently,

they rush in upon thee more tumultuously, so as to make me apprehensive lest thou shouldst be sometimes overwhelmed. I have no doubt that thine own experience has taught thee sufficiently what need there is for the most careful and earnest consideration with regard to these things. . . . I am speaking now of that "daily instance" (II Cor. xi. 28) which thou sufferest from the city, from the court, and from thine own particular church. These, I say, are what I mean by the things about thee: the clergy and people of whom thou art bishop in a more especial manner, and with the care of whom, consequently, thou art more especially charged; also those who are constantly at thy side, the seniors of the people and the judges of the earth; likewise they that are of thy household and sit at thy table, thy chaplains, chamberlains, and the other officers who serve thee in thy palace. . . .

Chapter II

I say, then, in the first place, that the Roman clergy ought to be the most irreproachable of all, because it is to them principally that the clergy of every other church look for their models. Moreover, any abuses amongst the clergy over whom thou dost more especially preside, will redound more particularly to thy discredit. It therefore concerns the honour of thy name to see to it that those ecclesiastics who live with thee shall be so well disciplined and so well regulated as to be worthy to serve as mirrors and models of all virtues and good behaviour. They should be found distinguished from the rest by greater devotion to their sacred functions, by greater fitness for the administration of the sacraments, by greater zeal for the instruction of the people, and by greater care and solicitude to keep themselves in all purity. But what shall I say of thy people? They are the Roman people! I cannot express what I think of them more briefly and forcibly than by giving them this title. What fact has been so well known to every age as the arrogance and pride of the Romans? They are a people who are strangers to peace and accustomed to tumult; a people ferocious and intractable even until now; a people that know not how to submit whilst resistance is possible. Behold thy cross. The care of this people has been entrusted to thee, and that charge thou mayest not neglect. Perchance thou wilt only laugh at me for speaking thus, as being fully persuaded that the Romans are absolutely incorrigible. Nevertheless, do not lose heart. What is required of thee is not the *cure* of the patient but the solicitous *care* of him. "Take care of him," said the Good Samaritan to the innkeeper, not "cure him" or "heal him" (Luke x. 35). And one of the poets [Ovid] has said:—

> The patient oft is found so ill
> That naught avails the doctor's skill. . . .

I have now come to a delicate and difficult part of my subject. And I see plainly what will happen the moment I begin to express my sentiments. What I suggest will be denounced as a novelty, because it cannot be condemned as unjust. But that it is even a novelty I refuse to admit. For I know that it was even a common practice in former times. . . . Well then, amongst thy predecessors there have been those who devoted themselves unreservedly to the care of their flocks, who gloried in the shepherd's name and functions, who thought nothing unworthy of them except what they regarded as prejudicial to the salvation of souls, who, so far from seeking the things that were their own (Philipp. ii. 21), rather sacrificed their personal interests to the good of their people. They were sparing neither of their pains nor of their means, yea, not even did they spare themselves. Hence thou hearest one of them crying out to his sheep, "I most gladly will spend and be spent myself for your souls" (2 Cor. xii. 15). . . .

Where, I ask, is that custom now? It has given place to another very different in kind. . . . Nowadays—and surely it is an intolerable scandal—very few look to the lawgiver's mouth, but all bend their eyes on his hands. And not without good reason. For of late it is by means of the bribes and gifts of their hand that the Sovereign Pontiffs have been accustomed to transact all their business. Canst thou point to a single person amongst the immense population of Rome who would have acknowledged thee as Pope without either a bribe or the expectation of a bribe? . . . Silver coins are seen to glitter in the mud. There is a rush from all directions. But it is not the more indigent that secures the prize, but rather he who has the advantage in bodily strength, or who in fleetness of foot is superior to his competitors. I cannot say that this usage, or better, this crying abuse, began with thee: but God grant that it may end with thee.

But I must go on to speak of other scandals. In the midst of these depressing scenes I behold thee, the supreme Shepherd of the flock, advancing majestically, "in gilded clothing surrounded with variety" (Ps. xliv. 10). Tell me, what profit does the flock derive from such magnificent pageants? If I may venture to say it: they are better calculated to provide food for the wolves than pasture for the sheep. Thinkest thou that St. Peter loved to surround himself with this pomp and display, or St. Paul? Alas! the only object for which ecclesiastics show any zeal nowadays is the maintenance of their dignity. All their solicitude is for external honour and decorum, whilst for interior sanctity they care little, if anything at all.

Chapter III

. . . Now we nowhere find that Peter ever appeared in public adorned with silk and jewels, covered with cloth of gold, riding on a white horse, surrounded by a military escort, and a throng of clamorous attendants. And nevertheless it seemed to him that even without such aids he could accomplish sufficiently well the task enjoined him in the words, "If thou lovest Me, feed My sheep" (John xxi. 17). In all that belongs to earthly magnificence thou hast succeeded not Peter, but Constantine. However, I would counsel thee to tolerate this pomp and this splendour at least for a time, yet not to desire them as if they were essential to thy state. But I exhort thee more particularly to attend to those things which I know to fall within the scope of thy duties. Even though thou art clothed in purple and gold, that is no reason why thou, who art a shepherd's heir, shouldst avoid the labours and solicitude of a shepherd; that, I say, is no reason why thou shouldst be ashamed of the Gospel. But if, so far from being ashamed of the Gospel, thou dost preach it with a willing heart, thou hast glory even amongst the great apostles. To preach the Gospel is to pasture the flock. Consequently, "do the work of an evangelist" (2 Tim. iv. 5), that is, of a Gospel preacher, and thou hast also discharged the duties of a shepherd.

"What?" thou wilt say, "dost thou tell me to pasture these who are not sheep but dragons and scorpions?" All the more reason why thou shouldst endeavour to subdue them, not indeed with the sword, but with the word of God. For wherefore shouldst thou try again to wield that sword which thou wert commanded of old to replace in its scabbard? Nevertheless, he who would deny that the sword belongs to thee, has not, as I conceive, sufficiently weighed the words of the Lord, where He said, speaking to Peter, "Put up *thy* sword into the scabbard" (John xviii. 11). For it is here plainly implied that even the material sword is thine, to be drawn at thy bidding, although not by thy hand. Besides, unless this sword also appertained to thee in some sense, when the disciples said to Christ, "Lord, behold here are two swords" (Luke xxii. 38), He would never have answered as He did, "It is enough," but rather, "it is too much." We can therefore conclude that both swords, namely the spiritual and the material, belong to the Church, and that although only the former is to be wielded by her own hand, the two are to be employed in her service. It is for the priest to use the sword of the word, but to strike with the sword of steel belongs to the soldier, yet this must be by the authority and will (*ad nutum*) of the priest and by the direct command of the emperor, as I have said elsewhere.[1] . . .

Chapter IV

Let us come now to those who sit at thy side and share with thee the solicitudes of government. They are thy constant and trusted associates. Wherefore, if they be good, thou more than others shalt benefit by their goodness; as on the contrary, if they be evil, they shall be evil especially for thee. . . . It is thy duty to summon from all parts of the world and to associate to thyself, after the example of Moses (Numb. xi. 16), not youths, but men of mature age, such as thou knowest to be the ancients of the people, reckoning age more by virtues than by years. Is it not reasonable that they should be selected from every nation whose office it shall be to judge all nations? No one should ever obtain this dignity by his own solicitation. In making such appointments thou oughtest to be influenced not at all by entreaty, but solely by considerations of prudence. . . . Consequently, so far as may be practicable, thou oughtest to select, not such as require to be proved, but rather such as have already proved themselves. . . .

Therefore, it is neither he that willeth nor he that runneth

---

1. This passage was often cited in later times by exponents of the superiority of the spiritual power over the temporal.

(Rom. ix. 16) whom thou oughtest to select, but rather he that hesitates and he that refuses. These thou must even constrain and oblige to enter. It is on such, it seems to me, that thy spirit shall rest; on such, namely, as are not of a hardened forehead, but modest and diffident; who will fear nothing except to offend God, and hope for nothing except from God; who will look not to the hands but to the necessities of those that claim their assistance; who will manfully take the side of the persecuted, and "reprove with equity for the meek of the earth" (Is. xi. 4); whom thou shalt find to be men of irreproachable character and of true sanctity, prompt in obedience, exercised in patience, submissive to rule, rigorously just in their censures, orthodox in faith, conscientious in their administration, devoted to peace, lovers of unity and concord, righteous in their judgments, provident in their counsels, prudent in their commands, diligent in preparing, strenuous in acting, modest in speech, confident in adversity, faithful in prosperity, sober in their zeal; whose mercy will not degenerate into softness; whose leisure will not be a time of sloth; who will show hospitality without going to excess, and who will know how to restrain themselves at the banquet; who will not be over solicitous concerning temporalities, neither covetous of their neighbour's goods nor prodigal of their own, but always and in everything circumspect; who will not refuse to act as "ambassadors for Christ" (II Cor. iv. 20) whenever necessity or obedience requires it, yet may be equally trusted not to undertake anything such on their own responsibility; who will not obstinately reject what modesty may lead them to avoid; who, when despatched on any embassy, will not seek their own profit, but will walk in the Saviour's footsteps— will not look upon their mission as an opportunity for gain, but will be more concerned for the success of that mission than for any advantage to themselves; who will act the part of John Baptist in the presence of kings (Matt. xiv.), of Moses before tyrants (Exod. v.-xii.), of Phinees towards libertines (Numb. xxv.), of Elias towards idolators (III Kings xviii.), of Eliseus towards the avaricious (IV Kings v.), of Peter towards liars (Acts v.), of Paul towards blasphemers (Acts xiii.), of Christ towards sacrilegious traffickers (Matt. xxi. 12); who, instead of contemning will instruct the people, instead of flattering will terrify the rich, instead of oppressing will relieve the poor, instead of fearing will despise the threats of princes; who will not enter with uproar nor depart in wrath; who will not despoil but reform the churches; who will not empty the purses of the faithful, but will rather study how they may strengthen their hearts and purify them from their stains; who will be jealous of their own good name, without envying the reputation of others; whom thou shalt find possessed of both the love and the habit of prayer, and relying upon it for success more than upon their own labour and industry; whose coming shall bring peace, and whose going shall leave sorrow; whose speech shall be edifying, whose life shall be a pattern of all justice, whose presence shall give gladness, and whose memory shall be in benediction; who will make themselves amiable, not so much by words as by deeds, and excite men's wonder more by great actions than by magnificent displays; who will be humble with the humble, and innocent with the innocent (Ps. xvii. 26), yet will sternly reprove the obdurate, will curb the malignant, and will "render a reward to the proud" (Ps. xciii. 2); who will not make haste to enrich themselves and their dependents from the dowry of the widow and the patrimony of the Crucified, but will freely give what they have freely received (Matt. x. 8), will freely "execute judgment for them that suffer wrong" (Ps. cxlv. 7), "vengeance upon the nations, chastisement among the people" (Ps. cxlix. 7), who shall seem to have received of thy spirit, as the seventy ancients received of the spirit of Moses (Numb. xi. 17), by which, whether absent or present, they will labour to please God (2 Cor. v. 9) and thee; who will always come back from their legatine missions, weary indeed with labour, but not burdened with spoil; glorying not in that they have brought home with them whatever they found most curious and precious in the countries they visited, but because they have given peace to nations, laws to barbarians, tranquillity to monasteries, order to the churches, discipline to the clergy, and to God an acceptable people, zealous, in the practice of good works. . . .

Chapter VI

We are now tired of the court. Let us therefore go out into the palace: they are awaiting us at home. There we shall find those who belong rather to thine interior than to thine entourage, if I may so speak. Do not regard it as superfluous to consider how thou oughtest to regulate thy household and to provide for them who live under thy roof and belong to thy family. In my judgment, this is an indispensable consideration. . . . But thou must attend personally to the more important matters; as for the rest, it is also a personal obligation for thee to appoint subordinates who shall faithfully administer them in thy name. . . .

But there are certain matters concerning which I would have thee to keep thyself well informed, I mean the character and conduct of each member of thy household. The priests of thy household must either be a model or a by-word and a scandal to all. Never suffer anything improper, anything unbecoming, to appear in the countenance, in the conduct, or in the carriage of those with whom thou livest. Let thy brother-bishops learn from thy example not to keep in their palaces long-haired boys or foppish young men: curly-headed coxcombs look particularly out of place in the midst of mitred prelates. And remember also the Wise Man's admonition, "Hast thou daughters? Shew not they countenance gay towards them" (Eccli. vii. 25).

Nevertheless, I would not have thee to be austere in thy manner, but only grave. Austerity is wont to repel the timid, whereas the effect of gravity is to sober the frivolous. The presence of the former disposition would render thee odious, the absence of the latter would make thee contemptible. Herein as in all things else thou wilt do best to observe moderation. Therefore avoid over-severity as much as excessive lightness. What can be more pleasing than such manners as are equally removed from the stiffness which freezes and from the familiarity which breeds contempt? Be the Pope in the palace, but at home show thyself more as a father. Make thyself loved, if possible, by thy domestics; otherwise let them fear thee. It is always good to keep a guard over thy lips, yet not so as to exclude the grace of affability. Consequently, I counsel thee to bridle the imprudence of thy tongue at all times, but most especially at table. But if thou wouldst regulate thy exterior in the best possible manner, let thy conduct be always grave, thy looks benign, and thy conversation serious. . . .

Chapter VII

It is now time to bring this fourth book to an end. However, I should like before concluding to repeat by way of epilogue something of what has been said, and to add something more which has been omitted. Remember above all things that the holy Roman

Church, of which God has made thee ruler, is the *mother*, not the *mistress* of the other churches; and that thou art not the lord and master of the bishops, but one of their number, the brother of those that love God, and "a partaker with all them that fear Him" (Ps. cxviii. 63). For the rest, consider thyself obliged to be the model of justice, the mirror of sanctity, the pattern of piety, the oracle of truth, the defender of the faith, the doctor of nations, the guide of Christians, the friend of the Bridegroom, the paranymph of the Bride, the regulator of the clergy, the pastor of the people, the instructor of the unwise, the refuge of the oppressed, the advocate of the poor, the hope of the miserable, the guardian of orphans, the protector of widows, the eye of the blind, the tongue of the speechless, the support of the aged, the avenger of crime, the terror of evildoers, the glory of the good, the rod of the powerful, the hammer of tyrants, the father of kings, the moderator of laws, the administrator of canons, the salt of the earth, the light of the world, the priest of the Most High, the vicar of Christ, the anointed of the Lord, and finally the God of Pharaoh. Understand aright what I say. The Lord will give thee understanding. Whenever, therefore, power is united to malice it is thy duty to oppose it with a superhuman daring and a divine authority. Let thy "countenance be against them that do evil things" (Ps. xxxiii. 17). Let him who fears not man nor dreads the sword be afraid of the spirit of thine anger. Let him fear the power of thy prayers who has only contempt for thy warnings. Let him who provokes thy indignation be made sensible that he has incurred the anger, not of man, but of God. And let him who refuses to listen to thy remonstrances be afraid lest the Lord should listen to thy complaints.

Book V

[From consideration to contemplation.]

CHAPTER I

Although the four preceding books are included with the present under the title "On Consideration," they are to a great extent concerned with action, because with regard to many particulars they are intended to teach and admonish thee not only of what thou shouldst consider, but likewise of what thou oughtest to do. This fifth book, which I am now beginning, shall treat of consideration alone. For the things that are above thee—which is the part of my subject remaining to be discussed—have no need of thy action, but only invite thy contemplation. There is nothing for thy activity to effect in those objects which abide always in the same state and shall so abide for ever, and some of which have existed from everlasting. Therefore, my most wise and holy Father, I would have thee to understand clearly that as often as thy consideration descends from such high and heavenly things to those that are earthly and visible, whether to study them as sources of knowledge, or to desire them as useful, or to compose and regulate them as thy duty demands: so often does it enter into a land of exile. However, if it occupies itself with material realities in such a way as to make them the means of attaining to the spiritual, its exile will not be very remote. Indeed I may say that by this mode of application to sensible objects it begins to return to its native sphere. For this is the most sublime and worthy use to which earthly creatures can be put, when, as St. Paul of his wisdom tells us, "the invisible things of God are clearly seen, being understood by the things that are made" (Rom. i. 20). . . .

Chapter II

Great is he who, according to what has been said, regards the service of the senses as the wealth belonging to the natives of this land of his exile, and so endeavours to put it to the best use by employing it for his own and his neighbour's salvation. Nor less great is he who, by philosophising, uses the senses as a stepping-stone for attaining to things invisible. The only difference is that the latter occupation is manifestly the more pleasant, the former the more profitable: the one demands more fortitude, the other yields greater delight. But greatest of all is he who, dispensing altogether with the use of the senses and of sensible objects, so far at least as is possible to human fragility, is accustomed, not by toilsome and gradual ascents but by sudden flights of the spirit, to soar aloft in contemplation from time to time, even to those sublime and immaterial realities. To this last kind of consideration as I think, belong the transports of St. Paul. For they were rather raptures than ascents: he does not say that he mounted, but that "he was caught up into paradise" (2 Cor. xii. 4). And in another place he writes, "Whether we be transported in mind, it is to God" (ibid. v. 13). Now these three degrees are attained in the following manner. Consideration, even in the place of its banishment, by the pursuit of virtue and the help of grace, rises superior to the senses; and then either represses them lest they should wax wanton, or keeps them within due bounds lest they should wander away, or it avoids them altogether lest they should tarnish its purity. In the first it appears more powerful, in the second more free, and more pure in the third. For purity and fervour are the two wings which it uses in its flight. . . .

Chapter III

Perchance thou wilt tell me here that I have explained clearly enough by what way thou art to ascend, and that it now remains to say what is the term of the ascent. Thou art deceived if thou hopest to obtain from me any information concerning this, because it is ineffable. Dost thou think that I shall be able to describe what "eye hath not seen, nor ear heard, neither hath it entered into the heart of man" (II Cor. ii. 9)? "But to us," as the Apostle goes on to say, "God hath revealed it by His Spirit" (ibid.). Consequently, the things that are above thee cannot be described in words but must be revealed by the Spirit. Seek, then, by consideration for that which thou canst not learn from language, solicit it in prayer, merit it by thy life, attain to it by thy purity. . . .

Chapter XIII

Once more: What is God? He is Height and He is Depth. As Height, He is above all things; as Depth, He is beneath all. It is evident that amongst the divine attributes there exists the most perfect equality, firmly established on all sides, and persevering immutably the same. By Height, we are to understand the divine power; by Depth, the divine wisdom. Between these two also there is a relation of correspondence similar to that between Length and Breadth; for we know that the Height is as inaccessible as the Depth is unfathomable, St. Paul bearing witness to this where he utters that cry of wonder and admiration, "O the depth of the riches of the wisdom and of the knowledge of God! How incomprehensible are His judgments, and how unsearchable His ways!" (Rom. xi. 33). And we ourselves also, seeing, although but dimly, the most absolute unity of these perfections in God and with God, may cry out like the Apostle, and say, "O Wisdom all-powerful, 'reaching from end to end' mightily! O Power all-wise, 'disposing all things sweetly' "! (Wisdom viii. 1). The Thing is one in Itself, but It is manifold in Its effects, multiform in Its operations. And this one Thing is Length because of Its eternity, Breadth because of Its charity, Height because of Its majesty, Depth because of Its wisdom. . . .

Chapter XIV

These things are known to us. But are we therefore to believe that we also comprehend them? Surely not. It is by sanctity of life, not by discourse of reason, that we must attain to a comprehension of the things of God: if yet it is possible in any sense to comprehend the incomprehensible. But unless this were in some sense possible, the Apostle would not have said, "That you may be able to comprehend with all the saints." For his words imply that the saints have arrived at comprehension. In what way, dost thou ask? If thou art a saint, thou also hast arrived at this and knowest the way. If thou art not a saint, make thyself one, and so thou shalt know by the experience. A man is made a saint by two holy affections, the holy fear and the holy love of the Lord. The soul that possesses these virtues in their perfection can employ them as two arms to comprehend God, to embrace Him, to draw Him close to herself, and to hold Him fast, so that she can say with the Spouse in the Canticle, "I held Him and I will not let Him go" (Cant. iii. 4). Holy fear corresponds to Height and Depth, holy love to Length and Breadth. . . .

Observe now that to these four attributes of God, there correspond as many different kinds of contemplation. The first and loftiest contemplation is admiration of the Divine Majesty. This requires a purified soul, which, as being free from vices and unburdened of sin, it may easily lift up to things supernal, yea, and sometimes hold suspended—even though but for a short space—in a very transport and ecstasy of delighted wonder. Indispensable to this first kind of contemplation is the second, which has its gaze fixed upon the judgments of God. For whilst it grievously troubles the soul by this most terrifying prospect, it extinguishes vices, implants virtues, leads the way to wisdom, preserves humility. Now humility is the true and firm foundation of all the virtues, and the result of its shaking would be the ruin of the whole spiritual edifice. The third species of contemplation occupies itself, or rather takes its repose, in the memory of the divine benefits; and, lest we should remain ungrateful, it not only represents to our minds the favours we have received, but also inspires us with love for our Benefactor. It is of souls devoted to this that the Psalmist says, "They shall publish the memory of the abundance of Thy sweetness" (Ps. cxliv. 7). The fourth kind, "forgetting the things that are behind" (Philipp. iii. 13), rests only in the expectation of the promises; and as this is nothing else but a meditation on eternity—inasmuch as the things promised are eternal—it at the same time nourishes patience and gives us the strength required for perseverance. It is now easy, as I think, to correlate these four kinds of contemplation with the four attributes mentioned by the Apostle: for by meditation on the promises we attain to Length, by recollection of the divine benefits we comprehend Breadth; the contemplation of God's Majesty brings us to Height, and we reach Depth by pondering His judgments.

We must still go on seeking Him Who has not yet been sufficiently found and Who can never be too much sought. But perhaps it will be more becoming to seek Him, yea, and more easy to find Him, by fervent prayer than by argumentation. Therefore let me now put an end to the book, although not to the seeking.

IV

The High Middle Ages (1150–1300)

The century or more after the middle years of the twelfth century has commonly been considered as marking the climax of medieval civilization. Economic expansion continued and these years brought to fruition in the medieval universities the promise of the twelfth-century renaissance. This was the period of the Gothic cathedrals, of new forms in art, in music, and of a vigorous literature in different vernacular languages; in short, a period of growth in all fields of human endeavor. Yet toward the end of the thirteenth century signs were not wanting, especially in economic concerns, that some sort of recession had begun. Thus the High Middle Ages have often been contrasted with the subsequent age of transition to a more modern civilization.

The Church shared in the general progress characteristic of thirteenth-century civilization and was affected by the decline during its later years. Throughout the period of growth its purposes were far-reaching and its achievements impressive. Its ideal was high indeed, nothing short of a total Christian orientation of society. What the Carolingians had envisaged under royal auspices, what the Gregorians had sought to renew under papal direction—the *respublica christiana*—was to be thoroughly integrated under the aegis of a law whose ultimate authority rested in the papal curia.

Such a goal was not, however, easy to attain. The European world which the popes and bishops sought to guide in the thirteenth century was in many ways markedly different from that of even a century earlier (the world in which St. Bernard had grown up), and it presented many new difficulies. If ecclesiastical government and canon law were better administered, so also were secular government and civil law. Conflicts of jurisdiction continued to disturb the peace, as popes occasionally found it necessary to discipline secular rulers or oppose their policies. Certain of the controversies which resulted—for example, those between Innocent III and the kings of England and France, or the determined resistance of the Emperor Frederick II to Popes Gregory IX and Innocent IV—were long and bitter. How all these things affected the course of European history is well known. However necessary and justified each of these may have seemed to the authorities of either side, their combined effect on religious life was disastrous.

Heresy presented a much more serious threat to religious unity than had been the case for centuries. Whereas most of the heresies of the earlier Middle Ages had been local, Catharism (a dualist, neo-Manichaean belief brought from the East to western Europe during the twelfth century) produced a formidable organization and spread widely, especially in southern France. Since efforts on the part of bishops and occasional special preachers—St. Bernard himself had been one of them—were unavailing, Pope Innocent III organized military action, the Albigensian Crusade. This was primarily designed to force recalcitrant lay magnates, notably the count of Toulouse, to provide the requisite assistance of the secular power. An important decree of the Fourth Lateran Council (1215) outlined in detail the judicial measures to be taken against individual heretics or those who aided them. These were supplemented in subsequent decades by even severer methods and by the authorization of special tribunals under the direction of papally appointed judges.

The growth in number and size of urban communities created new problems in parochial organization, hitherto predominantly rural. Further, the increased volume of industry and interregional trade brought new or aggravated old moral problems. Traffic in money was now a normal activity, and the Church continued, even made more severe, its strictures against usury. In general, town dwellers remained loyal to the faith. Yet as an ever-growing number of bourgeois received some sort of education, they became more articulate in their criticism of ecclesiastical shortcomings. This is but one of the many striking contrasts found in the thirteenth century.

The religious life of the nobility was also showing signs of change, and it too presents many contrasts. In an age when local feudal wars were becoming less frequent, chivalry tended to become highly ceremonialized. To judge from vernacular literature, aristocratic society was beginning to give evidence of greater sophistication. Least affected by change were the rural peasants, among whom, to judge from repeated condemnations by local councils, pagan superstitions and practices still survived. That this continued to be so resulted largely from the fact that although educational opportunities were increasing, they were still not sufficient to ensure either an adequately trained parish clergy or a lay religion which was much more than elementary.

Clearly, therefore, the greatest problem confronting the Church in the thirteenth century (as indeed in any century) was pastoral care: how to bring a meaningful religious life to the laity. In fact, it has sometimes been said that while the Gregorians of the eleventh century attacked the problem of a feudalized episcopate, it remained for their successors to reach down to the parish priest. Certainly any estimate of the Church in the High Middle Ages must be based in large measure on its achievements in this area.

The most conspicuous evidence of the Church's efforts to confront these manifold problems is the series of six ecumenical councils assembled by the popes over a period from the First Lateran Council of

1123 to the Second Council of Lyons in 1274. The greatest of these was the Fourth Lateran Council convoked by Pope Innocent III in 1215.[1] Moreover, it is evident from the council's decrees that Innocent fully understood that a healthy religious life depended on a dedicated as well as a well-trained clergy.

Since enacting decrees is one thing and implementing them another, what happened after the bishops return to their dioceses is just as important as the sessions of a general council. Accordingly, the records of local councils and episcopal visitations are equally, perhaps more, significant as evidence of the Church's action. A number of these local records have survived and been studied; from them it appears that, though bishops differed in their zeal and competence, local councils did, in fact, meet and many bishops regularly made inspection tours of their jurisdictions. Local councils commonly repeated certain of the decrees of the general councils, and they were also able to utilize the compilations of papal decretals such, for example, as those issued by Gregory IX in 1234.

The appearance of Gregory's IX's book, the *Liber extra,* is an example of another, somewhat less spectacular though equally important aspect of the Church's overall influence, the increasing impact of canon law on the routine affairs of life. A series of legally trained men occupied the papal office beginning with Alexander III (1159–81). Their opinions, often instructions to judge-delegates,[2] added considerably to the growing number of papal decretals which, together with conciliar legislation, necessitated revision and compilation of the material not included in Gratian's *Decretum.*[3]

Innocent III, in addition to presiding over the Fourth Lateran Council, gave the first tentative authorization to two men who saw more clearly than most of their contemporaries the needs of the time, Francis of Assisi and Dominic, a native of Castile. For the orders these two men founded were destined in their respective though different ways to enrich the hitherto meager religious life of the average Christian layman.

The story of the young Francis's conversion from a gay and carefree life to one dedicated to "Lady Poverty" as "God's troubadour" is too well known to require detailed elaboration here. Probably around 1209 he appeared before Innocent III, who seems to have been impressed by Francis's sincerity and zeal, or was persuaded of them by others, but hesitated to grant him permission to found a new order, largely because he felt that Francis and his followers lacked adequate schooling. In a second interview, however, he gave a qualified permission.

---

1. The others were: Second Lateran (1139), Third Lateran (1179), and First Lyons (1245).
2. A judge-delegate was a local ecclesiastic appointed to settle a case in the place of origin and thus obviate the necessity of a trip to Rome to lodge an appeal.
3. Two later collections were the *Liber sextus* of Boniface VIII (1298) and the *Clementines* of John XXII (1317).

In their attempt to establish an organization, Francis and his first associates encountered difficulties. The Fourth Lateran Council legislated against the founding of new religious orders. Moreover, the primitive simple dedication to poverty might be feasible for Francis and a few companions, but it soon proved impractical for a rapidly growing society. However, a rule for what, in fact, proved to be a new order, the Order of Friars Minor, was officially promulgated in 1223. It was an adaptation of the ideal of Francis to the practical exigencies of thirteenth-century life. Meanwhile, Francis had also prepared a rule for St. Clare and her associates, who formed the Franciscan "Second Order."

Franciscans were soon found everywhere in Europe and the order became the largest of all. They brought to medieval religion new dimensions, above all a spontaneous joy and love, joy in God's creatures as taught by Francis, love for all men, and a deep devotion to the human nature of Christ and His Mother. Francis, we are told, made the first Christmas crib. Indeed, Franciscan preachers made real and vivid the whole of Christ's life, and Franciscan poets composed both popular poetry in the vernacular and formal liturgical hymns in Latin.

Meanwhile, Dominic adapted to his needs the Augustinian rule for canons regular, a step approved by Pope Honorius III in 1216. The new organization, the Order of Friars Preachers, grew rapidly; by 1221, when Dominic died, there were some 500 members and 100 Dominican nuns. What particularly distinguished the Dominicans was their dedication to preaching. It figures prominently in their rule, and even architecture was affected as Dominican churches were designed to open up all available space in order to make the pulpit more widely visible. Study for the purpose of more intelligent preaching also led to deeper scholarship, and Dominicans were soon to be found at the universities.

The very popularity of the friars eventually aroused the jealousy of the local clergy. They were soon in great demand not only as preachers but as confessors. It became necessary, therefore, to regulate carefully their relations with the diocesan bishops. Despite all difficulties of this kind, however, the friars persevered.[4] They continued throughout this and later periods to exert a profound influence on the religious life of Europe, and they also gave a new impetus to missions. The Franciscan rule included a clause outlining the procedures to be followed by brothers who wished to go out to "Saracens and other unbelievers." It was not long before members of both orders began to journey to North Africa, Asia, even to the Far East.

Thus it was that the traditional ecclesiastical establishment, now enormously aided by the friars, was able to affect the religious life of the ordinary person somewhat more deeply than in the past. This was perhaps most evident in the towns, as it was the town dwellers who were most influenced by the friars. The resurgence of preaching in the

---

4. It should be noted that two other orders of friars were established during this period, the Augustinian Friars and the Carmelites.

thirteenth century is particularly important. In fact, it is not easy for those accustomed to modern situations where the sermon is a more or less normal occurrence to appreciate the impact of the friars and of the other preachers who imitated them. Preaching, it must be remembered, had been neither very regular nor uplifting.

Other religious practices developed either spontaneously or with clerical assistance. Religious drama, for example, became far more elaborate and entirely separated from the liturgy in which it had originated. Both Franciscans and Dominicans had lay associates who were organized into what were called Third Orders whose members undertook certain religious observances without actually embracing a monastic type of life. Confraternities dedicated to charitable enterprises and the maintenance of hospitals were numerous, and craft guilds invariably placed themselves under the aegis of a patron saint. Semi-religious orders of men and women, such as the Beguinages which originated in Flanders, were also dedicated to the performance of works of charity.

It is evident from the art which adorned Gothic churches that saints and their images were more popular then ever. Among the saints, the Virgin Mary occupied a special place. Devotion to the "Mother of God" had always been central in Christian religious life. But during the thirteenth century, perhaps owing much to St. Bernard's influence and later to the friars, her cult became greatly intensified. Many cathedrals and churches were erected in her name and she was the inspiration for various forms of religious literature. Some of this was of a popular nature, for example, the charming story of *Our Lady's Tumbler*.[5] But Mary also inspired serious liturgical poets and some of the greatest medieval hymns were composed in her honor.

Despite considerable progress there remained much that was imperfect in the popular religion of the age. Examples of sermons which have come down to us are obviously addressed to a public still uneducated and seem to the modern reader almost childish. Frequent reception of the sacraments was rare, and such books of devotion for the more literate as have survived speak of "hearing" mass. An important canon of the Fourth Lateran Council required, as a minimum and under pain of excommunication, confession and communion at least once a year. There were strange contrasts of reverence and irreverence. Many were the complaints of misbehavior, even of sacrilege, in church buildings. People jostled one another to glimpse the consecrated host when it was elevated by the priest at mass, a custom which was introduced during the thirteenth century. Doubtless it was to correct such abuses and to promote a more genuine reverence to the sacrament that the feast of Corpus Christi was instituted in 1264.

It is not strange, therefore, that thoughtful persons living in the middle and later years of the thirteenth century were dismayed. The

5. This is included in another volume of the present series, D. Herlihy, *Medieval Culture and Society* (New York, 1968), pp. 292-302.

hopes raised by the Fourth Lateran Council were not fulfilled and the enthusiasm generated by the friars diminished. Discontent and criticism of ecclesiastical policies mounted, and certain modern historians, viewing the state of ecclesiastical society in the later years of the century, speak of "*le malaise occidental.*"[6] Why was this so? Doubtless political and economic turmoil was a major contributing factor. Doubtless, too, human frailty played a part. A judicial and administrative system centered in the Roman curia was expensive. There were delays and frustrations and, it appears, not a little venality. Moreover, for some devout souls the very effectiveness of the Church's administration and the sophistication of its juridical procedures produced misgivings. How could so highly organized a structure claim to be the Church of the Apostles? St. Bernard had pondered this question a century earlier. It disturbed the Franciscans and prompted the extreme faction to an almost utopian search for poverty and the realm of the spirit.

The primitive zeal and enthusiasm of the friars in their early days gave way to more settled attitudes as they became established in houses and convents and organized into provinces. A serious rift began to appear within the Franciscan order between the strict observants, those who aspired to retain the total abnegation of property which Francis and his first associates had practiced, and the others, ultimately the majority, who felt that a large organization, even one dedicated to an evangelical purpose, must make some compromises with the world as it existed. The entrance of the friars into the university community at Paris was vehemently, albeit unsuccessfully, resisted and added another element of friction to the difficulties already developing over certain works of Aristotle and the commentaries by the Moslem scholar, Averroës.

To those who are accustomed to regarding the thirteenth century as the climax of medieval civilization the difficulties and frustrations of the Church may seem extremely puzzling. One or two observations are perhaps in order here. First, the great achievements of the age in philosophy, theology, law, art, and literature, however significant, were the work of a comparatively small number of persons. Second, if it is true that the Church had not been able either to supply a sufficient number of adequately trained priests or to give real depth to the layman's religious life, it must be emphasized that its efforts in this regard represented only a beginning. The Fourth Lateran Council was the first in the Middle Ages which really attempted to grapple with the problem of the parish priest and his people.

And finally it must also be pointed out that much of the criticism, outspoken though it was, was directed at persons and institutions and not at the Church's fundamental teachings. In short, perhaps the malaise was caused less by disillusionment than by a greater awareness

6. The title of Chapter III, A. Fliche and V. Martin (eds.), *Historie de l'église*, vol. X (Paris, 1950), by A. Fliche and Yvonne Azais.

of the magnitude of the problems to be confronted, together with an impatience that progress was so slow. At any rate, the picture is one of many contrasts.

A book of this kind cannot resolve such questions. But stating them may help to explain the varied nature of the selections which follow.

Suggested Readings

(In addition to the works of Bainton, Cannon, Deanesley, Hughes, Knowles, Leff, and Russell mentioned above)

Bennett, R. F., *The Early Dominicans* (Cambridge, 1937).

Brooke, R., *Early Franciscan Government, Elias to Bonaventure* (Cambridge, 1959).

Englebert, O., *Saint Francis of Assisi* (new ed., Chicago, 1965), includes a comprehensive bibliography of Franciscan literature.

Gibbs, M. and J. Lang, *Bishops and Reform, 1215–72* (London, 1934).

Hinnebusch, W. A., *The Early English Friars Preachers* (Rome, 1961).

Moorman, J. R. H., *Church Life in England in the Thirteenth Century* (Cambridge, 1955).

———, *A History of the Franciscan Order from Its Origins to the Year 1515* (London and New York, 1968).

Powell, J. M., *Innocent III, Vicar of Christ or Lord of the World?* (Boston, 1963).

Smith, C., *Innocent III, Church Defender* (Baton Rouge, La., 1951).

Pope Innocent III

41. Letter to Archbishop Hubert of Canterbury

Historians continue to differ in their interpretation of the career and character of Pope Innocent III (1198–1216). Traditionally, he has been viewed as a pope-diplomat, highly skilled in the art of ecclesiastical power politics. In recent years, however, the opinion that he was in fact genuinely dedicated to the cause of reform has gained adherents. The first letter presented here would seem to lend support to this contention, for it reveals both the pope's scrupulous regard for proper legal procedure in bestowing a benefice and his deep concern for the promotion of worthy candidates. As the editors of the letter note, Master Mauger, the candidate in question, was in point of fact named after canonical postulation, a process whereby the electors could, and in this case did, request dispensation from a canonical impediment.

The translation is by C. R. Cheney and W. H. Semple, *Selected Letters of Pope Innocent III Concerning England (1198–1216)* (London, 1953), pp. 16–22. Reprinted by permission of Thomas Nelson & Sons Ltd., Publishers.

It became known to us some time since, by letters both from you and from certain of your suffragans and from our beloved sons the prior and chapter of the church of Worcester that, the church having lost its pastor, the prior and chapter unanimously elected as pastor of their souls our beloved son, Master Mauger, archdeacon of Évreux; and that, on his election being presented to you, you postponed confirmation of it until his arrival in person—he having been elected in his absence and without his knowledge. When at length he learnt what had been done, he devoutly came into your presence and (contrary to the general opinion, since all believed there was no impediment to the prompt confirmation of a unanimous and canonical election) he revealed to you in a voluntary and private confession that for some time he had been conscience-stricken in respect of his birth; and he stated that, without the indulgence of the Apostolic See, he refused to advance a single step towards an office so exalted and important, even though he should find the promoter to be well-disposed and willing.

You as a prudent and discreet man, on learning of his conscientious scruple, decided not to proceed immediately to the confirmation, but in a letter to us you both indicated the history of the case and commended Master Mauger's merits and learning. The chapter of the church in its letter to us stated that it did not know why you had postponed confirmation of the election, and, presenting to us the decree of election supported by the electors' signatures, asked to have it confirmed by the Apostolic See. Some of your suffragans stated explicitly in their letter what in your letter seemed rather obscurely suggested—that he was the son of a certain knight by an unmarried woman of free birth. Meantime, Master Mauger unexpectedly arrived in our presence: he set out the circumstances of his birth exactly as they had been reported in your suffragans' letter, and added that his father had never been married, but had secretly seduced his mother as a virgin, and that she was not married until four years after his birth.

We have discussed this matter carefully with our brethren. On reviewing the canons, we have found some that forbid the elevation to pastoral office of men not born in wedlock: these are doubtless based on the divine law by which illegitimate children and bastards are prohibited from entering the Church until the tenth generation. We have also found others that raise no objection to the taking of holy orders by individuals no matter from what source sprung, provided they have merits to support them; these hold that the sin of the parents should not be visited on the children, and in proof they adduce the argument that 'our Lord, Jesus Christ, who is a priest after the order of Melchisedech for ever, chose to be born of a line which had included not only foreign but even adulterous unions.' This second group of canons also seems to depend on Holy Writ where it says, 'the son shall not bear the iniquity of the father and the father shall not bear the iniquity of the son' (Ezek. 18:20).—a passage which appears to set aside the ancient proverb once current among the children of Israel, 'the fathers have eaten sour grapes and the children's teeth are set on edge' (Ezek. 18:2). A third group of canons, trying to harmonise differences, seemed partly to reconcile the discrepancy between the first two groups by saying that the illegitimate are not to be barred from holy offices if they have lived religious lives in monasteries or in canonries; and some in this group assert that among the illegitimate only those who follow their fathers' incontinence should be barred from sacred offices. These canons, too, appear to have the support of the divine law, where it says, 'I am a jealous God, visiting the iniquities of the fathers upon the children unto the third and fourth generation of those who hate me without cause' (Exod. 20:5)—which is as if God said, 'those who follow their fathers' hatred of me.'

But there is a canon of the Lateran Council, issued in general synod by our predecessor Alexander of happy memory, which agrees with the first group of canons mentioned above: it not only forbids such men to be advanced to bishoprics but also imposes a penalty on the electors, and, in fact, declares that the electors have thereby incurred the penalty—which seems to shew that the condemnation in the canon applies generally: it runs as follows, 'Lest action taken in individual cases to meet the necessities of the time should be interpreted as a precedent by posterity, no one is to be elected bishop except a man born in lawful wedlock'; and again at the end it adds, 'If the clergy have elected any man contrary to this ruling, they are to know that they are immediately deprived of their power of electing and suspended from ecclesiastical benefices for three years.' This canon was issued, in a council of many canon lawyers, not by a man without knowledge of the ancient canons, but by one fully acquainted with canonical sanctions, and it was affirmed by the council's approval. It appears to stop all possibility of promoting the illegitimate to episcopal rank, since it prohibits making a precedent of any action which, it hints, was taken in earlier times to meet a special necessity—even though special necessity be the sole motive influencing the dispensing authority to allow the dispensation. Moreover, it implicitly declares the election of illegitimates to be null and void, when it fixes as penalty for the electors the instant loss of their power to elect—a meaningless penalty, unless the election were still pending, which it could not be if the previous election or nomination still held good. Clearly then, such an election was invalidated by this canon.

Now although this canon penalizes the illegitimate by implying that such an election is null, nevertheless it did not take from us the power of dispensation: that was not Alexander's purpose in the prohibiton: he could not, in the matter of dispensation, establish a decision prejudicial to his successors who after him were to exercise power equal to, or rather, identical with his own; for equal has no authority over equal. His purpose was solely to prohibit such elections because, as a result of action occasionally taken by dispensation to meet a necessity of the time, certain persons (extending a concession into a general permission, and regarding it as a precedent) believed they were legally entitled to elect the illegitimate and in fact did elect them without concern: hence the heavy penalty he imposed on the electors.

However, we have discussed with our brethren whether in such a case involving such a person we ought to grant a dispensation from pity or whether we should maintain the rigour of the law. We found that, in a much more difficult case, our predecessor, Pope Urban of happy memory, granted a dispensation to the bishop-elect of Le Mans who was the son of a priest, and also to a bishop of Leon who after his consecration had humbly and voluntarily confessed that he was the son of an unmarried mother with whom his father had associated while his lawful wife was still alive. But Urban forbad this decision to be regarded as a rule of law or made a precedent for the future. It was clear to us that, though for some time back dispensations had been granted to the illegitimate and might possibly in the future have to be granted for a specific reason, the dispensation ought to be given more readily in a case of this type, namely, where the person's perfection exceeded his imperfection. In Master Mauger there were many qualities that seemed to prompt us to a dispensation—his education, his honourable character, his virtuous life, and his personal reputation vouched for by some of our brethren who knew him in the schools. Other points which added no little weight were his unanimous election by the chapter of Worcester, the petition of the laity, the king's assent, your own prayer, the suffragans' support, and the man's humble devotion in making his confession, for voluntarily and humbly he chose to confess his defect rather than mount the episcopal throne with guilt on his conscience.

Having thoroughly discussed all this with our brethren, and knowing that the chapter of Worcester had not humbly postulated Master Mauger but had elected him without due thought—though, to obtain the benefit of dispensation, they ought to have proceeded not by the forbidden way of election, but by the approved method of postulation: we declare this election (invalidated already by the authority of the above canon) to be null and void: and to the chapter of Worcester we shew much forbearance in not inflicting on them the penalty named in the above canon, and in not compelling them to prove their plea of ignorance. And although after the quashing of the election many have humbly supplicated us to deign, for the reasons stated above, to grant him a dispensation out of pity since no more suitable case for a dispensation under this head could present itself, yet because we wish to reserve to the said chapter complete freedom to elect or to postulate, we have decided not to allow such a supplication for the present, because it was not made in the name of the chapter, whose envoys were sent, not to postulate a dispensation, but to seek confirmation of the election; but at the same time we decree to be null and void any step which may have been taken to fill the see before the receipt of this letter. Wherefore we will and command that, on our behalf, you should cause a strict prohibition to be issued throughout the province of Canterbury to the effect that in future there should not be attempted, contrary to the above ruling, any such irregular action as is known (and with shame we mention it) to have been taken in respect of many persons in that province. But if the chapter of Worcester should think fit to postulate Master Mauger on his exceptional merits, let it arrange to present the postulation to the Apostolic See.

42. *Letter to the Bishop of Ely*

One of the most extraordinary letters to issue from the pope's chancery, as well as one of the most significant illustrations of the judge-delegate system, was written in 1204 to the bishop of Ely. That Innocent in the midst of his manifold concerns could take the time to write such a detailed letter in which he answers some fifteen questions is in itself remarkable. Further, his answers, in abridged form or in full, were included under various headings in the decretal collection of Gregory IX. A number of the paragraphs deal with procedural details, in particular the perennial legal problem of appeals. The paragraphs cited here are for the most part concerned with typical, routine matters of ecclesiastical administration. The translation is by C. R. Cheney and W. H. Semple, *op. cit.*, pp. 69–78. Reprinted by permission of Thomas Nelson & Sons Ltd., Publishers. Footnote references to the decretal collection of Gregory IX have been included.

The diligent attention to pastoral duty which you shew in discharging our mandates, and your scrupulous avoidance of error, prompt us, though harassed by many claims of business, to lay them aside for a while and give our mind to answering your points of enquiry.

As a judicious man you have consulted us on the question whether, if a delegate from the highest authority has chosen to depute to another the case committed to him, he can compel an unwilling person to undertake the deputed case.[1] On this we have taken our brethren's advice and think it right to reply as follows: since a delegate from the highest authority has by law been granted the legal right of appointing a judge, provided he has no evil motive in seeking to divest himself of the duty, he can compel an unwilling person on the ground that the legal right would seem meaningless if it carried no power of compulsion. The said delegate, however, ought carefully to provide that if, through necessity, he has seen fit to depute the business to persons of higher status he should have consideration for their rank and person in applying measures of compulsion. Following on this, you have further asked whether the delegate, if he thinks it expedient, can order anyone he pleases to summon the parties to his presence and can inflict a penalty for contempt on such a person if recalcitrant. To this we briefly reply that, since he can commit the whole business to another (as stated above), he can, with discretion, depute the duty of summoning to anyone he pleases and can properly punish for contempt.

You have also enquired whether, if a case has been referred to the archbishop by appeal, the archbishop on the strength of his ordinary power can delegate it to a subordinate of his suffragan or punish such a subordinate if he refuses to undertake the case thus delegated.[2] To this we reply that the archbishop cannot compel him, if unwilling, to undertake such a delegation, for (apart from certain definite provisions) he has no power over him, though his bishop is subject to the archbishop by metropolitan law. . . .

Because it often happens that execution of a sentence is entrusted to the ordinary, you have thought fit to ask the Apostolic See whether, if the ordinary has discovered the sentence to be unjust,

1. *Decretals*, I, 29, 28.
2. *Ibid.*, I, 31, 11.

he ought to put it into effect or should refrain.[3] Considering, therefore, that he has been entrusted not with cognizance of the case, but with execution of the sentence, we have chosen to answer your point thus: since an ordinary is bound to obey, even though he knows the sentence to be unjust he is nevertheless bound to execute it—unless by making representations to the judge, he can obtain release from the duty.

You have also asked to be informed whether, on the death of a delegate who has excommunicated a defendant for manifest disobedience or, for the sake of preserving the property, has given the plaintiff possession of the things he claimed, it is lawful for anyone, without a special mandate from the Apostolic See, to grant this defendant the benefit of absolution if he is willing to obey the law, or to restore possession within a twelvemonth on receipt of a suitable guarantee.[4] To this we reply that, since a delegate (as far as concerns his commission) is greater than an ordinary, a person excommunicated by such a delegate cannot, except at the point of death, be given the grace of absolution by another, without the mandate of the Pope—unless the delegate were such as to have a successor in his onerous and honourable office; nor will the defendant be able to recover the lost possession through any other than the Pope. But, so that after a twelvemonth another may not become the lawful possessor, he will be able before the ordinary (or if unable to reach him, before worthy officials) to offer and furnish a guarantee that he will obey the law: thus he may break the prescription of a twelvemonth and deserve after a year to recover possession by leave of the Apostolic See. . . .

Since it often happens that lay patrons of churches present for vacant churches now one individual and now another, you have earnestly asked to have it explained by the Apostolic See whether a clerk, presented by a lay patron for a church, acquires any rights in it from this presentation if his diocesan has ruled him to be inadmissible; and if he has appealed to the Apostolic See and, after the lodgment of his appeal, the patron has presented another and the bishop has installed this second presentee, can the first properly be removed from that church? As our predecessor, Pope Alexander of good memory, in distinguishing between those presented by lay

3. *Ibid.*, I, 29, 28.
4. *Ibid.*, I, 1, 11, 31; cf. II, 15.

and clerical patrons, ruled that the situation of the possessor was better in the case of those presented by a layman, we follow closely in his steps (such is our reverence for him) and reply that the installation of a lay patron's second presentee has firm validity. We decree, however, that a bishop who from malice has refused to admit a suitable presentee should be compelled to provide him with an appropriate benefice, so that the bishop may be punished in the same respect in which clearly he has offended.[5]

You have put a further question: if monks have been given permission by the Apostolic See to convert their churches to their own uses when the pastors of these churches die, is it then lawful for the monks on their own authority to take possession of them or should they be put in possession by the diocesan?[6] To this we reply that, unless the Pope's indult specifically says 'without consulting their bishop,' it is not lawful for them to take possession; for we do not believe that such an indult impairs a bishop's jurisdiction.[7]

And you have earnestly put another question: because by Denis' authority[8] parishes were delimited so that the revenues of individual parishes might be devoted to the essential needs of the church and with stipends of the ministers, is it lawful for a bishop, without the Pope's authority or, at least, without the concurrence of his chapter, to confer on monks the obventions of a parish church, the vicar's stipend being reserved? And, since the decrees of the [Third] Lateran Council forbid the imposition of a new pension on churches or the increase of an old pension, you ask to be informed whether a bishop, with the patron's consent, can confer on religious houses a whole church or, as a new charge, a portion of it. To these questions we briefly reply that, saving the canonical decree regarding the payment of a fiftieth to religious houses, a bishop can do neither of these things, except by permission of the Roman pontiff, without his chapter's consent. . . .

You have also enquired by what proofs decretals should be tested for genuineness: for a judge can reasonably question their authority when some are to be found in a text-book for students and are cited in law-suits, though their authenticity is not attested

5. *Ibid.*, III, 38, 29; 38, 24; 38, 5.
6. *Ibid.*, V, 33, 19.
7. *Ibid.*, III, 10, 9.
8. Pope Dionysius (259–68) (Pseudo-Isidorian).

by a seal and they have not been published by metropolitan authority.[9] Because, therefore, it often happens that even in our court decretals are cited the genuineness of which we doubt, in graciously answering your enquiry we have thought fit, by the authority of this letter, to rule that, when a decretal is cited about which a judge can have reasonable doubt, he should not fear to judge by it if it is in keeping with the common law, since clearly he is proceeding not so much on the authority of the decretal as of the common law: but, if it seems to be at variance with the common law, he should not judge by it but consult his superior about it.

Since sometimes the termination of cases is maliciously postponed by delaying exceptions, in replying to your enquiry we decree that all delaying exceptions should be presented by a definite date to be fixed by the judge, so that if the parties thereafter decide to present any exceptions not previously notified they should not be heard, unless an exception has arisen on a new point or the litigant who has decided to present it gives an affidavit that it came to his notice after the appointed date.[10]

Further, we decree that the principals in a suit should state their case to the court not by advocates but personally—unless they have been so incompetent that their deficiency, on the judge's permission, requires to be made good by others.[11]

Because it often happens that on the day,[12] which a judge appointed by us has fixed for the parties to a suit, the judge himself is summoned by the king or archbishop as a result of one party's scheming contrivance to have the hearing postponed: therefore, wishing to thwart the wicked devices of unscrupulous men, we decree that, if our delegate is satisfied that this has been contrived by the malice of a party to the suit, he should punish that party with a fitting penalty and, so that no advantage may be gained from such deceit, he should entrust that day's hearing of the case to a person acceptable to both parties, this person to proceed without appeal on the said day unless the parties have themselves agreed on a postponement.

Further,[13] you wished to consult us whether a man appointed

9. *Ibid.*, II, 22, 28.
10. *Ibid.*, II, 25, 4.
11. *Ibid.*, II, i, 14.
12. *Ibid.*, II, 1, 14.
13. *Ibid.*, I, 29, 28.

deacon without the laying-on of hands should be allowed to act as minister, and whether in the case of one who has been anointed in error with oil instead of chrism the sacrament of confirmation should be repeated. In reply we have chosen briefly to say that in such cases nothing should be repeated, but whatever was carelessly omitted should be carefully made good.

The Fourth Lateran Council (1215)

The Fourth Lateran Council, convoked in 1215 by Pope Innocent III, represents the medieval Church's most determined and far-reaching effort to implement the religious renewal which had been gaining momentum since the mid-eleventh century. It met at a troubled time in the Church's history. The Catharist heresy persisted despite the crusade which Innocent had launched in 1209. On the frontiers of Christendom the Moors had been thrust back in Spain (1212), but the diversion of the Fourth Crusade to Constantinople (1204) had not only left the Saracens in possession of the Holy Land, but had further embittered Greek Christians. Within the western Church the reforms of earlier days, further implemented by the three preceding Lateran councils, and especially by the Third under Alexander III, left much still to be done, particularly in the matter of raising the standards of the parish priests.

Innocent had evidently considered for some time the possibility of summoning a general council; and in 1213 when he sent out the letters of convocation he apparently felt the time was ripe. The Spanish situation (as mentioned above) was stabilized, the problem of the succession to the throne of the Holy Roman Empire seemed on the way to solution, and the Albigensian war was, temporarily as it turned out, halted. In his letters of convocation and in the sermon with which he opened the council, Innocent stated clearly that he was motivated by two overriding concerns: the reform of the Church, and the crusade. It is significant that he linked these two ideals together. There is no doubt that he was well aware of European conditions and the tremendous efforts needed to carry through the remedial measures necessary. Yet he associated Christendom's struggle against Islam with these and gave it equal weight.

The council, which opened in November, 1215, was one of the most impressive gatherings in the Church's history: 412 bishops, some 800 abbots and priors, and the delegates of most of the rulers of Europe were present. Although the Latin occupation of Constantinople and parts of the Byzantine empire gave the council a somewhat more geographically ecumenical aspect than its predecessors, the Greek bishops, for the most part, did not attend. Evidently the organization and preparation of agenda, etc., were managed with exceptional efficiency, and most of the business was accomplished in small meetings before and between the three plenary sessions (November 11, 20, 30). The council completed its work in less than a month and at the final session promulgated 70 decrees, a veritable blueprint for a revivified Christian society. Following these decrees came a detailed series of provisions for a new crusade.

43. Innocent III and the Fourth Lateran Council

Letter of Convocation

From the translation by C. R. Cheney and W. H. Semple, *op. cit.*, pp. 144–147. Reprinted by permission of Thomas Nelson Sons Ltd., Publishers.

Beasts of many kinds are attempting to destroy the vineyard of the Lord of Sabaoth, and their onset has so far succeeded against it that over no small area thorns have sprung up instead of vines, and (with grief we report it!) the vines themselves are variously infected and diseased, and instead of the grape they bring forth the wild grape. Therefore we invoke the testimony of Him, who is a faithful witness in the heavens, that of all the desires of our heart we long chiefly for two in this life, namely, that we may work successfully to recover the Holy Land and to reform the Universal Church, both of which call for attention so immediate as to preclude further apathy or delay unless at the risk of great and serious danger. Hence we have often poured forth our tears and supplications before God, humbly beseeching Him that in these matters He would reveal to us His good pleasure, and would inspire affection, kindle desire, and strengthen purpose by granting an opportunity and occasion to achieve these objects with success. Therefore (as concern for so great a purpose required) we have had much careful discussion on these matters with our brethren and other prudent men, and on their advice we have finally decided that to attain these objects one thing must be done, namely, that, since these objects affect the condition of the whole body of the faithful, we should summon a general council according to the ancient custom of the Holy Fathers—this council to be held at a convenient time and to be concerned only with the spiritual good of souls. It will be a council in which (in order to uproot vices and implant virtues, to correct abuses and reform morals, to eliminate heresies and strengthen faith, to allay differences and establish peace, to check persecutions and cherish liberty, to persuade Christian princes and peoples to grant succour and support for the Holy Land from both clergy and laymen, and for other reasons which it would be tedious to enumerate here), whatever, with the council's approval, shall have seemed expedient for the honour and glory of the Divine Name, for the healing and salvation of our souls, and for the good and benefit of Christian people, may be wisely established as decrees of inviolable force affecting prelates and clergy regular and secular.

But because a general council could not be conveniently assembled until two years from now, we have arranged in the meantime for discreet men in the several provinces to investigate fully matters which require the corrective of an apostolic ordinance, and for the sending of suitable agents to organize preparations for a Crusade so that, if in response to necessity the sacred council approves, we personally may take over control and prosecute the business the more effectively. Believing, therefore, that this wholesome proposal cometh down from Him from whom is derived every good and perfect gift, by apostolic letter we charge and command you all to make such preparation as will enable you, within two and a half years from this 1213th year of our Lord's Incarnation and on the 1st November, to present yourselves before us in modesty and prudence; and you will arrange that in your province one or two suffragan bishops should remain to carry on ecclesiastical administration, but so that both they and any others who, being detained for a canonical reason, cannot come in person shall send suitable deputies in their place. You will observe such moderation in your retinue and equipage as has been appointed by the [Third] Lateran Council[1]: no one is to bring more than is permitted, anyone may bring less: no one is to incur excessive and ostentatious expenditure, but only such as is essential and moderate: each must prove himself in deed and in bearing to be a true

---

1. Third Lateran Council, Canon 4.

worshipper of Christ, for it is not worldly applause but spiritual advancement that is to be sought in this matter. You, brothers archbishops and bishops, are to command, as from us, all chapters of churches, cathedral and otherwise, to be represented at the council by their provosts or deans or by other suitable persons; for certain matters will be treated at the council which particularly concern the chapters of churches. Meantime, both personally and by discreet agents, you will enquire precisely about all matters which seem to call for energetic correction or reform, and conscientiously writing a report you will deliver it for the scrutiny of the sacred council. As regards the necessary aid for the Holy Land, where God our King of old deigned to work salvation in the midst of the earth, you must earnestly devote to it your help and labour, faithfully and wisely assisting those whom we shall have deputed for the special management of the business.

Wherefore, let no one deceitfully excuse himself and withdraw from the execution of so holy a work, if he would escape canonical punishment. Let no one plead the difficulties caused by dissensions or by the roads; for, since the Lord now shews a token for good, these troubles for the most part are beginning to abate: the greater the dangers that threaten, the stronger the remedies that should be applied. No man will ever cross the ocean if he is always waiting for the sea to cease its turmoil.

The Lateran, the 19th of April, in the sixteenth year of our Pontificate.

Opening Sermon at the Lateran Council

The following selections from Innocent's sermon represent roughly one half of the entire discourse. The sermon is replete with symbolism and imagery, mostly taken from Scripture, and can be regarded as somewhat over elaborate, if not florid. It is possible, therefore, to dismiss it as a *pro forma* homily composed by a busy and, as some would say, politically oriented pope. It is also possible, however, to see beneath the rhetoric a genuine earnestness and sincerity. To distinguish between these interpretations is precisely the problem which is today confronting the historians of Innocent's pontificate. The text is translated from *MPL*, 217, cols. 673–680.

"With desire I have desired to eat his pasch with you before I suffer" (Luke 22:15), that is before I die.

Because "for to me, to live is Christ, and to die is gain" (Philippians 1:21), I do not refuse to drink the cup of suffering if it is the will of God, whether it is offered to me for the defense of the Catholic faith, or for aid to the Holy Land, or for the maintaining of ecclesiastical liberty, although I desire to remain in the flesh until the work begun is consummated. Truly, God's will, not mine, be done. And therefore I have said to you, "I have longed to eat this passover with you before I suffer." . . .

And I also invoke His testimony who is the faithful witness in heaven, because not with a carnal but with a spiritual "desire have I desired to eat this passover with you"; not because of earthly convenience or temporal glory, but for the reformation of the whole church, and above all for the liberation of the Holy Land. On account of these two things principally and particularly I have convoked this sacred council. But perhaps you say: what is this passover which you desire to eat with us? . . .

Passover in Hebrew is called *phase*, that is crossing over (Exodus 12). In Greek it is πάσχειν which is to suffer; because through sufferings we must cross over to glory, according to what the Truth itself said, "Ought not Christ to have suffered these things, and so to enter into his glory?" (Luke 24:16). Wherefore, if we wish to co-reign, we must suffer, since "the sufferings of this time are not worthy to be compared with the glory to come, that shall be revealed in us" (Romans 8:18). This passover, which is *phase*, that is crossing, I have with desire desired to eat with you. Of this it is said in Exodus (12:11), "you shall eat it in haste: for it is the phase (that is the passage) of the Lord." For it is recited in the book of Kings and is openly included in Paralipomenon that the temple was restored in the eighteenth year of the reign of Joseph the king and the passover was celebrated as it was not in Israel since the days of the judges and the kings (IV Kings 14; Paral. 35). If only this history might be a parable of our own time, so that in the eighteenth year of our pontificate the temple of the Lord, that is the church, might be restored, and the *phase*, that is the passover might be celebrated, namely this solemn council, through which there might be a crossing from vices to virtues, as in truth has not been done in Israel since the days of judges and kings, that is to say, in the Christian people living to see God, from the time of the holy fathers and catholic rulers. And I, indeed, have hope in Him who promised to his faithful, saying, "Where there are two or three gathered together in my name, there am I in the midst of them"

(Matt. 28:20), because He himself is indeed present in the midst of us who are have assembled in this basilica of the Savior in the name of the Savior to celebrate this passover in behalf of those things which pertain to salvation. It is a triple passover or *phase* which I desire to celebrate with you, bodily, spiritual, eternal; bodily, that it may be a crossing to the place to liberate unhappy Jerusalem; spiritual, that it may be a crossing from one condition to another to reform the universal church; eternal, that it may be a crossing from one life to another, to obtain the glory of heaven. Concerning the bodily crossing, Jerusalem calls to us plaintively through Jeremiah in the *Lamentations* (1:12), "O all ye that pass by the way, attend, and see if there be any sorrow like to my sorrow." There, cross over to me, all you who love me, to liberate me from such misery. For I, who used to be the mistress of the people, am now placed under tribute; I who was wont to be thronged with people now sit as it were alone. "The ways of Sion mourn because there are none that come to the solemn feast." (*ibid.* 1:4). Her enemies are placed over her, the holy places have all been profaned, and the sepulcher of the Lord, once glorious, is shamed. Where once the only be-gotten Son of God, Jesus Christ, was worshipped, now is venerated the son of perdition, Mohammed. The sons of strangers taunt me and reproach the wood of the cross, saying, "You trusted in wood, now let it save you if it can." O what shame, what disorder, what scandal, that the sons of a slave, the base Agarenes, hold our mother, the mother of all the faithful enslaved! . . .

What then shall we do? Indeed, O beloved brethren, I commit myself entirely to you. I show myself wholly to you, ready, according to your counsel, if you deem it expedient, to undertake personal labor and cross over to kings and peoples, to peoples and nations; and even beyond, if by a strong shout I could excite them to arise to fight the battle of the Lord, and avenge the injury to the Crucified who for our sins was cast out of the land and out of his seat which he purchased with blood and in which he accomplished all the sacraments of our redemption. Whatever others may do, let us priests especially assume this business of the Lord, helping and succoring with our persons and our possessions the needs of the Holy Land in such a way that no one remains who is not a partici-pant in so great a work, or has no share in so great a reward. For once in a similar case God brought safety to Israel through the priests when through the Maccabees, indeed priests, sons of

Mathatia, he liberated Jerusalem and the temple from the hands of the godless (Macc. 9).

Of the spiritual crossing, the Lord said to the man clothed in linen with an inkhorn at his loins, "Go through the midst of the city, through the midst of Jerusalem: and mark [the letter] Thau upon the foreheads of the men that sigh, and mourn for all the abominations that are committed in the midst thereof" (Ezek. 9:4). Then he said to six men having the weapons of destruction in their hands, "Follow him through the city and strike all on whom you do not find the Thau. Let your eye miss no one, and begin at my sanctuary." The man clothed in linen with the inkhorn at his loins must be he who speaks, the man strong in virtue, such as he of whom the Scripture speaks, "There was a man in the Land of Hus, whose name was Job, and that man was simple and upright, and fearing God and avoiding evil" (Job 1:1) clothed in linen, that is in honest ways, and adorned by good works. . . .

This crossing through the midst of the city and marking Thau on the foreheads of those living in tears and sorrow is commanded because T is the last letter of the Hebrew alphabet and represents the form of the cross as it was before Pilate placed the inscription over the crucified Lord, which the blood of the lamb on each doorpost and on the lintels of homes wondrously signified. . . .

The supreme pontiff who is made watcher over the house of Israel ought to pass through the universal church, which is the city of the great king, the city placed on a mountain, investigating and inquiring into the merits of all, lest they call the good evil and the evil good, lest they put darkness for light and light for darkness (Isa. 5:20); lest they cause death to the souls which are not dying and give life to the souls which do not live (Ezek. 11). And, therefore, so that he may distinguish and set off the former from the latter he has to place the sign of Thau on the foreheads of the men who weep and lament, in order to designate those who weep and lament over the abominations which are perpetuated in the midst of the church as signed with Thau on their foreheads. Such, indeed, weep for the sins and they sigh with shame over the abominations which are made in the midst of the city. . . .

Here also evils come forth in the Christian people. Faith perishes, religion is deformed, liberty is confounded, justice is trampled under foot, heretics burgeon, schismatics grow insolent, the perfidious rage, the Agarenes prevail. Yet regarding the eternal crossing over Our Lord said, "Blessed are those servants whom the Lord when he cometh shall find watching. Amen, I say to you, that he will gird himself, and make them sit down to meat, and passing will minister unto them" (Luke 12:37). Concerning this crossing surely the martyrs glory in the Psalm, saying, "We have crossed through fire and water, and thou hast brought us out into a refreshment" (Ps. 45:12). This passover, above all others I desire to eat with you in the kingdom of God. It is, moreover, both a bodily and a spiritual eating. . . . There is besides a consuming of the eucharist and a consuming of glory. . . . Of the former it is said, "He who eats Me shall have life because of Me" (John 6); of the latter it is read, "Blessed is he that shall eat bread in the kingdom of God" (Luke 14:15). With this last consuming I most particularly desire to eat the passover with you, that we may cross from labor to rest, from sorrow to joy, from death to life, from corruption to eternity; with Our Lord Jesus Christ as our surety, to Whom is honor and glory for all ages. Amen.

44. Canons of the Council

The council issued 71 canons, the final one being a detailed series of provisions for a new crusade. Several dealt with judicial procedures and were designed to ensure a fair hearing for every person concerned and to define more precisely the conditions justifying appeals. The canons included here are principally concerned with the state of the Church and the appropriate disciplinary measures which were considered necessary to ensure a healthy religious life. The translation of these canons is by H. R. Schroeder, *The Disciplinary Decrees of the Ecumenical Councils* (St. Louis, Mo., 1937), pp. 237–292. Reprinted by permission of B. Herder Book Company. The translation of the Constitution for the Jews is taken from E. A. Synan, *The Popes and the Jews in the Middle Ages* (New York, 1965), pp. 230–232, reprinted with permission of The Macmillan Co.

Canon 1

Owing to the prevalence of heresy the council fathers in Canon 1 redefined the traditional doctrines of the Trinity, the incarnation of Christ, the last judgment, and the final resurrection, etc. They then added an important definition, cited here, of the eucharistic miracle as being a "transubstantiation" of the bread and wine into the body and blood of Christ. The term had been used before by theologians, but had not been officially sanctioned.

The following statement on baptism and on penance for sin committed after baptism should be read in connection with Canons 21 and 22 below which deal with the religious obligations of lay persons. It has been suggested that the reference to married persons was prompted by the prevalence of the dualist ideas of the Cathari.

. . . There is one Universal Church of the faithful, outside of which there is absolutely no salvation. In which there is the same priest and sacrifice, Jesus Christ, whose body and blood are truly contained in the sacrament of the altar under the forms of bread and wine; the bread being changed (*transsubstantiatis*) by divine power into the body, and the wine into the blood, so that to realize the mystery of unity we may receive of Him what He has received of us. And this sacrament no one can effect except the priest who has been duly ordained in accordance with the keys of the Church, which Jesus Christ Himself gave to the Apostles and their successors.

But the sacrament of baptism, which by the invocation of each Person of the Trinity, namely, of the Father, Son, and Holy Ghost, is effected in water, duly conferred on children and adults in the form prescribed by the Church by anyone whatsoever, leads to salvation. And should anyone after the reception of baptism have fallen into sin, by true repentance he can always be restored. Not only virgins and those practicing chastity, but also those united in marriage, through the right faith and through works pleasing to God, can merit eternal salvation.

Canon 3

Canon 3 is an important landmark in the Church's efforts to stamp out the heresy of Catharism. In addition to authorizing the Albigensian Crusade, Innocent had elaborated certain judicial procedures, some of which were repeated here. Although this decree provides for recourse to the secular power and indicates suitable punishments, it clearly leaves the responsibility for discovering and proceeding against heretics in the hands of the bishops. No separate tribunals are envisaged and the death penalty is not stipulated. Courts presided over by specially appointed papal judges as well as more severe procedures and punishments were to come in subsequent decades.

Since Innocent by 1213 had renewed his efforts to organize a crusade to the Holy Land and was presumably attempting to liquidate the

Albigensian problem, it is remarkable that Canon 3 offers the crusade indulgence to the opponents of heresy. It is possible that the bishops' opinion in this matter prevailed over that of the pope.

We excommunicate and anathematize every heresy that raises itself against the holy, orthodox and Catholic faith which we have above explained; condemning all heretics under whatever names they may be known, for while they have different faces, they are nevertheless bound to each other by their tails, since in all of them vanity is a common element. Those condemned, being handed over to the secular rulers or their bailiffs, let them be abandoned, to be punished with due justice, clerics being first degraded from their orders. As to the property of the condemned, if they are laymen, let it be confiscated; if clerics, let it be applied to the churches from which they received revenues. But those who are only suspected, due consideration being given to the nature of the suspicion and the character of the person, unless they prove their innocence by a proper defense, let them be anathematized and avoided by all until they have made suitable satisfaction; but if they have been under excommunication for one year, then let them be condemned as heretics. Secular authorities, whatever office they may hold, shall be admonished and induced and if necessary compelled by ecclesiastical censure, that as they wish to be esteemed and numbered among the faithful, so for the defense of the faith they ought publicly to take an oath that they will strive in good faith and to the best of their ability to exterminate in the territories subject to their jurisdiction all heretics pointed out by the Church; so that whenever anyone shall have assumed authority, whether spiritual or temporal, let him be bound to confirm this decree by oath. But if a temporal ruler, after having been requested and admonished by the Church, should neglect to cleanse his territory of this heretical foulness, let him be excommunicated by the metropolitan and the other bishops of the province. If he refuses to make satisfaction within a year, let the matter be made known to the supreme pontiff, that he may declare the ruler's vassals absolved from their allegiance and may offer the territory to be ruled by Catholics, who on the extermination of the heretics may possess it without hindrance and preserve it in the purity of faith; the right, however, of the chief ruler is to be respected so long as he offers no obstacle in this matter and permits freedom of action. The same law is to be observed in regard to those who have no chief rulers (that is, are independent). Catholics who have girded themselves with the cross for the extermination of the heretics, shall enjoy the indulgences and privileges granted to those who go in defense of the Holy Land.

We decree that those who give credence to the teachings of the heretics, as well as those who receive, defend, and patronize them, are excommunicated; and we firmly declare that after any one of them has been branded with excommunication, if he has deliberately failed to make satisfaction within a year, let him incur *ipso jure* the stigma of infamy and let him not be admitted to public offices or deliberations, and let him not take part in the election of others to such offices or use his right to give testimony in a court of law. Let him also be intestable, that he may not have the free exercise of making a will, and let him be deprived of the right of inheritance. Let no one be urged to give an account to him in any matter, but let him be urged to give an account to others. If perchance he be a judge, let his decisions have no force, nor let any cause be brought to his attention. If he be an advocate, let his assistance by no means be sought. If a notary, let the instruments drawn up by him be considered worthless, for, the author being condemned, let them enjoy a similar fate. In all similar cases we command that the same be observed. If, however, he be a cleric, let him be deposed from every office and benefice, that the greater the fault the graver may be the punishment inflicted.

If any refuse to avoid such after they have been ostracized by the Church, let them be excommunicated till they have made suitable satisfaction. Clerics shall not give the sacraments of the Church to such pestilential people, nor shall they presume to give them Christian burial, or to receive their alms or offerings; otherwise they shall be deprived of their office, to which they may not be restored without a special indult of the Apostolic See. Similarly, all regulars, on whom also this punishment may be imposed, let their privileges be nullified in that diocese in which they have presumed to perpetrate such excesses.

But since some, under "the appearance of godliness, but denying the power thereof," as the Apostle says (II Tim. 3:5), arrogate to themselves the authority to preach, as the same Apostle says: "How shall they preach unless they be sent?" (Rom. 10:15), all those prohibited or not sent, who, without the authority of the Apostolic See or of the Catholic bishop of the locality, shall presume to usurp the office of preaching either publicly or privately, shall be excommunicated and unless they amend, and the sooner the better, they shall be visited with a further suitable penalty. We add, moreover, that every archbishop or bishop should himself or through his archdeacon or some other suitable persons, twice or at least once a year make the rounds of his diocese in which report has it that heretics dwell, and there compel three or more men of good character or, if it should be deemed advisable, the entire neighborhood, to swear that if anyone know of the presence there of heretics or others holding secret assemblies, or differing from the common way of the faithful in faith and morals, they will make them known to the bishop. The latter shall then call together before him those accused, who, if they do not purge themselves of the matter of which they are accused, or if after the rejection of their error they lapse into their former wickedness, shall be canonically punished. But if any of them by damnable obstinacy should disapprove of the oath and should perchance be unwilling to swear, from this very fact let them be regarded as heretics.

We wish, therefore, and in virtue of obedience strictly command, that to carry out these instructions effectively the bishops exercise throughout their dioceses a scrupulous vigilance if they wish to escape canonical punishment. If from sufficient evidence it is apparent that a bishop is negligent or remiss in cleansing his diocese of the ferment of heretical wickedness, let him be deposed from the episcopal office and let another, who will and can confound heretical depravity, be substituted.

Canons 6, 7, 10, 11, 14, 15, 16, 17, 18, 23, 26, 27, 29, 30, 31, 32

All of these canons are concerned with the morale and standards of conduct of the clergy. They reveal the council's awareness of the difficulties still encountered in providing suitable candidates for ecclesiastical positions as well as in maintaining discipline. Canon 6 repeats an injunction which dates from the Council of Nicea in 325 (cf. above). Others re-enact measures promulgated by recent councils, in particular the Third Lateran Council of 1179.

CANON 6

In accordance with the ancient provisions of the holy Fathers, the metropolitans must not neglect to hold with their suffragans the annual provincial synods. In these they should be actuated with a genuine fear of God in correcting abuses and reforming morals, especially the morals of the clergy, familiarizing themselves anew with the canonical rules, particularly those that are enacted in this general council, that they may enforce their observance by imposing due punishment on transgressors. . . .

. . . Whoever shall neglect to comply with this salutary statute, let him be suspended from his office and benefices till it shall please his superior to restore him.

Canon 7

By an irrefragable decree we ordain that prelates make a prudent and earnest effort to correct the excesses and reform the morals of their subjects, especially of the clergy, lest their blood be demanded at their hands. But that they may perform unhindered the duty of correction and reform, we decree that no custom or appeal shall stand in the way of their efforts, unless they shall have exceeded the form to be observed in such cases. The abuses, however, of the canons of the cathedral church, the correction of which has by custom belonged to the chapter, shall, in those churches in which such a custom has hitherto prevailed, by the advice or command of the bishop be corrected within a reasonable time specified by the bishop. Otherwise the bishop, having in mind the interests of God, opposition notwithstanding, shall not delay to correct them by means of ecclesiastical censure according as the *cura animarum* demands. . . .

Canon 10

Among other things that pertain to the salvation of the Christian people, the food of the word of God is above all necessary, because as the body is nourished by material food, so is the soul nourished by spiritual food, since "not in bread alone doth man live, but in every word that proceedeth from the mouth of God" (Matt. 4:4). It often happens that bishops, on account of their manifold duties or bodily infirmities, or because of hostile invasions or other reasons, to say nothing of lack of learning, which must be absolutely condemned in them and is not to be tolerated in the future, are themselves unable to minister the word of God to the people, especially in large and widespread dioceses. Wherefore we decree that bishops provide suitable men, powerful in work and word, to exercise with fruitful result the office of preaching; who in place of the bishops, since these cannot do it, diligently visiting the people committed to them, may instruct them by word and example. And when they are in need, let them be supplied with the necessities, lest for want of these they may be compelled to abandon their work at the very beginning. Wherefore we command that in cathedral churches as well as in conventual churches suitable men be appointed whom the bishops may use as coadjutors and assistants, not only in the office of preaching but also in hearing confessions, imposing penances, and in other matters that pertain to the salvation of souls. If anyone neglect to comply with this, he shall be subject to severe punishment.

Canon 11

Since there are some who, on account of the lack of necessary means, are unable to acquire an education or to meet opportunities for perfecting themselves, the Third Lateran Council in a salutary decree [Canon 18] provided that in every cathedral church a suitable benefice be assigned to a master who shall instruct *gratis* the clerics of that church and other poor students, by means of which benefice the material needs of the master might be relieved and to the students a way opened to knowledge. But, since in many churches this is not observed, we, confirming the aforesaid decree, add that, not only in every cathedral church but also in other churches where means are sufficient, a competent master be appointed by the prelate with his chapter, or elected by the greater and more discerning part of the chapter, who shall instruct *gratis* and to the best of his ability the clerics of those and other churches in the art of grammar and in other branches of knowledge. In addition to a master, let the metropolitan church have also a theologian, who shall instruct the priests and others in the Sacred Scriptures and in those things especially that pertain to the *cura animarum*. To each master let there be assigned by the chapter the revenue of one benefice, and to the theologian let as much be given by the metropolitan; not that they thereby become canons, but they shall enjoy the revenue only so long as they hold the office of instructor. If the metropolitan church cannot support two masters, then it shall provide for the theologian in the aforesaid manner, but for the one teaching grammar, let it see to it that a sufficiency is provided by another church of his city or diocese.

CANON 14

That the morals and general conduct of clerics may be better reformed, let all strive to live chastely and virtuously, particularly those in sacred orders, guarding against every vice of desire, especially that on account of which the anger of God came from heaven upon the children of unbelief, so that in the sight of Almighty God they may perform their duties with a pure heart and chaste body. But lest the facility to obtain pardon be an incentive to do wrong, we decree that whoever shall be found to indulge in the vice of incontinence, shall, in proportion to the gravity of his sin, be punished in accordance with the canonical statutes, which we command to be strictly and rigorously observed, so that he whom divine fear does not restrain from evil, may at least be withheld from sin by a temporal penalty. If therefore anyone suspended for this reason shall presume to celebrate the divine mysteries, let him not only be deprived of his ecclesiastical benefices but for this twofold offense let him be forever deposed. Prelates who dare support such in their iniquities, especially in view of money or other temporal advantages, shall be subject to a like punishment. But if those, who according to the practice of their country have not renounced the conjugal bond, fall by the vice of impurity, they are to be punished more severely, since they can use matrimony lawfully.[1]

CANON 15

All clerics shall carefully abstain from drunkenness. Wherefore, let them accommodate the wine to themselves, and themselves to the wine. Nor shall anyone be encouraged to drink, for drunkenness banishes reason and incites to lust. We decree, therefore, that that abuse be absolutely abolished by which in some localities the drinkers bind themselves *suo modo* to an equal portion of drink and he in their judgment is the hero of the day who outdrinks the others. Should anyone be culpable in this matter, unless he heeds the warning of the superior and makes suitable satisfaction, let him be suspended from his benefice or office.

We forbid hunting and fowling to all clerics; wherefore, let them not presume to keep dogs and birds for these purposes.

1. The final sentence refers to Byzantine clergy under Latin jurisdiction as a consequence of the Fourth Crusade (1204).

CANON 16

Clerics shall not hold secular offices or engage in secular and, above all, dishonest pursuits. They shall not attend the performances of mimics and buffoons, or theatrical representations. They shall not visit taverns except in case of necessity, namely, when on a journey. They are forbidden to play games of chance or be present at them. They must have a becoming crown and tonsure and apply themselves diligently to the study of the divine offices and other useful subjects. Their garments must be worn clasped at the top and neither too short nor too long. They are not to use red or green garments or curiously sewed together gloves, or beak-shaped shoes or gilded bridles, saddles, pectoral ornaments (for horses), spurs, or anything else indicative of superfluity. At the divine office in the church they are not to wear cappas with long sleeves, and priests and dignitaries may not wear them elsewhere except in case of danger when circumstances should require a change of outer garments. Buckles may under no condition be worn, nor sashes having ornaments of gold or silver, nor rings, unless it be in keeping with the dignity of their office. All bishops must use in public and in the church outer garments made of linen, except those who are monks, in which case they must wear the habit of their order; in public they must not appear with open mantles, but these must be clasped either on the back of the neck or on the bosom.

CANON 17

It is a matter for regret that there are some minor clerics and even prelates who spend half of the night in banqueting and in unlawful gossip, not to mention other abuses, and in giving the remainder to sleep. They are scarcely awakened by the diurnal concerts of the birds. Then they hasten through matins in a hurried and careless manner. There are others who say mass scarcely four times a year and, what is worse, do not even attend mass, and when they are present they are engaged outside in conversation with lay people to escape the silence of the choir; so that, while they readily lend their ears to unbecoming talk, they regard with utter indifference things that are divine. These and all similar things, therefore, we absolutely forbid under penalty of suspension, and strictly command in virtue of obedience that they celebrate diligently and devoutly the diurnal and nocturnal offices so far as God gives them strength.

CANON 18

No cleric may pronounce a sentence of death, or execute such a sentence, or be present at its execution. If anyone in consequence of this prohibiton (*hujusmodi occasione statuti*) should presume to inflict damage on churches or injury on ecclesiastical persons, let him be restrained by ecclesiastical censure. Nor may any cleric write or dictate letters destined for the execution of such a sentence. Wherefore, in the chanceries of the princes let this matter be committed to laymen and not to clerics. Neither may a cleric act as judge in the case of the Rottarii,[1] archers, or other men of this kind devoted to the shedding of blood. No subdeacon, deacon, or priest shall practice that part of surgery involving burning and cutting. Neither shall anyone in judicial tests or ordeals by hot or cold water or hot iron bestow any blessing; the earlier prohibitions in regard to dueling remain in force.[2]

CANON 23

That the ravenous wolf may not invade the Lord's flock that is without a pastor, that a widowed church may not suffer grave loss in its properties, that danger to souls may be averted, and that provision may be made for the security of the churches, we decree that a cathedral or regular church must not be without a bishop for more than three months. If within this time an election has not been held by those to whom it pertains, though there was no impediment, the electors lose their right of voting, and the right to appoint devolves upon the next immediate superior. Let the one upon whom this right to appoint devolves, having God before his eyes, not delay more than three months to provide canonically and with the advice of the chapter and other prudent men the widowed church with a suitable pastor, if he wishes to escape canonical punishment. This pastor is to be chosen from the widowed church itself, or from another in case a suitable one is not found therein.

CANON 26

Nothing is more injurious to the Church of God than the selection of unworthy prelates for the direction of souls. Wishing,

1. *Routiers:* companies of mercenary soldiers.
2. This decree effectively ended the ancient practice of the judicial ordeal.

therefore, to apply the necessary remedy to this evil, we decree by an irrefragable ordinance that when anyone has been elected for the guidance of souls, he to whom the confirmation of the election belongs shall carefully investigate the process and circumstances of the election as well as the person of the one elected, and only when everything proves to be satisfactory may he confirm. If through carelessness the contrary should take place, then not only the one unworthily promoted is to be removed, but the one also who furthered such promotion (by confirmation) is to be punished. The latter's punishment, we decree, shall consist in this, that when it is agreed that through negligence he confirmed a person who lacks sufficient knowledge or is wanting in integrity of morals or is not of legitimate age, not only is he to lose the right of confirming the first successor of such a person, but, that he may not in some case escape punishment, he is also to be deprived of the revenues of his benefice till he be deemed worthy of pardon. If, however, the evidence shows that his action was inspired by malice, a severer punishment is to be imposed on him. Bishops also, if they wish to escape canonical punishment, shall take the necessary precaution to promote to sacred orders and ecclesiastical dignities only such as are qualified to discharge worthily the duties of the office committed to them. . . .

CANON 27

Since the direction of souls is the art of arts, we strictly command that bishops, either themselves or through other qualified men, diligently prepare and instruct those to be elevated to the priesthood in the divine offices and in the proper administration of the sacraments of the Church. If in the future they presume to ordain ignorant and unformed men (a defect that can easily be discovered), we decree that both those ordaining and those ordained be subject to severe punishment. In the ordination of priests especially, it is better to have a few good ministers than many who are no good, for if the blind lead the blind both will fall into the pit (Matt. 15:14).

CANON 29

With much foresight it was prohibited in the Lateran Council that no one should, contrary to the sacred canons, accept several ecclesiastical dignities or several parochial churches; otherwise the one receiving should lose what he received, and the one who bestowed be deprived of the right of collation. But since, on account of the boldness and avarice of some, the aforesaid statute has thus far produced little or no fruit, we, wishing to meet the situation more clearly and emphatically, declare in the present decree that whoever shall accept a benefice to which is annexed the *cura animarum* after having previously obtained such a benefice, shall *ipso jure* be deprived of this (the first one); and if perchance he should attempt to retain it, let him be deprived of the other one also. He to whom the collation of the first benefice belongs may freely confer it, after the incumbent has accepted a second, on anyone whom he may deem worthy; should he delay to do so beyond a period of six months, then in accordance with the decree of the Lateran Council, let not only its collation devolve on another, but also let him be compelled to indemnify the church in question from his own resources equal to the amount of the revenues drawn from it during its vacancy. . . .

Canon 30

It is a very inconsistent and grave matter that some bishops, when they can promote suitable men to ecclesiastical benefices, do not fear to choose unworthy ones, who lack integrity of morals and sufficient knowledge, following the carnal and inordinate affections for their kindred rather than the judgment of reason. The great detriment that thus accrues to the churches no one of sound mind is ignorant of. Wishing, therefore, to cure this disease, we command that unworthy persons be rejected and suitable ones, who will and can render to God and the churches an acceptable service, be chosen; and let a careful investigation in regard to this matter be made in the annual provincial synod. Anyone who has been found culpable after the first and second admonition, let him be suspended by the synod from conferring benefices, and in the same synod let a prudent and upright person be appointed who may take the place of the one suspended. The same is to be observed in regard to the chapters that prove delinquent in this matter. An offense of this kind on the part of a metropolitan must be made known by the synod to a higher superior. That this salutary provision may be more effectively observed, such a sentence of suspension may by no means be removed except by the authority of the Roman pontiff or by the patriarch of the one suspended, that in this matter also the four patriarchal sees may be specially honored.[1]

CANON 31

To destroy that worst of corruptions that has grown up in many churches, we strictly forbid that the sons of canons, especially the illegitimate ones, be made canons in the same secular churches in which their fathers have been appointed. Such appointments, we decree, are invalid; those who presume to make them, let them be suspended from their benefices.

CANON 32

In some localities a vice has grown up, namely, that patrons of parochial churches and some other persons (including bishops) arrogate to themselves the revenues of those churches, leaving to the priests attached to them such a meager portion as to deprive them of a decent subsistence. For we have learned from a source the authority of which is unquestionable that in some places the parochial clergy receive for sustenance only a *quarta quartae*, that is, one sixteenth of the tithes.[2] Whence it is that in these localities there seldom is found a parochial priest who possesses more than a very limited knowledge of letters. Since therefore the mouth of the ox that threshes should not be muzzled, and he who serves the altar should live by the altar, we decree that no custom on the part of a bishop, patron, or anybody else shall stand in the way of priests receiving a *portio sufficiens*.

He who has a parochial church must serve it himself and not entrust its administration to a vicar, unless perchance there be a parochial church annexed to the prebend or dignity, in which case we grant that he who has such a prebend or dignity, since it behooves him to serve in the major church, may ask to have appointed for the parochial church a suitable and irremovable vicar, who, as was said before, shall enjoy a *portio congruens* of the revenues of that church; otherwise by the authority of this decree let him be deprived of it and let it be conferred on another who

1. Canon 5 established a hierarchy of patriarchates after Rome: Constantinople (then in Latin hands), Alexandria, Antioch, Jerusalem.
2. Instead of the full quarter customarily due him.

will and can fulfil the aforesaid requirements. We also absolutely forbid that anyone presume to confer fraudulently on another a pension as a benefice from the revenues of a church that ought to have its own priest (*proprius sacerdos*).

Canons 63, 65, 66

These decrees reveal that simony or comparable forms of financial corruption were still a problem. Canon 66 which prohibits financial exactions for sacerdotal ministrations should be studied in connection with Canon 32, above. For it is clear that parish priests were often deprived of adequate material support.

CANON 63

We have learned with certainty that in many places and by many persons exactions and base extortions are made for the consecration of bishops, the blessing of abbots, and the ordination of clerics, and that a tax is fixed as to how much this one or that one is to receive and how much this one or that one is to pay; and what is worse, some endeavor to defend such baseness and depravity by an appeal to a custom of long standing. Therefore, wishing to abolish such abuse, we absolutely condemn a custom of this kind, which ought rather to be called corruption, firmly decreeing that neither for those conferring nor for the things conferred shall anyone presume to demand or to extort something under any pretext whatsoever. Otherwise both he that has received and he that has given a price of this kind, shall share the condemnation of Giezi and Simon. (Cf. IV Kings, 5:20–27; Acts 8:9–24.)

CANON 65

We have heard it said of some bishops that on the death of rectors of churches they place the churches under interdict and will not allow any persons to be appointed to the vacancies till a certain sum of money has been paid them. Moreover, when a soldier or cleric enters a monastery or chooses to be buried among religious, though he has left nothing to the religious institution, difficulties and villainy are forced into service till something in the nature of a gift comes into their hands. Since, therefore, according to the Apostle we must abstain not only from evil but also from every appearance of evil, we absolutely forbid exactions of this kind. If any transgressor be found, let him restore double the amount exacted; this is to be placed faithfully at the disposal of those localities to whose detriment the exactions were made.

CANON 66

It has frequently come to the ears of the Apostolic See that some clerics demand and extort money for burials, nuptial blessings, and similar things, and, if perchance their cupidity is not given satisfaction, they fraudulently interpose fictitious impediments. On the other hand, some laymen, under the pretext of piety but really on heretical grounds, strive to suppress a laudable custom introduced by the pious devotion of the faithful in behalf of the church (that is, of giving freely something for ecclesiastical services rendered). Wherefore, we forbid that such evil exactions be made in these matters, and on the other hand command that pious customs be observed, decreeing that the sacraments of the Church be administered freely and that those who endeavor maliciously to change a laudable custom be restrained by the bishops of the locality when once the truth is known.

Canon 8

One of the more significant achievements of medieval canonists was to elaborate procedures for determining the extent of guilt. This problem, it will be recalled (cf. above, Document 31), had concerned Gratian early in the twelfth century. Canon 8 is an essential concomitant to the disciplinary decrees just cited, outlining a due process formula for ecclesiastical courts.

How and when a prelate ought to proceed in the inquiry and punishment of the excesses of subjects (that is, of clerics) is clearly deduced from the authority of the New and Old Testament, from which the canonical decrees were afterward drawn, as we have long since clearly pointed out and now with the approval of the holy council confirm. For we read in the Gospel that the steward who was accused to his master of wasting his goods, heard him say: "How is it that I hear this of thee? Give an account of thy stewardship, for now thou canst be steward no longer" (Luke 16:2). And in Genesis the Lord said: "I will go down and see whether they have done according to the cry that is come to me" (Gen. 18:21). From these authorities it is clearly proved that not only when a subject (that is, a cleric of a lower rank) but also when a prelate is guilty of excesses and these should come to the ears of the superior through complaint and report, not indeed from spiteful and slanderous persons, but from those who are prudent and upright persons, and not only once but often, he must in the presence of the seniors of the church carefully inquire into the truth of such reports, so that if they prove to be true, the guilty party may be duly punished without the superior being both accuser and judge in the matter. But, while this is to be observed in regard to subjects, the observance must be stricter in reference to prelates, who are, as it were, a target for the arrow. Because they cannot please all, since by their very office they are bound not only to rebuke but also at times to loose and bind, they frequently incur the hatred of many and are subject to insidious attacks. The holy fathers, therefore, wisely decreed that accusations against prelates must be accepted with great reserve lest, the pillars being shattered, the edifice itself fall unless proper precaution be exercised by which recourse not only to false but also malicious incrimination is precluded. They wished so to protect prelates that on the one hand they might not be unjustly accused, and on the other hand that they might be on their guard, lest they should become haughtily delinquent; finding a suitable remedy for each disease in the provision that a criminal accusation which calls for *diminutio capitis*, that is, degradation, is by no means to be accepted, *nisi legitima praecedat inscriptio*. But when anyone shall have been accused on account of his excesses, so that the reports and whisperings arising therefrom cannot any longer be ignored without scandal or tolerated without danger, then steps, inspired not by hatred but by charity, must be taken without scruple toward an inquiry and punishment of his excesses. If it is a question of a grave offense, though not one that calls for a *degradatio ab ordine*, the accused must be deprived absolutely of all administrative authority, which is in accordance with the teaching of the Gospel, namely, that the steward who cannot render a proper account of this office as steward be deprived of his stewardship. He about whom inquiry is to be made must be present, unless he absents himself through stubbornness; and the matter to be investigated must be made known to him, that he may have opportunity to defend himself. Not only the testimony of the witnesses but also their names must be made known to him, that he may be aware who testified against

him and what was their testimony; and finally, legitimate exceptions and replications must be admitted, lest by the suppression of
names and by the exclusion of exceptions the boldness of the
defamer and the false witness be encouraged. The diligence of the
prelate in correcting the excesses of his subjects ought to be in
proportion to the blameworthiness of allowing the offense to go
unpunished. Against such offenders, to say nothing of those who
are guilty of notorious crimes, there can be a threefold course of
procedure, namely, by accusation, by denunciation, and by inquiry, in all of which, however, proper precaution must be exercised lest perchance by undue haste grave detriment should result.
The accusation must be preceded by the *legitima inscriptio*, denunciation by the *caritativa admonitio*, and the inquiry by the
clamosa insinuatio (*diffamatio*); such moderation to be always used
that the *forma sententiae* be governed by the *forma judicii*. The
foregoing, however, does not apply to regular clerics, who, when a
reason exists, can be removed from their charges more easily and
expeditiously.

Canons 12, 13, 60

Canons 12, 13, and 60 concern the regular clergy. In Canon 12 the
Cistercian system of provincial chapters outlined in their constitution,
the *Carta caritatis*, is extended to other orders.

CANON 12

In every ecclesiastical province there shall be held every three
years, saving the right of the diocesan ordinaries, a general chapter
of abbots and of priors having no abbots, who have not been accustomed to celebrate such chapters. This shall be held in a monastery
best adapted to this purpose and shall be attended by all who are
not canonically impeded, with this restriction, however, that no
one bring with him more than six horses and eight persons. In
inaugurating this new arrangement, let two neighboring abbots of
the Cistercian order be invited to give them counsel and opportune
assistance, since among them the celebration of such chapters is of
long standing. These two Cistercians shall without hindrance
choose from those present two whom they consider the most
competent, and these four shall preside over the entire chapter, so
that no one of these four may assume the authority of leadership;

should it become expedient, they may be changed by prudent deliberation. Such a chapter shall be celebrated for several consecutive days according to the custom of the Cistercian order. . . . Moreover, the diocesan ordinaries must strive so to reform the monasteries subject to them, that when the aforesaid visitors come to them they will find in them more that is worthy of commendation than of correction, taking special care lest the monasteries be oppressed by them with undue burdens. For, while we wish that the rights of the superiors be respected, we do not on that account wish that injury be sustained by inferiors. We strictly command diocesan bishops and persons attending the chapters, that with ecclesiastical censure—every appeal being denied—they restrain advocates, patrons, vicegerents, rulers, consuls, nobles, and soldiers, and all others, from molesting the monasteries either in persons or properties and if perchance these persons should so molest, let the aforesaid bishops and chapter members not neglect to compel these latter to make satisfaction, that the monasteries may serve Almighty God more freely and peacefully.

Canon 13

[A multiplicity of religious orders, some of them small, proved to be a serious problem. This explains the following canon.]

Lest too great a diversity of religious orders lead to grave confusion in the Church of God, we strictly forbid anyone in the future to found a new order, but whoever should wish to enter an order, let him choose one already approved. Similarly, he who should wish to found a new monastery, must accept a rule already approved. We forbid also anyone to presume to be a monk in different monasteries (that is, belong to different monasteries), or that one abbot preside over several monasteries.

Canon 60

[Since many monasteries were exempt from episcopal jurisdiction, some abbots appropriated to themselves episcopal functions. This decree may be taken as an example of Innocent's awareness of the problem of diminishing episcopal authority.]

From different parts of the world complaints of bishops come to us in regard to grave excesses of some abbots, who, not content within their own spheres, extend their hands to those things that concern the episcopal office, deciding matrimonial cases, imposing public penances, granting letters of indulgences, and similar things, whence it sometimes happens that the episcopal authority is looked upon by many as something of trifling importance. Wishing, therefore, in these matters to safeguard the dignity of the bishops and the welfare of the abbots, we absolutely forbid in the present decree that abbots presume to overreach themselves in such matters if they wish to escape canonical penalties, unless they can by a special concession or other legitimate reason defend themselves in matters of this kind.

Canons 21, 22, 51

These three canons concern the laity. Canon 21 is one of the most celebrated measures taken by the council. It enjoins a minimum level of lay participation in the sacramental life of the Church. It probably reflected in part the contemporary fear of heresy and in part, also, the tendency for people to avoid their own parish priest and wander elsewhere. And it dramatically illustrates the difficulties still encountered in reaching the laity on any but the most elementary plane. Frequent reception of the sacraments was not a feature of medieval religion, even among the clergy. For the laity, the problem was accentuated by the dearth of adequately trained clerics. Note the severe penalty imposed on a priest who violates the secrecy of confession.

CANON 21

All the faithful of both sexes shall after they have reached the age of discretion faithfully confess all their sins at least once a year to their own (parish) priest and perform to the best of their ability the penance imposed, receiving reverently at least at Easter the sacrament of the Eucharist, unless perchance at the advice of their own priest they may for a good reason abstain for a time from its reception; otherwise they shall be cut off from the Church (excommunicated) during life and deprived of Christian burial in death. Wherefore, let this salutary decree be published frequently in the churches, that no one may find in the plea of ignorance a shadow of excuse. But if anyone for a good reason should wish to confess his sins to another priest, let him first seek and obtain permission from his own (parish) priest, since otherwise he (the other priest) cannot loose or bind him.

Let the priest be discreet and cautious that he may pour wine and oil into the wounds of the one injured after the manner of a skilful physician, carefully inquiring into the circumstances of the sinner and the sin, from the nature of which he may understand what kind of advice to give and what remedy to apply, making use of different experiments to heal the sick one. But let him exercise the greatest precaution that he does not in any degree by word, sign, or any other manner make known the sinner, but should he need more prudent counsel, let him seek it cautiously without any mention of the person. He who dares to reveal a sin confided to him in the tribunal of penance, we decree that he be not only deposed from the sacerdotal office but also relegated to a monastery of strict observance to do penance for the remainder of his life.

CANON 22

Since bodily infirmity is sometimes caused by sin, the Lord saying to the sick man whom he had healed: "Go and sin no more, lest some worse thing happen to thee" (John 5:14), we declare in the present decree and strictly command that when physicians of the body are called to the bedside of the sick, before all else they admonish them to call for the physician of souls, so that after spiritual health has been restored to them, the application of bodily medicine may be of greater benefit, for the cause being removed the effect will pass away. We publish this decree for the reason that some, when they are sick and are advised by the physician in the course of the sickness to attend to the salvation of their soul, give up all hope and yield more easily to the danger of death. If any physician shall transgress this decree after it has been published by the bishops, let him be cut off (*arceatur*) from the Church till he has made suitable satisfaction for his transgression. And since the soul is far more precious than the body, we forbid under penalty of anathema that a physician advise a patient to have recourse to sinful means for the recovery of bodily health.

CANON 51

[Canon 50 removed the previously existing prohibitions against marriages in the second and third degrees of affinity. Canon 51 prescribes measures for determining the facts regarding consanguinity; it reinforces the prohibitions which remain and condemns clandestine marriages. Peter Lombard, it will be recalled, had included marriage among the sacraments. Although discussion as to the nature of marriage continued, it was expected that marriage would be contracted in the presence of a priest.]

Since the prohibition of the conjugal union in the three last degrees has been revoked, we wish that it be strictly observed in the other degrees. Whence, following in the footsteps of our predecessors, we absolutely forbid clandestine marriages; and we forbid also that a priest presume to witness such. Wherefore, extending to other localities generally the particular custom that prevails in some, we decree that when marriages are to be contracted they must be announced publicly in the churches by the priests during a suitable and fixed time, so that if legitimate impediments exist, they may be made known. . . .

Canons 67–70

These canons renew or clarify earlier local or general decrees concerning the position of Jews in Christian society and, also, presumably reflect the views of Innocent III. Moreover, although popular anti-Jewish feeling certainly existed in the Middle Ages and the tone of these canons seems scarcely charitable to modern ears, their primary purpose was not mere anti-Semitism as that term is understood today. Rather, it was pastoral, the protection of the Christian community from any form of distraction, even, as in Canon 68, which is directed against Saracens as well as Jews, immoderate dress. It is evident, too, that the council fathers considered usury to be an important aspect of Jewish-Christian relations.

These decrees should be considered in connection with two preceding measures which are cited first here, Canon 25 of the Third Lateran Council (1179) on usury, which illustrates how seriously this matter was regarded, and Innocent III's Constitution for the Jews, issued in 1199, a slightly modified version of an earlier constitution of Alexander III.

THIRD LATERAN COUNCIL, CANON 25

Since almost everywhere the crime of usury has developed to such an extent that many, heedless of the strict Scriptural prohibition, pass over other professions to devote themselves to the business of usury, as if it were lawful, we decree that notorious usurers be not admitted to the communion of the altar and, if they die in that sin, that they shall not receive Christian burial. Neither shall anyone accept their offering. He who has taken such an offering or given them Christian burial, shall be compelled to return what he has taken, and, till he has satisfied the wishes of the bishop, let him remain suspended from his office.

CONSTITUTION FOR THE JEWS

Although in many ways the disbelief of the Jews must be reproved, since nevertheless through them our own faith is truly proved, they must not be oppressed grievously by the faithful, as the prophet says: "Do not slay them, lest these be forgetful of Thy Law," [Ps. 58 (59):12] as if he were saying more openly: "Do not wipe out the Jews completely, lest perhaps Christians might be able to forget Thy Law, which the former, although not understanding it, present in their books to those who do understand it."

Just as, therefore there ought not to be license for the Jews to presume to go beyond what is permitted them by law in their synagogues, so in those which have been conceded to them, they ought to suffer no prejudice. These men, therefore, since they wish rather to go on in their own hardness than to know the revelations of the prophets and the mysteries of the Law, and to come to a knowledge of the Christian faith, still, since they beseech the help of Our defense, We, out of the meekness proper to Christian piety, and keeping in the footprints of Our predecessors of happy memory, the Roman Pontiffs Calixtus, Eugene, Alexander, Clement, and Celestine, admit their petition, and We grant them the buckler of Our protection.

For We make the law that no Christian compel them, unwilling or refusing, by violence to come to baptism. But, if any one of them should spontaneously, and for the sake of the faith, fly to the Christians, once his choice has become evident, let him be made a Christian without any calumny. Indeed, he is not considered to possess the true faith of Christianity who is recognized to have come to Christian baptism, not spontaneously, but unwillingly.

Too, no Christian ought presume, apart from the juridical sentence of the territorial power, wickedly to injure their persons, or with violence to take away their property, or to change the good customs which they have had until now in whatever region they inhabit.

Besides, in the celebration of their own festivities, no one ought disturb them in any way, with clubs or stones, nor ought any one try to require from them or to extort from them services they do not owe, except for those they have been accustomed from times past to perform.

In addition to these, We decree, blocking the wickedness and avarice of evil men, that no one ought to dare mutilate or diminish a Jewish cemetery, nor, in order to get money, to exhume bodies once they have been buried.

If anyone, however, shall attempt, the tenor of this decree once known, to go against it—may this be far from happening!—let him be punished by the vengeance of excommunication, unless he correct his presumption by making equivalent satisfaction.

We desire, however, that only those be fortified by the guard of this protection who shall have presumed no plotting for the subversion of the Christian faith.

Given at [the palace of] the Lateran, by the hand of Raynaldus, Archbishop of Acerenza, acting for the Chancellor, on the seventeenth day before the Kalends of October, in the second indiction, and the 1199th year of the Incarnation of the Lord, and in the second year of the pontificate of the Lord Pope, Innocent III.

CANON 67

The more the Christians are restrained from the practice of usury, the more are they oppressed in this matter by the treachery of the Jews, so that in a short time they exhaust the resources of the Christians. Wishing, therefore, in this matter to protect the Christians against cruel oppression by the Jews, we ordain in this decree that if in the future under any pretext Jews extort from Christians oppressive and immoderate interest, the partnership of the Christians shall be denied them till they have made suitable satisfaction for their excesses. The Christians also, every appeal being set aside, shall, if necessary, be compelled by ecclesiastical censure to abstain from all commercial intercourse with them. We command the princes not to be hostile to the Christians on this account, but rather to strive to hinder the Jews from practicing such excesses. Lastly, we decree that the Jews be compelled by the same punishment (avoidance of commercial intercourse) to make satisfaction for the tithes and offerings due to the churches, which the Christians were accustomed to supply from their houses and other possessions before these properties, under whatever title, fell into the hands of the Jews, that thus the churches may be safe-guarded against loss.

CANON 68

In some provinces a difference of dress distinguishes the Jews and Saracens from the Christians, but in others confusion has developed to such a degree that no difference is discernible. Whence it happens sometimes through error that Christians mingle with the women of Jews and Saracens, and, on the other hand, Jews and Saracens mingle with those of the Christians. Therefore, that such ruinous commingling through error of this kind may not serve as a refuge for further excuse for excesses, we decree that such people of both sexes (that is, Jews and Saracens) in every Christian province and at all times be distinguished in public from other people by a difference of dress, since this was also enjoined on them by Moses. On the days of the Lamentations and on Passion Sunday they may not appear in public, because some of them, as we understand, on those days are not ashamed to show them-selves more ornately attired and do not fear to amuse themselves at the expense of the Christians, who in memory of the sacred passion go about attired in robes of mourning. That we most strictly forbid, lest they should presume in some measure to burst forth suddenly in contempt of the Redeemer. And, since we ought not to be ashamed of Him who blotted out our offenses, we command that the secular princes restrain presumptuous persons of this kind by condign punishment, lest they presume to blaspheme in some degree the One crucified for us.

CANON 69

Since it is absurd that a blasphemer of Christ exercise authority over Christians, we on account of the boldness of transgressors renew in this general council what the Synod of Toledo (589) wisely enacted in this matter, prohibiting Jews from being given preference in the matter of public offices, since in such capacity they are most troublesome to the Christians. But if anyone should commit such an office to them, let him, after previous warning, be restrained by such punishment as seems proper by the provincial synod which we command to be celebrated every year. The official, however, shall be denied the commercial and other intercourse of the Christians, till in the judgment of the bishop all that he acquired from the Christians from the time he assumed office be restored for the needs of the Christian poor, and the office that he irreverently assumed let him lose with shame. The same we extend also to pagans.

CANON 70

Some (Jews), we understand, who voluntarily approached the waters of holy baptism, do not entirely cast off the old man that they may more perfectly put on the new one, because, retaining remnants of the former rite, they obscure by such a mixture the beauty of the Christian religion. But since it is written: "Accursed is the man that goeth on the two ways" (Ecclus. 2:14), and "a garment that is woven together of woolen and linen" (Deut. 22:11) ought not to be put on, we decree that such persons be in every way restrained by the prelates from the observance of the former rite, that, having given themselves of their own free will to the Christian religion, salutary coercive action may preserve them in its observance, since not to know the way of the Lord is a lesser evil than to retrace one's steps after it is known.

45. *Implementation of the Decrees: Robert Grosseteste*

No study of the canons of ecumenical councils or of papal decretals can be complete without some consideration of the extent to which such decrees were implemented, for the mere promulgation of decrees does not ensure their observance. Many provincial councils were held throughout western Europe during the thirteenth century in which the ordinances of general councils as well as collections of papal decretals were received and repeated. Moreover, the investigation can be carried one step further by examining the activities of individual bishops. Such evidence is not always available; and the most carefully preserved records are likely to be those of the most conscientious bishops and, therefore, not entirely typical. Two such records, however, are presented here as illustrations of ecclesiastical conditions in the decades following the Fourth Lateran Council. Both mention the assembling of provincial or diocesan councils.

The first set of documents records the instructions and visitations of Robert Grosseteste, bishop of Lincoln (1235-53). Grosseteste was a celebrated scholar and had been a teacher at Oxford where he was closely associated with the Franciscans. He is especially noted for his explorations into the scientific method which Roger Bacon carried further and for his role in introducing Aristotelian studies into Oxford.

As bishop, Grosseteste was both conscientious and efficient. Moreover, when he took over the see of Lincoln, there were available not only the Lateran decrees but Pope Gregory IX's collection of decretals. Grossseteste was not content simply to issue instructions. As he said himself, a bishop's pastoral responsibility required that he take steps to see that instructions were carried out. Hence the importance of his visitations.

Grossseteste was also active in opposing royal encroachments on ecclesiastical liberties, and he was not afraid to protest, and in one instance to refuse to accept, the abuse of papal provisions to local benefices during the pontificate of Innocent IV.[1] Not many bishops approached the stature of this bishop of Lincoln. He was one of the outstanding prelates of the period.

Three selections from Grosseteste's writings are included here: instructions to the archdeacons of the diocese on whom fell the burden of implementing the reforms; the bishop's description of his visitations; and a set of statutes for the diocese. All three reveal a great deal about the conditions of the lower clergy, especially perhaps its minimal education, as well as about the religious life of the laity. Both, apparently, left much to be desired. It is worth noting, too, that Grosseteste made use of the friars. Moreover, pastoral care in the thirteenth century evidently occasionally included giving advice on matters of public peace and household safety.

The selections are translated from the Latin text in F. M. Powicke and C. R. Cheyney (eds.), *Councils and Synods*, vol. II (Oxford, 1964), Part I, pp. 203–205; 265–266; and 267 ff.

Instructions to Archdeasons (1235–36)

Because it pertains to the office of shepherd to suffer with those who are ignorant and in error and watch over the flock committed to his care . . . and to feed that flock with wisdom and teaching . . . we have considered it necessary to include in the present letter certain very pernicious errors which lead through a dark, erroneous, and slippery path . . . that these errors may be exposed and warned against . . . throughout your archdeaconries . . . and others, indeed, prohibited and curbed by canonical censure. . . .

And because he struggles in vain to curb other vices who has not subdued gluttony and drunkenness, we command first, strictly

1. See below, Document 56.

enjoining you to forbid the drinking parties, popularly called *scot-ales*, in your synods as well as in your chapter meetings, and that you frequently see that they are forbidden in all churches of your archdeaconries, and that you discipline canonically those who presume to go against the aforesaid prohibitions, imposing canonical censure on them. For it is written, "Wine, that is everything that inebriates, drunken with excess raiseth quarrels, and wrath, and many ruins, is bitterness of the soul, the stumbling block of the fool, lessening strength, and causing wounds" (Eccles., xxxi, 38–40). Besides, it deforms the image of God in man by depriving him of the use of his reason, it constricts natural actions, induces the worst diseases, shortens life; it is the principle of apostasy, and creates innumerable other evils. We who are appointed to tear out, destroy, ruin and scatter things of this kind ought not to be remiss in rooting out such great evils.

In addition to this we decree that, according to the form indicated above, you prohibit and cause to be prohibited by disciplining and punishing those who scorn the prohibition, the quintain revolving on poles[1] and other similar games where there is competition for a prize, since both the participants and the spectators at such games, as Isidore clearly shows, sacrifice to demons—the inventors of such games—and because such games frequently give opportunities for anger, hatred, violence, and homicide. Other games played on feast days which have not ordinarily fomented discord you are to dissuade by healthful preaching. For, as blessed Augustine bears witness, women spin and weave and men plow and do other things necessary and useful for the maintenance of life on feast days with much less sin than by indulging in purely pleasurable and useless things of this kind. For holy days are hallowed to divine observances and holy works which are directly profitable to the salvation of souls; from these the things which are for ease and pleasure are incomparably more distant than are those of necessity and utility.

By frequent preaching remind those who assemble for the night vigils on the eve of saints' days at their churches or memorials or for the services for the dead that they occupy themselves with divine services and prayers only; so that they may not by being

1. The quintain was a sort of revolving target used to train young men in jousting.

intent on games or perhaps worse, as has been the custom, provoke against themselves the wrath of the saints whose suffrages they have come to beseech; and so that in the services for the dead they do not make the home of sorrow and recollection of those departed and as a warning against sins into a house of laughter and joking to the increase of sins. For eternal mourning shall take hold of the end of these and a dark forgetfulness, which wisdom or knowledge or reason will demonstrate.[2]

By suitable warning and ecclesiastical censure see that all such games are kept away from churches and cemeteries, for holy places are to be freed from human uses, not to mention human mirth-making, and turned to divine uses. And those who presume the contrary make the house and place of prayer into a den of thieves (Matt., xxi, 13).

Also give warning by frequent preaching in each church that mothers and nurses are not to keep little babies beside them in bed, lest by chance they carelessly smother them, as often happens, and as a consequence what is thought to be giving affection to a tender life is the occasion of death.

Strictly forbid clandestine marriages by assiduous preaching, and clearly and carefully explain the dangers which follow, so that by a foreknowledge of the peril of evil to come, its occasion may more forcefully and carefully be avoided.

In addition, in each church give a strict order that in the annual visitation and veneration of the mother church no parish is to strive with its banners to get ahead of those of another parish, because it often happens from this that there are not only altercations but serious bloodshed. Indeed, rather on the contrary give canonical warning to those who so presume, for contenders of this kind thereby violate and dishonor the mother church which they should venerate and honor. Nor should those be immune from some sort of punishment who dishonor their spiritual mother, when those who dishonor their human mothers are cursed by divine law and punished by death.

Further, we have found in certain churches this bad practice to have grown into a custom, that on Easter day the offerings of the parishioners are not received except after mass has been celebrated when they come to receive the sacrament of the body and blood of

2. Cf. Prov., xiv 13; Wisd., xvii, 3; Eccles., vii, 26, ix, 10 (eds.).

the Lord. This corrupt practice you must root out strictly under heavy penalty, since there arises from this grave scandal and the mark of base cupidity on the part of the priests of the church; and the devotion of the people approaching this great sacrament is very much hindered.

Moreover, because we have found in some places, contrary to the general as well as provincial council,[3] that the sacraments of the church are denied if money is not given, and even the sacrament of the Eucharist on Easter day, lest anyone in this matter pretend that some sort of excuse is valid as though through ignorance, see to it that on this the decree of the councils is frequently recited not only in synods but also in chapter meetings and punish with canonical severity those who presume otherwise.

Description of Visitations

In past times the bishops of Lincoln have been accustomed to visit the religious houses of the diocese subject to them, and because of this visit to receive procurations from these houses. It is not, however, our present intention to speak of those things which are customary and approved and acceptable from longstanding use. Rather, if it is pleasing, may a few things be graciously heard concerning unusual matters. Since my elevation to the episcopate I have considered myself to be the pastor of souls and, lest in the final judgement the blood of the sheep be required of my hand, obligated to visit the sheep committed to me with all diligence as scripture prescribes and lays down. Accordingly, I have begun to go about my diocese through each rural deanery, requiring the clergy of each deanery in turn to assemble at a certain day and place, and the people instructed to be present on that same day with children to be confirmed, to hear the word of God, and to confess. When the clergy and people are assembled I myself would often expound the word of God to the clergy and a friar or lesser preacher to the people. Following this, four friars would hear confessions and enjoin penances. When the children had been confirmed, on the same day or the day following I with my clergy continually attended to questions, corrections, and reforms as it pertains to the duty of inquiry. In my first round certain persons came to me and said, as though reproaching me for these things I

3. IV Lateran, 66; Oxford (1222) (eds.).

have mentioned, "My Lord, you are doing something new and exceptional." To which I replied, "Every new thing which implants and promotes and perfects the new man, corrupts and destroys the old. Blessed is the new and in every way welcome to Him who comes to recreate the old man in newness."

Statutes of Bishop Robert Grosseteste for the Diocese of Lincoln

Since we ought to render a good accounting concerning you which, according to Augustine, is to speak and not keep silent, to weep when we speak and are not heard, we cannot pass over in silence the things which we believe it necessary for you to know and observe.

(1) Therefore, because the safety of souls is not established without the observance of the decalogue, we exhort in the Lord, urgently enjoining each pastor of souls and parish priest to know the decalogue, that is, the ten commandments of the Mosaic Law, and frequently to preach and explain them to the people in his care. He should know also what are the seven deadly sins and likewise preach that they must be avoided by the people. In addition, let him know, at least in simple form, the seven sacraments of the church, and most of all, those who are priests should know what things are required for a valid sacrament of confession and penance; and they should often teach the laity the form for baptizing in the common speech. Let each one also have at least a simple understanding of the faith as is contained in the creed, both the longer and the shorter, and that in the tract "Whoever wishes (*Quicunque vult*)" which is daily chanted in the church at Prime.[1]

(2) Further, the eucharist which is the sacrament of the Lord's body is always to be kept respectfully, devoutly, and faithfully in a special place, clean and designated. Each priest should teach his people often that, when in the celebration of the mass the host of salvation is elevated, they should bow reverently and do likewise when the priest carries it to the sick. Let him, properly vested, carry and return it with a clean covering placed over it, openly and respectfully before his breast with reverence and fear, with a little light always preceding, since it is the brightness of eternal light

1. The Creed of Athanasius.

(Wisd., vii, 26), so that by this faith and devotion may be increased among all people, as it is written in the general council. A bell as well as the light should always precede the host of the body of Christ, always to be venerated, so that by its sound the devotion of the faithful may be aroused to a due adoration of so great a sacrament. Let priests also diligently see to it that the holy eucharist does not become moist or mouldy because of a defect in the vessel or from being kept too long, so that it become unpleasant in appearance and of disagreeable taste.

(3) Priests, moreover, must be especially prompt and ready not only during the day but also at night to visit the sick when they require it, lest a sick person, *quod absit!* because of their negligence die without confession or communion of the body of the Lord or extreme unction.

(4) Also altar slabs are to be in good taste and of proper size and firmly attached to the surrounding wood so that they do not move from it, nor are they to be taken for any other use than for the celebration of the divine services; for example, colors are not to be ground on them or anything of that sort done.

(5) Chrism cloths are not to be put to secular uses.

(6) Likewise, let the divine office be carried out in church fully and devoutly, so that, for example, readings, hymns, psalms, and other things which are recited in praise of God, may have the full pronunciation of the words and strict attention of the mind to the sense of the words, lest, *quod absit!* instead of a complete and living victim there is offered one mutilated or dead.

(7) Also, all pastors of souls and parish priests on finishing the divine services in church are to devote themselves diligently to prayer and the reading of holy scripture, as it pertains to their duties, [that] they may always be prepared to satisfy anyone requesting an explanation concerning hope and faith; and let them be always "inserted" in the teaching and work of scripture as levers in the ring of the ark,[2] so that by assiduous reading, as though it were daily food, prayer may be nourished and grow fertile.

(8) Let rectors of churches and parish priests also provide attentively that the young men of their parishes are taught carefully and know the Lord's Prayer, the creed, the Hail Mary, and how to sign themselves with the sign of the cross correctly. And because

2. Cf. Exodus ccv, 15 (eds.).

we have heard that even certain adults do not know these things, we order that when lay persons come to confession they be examined carefully as to whether they do know these things; and after this it is expedient for them to be instructed in these matters by the priests.

(9) And because Isaiah says (liii, 11) those who carry the vessels of the Lord must be clean and touch no unclean things, we exhort and admonish all those beneficed and in holy orders to shun the vice of self-indulgence and all willful uncleanness of the flesh, maintaining the purity of continence.

(10) Let none of them take a wife; let anyone, moreover, who took a wife before he was raised to holy orders not hold an ecclesiastical benefice, nor presume to minister in holy orders, if he received them afterwards.

(11) Since not only evil, but every kind of evil must be shunned, we emphatically forbid clerics to frequent the convents of nuns without clear and reasonable cause.

(12) No priest should maintain a woman in his house, whether a relative or otherwise, whence suspicion can reasonably arise.

(13) And because in Leviticus the Lord said to Aaron, "You shall not drink wine or anything that may make you drunk, you and your sons when you enter into the tabernacle of the testimony, lest you die" (x, 9), and since Aaron and his sons, priests of the old law, show forth as the image of the priest of that time, and wine and other intoxicating drinks as the figure of drunkenness, since also priests must remain symbolically day and night in the tabernacle, the watchful sentinels of the Lord, lest they die, as it is written in that same book (*ibid.*, viii, 35), we firmly forbid any beneficed person or anyone in holy orders to be intoxicated or gluttonous or to frequent taverns, lest they die an eternal death, according to the threat of the law, but by abstinence and sobriety keep themselves fit so that according to the teaching of the Lord they may have the wisdom to distinguish between holy and unholy, between clean and unclean, and teach the people all the ordinances of the Lord which He spoke by the hand of Moses (*ibid.*, x, 10–11).

(14) And because it was said of the Levites that they will have no part in the inheritance of the children of Israel; wherefore every spark of avarice and base gain is removed by the ministers of the church; we strongly urge and warn beneficed [clergy] and those in holy orders not to enter into financial transactions, not to lend at

interest (usury), but as evangelical teaching admonishes, give a loan expecting nothing in return.

(15) Nor shall they [priests] give or receive churches or church property in farm, except in cases permitted by the councils.

(16) In order to remove any kind of cupidity we firmly prohibit, not only by ordinary but also by special apostolic authority, any beneficed person or one in holy orders to be promoted as viscounts[3] or secular judges or to hold jurisdiction over wards for which they may be obliged to render account of their jurisdictions to lay authorities.

(17) We most strictly forbid any rector of a church to make an agreement with his priests such that the priest will be able to receive, over and above the allotted stipend, payments for annual or triennial masses,[4] because such an agreement is clear indication that the priest, according to this, is being definitely underpaid. It also follows that he does not fulfil the annual or triennial anniversaries which he has accepted or that he does not properly carry out the religious observances in the parish church.

(18) An adequate and honest living must be given to these priests by the rectors of churches lest on account of inadequate living the churches should lack divine services or that these priests should covet dishonest money or beg their bread.

(19) We emphatically forbid any free lands of the churches of the Lord to be given in farm to any layman, unless perhaps such laymen are servants of the same churches. In this case let it be done with the license of the diocesan.

(20) No rectors or vicars are to build out of the resources of the church in a lay fief outside of the estate of the church; and likewise no tithes are to be placed in lay fief, but in the estate of the church itself.

(21) We also decree that revenues for candles or for other proper uses in these churches consigned through the devotion of the laity are not to be converted by these rectors or vicars to their own use or profit.

(22) We also firmly prohibit offerings to be received of lay persons after the mass on Easter day when they communicate, because this is a clear indication of avarice and an evident detriment to the devotion of the communicants.

3. Presumably sheriffs.
4. Possibly thirty-day or month's mind masses or 30 masses (*tricennaria, tricennalia*)?

(23) We urge and advise that [they] do not watch mimes, jesters or actors, or play at dice or games of chance, or sit by the players; because although it may seem a small thing to some, nevertheless, according to the teachings of the holy fathers, those who do such things give sacrifices to demons.

(24) And because in the clergy nothing ought to shine forth except the humility of Jesus Christ and evangelic perfection which counsels that if anyone strikes you in the right cheek turn the other to him, we warn and admonish the clergy not to bear arms, but to have the shaven head and tonsure of their order and appropriate attire both for themselves and for their mounts according to what the sacred councils lay down.[5]

(25) We also order not only by our own but by special apostolic authority that no one retain more cures [care of souls] than is permitted by the apostolic see.

(26) Similarly, that sons serving churches in which they have directly succeeded their fathers resign entirely and the patrons present suitable persons to those churches.

(27) We have heard and are not a little grieved that certain priests exact money from the laity for penance or for administering other sacraments, and that certain priests enjoin penances with base profit attached: for example, that a woman known by her husband after childbirth and before her purification (churching) should carry an offering to the altar with whatever woman in the same parish is to be purified; or that a murderer or anyone who encompassed the death of another offer for any dead person in the same parish. These and things of this kind which are filled with avarice we entirely forbid.

(28) And no priest is to charge for annual or triennial anniversaries with similar greediness so that he himself obviously makes profit.

(29) We have also heard that some priests make their deacons hear the confessions of the parishioners. It is not necessary to call to mind that this is out of place, since it is clearly true that the power of binding and loosing is not bestowed on the deacon, and the priests themselves would not seek [to avoid] this unless they were intent on ease or time for secular affairs. Therefore, we firmly forbid deacons to hear confessions or impose penances or administer other sacraments which priests alone are allowed to administer.

5. IV Lateran, 16; Oxford (1222); London (1237) (eds.).

(30) We also desire and order that all beneficed persons be raised to the orders which the cure they have undertaken requires.

(31) Moreover, by special apostolic authority we warn and order that all rectors of churches and vicars reside in their benefices, devoting themselves to these laudably and honorably, unless it be from some reasonable cause that they are dispensed from residing in their churches.

(32) Also in all churches whose facilities are sufficient for it there should be one deacon and one subdeacon as is proper for the [i.e., as] ministers. In other churches, let there be at least one clerk fit and honorable to serve in the divine offices in appropriate clerical attire.

(33) We also strongly order by evangelical authority and even by special apostolic indulgence that no markets be held in sacred places since the Lord cast out from the temple those buying and selling, so that the house of prayer might not become a den of thieves.

(34) In addition, let cemeteries be well enclosed, and churches and houses pertaining to them properly constructed according to the resources of the churches. And let the churches be fittingly furnished with books and sacred vessels and vestments, and the ornaments and sacred vessels be in safe and reliable custody at night and not be placed in the homes of lay persons or in their custody unless clear and reasonable necessity requires.

(35) The execrable custom which has been usual in certain churches of observing the Feast of Fools we forbid altogether by the special authority of apostolic rescript, so that a house of sport may not be made out of the house of prayer, and the pain of the Circumcision of Our Lord Jesus Christ may not be mocked by jests and public shows.

(36) We also forbid any priests to celebrate [mass] with vinegar.

(37) And because each craftsman should dedicate his skill rather to another, we decree that the rectors of souls devote themselves vigilantly to the art of government of souls, since, as blessed Gregory is witness, this is the art of arts. And so that they are not diverted from this we strictly forbid any of them to attend lectures [on] or to teach secular law.

(38) We also decree that in any church whatsoever the canon of the mass be set in proper order.

(39) We also order that in each church it be solemnly an-

nounced that no one is to play at the quintain or set up other games in which there is competition for a prize, nor is anyone to be present at such games. Likewise, we forbid the drinkings which are popularly called *scotales*.

(40) Also let all games and secular amusements be entirely removed from sacred precincts.

(41) Let mothers and nurses be frequently warned not to keep little babies close to them in bed.

(42) Clandestine marriages are to be strictly forbidden.

(43) Rectors of churches and priests must not allow their parishes, in the annual visitation to the mother church, to strive to lead the way with their banners, because fights and death often result.

(44) We also strictly decree that in each church it be solemnly announced that no one is knowingly and intentionally to receive as guests the concubines of clerics, except possibly in travelling, and then taking especial care that no cleric guilty of fornication be given hospitality in the same place.

(45) Moreover, laymen are not to stand or sit among the clergy in the chancel while divine service is being celebrated there, except possibly out of courtesy or some other reasonable and clear cause this is permitted the patrons alone.

(46) A list of excommunications from the Council of Oxford (1222) . . .

These, therefore, we wish and decree, and as they have been canonically decreed, they are to be firmly and reverently observed by you. And all contemners and transgressors thereof, if they are duly convicted or have confessed, we with Our Lord Jesus Christ's help will punish canonically to the extent of our power.

46. Eudes Rigaud's Record of Visitations

This selection is taken from the detailed day-by-day record of the visitations made by Archbishop Eudes Rigaud of Rouen (1248–69). Eudes was a distinguished prelate, a member of the Franciscan order and a respected counselor of King Louis IX of France, who entrusted him with the most delicate negotiations. Like Robert Grosseteste, he was an exceptionally conscientious bishop. He made periodic visitations throughout his archdiocese, and when unable to visit all places, assembled synods to receive local reports, repeat the decrees of general councils or the decretals of popes, or issue local ordinances.

Eudes's record is a remarkable medieval document which affords an unexampled picture of daily life in a large archdiocese. Moreover, the archbishop's frank reporting of conditions as he found them indicates the wide gap which still existed between the ideal laid down by conciliar canons and the actual. It is worth noting, however, that the normal conditions which needed little or no attention are often described in a line or two, whereas the lapses from discipline which required correction occupy more space in the record.

As the few sample passages cited here will show, the prelate's strenuous efforts to apply suitable remedies, his humanity, his tolerance, and sense of justice are also revealed. He is careful to account for his procurations, the charges for his visits (excessive procurations had been condemned by the Fourth Lateran Council along with unnecessarily large episcopal retinues). There is an interesting reference, too, to the Beguines, one of the semi-monastic charitable organizations of the period.

The translation is that of S. M. Brown in J. O'Sullivan (ed.), *The Register of Eudes of Rigaud*, Columbia University Records of Civilization (New York, 1964), pp. 18–23, 322 ff., 389–398, 400–409, 734. Reprinted by permission of Columbia University Press.

1248

January 4. We visited the monastery of St-Amand-de-Rouen, where we found forty-one veiled nuns and six due to take the veil. They make profession only when they receive the archbishop's blessing. We ordered that when they had reached the age for taking the vows, they should wait yet another year before making profession. Sometimes they sing the Hours of the Blessed Mary and the Suffrages with too much haste and jumbling of the words; we enjoined them to sing these in such a way that those beginning a verse should wait to hear the end of the preceding verse, and those ending a verse should hear the commencement of the following verse. Item, the monastery has one priory, to wit, at Saane[-St-Just], where there are four professed nuns. Item, they have the patronage of ten churches. There are three priests in perpetual residence. They confess five times a year. They do not keep the rule of silence very well; we enjoined them to correct this. They eat meat freely in the infirmary, to wit, three times a week. Sometimes the healthy ones eat with the sick in the infirmary, two or three with one sick sister. They have chemises, use feather beds and sheets, and wear cloaks of rabbits, hares, cats, and foxes; we utterly forbade the use of rabbit skins. The nuns sleep cinctured and in their chemises. Each nun receives a measure of wine, but more is given to one than to another; we ordered that wine should be given to each according to her needs and in equal measure, and if one of them should without permission give a portion of her wine to another outside the house she should compelled by the abbess to go without wine the next day. The monastery has debts amounting to two hundred pounds and an income of one thousand pounds. The abbess does not give detailed accounts to the community at large; we ordered her to cast her accounts each quarter.

This day Nicholas of St-Laurent, priest at Etalleville, came before us and appealed from our jurisdiction to that of the Apostolic See in the following letter:

> On the Monday following Christmas Day, you, the lord archbishop of Rouen, without reasonable cause, refused to confer the rectorship of the free and vacant church of St-Laurent upon me, Nicholas of St-Laurent, priest at Etalleville, when I was presented for the said church by William of St-Laurent, knight, who holds the right of advowson. You assumed that I was in some way unsuitable, although there was nothing canonically deficient in me. This you should not have done, for your predecessor promoted me to Holy Orders and likewise conferred upon me the care of the Church of Etalleville. Feeling that I have been unjustly injured in this matter, I appeal from your jurisdiction, in writing to the Apostolic See. Furthermore, I appeal lest you should take any action to my detriment, as in conferring the said church upon another, and I request that *apostoli* be given to me.[1]

Although we need not honor an appeal of this kind, we thought that the *apostoli* which he had requested should be given to him. . . .

January 18. We visited the priests of the deanery of Aumale, whom we had convoked at Coupigny. We found that Master John, priest of Haudricourt, was ill famed of incontinence with Amelota and with Martina and, although disciplined by the archdeacon, has persisted in his evil conduct. Item, the priest at La Fresnoye is ill famed of incontinence with a certain Emily, a married woman of Aumale; he has been disciplined by the archdeacon. Item, the priest at St-Pierre-d'Aumale, is ill famed of a

---

1. Letters to the judge of the next higher court.

certain woman, now married, who is said to have borne him a son. Item, the priest of Morvillers is publicly known for his drunkenness and for frequenting taverns; item, he also exacts fees for blessing marriages. Item, the priest at Escles [is ill famed] of a certain unmarried woman. Item, the priest at Villers [is ill famed] of a certain unmarried woman; he was disciplined by the archdeacon. Item, Peter, the priest at St-Valéry, rents arable land for sowing. Robert of Puys, priest, is publicly known for engaging in trade; he promised to give it up. We warned, rebuked, and threatened them all that if they did not correct their ways and if we should find them ill famed on the above faults, we would punish them more severely. Item, since some of the priests of this deanery rode horseback and appeared in public dressed in unseemly clothing, we instructed those who did not possess closed gowns to procure them before Assumption Day, under the penalty of twenty shillings, to be collected without mercy by the dean. Item, we forbade them to go any distance from their homes without a gown or to ride without one. We enjoined the dean to exact without fail a fine from those who did not attend the chapter meetings, unless they had some good reason for their absence.

This day we spent the night at Caule. We received a letter from the priest at Haudricourt and have inserted it on another page:

John, priest at Haudricourt, to all who may see this letter, greeting in the Lord. Know you that during his visitation of the deanery of Aumale the Reverend Father Eudes, by God's grace archbishop of Rouen, found me to be grievously defamed of incontinence, and after having been disciplined by the archdeacon of Eu I suffered a relapse. I have of my own free will promised the said archbishop that should he find me ill famed of this matter again, I would regard my church as resigned. In testimony whereof I place my seal on the present letter, as well as the sign which I made on it with my own hand. Given at Envermeu, on the feast of the Conversion of Saint Paul, in the year of our Lord 1248.

1257

September 5. At Aliermont. September 6. At Anglesqueville. September 7–8. At Jumièges. September 9–11. At Pont-Audemer. September 12. We presided over the sacred provincial council at Pont-Audemer. . . .

. . . We enacted the statutes which were read to the sacred council and which ran as follows:

> It is the pleasure of the sacred council that the [statutes] below be observed in strictness, in such manner that the Reverend Fathers, Eudes, by God's grace archbishop of Rouen, his suffragans, and their subjects are in no way obliged to observe them as newly enacted statutes, that is, as regards those which have already found expression in [canon] law, in the Statutes of Pope Gregory IX or in episcopal synods.

[A list of decrees follows, taken largely from the Fourth Lateran Council, the Council of Lyons (I), and the *Decretals* of Gregory IX.]

. . . With the common consent of our brothers, we decreed that the visitation of the province of Rouen may be recommenced by us whenever such shall seem expedient. The provincial council being thus celebrated, and without any discord, we retired singing *Te Deum laudamus* and came before the altar of St-Aniane, where, at the completion of the Psalm, we offered the suitable prayers.

It is to be noted that before we sat in council we celebrated Mass in pontificals, our suffragans standing by, but not vested as for the celebration of Mass; two canons of Rouen, one deacon, the other a subdeacon, were so vested. Mass being celebrated, we and our suffragans being properly clothed, we took our seats, and the deacon, in proper vestments, read the Gospel, beginning: "Jesus appointed," et cetera. We then with loud voice began the *Come Holy Spirit*. This completed, the precentor of Rouen and the precentor of Lisieux, both in surplices, sang the Litany. Then, having repeated the *Lord's Prayer* in a low voice, we uttered the prayer *Adsumus*. After this we preached our sermon, and then were carried out the other things in the order mentioned above. . . .

1259

September 21–October 1. At Paris. October 2. At St-Martin-de-Pontoise, at our own expense.

October 3. We visited there. Twenty monks were in residence; three others had gone to Rome and had appealed from the abbot and against him. They have twelve priories, in each of which there should be monks. At this time there were no monks at Boiriz; we ordered the abbot to place two monks there without delay. There was no prior; we ordered the abbot to appoint someone as prior. They had no provost, nor anyone in charge of the granary. Those who are not priests receive Communion once a month. We enjoined the abbot to impose such salutary penance as he deemed advisable upon those, especially in the outside priories, who ate meat when there was no need, and who did not observe the fasts of the Rule. They had a good deal of wine and wheat but did not know how to compute its worth. They owed thirteen hundred pounds after paying off interest and comparing the amount which they owe with the amount which is owed to them. Harduin, priest, was there, both by our mandate and with the consent of the abbot and community, to assist the abbot in handling and managing the business of the abbey. We received procuration there this day. Total for procuration: seven pounds, five shillings, seven pence.

October 4. We preached in the Franciscan cloister at Pontoise, and, with God's aid, we celebrated High Mass. We dined with them in community, it being the feast of St. Francis.

October 5. After expounding the Word of God, we visited the chapter of St-Mellon. Two canons were in residence, Dom Luke and Master Robert; [there were] nine vicars and two chaplains. There are ten prebends there. The [liturgy] books were badly bound. There was such a dearth of altar cloths that the altar often remained bare because of this defect. Item, Robert of Manières was contentious and quarreled with his associates; we warned him to restrain himself from quarreling and from using insulting words in the future. The vicars were in the habit of going about the town dressed in short coats; we expressly forbade them to wear them in the future, [threatening] otherwise that they would be taken away from them and employed for the support of the fabric of St. Mellon's church. We gave Dom Luke, canon of St-Mellon, the authority and power to coerce these [vicars] in this regard, by ecclesiastical censure if it should be necessary. The chaplain of Dom Richard, the sacristan, did not provide the church sufficiently with the things which he should provide for it, that is, candles for those singing in the choir. He was negligent, that is, in lighting the candles, in ringing the bells, and in preparing and bringing in the book of Lessons at the appropriate hours; we warned the said Dom Richard that he should attend to all of these things through his chaplain, and that he should work more diligently and better than was his practice. Item, Ralph, priest and vicar of John of Montluçon, voluntarily confessed that for a long time he had kept a woman called "La Maréchal", and that he had known her carnally within the past six weeks, and had been gravely ill famed of this. He admitted this ill fame and, with his hand on his breast, swore on the Holy Gospels that he would regard his benefice as resigned if we should find him again defamed of this "La Maréchal" or any other woman, and he could not purge himself canonically. Item, Peter, priest and vicar of Master William, was gravely defamed of a certain woman named Petronilla, and this ill fame was fully established by all the vicars of this church of whom we required an oath in this matter and carefully examined each one separately. We sentenced him to purge himself with the seventh hand of priests, which he was not willing to do, believing that he could not find suitable compurgators; however, he humbly besought us to deal mercifully with him. We, taking compassion upon him, imposed the following penance in writing, to wit, that he should take his way to Mont-St-Michel-in-Peril-of-the-Sea and to St-Giles before the coming feast of St. Andrew and bring back to us letters which would be worthy of belief and which showed that he had completed this pilgrimage as the law requires. Indeed, with hand on breast, he swore upon the Holy Gospels, as he had promised and sworn at our other visitation, touching the Holy Gospels and his hand on his breast, that without the publicity of a trial he would regard his benefice as resigned from that time on, if it should happen that he be found ill famed again of the said Petronilla or of any other woman, and the charge was provable; he also promised not to revive any claim to his benefice. Present at this visitation were: Master John of Neuilly-en-Thelle, canon of Rouen; Brother Harduin of the Franciscans; Master Gervais Rasoir and John of Morgneval, our clerks; and the two aforesaid resident canons.

This day we visited St. Peter's priory. Six monks were there; all were priests. The prior had but lately arrived. They used meat when there was no need. The sources of income were not written down; we ordered this done. They owed three hundred pounds. They complained greatly because women entered their choir and chancel and disturbed their prayers; they asked that we take this under advisement.

This day we spent the night at St-Martin, where for procuration we received from Dom Luke, canon of St-Mellon, in the name of the chapter of St-Mellon, one hundred shillings of Paris, which amount, together with wood, platters, cups, straw, beds, and cooking utensils, the said chapter owes us annually for procuration.

. . . December 12. We received procuration this day at the priory at Gaillonet, a Premonstratensian house. Total: six pounds, seven shillings, six pence.

December 13. With God's help, we bestowed our benediction upon Simon, abbot of Marcheroux, at Wy, and preached a sermon there to the entire parish. We spent the night there and received a *muid* of oats from the priest at Gadancourt, which this priest owes us once a year when we turn aside to Wy.

This day a certain priest, presented by us for the church at Château-Baudemont, and whom we found to be ill-equipped for the cure of souls, appealed to us in writing.

December 14. We received procuration at Sausseuse. Total for procuration: seven pounds, five shillings, two pence.

December 15. We entered the chapter of Sausseuse, and, having preached a sermon, we gave our attention to the election of Brother Peter of Liancourt, who had been elected as prior by five of the brothers proceeding by way of compromise instead of by all of them. Taking under advisement this election and the manner in which it was held, and having examined the prior-elect, we confirmed his election as valid, and enjoined the community to regard Peter as their prior and also to give him their obedience. We then investigated the state of the house but were unable to obtain complete information. However, we discovered that they owed forty pounds of Paris to Master Robert of Grainville, a canon of Rouen, that they had no money for pruning their vineyards, and that they lacked many horses. Not so long ago there had been eight good horses there. Then we ordered the prior to visit the outside priories and to see that their buildings were repaired, for it had been intimated to us that they were in a ruinous state.

This day we slept at Frênes.

December 16. We received procuration at Noyon-sur-Andelle. Total: . . . [*lacuna in MS*].

December 17. We visited there, where there were six monks from St-Evroult. The prior was ill. They ate meat freely; we forbade them to eat meat except as the Rule permits. They had suffered heavy losses in England. Because of the prior's illness, we were unable to get full information about the state of the house.

At this place John of Bray, priest, whom we had not wished to admit to the church at Baudemont, although he was presented by the king, withdrew the appeal he had entered against us at Wy. We were not obliged to defer to this appeal for, upon examination, we had found him to be too deficient in letters to have a cure of souls.

January 4. We received procuration at Graville. Total for procuration: eight pounds, sixteen shillings.

January 5. After preaching a sermon, we visited there. Nine canons were in residence. The prior had sent one to Bellevue to be the associate of the prior there. We forbade women to eat with the canons who had cure of souls. Alms are given thrice a week, and to lepers on Friday. About sixty pounds of collectible debts was owed to them in excess of what they owed. They intend, with God's aid, to invest two more canons before the coming feast of the Purification, and so there will be twelve.

This day spent the night at Montivilliers, at our own expense.

January 6. That is to say, on Epiphany, God helping us, we preached a sermon at the monastery at Montivilliers before the nuns and the people of the town, and we celebrated High Mass in pontificals. This day we received procuration there. They did not wish to compute.

January 7. We entered the chapter of the nuns and with God's aid preached His Word to them in chapter. Then, desiring, with God's help, to perform our duty of making a complete visitation, both in head and in members, as our office requires of us, it was urged on the part of the abbess and community that the archbishop of Rouen had never been in the habit of visiting them as a community, but only through the abbess. After a great deal of altercation, we asked them collectively and singly whether they would receive us for the purpose of making a full visitation; through their spokesman, Master Robert, their cleric, they replied, "No," adding that they would never consent that we exercise the office of visitation there, except in the matters concerning the abbess alone, and they rested their case upon charters, custom, and privilege. However, we warned them to make us amends for this disobedience, rebellion, and contempt before the coming Ash Wednesday.

February 12. We visited the shrine of Notre-Dame-de-Chartres, and spent the night at St-Pierre-en-Vaux.

This day sixty-six of the canons of Chartres assembled to elect a bishop, and proceeded by the method of scrutiny;[2] Master Peter of Mincy, dean of Chartres, was elected by thirty-nine votes. The others appealed.

February 13. Having heard and understood this discord which arose out of the election, we went to the cathedral, desiring to bring the canons into concord once again, and, God favoring us, we offered ourself as a mediator, actuated for the good of the peace and by zeal for charity. On this same business we remained there this day and during the following days, sleeping at the bishop's manor. Finally, in our presence, they unanimously consented to the said election.

1269

November 12. With God's grace we came to the monastery of St-Ouen-de-Rouen and exercised our office of visitation. Fifty monks were there; all but four were priests. We found the abbey in good condition as to spirituals. They owed five thousand pounds of Tours, fifteen hundred pounds of this at interest; three thousand in bad debts was owed to them. We spent this night at Déville.

November 13. We visited the monastery at St-Amand, where we found fifty-nine nuns, nine of whom were to be veiled. One lay brother was there; we gave orders that this lay brother should confess and receive Communion more often than was his practice, and that he should be punished if he did not obey well. Item, we ordered the abbess to strive as hard as she could to have the nuns live in peace and concord. Item, we ordered her to try to restore to the alms allotment the manor of Calcy, the income of which had been withdrawn from the almoness. They owed eleven hundred pounds. This day spent the night at Déville, at our own expense.

November 14. With God's aid, we came in person to Mont-aux-Malades and to the hospital of St. Mary Magdalene, and we received the permission of these places. Thence we returned to Déville.

November 15. This day we were at the Daughters of God, the Beguines, at Pré; at Salle-aux-Puelles; at the Sisters of St. Matthew; and at the Fratres Barrati, to wit, the Carmelite Brethren. We dined this day with the Friars Preachers of Rouen.

2. Ballot, as provided by Canon 24 of the Fourth Lateran Council.

With God's aid we visited the above-mentioned places, and, inquiring from them about their condition, we found that Mont-aux-Malades, the hospital, and the Salle-aux-Puelles were in good condition. Pré owed two thousand pounds and they had lost the year's harvest at Bures through bad weather. . . .

Franciscan Writings

---

47. The Rule of 1223

Because a first rule drawn up in 1221 had not been worded in language sufficiently precise for the canonists of the early thirteenth century, it was generally agreed that a new edition was necessary. Moreover, there were many difficulties to be encountered in adjusting the Franciscan ideal to actual conditions, especially as the community grew rapidly. Cardinal Ugolino (later Gregory IX), the protector of the new organization and a canonist of note, assisted in the necessary revision.

It was once held that Francis was out of sympathy with the organizational tendencies implied in the *Rule of 1223* and that this attitude in part explains his withdrawal to the mountain retreat at La Verna in the final years of his life. Although he was in later months disappointed by the attitudes of some of his brethren, there is no reason to believe that he did not actively participate in preparing the *Rule of 1223*. His withdrawal can be explained partly by the state of his health, but perhaps even more by an intense desire for the mystical contemplation which, indeed, was vouchsafed him. The translation is that of B. Fahy, O.F.M., *The Writings of St. Francis of Assisi, With Introduction and Notes by P. Hermann, O.F.M.* (Chicago, 1964), pp. 57–64. Reprinted by permission of Franciscan Herald Press.

Chapter 1. In the Name of the Lord Begins the Life of the Friars Minor

The Rule and life of the Friars Minor is this, namely, to observe the Holy Gospel of our Lord Jesus Christ by living in obedience, without property, and in chastity. Brother Francis promises obedience and reverence to his holiness Pope Honorius and his lawfully elected successors and to the Church of Rome. The other friars are bound to obey Brother Francis and his successors.

Chapter 2. Of Those Who Wish to Take Up This Life and How They Are to Be Received

If anyone wants to profess our Rule and comes to the friars, they must send him to their provincial minister, because he alone, to the exclusion of others, has permission to receive friars into the Order. The ministers must carefully examine all candidates on the Catholic faith and the sacraments of the Church. If they believe all that the Catholic faith teaches and are prepared to profess it loyally, holding by it steadfastly to the end of their lives, and if they are not married; or if they are married and their wives have already entered a convent or after taking a vow of chastity have by the authority of the bishop of the diocese been granted this permission; and the wives are of such an age that no suspicion can arise concerning them: let the ministers tell them what the holy Gospel says (Mt. 19:21), that they should go and sell all that belongs to them and endeavour to give it to the poor. If they cannot do this, their good will is sufficient.

The friars and their ministers must be careful not to become involved in the tempoal affairs of newcomers to the Order, so that they may dispose of their goods freely, as God inspires them. If they ask for advice, the ministers may refer them to some God-fearing persons who can advise them how to distribute their property to the poor.

When this has been done, the ministers should clothe the candidates with the habit of probation, namely, two tunics without a hood, a cord and trousers, and a caperon reaching to the cord, unless the ministers themselves at any time decide that something else is more suitable. After the year of the novitiate, they should be received to obedience, promising to live always according to this life and Rule. It is absolutely forbidden to leave the Order, as his holiness the Pope has laid down. For the Gospel tells us, *No one, having put his hand to the plough and looking back, is fit for the kingdom of God* (Lk. 9:62).

The friars who have already vowed obedience may have one tunic with a hood and those who wish may have another without a hood. Those who are forced by necessity may wear shoes. All the friars are to wear poor clothes and they can use pieces of sackcloth and other material to mend them, with God's blessing.

I warn all the friars and exhort them not to condemn or look down on people whom they see wearing soft or gaudy clothes and enjoying luxuries in food or drink; each one should rather condemn and despise himself.

Chapter 3. Of the Divine Office and Fasting, and How the Friars Are to Travel About the World

The clerics are to recite the Divine Office according to the rite of the Roman Curia, except the psalter; and so they may have breviaries. The lay brothers are to say twenty-four *Our Fathers* for Matins and five for Lauds; for Prime, Tierce, Sext, and None, for each of these, they are to say seven; for Vespers twelve and for Compline seven. They should also say some prayers for the dead.

All the friars are to fast from the feast of All Saints until Christmas. Those who voluntarily fast for forty days after Epiphany have God's blessing, because this is the period our Lord sanctified by his holy fast (cf. Mt. 4:2). However, those who do not wish to do so, should not be forced to it. All the friars are bound to keep the Lenten fast before Easter, but they are not bound to fast at other times, except on Fridays. However, in case of manifest necessity, they are not obliged to corporal fasting.

And this is my advice, my counsel, and my earnest plea to my friars in our Lord Jesus Christ that, when they travel about the world, they should not be quarrelsome or take part in disputes with words (cf. II Tim. 2:14) or criticize others; but they should be gentle, peaceful, and unassuming, courteous and humble, speaking respectfully to everyone, as is expected of them. They are forbidden to ride on horseback, unless they are forced to it by manifest necessity or sickness. *Whatever house* they *enter,* they should *first say,* "*Peace to this house*" (Lk. 10:5), and in the words of the Gospel they *may eat what is set before* them (Lk. 10:8).

Chapter 4. The Friars Are Forbidden to Accept Money

I strictly forbid all the friars to accept money in any form, either personally or through an intermediary. The ministers and superiors, however, are bound to provide carefully for the needs of the sick and the clothing of the other friars, by having recourse to spiritual friends, while taking into account differences of place, season, or severe climate, as seems best to them in the circumstances. This does not dispense them from the prohibition of receiving money in any form.

Chapter 5. The Manner of Working

The friars to whom God has given the grace of working should work in a spirit of faith and devotion and avoid idleness, which is the enemy of the soul, without however extinguishing the spirit of prayer and devotion, to which every temporal consideration must be subordinate. As wages for their labour they may accept anything necessary for their temporal needs, for themselves or their brethren, except money in any form. And they should accept it humbly as is expected of those who serve God and strive after the highest poverty.

Chapter 6. That the Friars Are to Appropriate Nothing for Themselves; on Seeking Alms; and on the Sick Friars

The friars are to appropriate nothing for themselves, neither a house, nor a place, nor anything else. As *strangers and pilgrims* (1 Pet. 2:11) in this world, who serve God in poverty and humility, they should beg alms trustingly. And there is no reason why they should be ashamed, because God made himself poor for us in this world. This is the pinnacle of the most exalted poverty, and it is this, my dearest brothers, that has made you heirs and kings of the kingdom of heaven, poor in temporal things, but rich in virtue. This should be your portion, because it leads to the land of the living. And to this poverty, my beloved brothers, you must cling with all your heart, and wish never to have anything else under heaven, for the sake of our Lord Jesus Christ.

Wherever the friars meet one another, they should show that they are members of the same family. And they should have no hesitation in making known their needs to one another. For if a mother loves and cares for her child in the flesh, a friar should certainly love and care for his spiritual brother all the more tenderly. If a friar falls ill, the others are bound to look after him as they would like to be looked after themselves.

Chapter 7. Of the Penance to Be Imposed on Friars Who Fall into Sin

If any of the friars, at the instigation of the enemy, fall into mortal sin, they must have recourse as soon as possible, without delay, to their provincial ministers, if it is a sin for which recourse to them has been prescribed for the friars. If the ministers are priests, they should impose a moderate penance on such friars; if they are not priests, they should see that a penance is imposed by some priest of the Order, as seems best to them before God. They must be careful not to be angry or upset because a frair has fallen into sin, because anger or annoyance in themselves or in others makes it difficult to be charitable.

Chapter 8. The Election of the Minister General of the Order and the Pentecost Chapter

The friars are always bound to have a member of the Order as Minister General, who is the servant of the whole fraternity, and they are strictly bound to obey him. At his death the provincial ministers and the custodes are to elect a successor at the Pentecost Chapter, at which the provincial ministers are bound to assemble in the place designated by the Minister General. This chapter should be held once every three years, or at a longer or shorter interval, if the Minister General has so ordained.

If at any time it becomes clear to all the provincial ministers and custodes that the Minister General is incapable of serving the friars and can be of no benefit to them, they who have the power to elect must elect someone else as Minister General.

After the Pentecost Chapter, the provincial ministers and custodes may summon their subjects to a chapter in their own territory once in the same year, if they wish and it seems worthwhile.

Chapter 9. Of Preachers

The friars are forbidden to preach in any diocese, if the bishop objects to it. No friar should dare to preach to the people unless he has been examined and approved by the Minister General of the Order and has received from him the commission to preach.

Moreover, I advise and admonish the friars that in their preaching, their words should be examined and chaste. They should aim only at the advantage and spiritual good of their listeners, telling them briefly about vice and virtue, punishment and glory, because our Lord himself kept his words short on earth.

Chapter 10. On Admonishing and Correcting the Friars

The ministers, who are the servants of the other friars, must visit their subjects and admonish them, correcting them humbly and charitably, without commanding them anything that is against their conscience or our Rule. The subjects, however, should remember that they have renounced their own wills for God's sake. And so I strictly command them to obey their ministers in everything that they have promised God and is not against their conscience and our Rule. The friars who are convinced that they cannot observe the Rule spiritually, wherever they may be, can and must have recourse to their ministers. The ministers, for their part, are bound to receive them kindly and charitably, and be so sympathetic towards them that the friars can speak and deal with them as employers with their servants. That is the way it ought to be; the ministers should be the servants of all the friars.

With all my heart, I beg the friars in our Lord Jesus Christ to be on their guard against pride, boasting, envy, and greed, against the cares and anxieties of this world, against detraction and complaining. Those who are illiterate should not be anxious to study. They should realize instead that the only thing they should desire is to have the spirit of God at work within them, while they pray to him unceasingly with a heart free from self-interest. They must be humble, too, and patient in persecution or illness, loving those who persecute us by blaming us or bringing charges against us, as our Lord tells us, *Love your enemies, pray for those who persecute and calumniate you* (Mt. 5:44). *Blessed are those who suffer persecution for justice' sake, for theirs is the kingdom of heaven* (Mt. 5:10). *He who has persevered to the end will be saved* (Mt. 10:22).

Chapter 11. The Friars Are Forbidden to Enter the Monasteries of Nuns

I strictly forbid all the friars to have suspicious relationships or conversations with women. No one may enter the monasteries of nuns, except those who have received special permission from the

Apostolic See. They are forbidden to be sponsors of men or women lest scandal arise amongst or concerning the friars.

Chapter 12. Of Those Who Wish to Go Among the Saracens and Other Unbelievers

If any of the friars is inspired by God to go among the Saracens or other unbelievers, he must ask permission from his provincial minister. The ministers, for their part, are to give permission only to those whom they see are fit to be sent.

The ministers, too, are bound to ask the Pope for one of the cardinals of the holy Roman Church to be governor, protector, and corrector of this fraternity, so that we may be utterly subject and submissive to the Church. And so, firmly established in the Catholic faith, we may live always according to the poverty, and the humility, and the Gospel of our Lord Jesus Christ, as we have solemnly promised.

48. The Rule of the Third Order

Early in his career Francis was pressed by many devout men and women who did not feel able to relinquish their normal occupations but who wanted to be associated with the renewal of Christian life which he and his followers were preaching. This was done, and Francis spoke of his "threefold army," indicating that a Third Order had been added to his own associates and those of St. Clare. Francis's original rule has been lost, but in 1221 Cardinal Ugolino, the protector of the Franciscans, published a more precisely legal set of regulations. Four ancient versions have survived, of which one, the so-called *Venice Rule*, is given here. The translation is by B. Fahy, O.F.M., *op. cit.*, pp. 168 ff. Reprinted by permission of t he Franciscan Herald Press.

First Rule of the Third Order

Here begins the Rule of the Continent Brothers and Sisters

In the name of the Father and of the Son and of the Holy Spirit: Amen.

The memorial of what is proposed for the Brothers and Sisters of Penance living in their own homes, begun in the year of our Lord 1221, is as follows.

CHAPTER I. DAILY LIFE

1. The men belonging to this brotherhood shall dress in humble, undyed cloth, the price of which is not to exceed six Ravenna soldi an ell, unless for evident and necessary cause a temporary dispensation be given. And breadth and thinness of the cloth are to be considered in said price.

2. They shall wear their outer garments and furred coats without open throat, sewed shut or uncut but certainly laced up, not open as secular people wear them; and they shall wear their sleeves closed.

3. The sisters in turn shall wear an outer garment and tunic made of cloth of the same price and humble quality; or at least they are to have with the outer garment a white or black underwrap or petticoat, or an ample linen gown without gathers, the price of an ell of which is not to exceed twelve Pisa denars. As to this price, however, and the fur cloaks they wear a dispensation may be given according to the estate of the woman and the custom of the place. They are not to wear silken or dyed veils and ribbons.

4. And both the brothers and the sisters shall have their fur garments of lamb's wool only. They are permitted to have leather purses and belts sewed in simple fashion without silken thread, and no other kind. Also other vain adornments they shall lay aside at the bidding of the Visitor.

5. They are not to go to unseemly parties or to shows or dances. They shall not donate to actors, and shall forbid their household to donate.

CHAPTER II. ABSTINENCE

6. All are to abstain from meat save on Sundays, Tuesdays, and Thursdays, except on account of illness or weakness, for three days at blood-letting, in travelling, or on account of a specially high feast intervening, namely, the Nativity for three days, New Year's, Epiphany, the Pasch of the Resurrection for three days, the holy Apostles Peter and Paul, St John the Baptist, the Assumption of the glorious Virgin Mary, the solemnity of All Saints and of St. Martin. On the other days, when there is no fasting, they may eat cheese and eggs. But when they are with religious in their convent homes, they have leave to eat what is served to them. And except for the

feeble, the ailing, and those travelling, let them be content with dinner and supper. Let the healthy be temperate in eating and drinking.

7. Before their dinner and supper let them say the Lord's prayer once, likewise after their meal, and let them give thanks to God. Otherwise let them say three *Our Fathers*.

CHAPTER III. FASTING

8. From the Pasch of the Resurrection to the feast of All Saints they are to fast on Fridays. From the feast of All Saints until Easter they are to fast on Wednesdays and Fridays, but still observing the other fasts enjoined in general by the Church.

9. They are to fast daily, except on account of infirmity or any other need, throughout the fast of St Martin from after said day until Christmas, and throughout the greater fast from Carnival Sunday until Easter.

10. Sisters who are pregnant are free to refrain until their purification from the corporal observances except those regarding their dress and prayers.

11. Those engaged in fatiguing work shall be allowed to take food three times a day from the Pasch of the Resurrection until the Dedication feast of St Michael. And when they work for others it will be allowed them to eat everything served to them, except on Fridays and on the fasts enjoined in general by the Church.

CHAPTER IV. PRAYER

12. All are daily to say the seven canonical Hours, that is, Matins, Prime, Terce, Sext, None, Vespers, and Compline. The clerics are to say them after the manner of the clergy. Those who know the Psalter are to say the *Deus in nomine tuo* and the *Beati immaculati* up to the *Legem pone* for Prime, and the other psalms of the Hours, with the *Glory be to the Father;* but when they do not attend church, they are to say for Matins the psalms the Church says or any eighteen psalms; or at least to say the *Our Father* as do the unlettered at any of the Hours.

The others say twelve *Our Fathers* for Matins and for every one of the other Hours seven *Our Fathers* with the *Glory be to the Father* after each one. And those who know the *Creed* and the *Miserere mei Deus* should say it at Prime and Compline. If they do not say that at the Hours indicated, they shall say three *Our Fathers*.

13. The sick are not to say the Hours unless they wish.

14. All are to go to Matins in the fast of St Martin and in the great fast, unless inconvenience for persons or affairs should threaten.

Chapter V. The Sacraments, Other Matters

15. They are to make a confession of their sins three times a year and to receive Communion at Christmas, Easter, and Pentecost. They are to be reconciled with their neighbours and to restore what belongs to others. They are to make up for past tithes and pay future tithes.

16. They are not to take up lethal weapons, or bear them about, against anybody.

17. All are to refrain from formal oaths unless where necessity compels, in the cases excepted by the Sovereign Pontiff in his indult, that is, for peace, for the Faith, under calumny, and in bearing witness.

18. Also in their ordinary conversations they will do their best to avoid oaths. And should anyone have sworn thoughtlessly through a slip of the tongue, as happens where there is much talking, he should the evening of the same day, when he is obliged to think over what he has done, say three *Our Fathers* in amends of such oaths. Let each member fortify his household to serve God.

Chapter VI. Special Mass and Meeting Each Month

19. All the brothers and sisters of every city and place are to foregather every month at the time the ministers see fit, in a church which the ministers will make known, and there assist at Divine services.

20. And every member is to give the treasurer one ordinary denar. The treasurer is to collect this money and distribute it on the advice of the ministers among the poor brothers and sisters, especially the sick and those who may have nothing for their funeral services, and thereupon among other poor; and they are to offer something of the money to the aforesaid church.

21. And, if it be convenient at the time, they are to have some religious who is informed in the words of God to exhort them and strengthen them to persevere in their penance and in performing

the works of mercy. And except for the officers, they are to remain quiet during the Mass and sermon, intent on the Office, on prayer, and on the sermon.

Chapter VII. Visiting the Sick, Burying the Dead

22. Whenever any brother or sister happens to fall ill, the ministers, if the patient let them know of it, shall in person or through others visit the patient once a week, and remind him of penance; and if they find it expedient, they are to supply him from the common fund with what he may need for the body.

23. And if the ailing person depart from this life, it is to be published to the brothers and sisters who may be present in the city or place, so that they may gather for the funeral; and they are not to leave until the Mass has been celebrated and the body consigned to burial. Thereupon each member within eight days of the demise shall say for the soul of the deceased: a Mass, if he is a priest; fifty psalms, if he understands the Psalter, or if not, then fifty *Our Fathers* with the *Requiem aeternam* at the end of each.

24. In addition, every year, for the welfare of the brothers and sisters living and dead, each priest is to say three Masses, each member knowing the Psalter is to recite it, and the rest shall say one hundred *Our Fathers* with the *Requiem aeternam* at the end of each.

25. All who have the right are to make their last will and make disposition of their goods within three months after their profession, lest anyone of them die intestate.

26. As regards making peace among the brothers and sisters or non-members at odds, let what the ministers find proper be done; even, if it be expedient, upon consultation with the Lord Bishop.

27. If contrary to their right and privileges trouble is made for the brothers and sisters by the mayors and governors of the places where they live, the ministers of the place shall do what they shall find expedient on the advice of the Lord Bishop.

28. Let each member accept and faithfully exercise the ministry of other offices imposed on him, although anyone may retire from office after a year.

29. When anybody wishes to enter this brotherhood, the ministers shall carefully inquire into his standing and occupation, and they shall explain to him the obligations of the brotherhood, especially that of restoring what belongs to others. And if he is content with

it, let him be vested according to the prescribed way, and he must make satisfaction for his debts, paying money according to what pledged provision is given. They are to reconcile themselves with their neighbours and to pay up their tithes.

30. After these particulars are complied with, when the year is up and he seems suitable to them, let him on the advice of some discreet brothers be received on this condition: that he promise he will all the time of his life observe everything here written, or to be written or abated on the advice of the brothers, unless on occasion there be a valid dispensation by the ministers; and that he will, when called upon by the ministers, render satisfaction as the Visitor shall ordain if he have done anything contrary to this condition. And this promise is to be put in writing then and there by a public notary. Even so nobody is to be received otherwise, unless in consideration of the estate and rank of the person it shall seem advisable to the ministers.

31. No one is to depart from this brotherhood and from what is contained herein, except to enter a religious Order.

32. No heretic or person in bad repute for heresy is to be received. If he is under suspicion of it, he may be admitted if otherwise fit, upon being cleared before the bishop.

33. Married women are not to be received except with the consent and leave of their husbands.

34. Brothers and sisters ejected from the brotherhood as incorrigible are not to be received in it again except it please the saner portion of the brothers.

Chapter VIII. Correction, Dispensation, Officers

35. The ministers of any city or place shall report public faults of the brothers and sisters to the Visitor for punishment. And if anyone proves incorrigible, after consultation with some of the discreet brothers he should be denounced to the Visitor, to be expelled by him from the brotherhood, and thereupon it should be published in the meeting. Moreover, if it is a brother, he should be denounced to the mayor or the governor.

36. If anyone learns that scandal is occurring relative to brothers and sisters, he shall report it to the ministers and shall have opportunity to report it to the Visitor. He need not be held to report it in the case of husband against wife.

37. The Visitor has the power to dispense all the brothers and sisters in any of these points if he finds it advisable.

38. When the year has passed, the ministers with the counsel of the brothers are to elect two other ministers; and a faithful treasurer, who is to provide for the need of the brothers and sisters and other poor; and messengers who at the command of the ministers are to publish what is said and done by the fraternity.

39. In all the above mentioned points no one is to be obligated under guilt, but under penalty; yet so that if after being admonished twice by the ministers he should fail to discharge the penalty imposed or to be imposed on him by the Visitor, he shall be obligated under guilt as contumacious.

Here ends the Rule of the Continent.

49. The Canticle of Brother Sun

Among other things St. Francis was a poet, and of all his poems none has remained more universally beloved than the *Canticle of Brother Sun,* so reminiscent of the canticle of the three young men in the fiery furnace (Dan. 3:57 ff.). Composed in the old Umbrian dialect, it is one of the earliest poems in the Italian vernacular. Although Francis wrote the poem while under intense suffering in the period before his death, it nonetheless evokes his unquenchable joy and love of the Creator and all that He created. The verses about pardon and peace were written after altercations had disrupted the peace in Assisi.

The text is taken from the translation by B. Fahy, O.F.M., *op. cit.,* pp. 130–131. Reprinted by permission of Franciscan Herald Press. Since there has been discussion about the meaning of the prepositions *cun* and *per* as used by Francis, the translator's note has been retained.

> Most high, all-powerful, all good, Lord!
>   All praise is yours, all glory, all honour
>   And all blessing.
> To you, alone, Most High, do they belong.
>   No mortal lips are worthy
>   To pronounce your name.
> All praise be yours, my Lord, through[1] all that you have made,
>   And first my lord Brother Sun,
>   Who brings the day; and light you give to us through him.

1. For a proper understanding of the poem it should be kept in mind that the praise is not directed to the creatures, nor is the praise directed to Al-

How beautiful is he, how radiant in all his splendour!
 Of you, Most High, he bears the likeness.
All praise be yours, my Lord, through Sister Moon and Stars;
 In the heavens you have made them, bright
 And precious and fair.
All praise be yours, my Lord, through Brothers Wind and Air,
 And fair and stormy, all the weather's moods,
 By which you cherish all that you have made.
All praise be yours, my Lord, through Sister Water,
 So useful, lowly, precious and pure.
All praise be yours, my Lord, through Brother Fire,
 Through whom you brighten up the night.
 How beautiful is he, how gay! Full of power and strength.
All praise be yours, my Lord, through Sister Earth, our mother,
 Who feeds us in her sovereignty and produces
 Various fruits with coloured flowers and herbs.
All praise be yours, my Lord, through those who grant pardon
 For love of you; through those who endure
 Sickness and trial.
Happy those who endure in peace,
 By you, Most High, they will be crowned.
All praise be yours, my Lord, through Sister Death,
 From whose embrace no mortal can escape.
Woe to those who die in mortal sin!
 Happy those She finds doing your will!
 The second death can do no harm to them.
Praise and bless my Lord, and give him thanks,
 And serve him with great humility.

50. *The* Stabat mater

This famous hymn, once thought to be the work of Jacopone da Todi, is of Franciscan origin and of the late thirteenth century. The Latin version is from F. J. E. Raby, *op. cit.*, no. 285; translation by E. Caswell and others, *Hymns Ancient and Modern*, no. 117, verses 1–3.

> *Stabat mater dolorosa*
> *iuxta crucem lacrimosa,*
> *dum pendebat filius;*

mighty God for the creatures, that is, for giving them to us. The prepositions *cun* and *per* are used in the meaning of instrumentality, that is, *by means of* or *through*. In his *Essays in Criticism* Matthew Arnold pointed this out already in 1875, though he used *of* as a simpler way of saying *by means of* or *through*. This is in accordance with the Italian meaning of these prepositions.

cuius animam gementem
contristantem et dolentem
pertransivit gladius

At the cross her station keeping
Stood the mournful mother weeping,
Where He hung, the dying Lord;
For her soul of joy bereavèd,
Bowed with anguish, deeply grievèd,
Felt the sharp and piercing sword.

O quam tristis et afflicta
fuit illa benedicta
mater unigeniti!
quae maerebat et dolebat,
et tremebat, cum videbat
nati poenas incliti.

Oh, how sad and sore distressèd
Now was she, that mother blessèd
Of the sole-begotten One;
Deep the woe of her affliction
When she saw the crucifixion
Of her ever-glorious Son.

Quis est homo qui non fleret
matrem Christi si videret
in tanto supplicio?
quis non posset contristari,
piam matrem contemplari
dolentem cum filio?

Who, on Christ's dear Mother gazing
Pierced by anguish so amazing
Born of woman, would not weep?
Who, on Christ's dear mother thinking
Such a cup of sorrow drinking,
Would not share her sorrows deep?

51. *Jacopone da Todi*, Donna del paradiso

Jacopone da Todi (d. 1306), the author of the *Donna del paradiso*, was
an ardent Franciscan who was once thought to have written the
preceding selection, the *Stabat mater*. Both compositions call forth the

anguish felt by Mary at her Son's crucifixion. But whereas the *Stabat mater* is a formal hymn in meter and rhyme, the *Donna del paradiso*, in the old Italian vernacular, must have had a wider appeal. It stirs the emotions even by the sound and rhythm of the words.

The text is taken from the *Penguin Book of Italian Verse*, edited with prose translation by G. B. Kay (Baltimore, 1958), pp. 8–13. Reprinted by permission of Penguin Books Ltd. Certain verses in Italian have been included here.

Messenger

Donna del paradiso,
lo tuo figliolo è priso . Iesu Cristo beato.

Acurre, donna, e vide . che la gente l'allide!
credo che llo s'occide, . tanto l'on flagellato.

Lady of Paradise, your son is taken, blessed Jesus Christ. Run, woman, and see for the people strike him. I believe he is being killed, they have so whipped him.

Virgin

Como esser porria, . che non fece mai follia,
Cristo, la spene mia, . omo l'avesse pigliato?

How could this be when he never did wrong? Christ, my hope, how could any one have seized him?

Messenger

Lady, he is betrayed: Judas has sold him, he has had thirty pieces of silver for it, he has struck a great bargain.

Virgin

Help, Magdalen, pain has come upon me! Christ, my son, is being led along, as was foretold me.

Messenger

Help, lady, lend aid! for they spit upon your son, and the people push him along: they have given him to Pilate.

Virgin

O Pilate, do not cause my son to be tormented: for I can show you how wrongly he is accused.

Crowd

Crucifige, crucifige! . Omo che se fa rege,
secondo nostra lege, . contradice al senato.

Crucify, crucify! A man who makes himself king, by our law, defies the senate.

Virgin

I beg you to hear me, think of my grief: perhaps even now you begin to have misgivings.

Messenger

They are dragging out the thieves to be his companions.

Crowd

Let him be crowned with thorns! he who called himself king.

Virgin

O figlio, figlio, figlio! . figlio, amoroso giglio,
figlio, chi dà consiglio . al cor mio angustiato?

Figlio, occhi giocondi, . figlio, co non respondi?
figlio, perchè t'ascondi . dal petto ove se'lattato?

O my son, son, son! my son, lovesome lily, who will counsel my heart in anguish?

Son, joyful eyes, son, why do you not answer? Son, why do you hide from the breast that has suckled you?

Messenger

Lady, here is the cross, being brought by the people, upon which the true light is to be raised.

Virgin

O cross, what will you do? Will you take my son? And what will you charge him with? That has no sin in him?

Messenger

O help, thou full of grief: for thy son is being stripped, and the people seem to wish that he be nailed to the cross.

Virgin

If they have taken off his clothes, let me see—how the cruel wounding has stained him all with blood.

Messenger

Lady, his hand has been taken and stretched upon the cross; it is pierced through by a nail, in such a way have they fixed him! The other hand is taken, and is being stretched upon the cross, and the pain burns that is ever more multiplied. Lady, his feet are taken and nailed to the wood; every joint is opened, they have so wrenched him.

Virgin

And I shall begin the lament: son, my comfort, son, who has made you dead to me, my delicate son?

They would have done better to have taken out my heart, than for it to be torn there, set upon the cross.

Christ

Mother, why have you come? You give me a mortal wound, since your weeping casts me down when I see it gripping you so.

Virgin

Figlio, che m'agio anvito, . figlio, patre e marito,
figlio, chi t'ha ferito? . figlio, chi t'ha spogliato?

My son, I have good cause, son, father, and husband, son, who has wounded you? my son, who has stripped you?

Christ

Mamma, perchè te lagni? . voglio che tu remagni,
che serve i miei compagni . ch'al mondo agio acquistato.

Mother, why do you lament? I want you to stay behind and care for the companions whom I have gained in the world.

Virgin

My son, do not say that: I want to die with you, I do not want to leave you, until, in a little while, my breath leaves me.

Let us have one burial, son of a darkened mother! Mother and son were found overcome by anguish.

Christ

Mother, with a stricken heart I put you into the hands of John, my chosen: let him be called your son.

John, keep this my mother in all love: have pity on her, for her heart has been pierced.

Virgin

Figlio, l'alma t'è uscita, . figlio de la smarrita,
figlio de la sparita, . figlio atossicato!

My son, your soul has gone, son of the lost woman, son of the lifeless one, who have been poisoned.

Figlio bianco e vermiglio, . figlio senza simiglio,
figlio, a chi m'apiglio? . figlio, pur m'hai lassato.

My son, white and red, son without compare, son, whom shall I hold to? son, you have left me then?

Figlio bianco e biondo, . figlio, volto iocondo,
figlio, perchè t'ha el mondo, . figlio, cusì sprezato?

My son, white and fair, son of joyful face, son, why has the world so despised you?

Figlio, dolce e piacente, . figlio de la dolente,
figlio, hatte la gente . malamente tratto!

My son, sweet and pleasant, son of the grieving one, son, the people have used you wickedly.

O John, my new son, your brother is dead: I have felt the blade
that was prophesied.
Which has killed son and mother, both seized by hard death: they
were found embraced, mother and son embraced.

Dominican Documents

---

52. Raymond of Peñafort, Constitutions

It was probably in the year 1205 that Innocent III granted an interview to two Spaniards, Bishop Diego of Osma and his companion,
Dominic, who were seeking permission to preach among the Cumans
on the eastern frontiers of Hungary. Apparently, the pope dissuaded
them from their original purpose, seeing in them the kind of persons
needed to preach in the Cathar areas of southern France. They first
joined with the Cistercians, but soon developed an entirely new
concept of itinerant preachers. After Diego died, Dominic carried the
work further with support from Bishop Fulk of Toulouse. Finally in
1215 Dominic and Fulk together proposed to the pope an organization
of preachers which might serve the needs of Christianity as a whole.

Dominic's first regulations, which he adapted from the Augustinian
rule for canons-regular, were revised after his death in the *Constitutions* of 1228, which retained the founder's ideas of what the organization should be. These were later codified by Raymond of Peñafort, a
distinguished canonist who was master-general of the order for two
years, 1238–40, and subsequently emended and modified by later
general chapters. Thus was created an order with divisions into
provinces under the general supervision of a master-general and a
system of representation in a general chapter.

The following selection, consisting of those chapters which concern
preaching and study, is prefaced by a remarkable passage from the
introductory statement. After insisting that the regulations must not be
altered by anyone of his own will, this prefatory statement then adds
that the superior may dispense with the strict observance of the *Constitutions* should these seem to hinder study, preaching, or the care of
souls. This indicates how seriously the Dominicans regarded this
external work of their order.

Chapters from the Constitutions *of the Order of Friars*
Preachers.

The text is translated from that of R. Creytens, O.P., "Les Constitutions des frères prêcheurs dans la rédaction de S. Raymond de Peñafort," *Archivum fratrum praedicatorum*, XVIII (1948), 63–67, with
later modifications as the editor indicates. These can be compared with
later versions and with the fourteenth-century *Constitutions* in G. R.
Galbraith, *The Constitutions of the Dominican Order* (Manchester,
1925), Appendix II.

FROM THE INTRODUCTION

. . . On this, however, let the superior have in his convent with
his brothers the power of dispensing, whenever it shall seem to him
expedient, especially in those things which will seem to hinder
study or preaching or the harvest of souls, since it is recognized
that our order was established from the beginning especially for
preaching and the safety of souls, and our study ought to be principally directed to this, so that we may be useful to the souls of our
neighbors. Let the priors avail themselves of dispensations as the
other brothers. . . .

XII CONCERNING PREACHERS

. . . No one is to be appointed to the office of preaching outside
the cloister or the company of brethren who is less than twenty-
five years old.[1] In fact, those who are suited, when they have to go
out to preach will be given companions by the prior according as
he judges it advantageous to their behavior and character. When,
after receiving a blessing, these go out, just as men who desire to
achieve their own salvation and that of others, let them everywhere
conduct themselves religiously and honorably as men of the Gospel, following in the footsteps of their Savior, speaking profitably
with God and about God with themselves and with their neighbor.
They will avoid the intimacy of questionable friendship.

Let them not take part in pleading cases unless on business of the
faith. When our brothers enter the diocese of any bishop to
preach, they shall first, if possible, visit the bishop so that according
to his counsel they may bring to the people the fruit they intend to

1. The phrase "without the license of his prior" was later added.

bring; and as long as they are in his diocese, they shall not meddle in those things which are irregular and themselves be faithfully obedient.

Let no one, indeed, dare to preach in the diocese of any bishop who has forbidden him to preach, unless he has letters from the supreme pontiff. Moreover, let our brothers beware, lest in raising their voices too high[2] they scandalize the religious and clergy by their preaching; but let them take care of those things which they see ought to be corrected in themselves by imploring the fathers to correct them separately. The companion given to a preacher must obey him as his prior in all things. We order that our brothers do not suggest in their preachings that money be given or taken for the house or for any particular person.

XIII Concerning the Brothers on a Journey

Those going to fulfil a mission of preaching or those who travel for other purposes shall not receive or carry gold, silver, money or gifts except food and the necessary clothing and books. If anyone receives anything of the abovementioned things let him hold it to present freely to his superior on his return. The brethren are not to receive little presents from women, nor give them, especially confessors. Likewise, brothers are not to be stewards of the possessions or money of others, nor receive deposits of things from outside except of books or ecclesiastical robes.

Preachers or travelers when they are en route must say their office as they know how and can, and be content with the office of those whom they are visiting at any time. Brothers are to take with them official travel letters and correct faults in the convents where they visit. . . .

XIV Concerning Students

Inasmuch as particular prudence must be observed toward students, let them have a special brother without whose permission they are not to write essays or hear lectures. He must correct those things which deserve correction which he has observed in them, and if it exceeds his powers, he should refer [it] to the superior.

They are not to study the books of the pagan philosophers even if they look at them for a short time; they must not learn the

2. *Ponendo os in celum:* putting on airs?

secular sciences of the arts which are called liberal, unless at some-time the master of the order or the general chapter wishes to order otherwise, but the young men as well as the others may read only theological books. Indeed, they must be so intent in study that day and night, at home, on the road, they read something or meditate and strive to retain as much as they can by heart.

If he has some [brothers] suited to teaching who can in a short time be capable of lecturing, the provincial prior should be sure to send them for study to the places where a studium (school) is well established. . . . Three brothers are to be sent from a province to the studium at Paris. Five provinces [with later changes and omissions] are to see to it that in some suitable convent there is a *studium generale (et solempne)* and to this any provincial prior should have the power to send two brothers suited to study.

We decree that each province shall be required to provide its brothers sent to the studium with at least three books of theology, namely the bible, the histories, and the sentences. They must study carefully in them and pay as much attention to the text as to the glosses. Likewise, no one is to have books written concerning the affairs of the house save for the common good. To no one must be conceded the definite use of books and no one must be disturbed if they are taken by anyone or assigned to the custody of anyone. On Sundays and feast days they are to refrain from writing essays. . . .

With regard to those who are studying, the superior must so arrange that they are not easily kept or prevented from study because of duty or anything else. A place must be established according as it shall seem appropriate to the master of students where, after the discussion or vespers or at some other time when he is unoccupied they may convene in his presence for raising questions or points of dispute. And when one is asking or making a suggestion, let the others be silent so as not to hinder the speaker. If anyone gives offense in questioning, objecting, or replying ungra-ciously or in a confused or clamorous or rude manner, he is to be immediately disciplined by whoever among them is presiding.

Let cells be assigned to those for whom the master of students thinks it expedient. But if anyone is found unproductive in his study, let his cell be given to another, and let him be set to work in other duties. In the cells, moreover, they can write, read, pray, sleep, and even stay awake at night if they desire on account of study. Moreover, no one may become a public doctor or debate unless with the license of the provincial prior and the diffinitors[3] of the provincial chapter. None of our brothers may read in the psalms or prophecies any literal meaning except that which the saints approve and confirm.

53. Provisions for the Friars Preachers at the University of Paris

The translation is by L. Thorndike, *University Records and Life in the Middle Ages,* Columbia University Records of Civilization (New York, 1964), pp. 68–70, from the *Chartularium universitatis Parisiensis,* vol. I, pp. 385–86. Reprinted by permission of Columbia University Press.

At Paris license of lecturing in theology should not be sought for any brother, nor should one licensed incept, nor one lecturing leave off, except by advice of the master, if he shall be in the province of France, or by advice of the provincial prior of France, if the master of the order is not in France.

At Valenciennes in the year of the Lord 1259 by mandate of the master and those on the committee for education it was ordained by brothers Bonhomme, Florentius, Albertus Teutonicus, Thomas Aquinas, Petrus de Tarantasia, masters of theology at Paris, who were present at the said chapter, that lecturers should not be occupied with acts and business by which they would be taken from their lectures.

Also, that provincial priors should seek diligently for youths apt for study, who could make rapid progress, and promote them in the university.

Also, that such a search be made annually by visitors in single convents and reported to the provincial chapter.

Also, that brothers should not be sent to universities, except those of good character and likely to make progress.

Also, that, if in any province lecturers cannot be had in all convents, it shall at least be provided that brothers, and especially

3. Elected representatives.

youths, do not remain always in those convents but be sent to places where there are lecturers.

Also that, if lecturers cannot be found qualified to lecture publicly, at least some be provided to give private lectures or histories or a *Summa* of cases, or something else of that sort, so that the brothers may not be idle.

Also, that young brothers apt for study be spared from discourses and other occupations, so as not to withdraw them from study.

Also, that there be established in provinces which require it some school of arts or place where youth are instructed.

Also, that brothers who stay away from classes be severely punished.

Also, that the brothers at the hour of lecture shall not be occupied in celebrating masses or other things of this sort nor go to town except for real necessity.

Also, that even the priors attend classes, like the other brothers, when they conveniently can.

Also, that lecturers on vacation attend classes and especially disputations.

Also, that lecturers be not made either preachers or confessors, unless they are capable of performing offices of this sort without notable peril.

Also, that priors and visitors and the masters of the brothers take pains to inquire carefully how the brothers and especially the young are occupied with study and what progress they are making, and punish the negligent.

Also, that lecturers continue their lectures as much as possible.

Also, that the visitors each year diligently inquire of the lecturers how much they lecture in a year and how many questions they have disputed and also determined, and how many convents of their visitation lack lecturers. And that whatever they shall find about this they shall report to the provincial chapter; and also the more notable defects which they have found the provincial prior and representatives shall refer afterwards to the chapter general.

Also, that in every province each year in each provincial chapter it be ordained how to provide for the students of their province who are sent to some university.

Also, the visitors shall diligently inquire how provision is made for the students and report notable defects to the provincial chapter by which an efficacious remedy shall be applied.

Also, provision shall be made that every lecturer occupying a professorial chair shall have a bachelor who shall lecture under him.

Also, that brothers carry to class the books which are read in class, if they have them, and no others.

Also, that in every convent where there is a lecturer there be instituted some brother who shall diligently repeat, provided there is anyone qualified in the convent.

Also, that repetitions be made concerning questions and collations concerning questions once a week, where this can be conveniently observed.

54. *Thomas Aquinas*, Summa theologica

The greatest of the thirteenth-century Dominican scholars was St. Thomas Aquinas (1225-1274). He studied with another distinguished Dominican, Albertus Magnus, and taught for a time at Paris. He was the author of several works, the best known being his *Summa contra gentiles* and the *Summa theologica*. The last named is a vast treatise summarizing systematically and in great detail the entire body of theological learning.

Thomas was able to take full advantage of the writings of Jewish, Arabian, and Greek philosophers which had been brought into western Europe in the preceding decades. He was also able to acquire a direct translation of some of Aristotle's works from his colleague, William Moerbeke. The influence of Aristotle's thought on Aquinas is evident throughout his works.

No excerpt can do justice to so prolific and so profound a writer, but the following selections may serve to illustrate Aquinas' method of posing a "question," stating various objections, giving his answer, and finally considering the objections one by one. The first selection consists of two articles taken from Part III, Question 63 of the *Summa theologica*, on *The Sacramental Character*, in which Thomas analyzes the character which a sacrament imprints on the soul. The second, taken from Part III, Question 75, *Of the Change of Bread and Wine into the Body and Blood of Christ*, explores the problem of the change of the bread and wine in the sacrament of the Eucharist, defined, it will be recalled, by the Fourth Lateran Council as "transubstantiation." It also shows how Aquinas uses the Aristotelian concepts of substance, form, matter, etc. The term "substance," it should be noted, has acquired a connotation in modern English almost totally at variance with its original philosophical meaning.

It should be noted that in the first selection Aquinas analyzes further the question proposed by Peter Lombard in Document 32, above. Reprinted from *Thomas Aquinas, The Summa theologica* (tr. Fathers of the English Dominican Province, London, 1911–22), with permission of Benziger, Inc., and Burns and Oates, Ltd.

Pt. III, Q. 63

SECOND ARTICLE. WHETHER A CHARACTER IS A SPIRITUAL POWER?

We proceed thus to the Second Article:—

Objection 1. It seems that a character is not a spiritual power. For *character* seems to be the same thing as *figure;* hence (Heb. i. 3), where we read *figure of His substance,* for *figure* the Greek has χαρακτήρ. Now *figure* is in the fourth species of quality, and thus differs from power which is in the second species. Therefore character is not a spiritual power.

Obj. 2. Further, Dionysius says (*Eccl. Hier.* ii.): *The Divine Beatitude admits him that seeks happiness to a share in Itself, and grants this share to him by conferring on him Its light as a kind of seal.* Consequently, it seems that a character is a kind of light. Now light belongs rather to the third species of quality. Therefore a character is not a power, since this seems to belong to the second species.

Obj. 3. Further, character is defined by some thus: *A character is a holy sign of the communion of faith and of the holy ordination, conferred by a hierarch.* Now a sign is in the genus of *relation,* not of *power.* Therefore a character is not a spiritual power.

Obj. 4. Further, a power is in the nature of a cause and principle (*Metaph.* v.). But a *sign* which is set down in the definition of a character is rather in the nature of an effect. Therefore a character is not a spiritual power.

On the contrary, The Philosopher says (*Ethic.* ii.): *There are three things in the soul, power, habit, and passion.* Now a character is not a passion: since a passion passes quickly, whereas a character is indelible, as will be made clear further on (A. 5). In like manner it is not a habit: because no habit is indifferent to acting well or ill: whereas a character is indifferent to either, since some use it well, some ill. Now this cannot occur with a habit: because no one abuses a habit of virtue, or uses well an evil habit. It remains, therefore, that a character is a power.

I answer that, As stated above (A. 1), the sacraments of the New Law produce a character, in so far as by them we are deputed to the worship of God according to the rite of the Christian religion. Wherefore Dionysius (*Eccl. Hier.* ii.), after saying that God *by a kind of sign grants a share of Himself to those that approach Him,* adds *by making them Godlike and communicators of Divine gifts.* Now the worship of God consists either in receiving Divine gifts, or in bestowing them on others. And for both these purposes some power is needed; for to bestow something on others, active power is necessary; and in order to receive, we need a passive power. Consequently, a character signifies a certain spiritual power ordained unto things pertaining to the Divine worship.

But it must be observed that this spiritual power is instrumental: as we have stated above (Q. LXII., A. 4) of the virtue which is in the sacraments. For to have a sacramental character belongs to God's ministers: and a minister is a kind of instrument, as the Philosopher says (*Polit.* i.). Consequently, just as the virtue which is in the sacraments is not of itself in a genus, but is reducible to a genus, for the reason that it is of a transitory and incomplete nature: so also a character is not properly in a genus or species, but is reducible to the second species of quality.

Reply Obj. 1. Configuration is a certain boundary of quantity. Wherefore, properly speaking, it is only in corporeal things; and of spiritual things is said metaphorically. Now that which decides the genus or species of a thing must needs be predicated of it properly. Consequently, a character cannot be in the fourth species of quality, although some have held this to be the case.

Reply Obj. 2. The third species of quality contains only sensible passions or sensible qualities. Now a character is not a sensible light. Consequently, it is not in the third species of quality as some have maintained.

Reply Obj. 3. The relation signified by the word *sign* must needs have some foundation. Now the relation signified by this sign which is a character, cannot be founded immediately on the essence of the soul: because then it would belong to every soul naturally. Consequently, there must be something in the soul on which such a relation is founded. And it is in this that a character essentially consists. Therefore it need not be in the genus *relation* as some have held.

Reply Obj. 4. A character is in the nature of a sign in comparison to the sensible sacrament by which it is imprinted. But considered in itself, it is in the nature of a principle, in the way already explained.

SIXTH ARTICLE. WHETHER A CHARACTER IS IMPRINTED BY EACH
SACRAMENT OF THE NEW LAW?

We proceed thus to the Sixth Article:—

Objection 1. It seems that a character is imprinted by all the sacraments of the New Law: because each sacrament of the New Law makes man a participator in Christ's Priesthood. But the sacramental character is nothing but a participation in Christ's Priesthood, as already stated (AA. 3, 5). Therefore it seems that a character is imprinted by each sacrament of the New Law.

Obj. 2. Further, a character may be compared to the soul in which it is, as a consecration to that which is consecrated. But by each sacrament of the New Law man becomes the recipient of sanctifying grace, as stated above (Q. LXII., A. 1). Therefore it seems that a character is imprinted by each sacrament of the New Law.

Obj. 3. Further, a character is both a reality and a sacrament. But in each sacrament of the New Law, there is something which is only a reality, and something which is only a sacrament, and something which is both reality and sacrament. Therefore a character is imprinted by each sacrament of the New Law.

On the contrary, Those sacraments in which a character is imprinted, are not reiterated, because a character is indelible, as stated above (A. 5): whereas some sacraments are reiterated, for instance, penance and matrimony. Therefore not all the sacraments imprint a character.

I answer that, As stated above (Q. LXII., AA. 1, 5), the sacraments of the New Law are ordained for a twofold purpose, namely, as a remedy for sin, and for the Divine worship. Now all the sacraments, from the fact that they confer grace, have this in common, that they afford a remedy against sin: whereas not all the sacraments are directly ordained to the Divine worship. Thus it is clear that penance, whereby man is delivered from sin, does not afford man any advance in the Divine worship, but restores him to his former state.

Now a sacrament may belong to the Divine worship in three ways: first in regard to the thing done; secondly, in regard to the agent; thirdly, in regard to the recipient. In regard to the thing done, the Eucharist belongs to the Divine worship, for the Divine worship consists principally therein, so far as it is the sacrifice of the Church. And by this same sacrament a character is not imprinted on man; because it does not ordain man to any further sacramental action or benefit received, since rather is it *the end and consummation of all the sacraments*, as Dionysius says (*Eccl. Hier.* iii.). But it contains within itself Christ, in Whom there is not the character, but the very plenitude of the Priesthood.

But it is the sacrament of Order that pertains to the sacramental agents: for it is by this sacrament that men are deputed to confer sacraments on others: while the sacrament of Baptism pertains to the recipients, since it confers on man the power to receive the other sacraments of the Church; whence it is called the *door of the sacraments*. In a way Confirmation also is ordained for the same purpose, as we shall explain in its proper place (Q. LXV., A. 3). Consequently, these three sacraments imprint a character, namely, Baptism, Confirmation, and Order.

Reply Obj. 1. Every sacrament makes man a participator in Christ's Priesthood, from the fact that it confers on him some effect thereof. But every sacrament does not depute a man to do or receive something pertaining to the worship of the priesthood of Christ: while it is just this that is required for a sacrament to imprint a character.

Reply Obj. 2. Man is sanctified by each of the sacraments, since sanctity means immunity from sin, which is the effect of grace. But in a special way some sacraments, which imprint a character, bestow on man a certain consecration, thus deputing him to the Divine worship: just as inanimate things are said to be consecrated forasmuch as they are deputed to Divine worship.

Reply Obj. 3. Although a character is a reality and a sacrament, it does not follow that whatever is a reality and a sacrament, is also a character. With regard to the other sacraments we shall explain further on what is the reality and what is the sacrament.

Pt. III, Q. 75

Second Article. Whether in This Sacrament the Substance of the Bread and Wine Remains After the Consecration?

We proceed thus to the Second Article:—

Objection 1. It seems that the substance of the bread and wine does remain in this sacrament after the consecration: because Damascene says (*De Fide Orthod.* iv.): *Since it is customary for men to eat bread and drink wine, God has wedded his Godhead to them, and made them His body and blood:* and further on: *The bread of communication is not simple bread, but is united to the Godhead.* But wedding together belongs to things actually existing. Therefore the bread and wine are at the same time, in this sacrament, with the body and the blood of Christ.

Obj. 2. Further, there ought to be conformity between the sacraments. But in the other sacraments the substance of the matter remains, like the substance of water in Baptism, and the substance of chrism in Confirmation. Therefore the substance of the bread and wine remains also in this sacrament.

Obj. 3. Further, bread and wine are made use of in this sacrament, inasmuch as they denote ecclesiastical unity, as *one bread is made from many grains and wine from many grapes,* as Augustine says in his book on the Creed (*Tract.* xxvi. *in Joan.*). But this belongs to the substance of bread and wine. Therefore, the substance of the bread and wine remains in this sacrament.

On the contrary, Ambrose says (*De Sacram.* iv.): *Although the figure of the bread and wine be seen, still, after the Consecration, they are to be believed to be nothing else than the body and blood of Christ.*

I answer that, Some have held that the substance of the bread and wine remain in this sacrament after the consecration. But this opinion cannot stand: first of all, because by such an opinion the truth of this sacrament is destroyed, to which it belongs that Christ's true body exists in this sacrament; which indeed was not there before the consecration. Now a thing cannot be in any place, where it was not previously, except by change of place, or by the conversion of another thing into itself; just as fire begins anew to be in some house, either because it is carried thither, or because it is generated there. Now it is evident that Christ's body does not begin to be present in this sacrament by local motion. First of all, because it would follow that it would cease to be in heaven: for what is moved locally does not come anew to some place unless it quit the former one. Secondly, because every body moved locally passes through all intermediary spaces, which cannot be said here. Thirdly, because it is not possible for one movement of the same body moved locally to be terminated in different places at the one time, whereas the body of Christ under this sacrament begins at the one time to be in several places. And consequently it remains that

Christ's body cannot begin to be anew in this sacrament except by change of the substance of bread into itself. But what is changed into another thing, no longer remains after such change. Hence the conclusion is that, saving the truth of this sacrament, the substance of the bread cannot remain after the consecration.

Secondly, because this position is contrary to the form of this sacrament, in which it is said: *This is My body*, which would not be true if the substance of the bread were to remain there; for the substance of bread never is the body of Christ. Rather should one say in that case: *Here is My body*.

Thirdly, because it would be opposed to the veneration of this sacrament, if any substance were there, which could not be adored with adoration of latria.

Fourthly, because it is contrary to the rite of the Church, according to which it is not lawful to take the body of Christ after bodily food, while it is nevertheless lawful to take one consecrated host after another. Hence this opinion is to be avoided as heretical.

Reply Obj. 1. God *wedded His Godhead*, i.e., His Divine power, to the bread and wine, not that these may remain in this sacrament, but in order that He may make from them His body and blood.

Reply Obj. 2. Christ is not really present in the other sacraments, as in this; and therefore the substance of the matter remains in the other sacraments, but not in this.

Reply Obj. 3. The species which remain in this sacrament, as shall be said later (A. 5), suffice for its signification; because the nature of the substance is known by its accidents.

FIFTH ARTICLE. WHETHER THE ACCIDENTS OF THE BREAD AND WINE REMAIN IN THIS SACRAMENT AFTER THE CHANGE?

We proceed thus to the Fifth Article:—

Objection 1. It seems that the accidents of the bread and wine do not remain in this sacrament. For when that which comes first is removed, that which follows is also taken away. But substance is naturally before accident, as is proved in *Metaph.* vii. Since, then, after consecration, the substance of the bread does not remain in this sacrament, it seems that its accidents cannot remain.

Obj. 2. Further, there ought not to be any deception in a sacrament of truth. But we judge of substance by accidents. It seems, then, that human judgment is deceived, if, while the accidents remain, the substance of the bread does not. Consequently this is unbecoming to this sacrament.

Obj. 3. Further, although our faith is not subject to reason, still it is not contrary to reason, but above it, as was said in the beginning of this work (P. I., Q. I., A. 6 *ad* 2; A. 8). But our reason has its origin in the senses. Therefore our faith ought not to be contrary to the senses, as it is when sense judges that to be bread which faith believes to be the substance of Christ's body. Therefore it is not befitting this sacrament for the accidents of bread to remain subject to the senses, and for the substance of bread not to remain.

Obj. 4. Further, what remains after the change has taken place seems to be the subject of change. If therefore the accidents of the bread remain after the change has been effected, it seems that the accidents are the subject of the change. But this is impossible; for *an accident cannot have an accident* (*Metaph.* iii.). Therefore the accidents of the bread and wine ought not to remain in this sacrament.

On the contrary, Augustine says in his book on the Sentences of Prosper (Lanfranc, *De Corp. et Sang. Dom.* xiii.): *Under the species which we behold, of bread and wine, we honour invisible things, i.e., flesh and blood.*

I answer that, It is evident to sense that all the accidents of the bread and wine remain after the consecration. And this is reasonably done by Divine providence. First of all, because it is not customary, but horrible, for men to eat human flesh, and to drink blood. And therefore Christ's flesh and blood are set before us to be partaken of under the species of those things which are the more commonly used by men, namely, bread and wine. Secondly, lest this sacrament might be derided by unbelievers, if we were to eat Our Lord under His own species. Thirdly, that while we receive Our Lord's body and blood invisibly, this may redound to the merit of faith.

Reply Obj. 1. As is said in the book *De Causis*, an effect depends more on the first cause than on the second. And therefore by God's power, which is the first cause of all things, it is possible for that which follows to remain, while that which is first is taken away.

Reply Obj. 2. There is no deception in this sacrament; for the accidents which are discerned by the senses are truly present. But the intellect, whose proper object is substance, as is said in *De Anima* iii., is preserved by faith from deception.

And this serves as answer to the third argument; because faith is not contrary to the senses, but concerns things to which sense does not reach.

Reply Obj. 4. This change has not properly a subject, as was stated above (A. 4 *ad* 1); nevertheless the accidents which remain have some resemblance of a subject.

SIXTH ARTICLE. WHETHER THE SUBSTANTIAL FORM OF THE BREAD REMAINS IN THIS SACRAMENT AFTER THE CONSECRATON?

We proceed thus to the Sixth Article:—

Objection 1. It seems that the substantial form of the bread remains in this sacrament after the consecration. For it has been said (A. 5) that the accidents remain after the consecration. But since bread is an artificial thing, its form is an accident. Therefore it remains after the consecration.

Obj. 2. Further, the form of Christ's body is His soul: for it is said in *De Anima* ii., that the soul *is the act of a physical body which has life in potentiality.* But it cannot be said that the substantial form of the bread is changed into the soul. Therefore it appears that it remains after the consecration.

Obj. 3. Further, the proper operation of a thing follows its substantial form. But what remains in this sacrament, nourishes, and performs every operation which bread would do were it present. Therefore the substantial form of the bread remains in this sacrament after the consecration.

On the contrary, The substantial form of bread is of the substance of bread. But the substance of the bread is changed into the body of Christ, as stated above (AA. 2, 3, 4). Therefore the substantial form of the bread does not remain.

I answer that, Some have contended that after the consecration not only do the accidents of the bread remain, but also its substantial form. But this cannot be. First of all, because if the substantial form of the bread were to remain, nothing of the bread would be changed into the body of Christ, excepting the matter; and so it would follow that it would be changed, not into the whole body of Christ, but into its matter, which is repugnant to the form of the sacrament, wherein it is said: *This is My body.*

Secondly, because if the substantial form of the bread were to remain, it would remain either in matter, or separated from matter. The first cannot be, for if it were to remain in the matter of the bread, then the whole substance of the bread would remain, which is against what was said above (A. 2). Nor could it remain in any other matter, because the proper form exists only in its proper matter.—But if it were to remain separate from matter, it would then be an actually intelligible form, and also an intelligence; for all forms separated from matter are such.

Thirdly, it would be unbefitting this sacrament: because the accidents of the bread remain in this sacrament, in order that the body of Christ may be seen under them, and not under its proper species, as stated above (A. 5).

And therefore it must be said that the substantial form of the bread does not remain.

Reply Obj. 1. There is nothing to prevent art from making a thing whose form is not an accident, but a substantial form; as frogs and serpents can be produced by art: for art produces such forms not by its own power, but by the power of natural energies. And in this way it produces the substantial forms of bread, by the power of fire baking the matter made up of flour and water.

Reply Obj. 2. The soul is the form of the body, giving it the whole order of perfect being, *i.e.*, being, corporeal being, and animated being, and so on. Therefore the form of the bread is changed into the form of Christ's body, according as the latter gives corporeal being, but not according as it bestows animated being.

Reply Obj. 3. Some of the operations of bread follow it by reason of the accidents, such as to affect the senses, and such operations are found in the species of the bread after the consecration on account of the accidents which remain. But some other operations follow the bread either by reason of the matter, such as that it is changed into something else, or else by reason of the substantial form, such as an operation consequent upon its species, for instance, that it *strengthens man's heart* (Ps. ciii. 15); and such operations are found in this sacrament, not on account of the form or matter remaining, but because they are bestowed miraculously upon the accidents themselves, as will be said later (Q. LXXVII., A. 3 *ad* 2, 3; AA. 5, 6).

55. *Thomas Aquinas*, Pange, lingua

Despite the rather dry and technical style which he used in writing about abstruse matters of theology or philosophy, Aquinas had a real poetic gift. When the feast of Corpus Christi was instituted officially in 1264, he was asked to arrange the office, that is, the liturgy for each of the hours, and the appropriate readings for the mass. In doing this he composed a number of hymns, including the *Pange, lingua* given here, as the hymn for First Vespers. It frankly imitates the *Pange lingua gloriosi* of Fortunatus (cf. Document 13 above). Aquinas' verse, as might be expected, is distinctly theological in content. The Latin version is that of F. J. E. Raby, *op. cit.*, No. 263, English translation by E. Caswall and others, *Hymns Ancient and Modern*, no. 309, verses 1–2, 5–6.

Pange, lingua gloriosi
corporis mysterium
sanguinisque pretiosi
quem in mundi pretium
fructus ventris generosi
rex effudit gentium.

Now, my tongue, the mystery telling
Of the glorious Body sing,
And the Blood, all price excelling,
Which the Gentiles' Lord and King,
In a Virgin's womb once dwelling,
Shed for this world's ransoming.

Nobis datus, nobis natus
ex intacta virgine
et in mundo conversatus
sparso verbi semine
sui moras incolatus
miro clausit ordine.

Given for us, and condescending
To be born for us below,
He with men in converse blending,
Dwelt the seed of truth to sow,
Till He closed with wondrous ending
His most patient life of woe.

Tantum ergo sacramentum
veneremur cernui,
et antiquum documentum
novo cedat ritui;
praestet fides supplementum
sensuum defectui.

Therefore we, before Him bending,
This great Sacrament revere;
Types and shadows have their ending,
For the newer rite is here;
Faith, our outward sense befriending,
Makes our inward vision clear.

Genitori genitoque
laus et jubilatio
salus, honor, virtus quoque
sit et benedictio,
procedenti ab utroque
compar sit laudatio.

Glory let us give, and blessing
To the Father and the Son,
Honor, might, and praise addressing,
While eternal ages run;
Ever too His love confessing,
Who from Both with Both is One.

The Literature of Protest

The spirit of protest in the High Middle Ages, as indeed in any period, inspired varied types of expression. It evoked from devoted bishops honest and sincere indignation together with constructive suggestions; it stimulated the sophisticated parody and satire of the scholar; it aroused the emotion of poets who wrote in the vernacular. Much of the thirteenth-century protest was extremely outspoken. But for the most part it was directed at the failures and shortcomings of the establishment and not against what it stood for. Certain special situations also had much to do with what was written. The Albigensian Crusade against heresy in southern France, and the classification of the resistance to Emperor Frederick II as a "crusade," for example, aroused considerable opposition even among the most loyal.

Curial venality was a favorite target of the critics. Since no adequate method had been devised to finance the central administration, the inevitable delays and frustrations were often avoided by informal payments. That corruption could and did result is all too obvious. Papal provision to local benefices, another object of widespread protest, had originally developed as a means of ensuring the promotion of suitably educated candidates as, for example, in the case of Peter Mauger and Innocent III cited above (cf. Document 41). During the struggles with the empire in the mid-thirteenth century, political motives often took precedence. Whatever the reason, the opposition to papal provisions was a symptom of the growing sense of national solidarity.

It is evident, too, that in the second half of the century the friars were encountering opposition and being subjected to serious criticism. Not all of the criticism was without bias. Men such as the French poet Rutebeuf, himself a university man, were outraged at what they regarded as the intrusion of the friars into the *studium* at Paris. Nevertheless, it remains true that some of the original ardor had cooled by the later years of the thirteenth century. The Franciscans were confronted with the threat of schism in their ranks; and the two orders were not always able to suppress their mutual rivalries.

The poets were often university-trained men, familiar with Latin. That they wrote in the vernacular indicates at once the importance of the new languages and the fact that they reached a wider audience. Those cited here are French. They are not, however, alone, for there are also many examples of protest in other languages.

56. Robert Grosseteste, Memoranda

Robert Grosseteste[1] to Pope Innocent IV and the Cardinals
(1250)

Cited in F. S. Stevenson, *Robert Grosseteste* (London, 1899), pp. 286–288.

As the life of the pastors is the book of the laity, it is manifest that such as these [bad priests] are the preachers of all errors and wickedness. They are in truth teachers of heresy, inasmuch as the word of action is stronger than the word of speech: they are worse than those who practice abominations, for they defile the soul.

1. On Grosseteste, see above, Document 45.

But what is the first cause and origin of these great evils? I fear
to speak it, but yet I dare not be silent, lest I should merit the
reproach of the prophet, "Woe is me, because I have held my
peace!" The cause, the fountain, the origin of all this, is this Roman
Court, not only because it does not put to flight these evils and
purge away these abominations, when it alone has the power to do
so, and is pledged most fully in that sense; but still more because by
its dispensations, provisions, and collations to the pastoral care, it
appoints in the full light of the sun men such as I have described,
not pastors, but destroyers of men; and, that it may provide for the
likelihood of some one person, it hands over to the jaws of death
many thousands of souls, for the life of each one of which the Son
of God was willing to be condemned to a most shameful death. He
who does not hinder this when he can is involved in the same
crime; and the crime is greater in proportion as he who commits it
is more highly placed, and the cause of evil is worse than its effect.
Nor let any one say that this Court acts thus for the common
advantage of the Church. This common advantage was studied by
the holy fathers who endured suffering on this account; it can
never be advanced by that which is unlawful or evil. Woe to those
who say, Let us do evil that good may come! The work of the
pastoral cure does not consist alone in administering the sacraments, repeating the canonical hours, and celebrating masses—and
even these offices are seldom performed by mercenaries—but in the
teaching of the living truth, the condemnation of vice, the punishment of it when necessary, and this but rarely can the mercenaries
dare to do. It consists also in feeding the hungry, giving drink to
the thirsty, clothing the naked, receiving guests, visiting the sick
and those in prison, especially those who belong to the parish and
have a claim on the endowment of the Church. These duties
cannot be performed by deputies or hirelings, especially as they
scarce receive out of the goods of the Church enough to support
their own lives. This bad use of their office is greatly to be
lamented in the case of the seculars, but in their case, at any rate,
there is always the possibility that others of a better mind may
follow them. When, however, parish churches are appropriated to
religious houses, these evils are made permanent. Those who preside in this See are in a special degree the representatives of Christ,
and in that character are bound to exhibit the works of Christ, and
to that extent are entitled to be obeyed in all things. If, however,

through favouritism or on other grounds they command what is opposed to the precepts and will of Christ, they separate themselves from Christ and from the conception of what a Pope should be; they are guilty of apostasy themselves and a cause of apostasy in others. God forbid that such should be the case in this See! Let its occupants, therefore, take heed lest they do or enjoin anything which is at variance with the will of Christ.

Robert Grosseteste to the Papal Notary (1253)

In this communication Grosseteste refuses to accept the appointment of Pope Innocent IV's nephew. He leaves no doubt either of his respect for the Apostolic See or of his sense of outrage at the appointment. The translation is taken from the chapter by W. A. Pantin in D. A. Collus, *Robert Grosseteste, Scholar and Bishop* (Oxford, 1955), pp. 189–190. Reprinted by permission of the Clarendon Press.

It is not possible that the most holy apostolic see, to which has been handed down by the Holy of Holies, the Lord Jesus Christ, all manner of power, according to the Apostle, for edification and not for destruction, can command or in any way attempt anything verging upon this kind of sin, which is so hateful to Jesus Christ, detestable, abominable, and pernicious to the human race. For this would be evidently a falling off and corruption and abuse of its most holy and plenary power. . . . No faithful subject of the Holy See, no man who is not cut away by schism from the body of Christ and the same Holy See, can submit to mandates, precepts or any other demonstrations of this kind, no, not even if the author were the most high body of angels. He must needs repudiate them and rebel against them with all his strength. Because of the obedience by which I am bound to the Holy See, as to my parents, and out of my love of my union with the Holy See in the body of Christ . . . as an obedient son I disobey, I contradict, I rebel. You cannot take action against me, for my every word and act is not rebellion, but the filial honour due by God's command to father and mother. As I have said, the Apostolic See in its holiness cannot destroy, it can only build. This is what the plenitude of power means; it can do all things to edification. But these so called provisions do not build up, they destroy. They cannot be the work of the Blessed Apostolic See, for 'flesh and blood,' which do not possess the Kingdom of God, 'hath revealed them,' not 'the Father of Our Lord Jesus Christ who is in Heaven.'

57. *Humbert of the Romans, Passage from the* Opus tripartitum

When Gregory X was preparing for the Second Council of Lyons (1274), he solicited suggestions and advice from the clergy. Two treatises have survived, one from Humbert de Romanis, the master-general of the Dominicans, and another from the bishop of Olmütz in Moravia. Humbert's work, the *Opus tripartitum*, was in three parts, dedicated respectively to the Greek schism, the crusade, and the re-form of the Church. All three of these matters were taken up subsequently by the council. The small excerpt from Part III cited here offers a number of practical suggestions as well as revealingly frank criticism of contemporary conditions.

The text is from Humbert de Romanis, *Opus tripartitum*, translated by G. G. Coulton, *Life in the Middle Ages*, vol. I (New York, 1930), pp. 199–200, reprinted with permission of The Macmillan Co.

With regard to divine service, it would seem wise to enact that men should not be compelled to keep new feast-days beyond the authority of the Roman Church; and that, except on the greater holy-days, instituted by the Church, men should be permitted to work after divine service, both because sins are the more multiplied on holy-days at the bidding of wicked sloth, in taverns, dances, and brothels; and also because the work-days are scarce enough now for the poor to earn their daily bread. . . . Fourthly, that divine service should be so abbreviated that it might be said and heard from end to end, and devoutly. Fifthly, that in great churches there should be a sufficient number of clerics at every service. . . .

In the parishes, the first thing blamable seems to be that some are too poor for any good parson to take. Secondly, the rich parishes are given to such as will not or cannot reside. Thirdly, vicars are put in, not of the best, but of the cheapest who will do the work. Fourthly, they are not given for God's sake to the best, but to unworthy men, sometimes for money from hand to hand, or for promises, or for services done. Fifthly, that [clergy] of evil fame are not corrected, but are oftentimes suffered to sin freely for the sake of bribes. Sixthly, some manual should be written for the instruction of the ignorant and unlearned in the duties of their office, seeing that they know not the Scriptures. As to the common run of the clergy, many of them are possessed with gluttony, lechery, vainglory, wastefulness, idleness, and many other evils, which should be corrected for the scandal that they give to the laity. Pardoners defile the Church with lies and filthiness, and render it a laughing-stock. Secondly, they bribe the prelates, who therefore suffer them to say whatsoever they will. Thirdly, in their briefs or cartels they lyingly feign so many indulgences, and expound them so ill, that scarce any man believeth. Fourthly, they gain much money, yet send little to headquarters; and they deceive the people with false relics.

58. Bruno of Olmütz, Memorandum to Pope Gregory X

The famous letter from Bishop Bruno of Olmütz to Pope Gregory X, written in 1273, refers to a number of situations peculiar to a diocese along the eastern frontier of western Christendom. The first part, which has been omitted here, deals with such matters as the Tartar menace, schismatic clergy, etc., as well as with the consequences of the long interregnum in the empire. In the passage cited here, despite the deplorable state of the secular clergy which he frankly describes, Bishop Bruno severely criticizes the intrusion of the friars into the normal functioning of the dioceses. He is especially indignant at their appropriation of burial fees, the dispensing of indulgences, and the like. It is possible that the bishop is overly severe, perhaps even inconsistent, in view of his own admissions concerning the local seculars. He does nevertheless clearly outline the kind of situation faced by many of the secular clergy as the friars settled within their jurisdictions. Further, some of his complaints, for example, the statement that the friars held their congregations by preaching, indicate certain positive improvements in parochial life. And it is to be noted that he does not advocate the removal of the friars.

The text is translated from the Latin text in *MGH, Leges*, IV, 591–593.

    . . . Concerning the clergy we write to you as follows: sufficient provision has been made in other councils about those things which have to do with their manner of life and character. Concerning those things, however, which are coming to light in our lands and those near us, we do not know whether they are the same everywhere; we believe it to be so, because in relation to the scarcity and poverty of benefices there is an excess of those who wish to enjoy the privilege of a cleric, and from this great difficulty has commonly arisen for those of us who are prelates. For since it is not possible for such persons to be provided for, they are forced to beg, to the disgrace of the clerical order, or what is worse, not wanting to dig and not possessing the necessary skills to lead a life of commerce, they turn themselves to theft, robbery, or sacrilege; and when they are caught in such things they are handed over to the bishops. Those, however, who escape from prison and persevere in evil-doing habitually, and are again apprehended, are assigned punishments at the corrupt hands of those judging in such a way that it sometimes happens that a crowd, aroused on account of this, has been given notice that it has incurred the penalty of excommunication. Because of this, scandal often arises between bishops and laity.

May it please your holiness, because for the bishops in our country the distance is so great that they cannot easily convene for the degradation of such persons, that in those cases where incorrigible clerics are found caught in reprehensible acts for the first, second, and third time, a bishop alone, without the convocation of bishops, be able to degrade them in solemn synod, and with the synod approving; otherwise, because of the large number of those seizing these clerics, that your paternity take steps to provide some means of absolution for such laymen without the difficult access to the Roman curia.

There are other things whereby it happens that the clergy and the secular conventual and parochial churches are so injured that the Apostolic See ought not to expect these of its daughters to grow, since we daily see them diminished and reduced in possessions and rights. For that exposing of the lepers which used to be the obligation of the priests, according to the Lord in the Gospel and Moses in the Old Testament, by which is understood the confession of sinners, is taken from [their] midst. The word of preaching which could once be heard by the people entrusted to [them] is spurned by them. These same conventual and parochial churches are no longer frequented by the people on Sundays and Holy Days, especially in the cities and towns where the Preachers and Minorities have their houses.[1] Except for one mass which they

---

1. I.e., Dominicans and Franciscans.

say silently in the convent, the aforementioned brothers usually say masses from dawn, not stopping until Tierce; reading rapidly they go through their several masses in succession. And since our moderns like brevity, the people prefer their masses and avoid the conventual and parish churches. The friars have been accustomed even at these masses to hold the people by means of a sermon. Therefore, they don't go to the other churches as they should. They have also been in the habit of giving an indulgence of two, three, four, ten, and even more years on their own feast days and throughout their octaves out of the indulgences they have been usually conceded by each of the bishops.[2] We have even seen certain papal letters which they have of daily indulgences of one hundred days for those who visit their churches.

In all these things there is no little loss not only to the churches of these cities, but even to the "threshold" of the apostles Peter and Paul and the other saints which, as a consequence, are not frequented as had previously been the custom. For it seems hardly to sit well with you, O reverend father, and your confreres and fellow bishops, and also the legates *a latere* you have sent that their authority appears to surpass ours, since in your daily preaching and ours we have habitually given no more than forty days. This, therefore, remains something that must be attended to, indeed, let nothing else be done daily, unless the name of the friars is to be preferred to that of the fathers, that is, the priests and bishops, even yourself, and unless from now on we ought not to be called shepherds nor it be fitting for us to recognize the countenance of our flock in confessions, nor to offer them the nourishment of preaching, nor care for the sick, nor restore the broken, when these same [friars] daily intrude themselves in all these concerns uninvited and unasked by us, asserting that in this they have received the privilege from the Apostolic See.

Moreover, because we have no share in the living, we do not even share in the dead, either in offerings or in the canonical portion. For the aforementioned friars have in the cities the burial of almost all the people. The clerical order which at one time depended on wills is now, on the contrary, known to have disap-

---

2. Indulgences of specific lengths of time were understood to symbolize the remission of penalty of corresponding importance in Purgatory. There was much misunderstanding about this, and when money was accepted for the granting of indulgences, corruption appeared.

peared from wills entirely, and legacies have been entirely relegated elsewhere. Such, indeed, are the losses which the clergy
suffer at the hands of these same people.

Furthermore, many related things follow in consequence.
Surely, since the Lord once bestowed the power of both binding
and loosing on Peter the apostle, and since there should be the same
discipline for both, we wonder by what right they claim to have
the power of loosing when they don't have the right of binding,
nor even want to have it; since even if it is conceded to them by the
bishops that they may excommunicate someone, they make themselves inaccessible, just as if they were excused. For, in this connection, they are afraid to discipline those against whom perhaps this
must be done. In fact, they want to drink the cup of pure wine
although it is full of diluted [wine] and its dregs are not emptied,
leaving that to be drunk by the clergy. For the aforesaid friars
seem to care without caring since they do not have the care of
souls. They take the usufruct of [pastoral] care while refusing to
have its perils; they preside without solicitude, having the honor of
care without its burden and without the hazard of its peculiar
danger, and they know the misdeeds of others. Likewise, their
authority in hearing confessions seems to exceed the power of your
penitentiaries [confessors]. Some of them turn over to us those
absolved for the imposition of penances; others, indeed, absolve
and enjoin penances without us. [Your] legates *a latere* after the
term of their legation, archbishops and bishops outside of their
dioceses, cannot intervene in absolving and binding. The friars, in
fact, in whatever lands they come to, impose penances and absolve,
exceeding in this jurisdiction all ordinary or even delegated jurisdictions.

Deliberation on all these matters surpasses our powers; rather it
is for yours to see to it that the authority of prelates and clergy is
preserved and that, at the same time, many religious orders can be
sustained, perhaps by taking a middle course between Pope Innocent IV and Pope Alexander IV, one of whom, as is known, issued
a statute for the clergy, the other for the friars.[3] Further, since you
have enjoined it on us, we have presumed to add a few drops of our
counsel to the great sea of your discernment, namely, that the

3. Innocent IV, in the bull *Etsi animarum*, curtailed the orders' privileges.
Alexander IV, the protector of the Franciscans, annulled this and issued
another in 1258 confirming and amplifying the privileges.

friars not be prohibited from hearing confessions as far as counselling is concerned, but for imposing penances and absolution, they, nevertheless, turn over the penitents to the proper priests. And although the friars otherwise are exempt, nevertheless, as far as hearing confessions and preaching are concerned, only those be chosen by the bishops whom they judge capable and suited to it; and that they [the bishops] have the power to restrain by ecclesiastical censure those who presume otherwise and even impose silence *in perpetuo* on those who in their preaching habitually disparage the clergy.

In order that the people, as was mentioned above, may not be drawn away by the preaching of these friars from hearing masses in their own parishes, you can order that preaching by the friars within the parishes be permitted only to a limited extent, for example on the feast day of the friars or the dedication of the patron saint under whose special title a church was founded. Moreover, it seems that since these orders were established on total poverty and mendicancy and do not work with their own hands, and since this [principle], that he who does not work may eat, cannot stand without the world's judgment, you rightly ought to prevent this among people overly aroused, and even give power to the bishops to prohibit them [the friars] from accepting convents wherever they please. Further, where it can and should be done, let it [the permission] be asked and received through the will of the bishops . . .

59. The Gospel According to Marks of Silver

This celebrated parody is a typical product of the schools, a bit of literary wit done with evident relish rather than bitterness by an author who, one almost suspects, would have been enormously disappointed if a curial housecleaning had robbed him of the object of his satire. The original and shortest version of the parody dates probably from the late twelfth century. Various expanded versions appeared in later years.

The parody begins with the usual liturgical formula for the beginning of the Gospel at mass: *Initium sancti evangelii* . . ., and uses several familiar passages from the four Gospels and other parts of the Bible. It belongs to a whole genre of literary funmaking on sacred themes—the mass, the office, Church councils, and the like—designed, perhaps among other things, simply to shock those of the devout who lacked a sense of humor.

The translation is by C. H. Haskins, *The Renaissance of the Twelfth Century* (Cambridge, 1927), pp. 185–186. Copyright 1927 by President and Fellows of Harvard College, 1955 by Clare Allen Haskins, reprinted by permission of Harvard University Press. For the original, with explanation, see P. Lehmann, *Die Parodie im Mittelalter* (new. ed., Stuttgart, 1963), pp. 32 ff., 183–184.

Here beginneth the Holy Gospel according to Marks of Silver. At that time the Pope said unto the Romans, "When the Son of Man shall come to the throne of our Majesty, say unto him first, 'Friend, wherefore art thou come?' But if he shall continue knocking without giving you anything, cast him out into outer darkness." And it came to pass that a certain poor clerk came to the court of the Lord Pope and cried out, saying, "Have pity upon me, O doorkeepers of the Pope, for the hand of poverty hath touched me. I am poor and needy, and therefore I beseech you to succor my misfortune and my misery." But when they heard him they were filled with indignation and said, "Friend, thy poverty perish with thee! Get thee behind me, Satan, because thou savorest not what the pieces of money savor. Verily, verily, I say unto thee, thou shalt not enter into the joy of thy Lord till thou hast paid the uttermost farthing."

So the poor man departed and sold his cloak and his tunic and all that he had, and gave unto the cardinals and the doorkeepers and the chamberlains. But they said, "What is this among so many?" and they cast him out, and he went out and wept bitterly and would not be comforted.

Then there came unto the curia a certain rich clerk, who had waxed fat and grown thick, and had committed murder in the insurrection. He gave, first to the doorkeeper, then to the chamberlain, then to the cardinals. But they thought among themselves that they should have received more. Then the Lord Pope, hearing that the cardinals and servants had received many gifts from the clergyman, fell sick nigh unto death; but the rich man sent him a medicine of gold and silver, and straightway he was healed. Then the Lord Pope called unto him the cardinals and the servants and said to them, "Brethren, see to it that no man deceive you with vain words; for, lo! I give you an example that even as I receive, so receive ye also."

60. Protest in Vernacular Poetry

Lines from the Besant de Dieu of Guillaume le Clerc

Guillaume lived and wrote in the first half of the thirteenth century. He was a Norman by birth, but his familiarity with the South is evident in his reference to the Albigensian Crusade. The prose translation is by Mary M. Wood, *The Spirit of Protest in Old French Literature*, Columbia University Studies in Romance Philology and Literature (New York, 1917), pp. 80–84. Reprinted by permission of Columbia University Press.

But I see priests who are rich, who have large incomes, but who spend them in evil ways and give little to God. And when a priest has risen so high through simony or sin that he has a bishopric in charge, immediately he thinks of a fortune. He heaps up treasure and begins to amass wealth, but if he has not entered by the door into the fold among the sheep, as a thief he shall be dishonored. Soon he shall have twenty thousand souls in his care, but let him see to it that he does not lose a single one. . . . And when he had great riches, the revenues of the holy church, the greater part of which, as I think, he ought to have dispensed for the love of God and to have kept the smaller share for himself, he did nothing of the kind. Instead he was more greedy than a dog that has in his mouth a big bone: . . . little he gave, little he distributed. What shall this wretch answer when the Judge shall come at the last day, the priest who has buried the treasures of holy church and the talents of God? . . . Archdeacons and deacons . . . who permit adultery, who in delivering judgment stoop to take bribes, who consent to fornication . . . who sell justice, these will be in very hard case; and those who have rich churches, three or four in a province, what will they do, what will they say before the Prince? They who have supported their mistresses on the great revenues of the church, and portioned their daughters and sons on the property of the Crucifix? And what will the parish priests say, those who are always ready to take money and receive confessions from the unhappy persons that they deceive by enjoining upon them masses, annuals and trentals, but then do not celebrate the offices. . . .

We ought to obey the Holy Father . . . but there are so many of the clergy covetous of gold and silver, that they make the ship creak and shake and depart from the right course. Those who are nearest the Master . . . love too much the red coin. I marvel greatly, I assure you, that our Master suffers such people to be in the ship. Through such men the Devil enters and all but causes the ship to founder. There are more thousands in the ship than one could count, who speak ill of it, and who cry out plainly that the blame of covetousness rests upon the head because he misdirects the ship, for if the master of the ship is surrounded by evil men, how can he possibly guard himself from their venom so carefully that he may receive no trace of it? But those who are about him, cardinals, legates, priests, are more covetous than the others. . . . Therefore it seems that the ship enjoys no mild, pleasant weather; I see storms sweeping up from over the sea from all quarters. For I see today throughout the world wars beginning and strife and people rising against people. I see pestilence and famine. . . .

When one of her sons has done wrong but is willing to make reparation, Rome ought not, I think, to send against him her older son to destroy him. It would be far better for her to summon him and talk gently with him and admonish him than to order his lands laid waste. When the French attack the people of Toulouse, whom they regard as heretics, and the Roman legates lead them, that, methinks, is not right at all.

Selected stanzas from the Romans de Carité of the "Renclus de Moiliens"

The first stanzas cited (paragraph 1) purports to tell the story of a pilgrimage in search of Charity. This allegorical satire of the "Hermit" is unlike the Gospel According to Marks of Silver in giving the impression of a real earnestness, so also the other stanzas (paragraphs 2 and 3), which are directed against unworthy priests. The poem can be dated around 1226. The prose translation is by Mary M. Wood, op. cit., pp. 100–104. Reprinted by permission of Columbia University Press.

First I went to Rome, for I thought to find thee [Charity] in that august abode with the Roman pope, who has the whole world under his sway; I thought surely I should find thee in his heart rather than in the heart of any other, since he is the sovereign father, who should be foremost in holiness, an example for others. O Charity, there I was told that long ago thou wast counselor in the house of the pope. Then the court was governed by reason; but thou wast there only for a season, for thou wast driven out by the advice of a good-for-nothing, Covetousness, the steward there, who hesitates at no treachery, so well she loves money. A false heart hides under a fair countenance, when she is offered a money potion. I heard naught but good said of the pope himself . . . but those who are about him often bring blame upon him; round him swarms a company whose ill repute echoes far. No poor man can enter the papal court; no one passes that door empty-handed. . . . When I had returned from the papal court, I directed my steps where the cardinals dwell; but I found them all of one kind, and everywhere mercenary. . . . Law is silent when gold whispers; justice retires before the clink of silver. . . . The Roman has a ready tongue; when it is oiled, it speaks glibly; but with tongue unlubricated he is mute. And whoever oils the hinges of his door, enters within; otherwise, he is turned away. The poor man retires in confusion, the rich is never refused entrance. You who have been at Rome know well how costly such ointment is. . . .

Priest, is it not a great wonder that you sleep and the layman wakes? What wonder is it if I wonder at the foolish pastor and the wise flock? These are clean, he is defiled; they are in the meadow, and he in the mud. . . .

Priest, when you took the *fanon*,[1] you made a harvester of yourself; you bound yourself to the sweat of labor in the harvest of God. Do then what you promised. . . . Priest, I have seen many years, and I have never seen two priests sweating blood. How does it happen that they do not sweat blood? How? Foul covetousness has made all priests recreants. They sweat at garnering in money. . . . I see few shepherds, many market-men; for, just as the tavern-keeper cares only for vendible goods for which men will give money, so these "shepherds" make profit of their flock. Venality has mounted so high that it has reached the greatest among those august abbots with the crozier and the episcopal mitre.

Lines from Rutebeuf, The Battle of Vices Against Virtues

Rutebeuf was one of the most talented poets of his day. A product of the schools, he was deeply involved in the controversy over the admission of the Dominicans to the Paris university and valiantly defended

---

1. The harvester's handkerchief, here used to symbolize his craft.

Guillaume de Saint-Amour who was finally banished for his opposition to the friars. These lines show the poet's feelings on this matter, but they also reflect a more general criticism of the friars.

Rutebeuf's poetry touched several genres. He wrote eloquently on the crusade and sharply condemned the failure of the nobles to respond. In his *Povreté Rutebeuf* he foreshadowed the later Villon. The poem cited here may be dated around 1270. The prose translation is by Mary M. Wood, *op. cit.*, pp. 126–128. Reprinted by permission of Columbia University Press.

It is not quite seventy years since these two holy orders came . . . to preach humility, which is the path of truth, to exalt it and to follow it, as they find in their book, these holy people came into the country. When they came at first, they came humbly; they begged their bread, such was the rule, to take away the sins of the world. . . . Humility was little, the virtue they had chosen for their own; now is Humility greater, for the friars are now lords of kings, of prelates and of counts. By my faith, now it would be a great shame if they had not other food than their rule prescribes. . . . Now is it right and reasonable that so great a dame should have great houses and beautiful halls and beautiful palaces, in spite of malicious tongues and that of Rutebeuf first of all, who was wont to blame them. . . . And the Friars who profess humility hold all the kingdom in their hands. They seek out and search into secrets. If they are admitted into men's houses, there is good reason for it. One is that they have sharp tongues, and every one fears slander. . . . The wicked man's flesh creeps when he sees them coming; it is hard for him to keep anything which they think good and beautiful, for they can tell many a tale. So he receives them with [pretended] joy and feasts them because he fears inquiry. . . .

Goodness and Dame Wrath . . . came with all their people ranged about them . . . before Pope Alexander.[1] . . . The Dominican Friars were there to hear judgment as they should, and Guillaume de Saint-Amour, for they had raised a great clamor about his sermons and his conversation. In my opinion the pope banished Master Guillaume from the land and kingdom of another. If he has everywhere such advantage, the lords have shame and harm from it, for they have no rights over their own land. . . . Now many good people say that it was neither good nor fitting to

---

1. Pope Alexander IV (1254–61), who supported the friars. Saint-Amour was permitted to return to Paris by Alexander's successor.

banish him, that he was wronged; but they know that, right or wrong, one may easily speak too much truth. This you may see from the case of him who was banished for this very thing, and so the question was not at all settled, but will last for a long time.

Priests and Laymen

---

61. Sermon Literature

Little is known of the actual character of preaching before the thirteenth century. As the pastoral functions passed from the bishop to the parish priests, presumably some sort of instruction arising out of the day's scriptural reading, the Epistle and Gospel, was given. Doubtless this was very rudimentary, though canonists continued to repeat ancient injunctions to priests to be supplied with suitable sermon material. Toward the end of the twelfth century, Maurice de Sully (d. 1196), bishop of Paris and an effective preacher in the vernacular, provided his priests with a collection of homilies. Presumably other bishops did likewise.

With the resurgence of popular preaching in the thirteenth century, there seems to have been a demand for pious stories to point up a moral or illustrate a religious truth. The use of *exempla,* as such anecdotes were called, was as old as preaching. Yet several new collections appeared during the thirteenth century. The typical *exemplum* was a brief tale, usually with allusions to contemporary life and making much use of the miraculous. Many of them seem crude, even childish, to the modern reader. Apparently they also offended thoughtful persons in the Middle Ages, and more than one voice, including that of Dante, was raised in criticism. What should be remembered in reading these stories, however, is that the anecdote presumably did not constitute the entire sermon. A story is after all a favorite device of the preacher who finds the attention of his audience wandering.

The three selections given here are taken from the collections of Jacques de Vitry (d. circa 1240), a French bishop, later a cardinal, and finally patriarch of Jerusalem; of Cesarius of Heisterbach, a monk who died around 1250; and of Étienne de Bourbon, a Dominican friar of considerable experience, who died around 1261. The passages are taken from the translation by D. C. Munro, *University of Pennsylvania, Translations and Reprints,* vol. II, no. 4 (Philadelphia, 1895).

Jacques de Vitry

Moreover, although poverty and other tribulations are advantageous, yet certain ones abuse them. Accordingly we read that when the body of St. Martin was borne in procession it healed all the infirm who met it. Now there were near the church two wandering beggars, one blind, the other lame, who began to converse together and said, "See, the body of St. Martin is now being borne in procession, and if it catches us we shall be healed immediately, and no one in the future will give us any alms, but we shall have to work and labor with our own hands." Then the blind man said to the lame, "Get up on my shoulders because I am strong, and you who see well can guide me." They did this; but when they wished to escape, the procession overtook them; and since, on account of the throng, they were not able to get away, they were healed against their will.

Cesarius of Heisterbach

A certain knight loved most ardently the above-mentioned martyr, St. Thomas of Canterbury, and sought everywhere to obtain some relic of him. When a certain wily priest, in whose house he was staying, heard of this he said to him, "I have by me a bridle which St. Thomas used for a long time, and I have often experienced its virtues." When the knight heard this, and believed it, he joyfully paid the priest the money which the latter demanded and received the bridle with great devotion.

God, truly, to whom nothing is impossible, wishing to reward the faith of the knight and for the honor of his martyr, deigned to work many miracles through the same bridle. The knight seeing this founded a church in honor of the martyr and in it he placed as a relic the bridle of that most wicked priest.

Étienne de Bourbon

For I have heard that a certain rustic, wishing to become wealthy and having many hives of bees, asked certain evil men how he could get rich and increase the number of his bees. He was told by some one that if he should retain the sacred communion on Easter and place it in one of his hives, he would entice away all of his neighbor's bees, which leaving their own hives, would come to the place where the body of our Lord was and there would make honey. He did this.

Then all the bees came to the hive where the body of Christ was, and just as if they had felt compassion for the irreverence done to it, by their labor they began to construct a little church and to erect foundations and bases and columns and an altar with like labor, and with the greatest reverence they placed the body of our Lord upon the altar. And within that little bee-hive they formed that little church with wonderful and the most beautiful workmanship. The bees of the vicinity leaving their hives came together at that one; and over that structure they sang in their own manner certain wonderful melodies like hymns.

The rustic hearing this, wondered. But waiting until the fitting time for collecting the swarm of bees and the honey-comb, he found nothing in his hives in which the bees had been accustomed to make honey; finding himself impoverished through the means by which he had believed that he would be enriched, he went to that one where he had placed the host, where he saw the bees had come together. But when he approached, just as if they had wanted to vindicate the insult to our Saviour, the bees rushed upon the rustic and stung him so severely that he escaped with difficulty, and suffering greatly. Going to the priest he related all that he had done and what the bees had done. The priest, by the advice of his bishop, collected his parishioners and went in procession to the place. Then the bees, leaving the hive, rose in the air, making sweet melody. Raising the hive they found within the noble structure of that little church and the body of our Lord placed upon the altar. Then returning thanks they bore to their own church that little church of the bees constructed with such skill and elegance and with praises placed it on the altar.

By this deed those who do not reverence but offer insult instead to the sacred body of Christ or the sacred place where it is, ought to be put to great confusion.

62. *Jacobus de Voragine*, The Golden Legend

The *Golden Legend* of Jacobus de Voragine, O.P., archbishop of Genoa, appeared sometime between 1270 and 1290. The original Latin version was designed to present material concerning the principal figures of the Old Testament, the major feasts of the Church, and the lives of all the saints on the liturgical calendar. In many cases, as for example in the extract cited here, the stories are preceded by a résumé of the appropriate scriptural passages and sometimes excerpts from a sermon by an earlier writer. Vernacular translations soon appeared and the *Golden Legend* inspired artists as well as preachers.

The selection given here is taken from the entry for the feast of the Purification which commemorates Mary's visit to the temple in Jerusalem—according to Mosaic law forty days after the birth of Jesus. The translation is that of William Caxton, who introduced the printing press into England in the fifteenth century, Jacobus de Voragine, *The Golden Legend* (London, 1900), Book III, pp. 25–27.[1]

This feast is called the purification of our Lady, not for that she had need ne ought make her purification, for she was pure and clean without having of any tatche of deadly sin ne venial, like as she that had, without company of any man, by the virtue of the Holy Ghost, conceived the Son of God, and was delivered without losing of her virginity, so she came with her blessed son at the fortieth day after his nativity for to obey the commandment of the law, after the manner of other women which had need of purification, and also for to show to us the example of humility. He is very humble that is worthy to be praised for his virtues. This glorious Lady is queen of heaven and Lady of angels, nevertheless she is pure and humble among the women like as a poor woman, without making any semblant of her great humility, ne of the high majesty of her son, whereof S. Bernard saith in this manner:

O who may make us to understand, glorious Lady, the thought of thine heart that thou haddest among the services that thou madest to thy blessed son in giving him suck, in laying down and raising, when thou sawest a little child of thee born on that one part, and of that other side thou knewest him to be God Almighty? And now thou believest and seest him created that had created all the world, now thou seest him feeble as a child which is Almighty and all puissant, now thou feedest him that all the world feedeth, and now thou seest him not speaking, that made man and speech. O who should con show hereupon the secrets of thine heart? How savoured thy courage when thou heldest thy child between thine

1. Another selection from the *Golden Legend* can be found in D. Herlihy, *Medieval Culture and Society*, Documentary History of Western Civilization (New York, 1968), pp. 308–314. On St. Bernard referred to at the end of the first paragraph, see above, Document 39.

arms whom thou lovedest as they Lord, and kissed him as thy son. Who should not marvel of this miracle, when a virgin and a clean maid hath enfanted and childed her maker and Lord of all the world? To him let us address our thoughts, and embrace we this child of one very belief, whom we ought to love because he hath humbled himself for us, and to doubt him, because he is our judge and our Lord, to whose commandments we owe to obey if we will be saved.

We read an example of a noble lady which had great devotion in the blessed Virgin Mary, and she had a chapel in which she did do say mass of our Lady daily by her chaplain. It happed that the day of the purification of our Lady, her chaplain was out, so that this lady might that day have no mass, and she durst not go to another church because she had given her mantle unto a poor man for the love of our Lady. She was much sorrowful because she might hear no mass and for to make her devotions she went into the chapel, and tofore the altar she kneeled down for to make her prayers to our Lady. And anon she fell asleep, in which she had a vision, and her seemed that she was in a church, and saw come into the church a great company of virgins, tofore whom she saw come a right noble virgin crowned right preciously. And when they were all set each in order, came a company of young men which sat down each after other in order like the other; after, entered one that bare a burden of candles, and departed them to them above first, and so to each of them by order he gave one, and at the last came this man to this lady aforesaid and gave to her also a candle of wax. The which lady saw also come a priest, a deacon and a subdeacon, all revested, going to the altar as for to say mass. And her seemed that S. Laurence and S. Vincent were deacon and sub-deacon, and Jesu Christ the priest, and two angels bearing tofore them candles, and two young angels began the introit of the mass, and all the company of the virgins sang the mass. And when the mass was sung unto the offering, her seemed that thilk virgin so crowned went tofore, and after, all the others followed, and offered to the priest, kneeling much devoutly, their candles. And when the priest tarried for this lady that she should also have come to the offering, the glorious queen of virgins sent to her to say that she was not courteous to make the priest so long to tarry for her. And the lady answered that the priest should proceed in his mass forth, for she would keep her candle and not offer it. And the glorious virgin sent yet once to her, and she said she would not offer her candle. The third time the queen said to the messenger: Go and pray her that she come and offer her candle, or else take it from her by force. The messenger came to this lady, and because in no wise she would not come and offer up her candle, he set hand on the candle that this lady held and drew fast, and she held fast, and so long he drew and haled that the candle brake in two pieces, and that one half abode still in the hand of the lady aforesaid, which anon awoke and came to herself, and found the piece of the candle in her hand, whereof she much marvelled, and thanked our Lord and the glorious Virgin Mary devoutly which had suffered her that day not to be without mass. And all the days of her life after she kept that piece of that candle much preciously, like an holy relic, and all they that were touched therewith were guerished and healed of their maladies and sicknesses. Let us pray then humbly to the glorious Virgin Mary, which is comfort to them that forsake their sins, that she will make our peace to the blessed Son and impetre and get of him remission of all our sins, and after this life to come to the glory and joy of heaven, to the which bring us the Father, the Son, and the Holy Ghost. Amen.

63. The Lay-Folks' Mass-Book

Even though the bulk of the medieval population remained illiterate, by the late twelfth century some nobles and a larger number of middle-class persons were able to secure some education. Few of them, however, knew any Latin, and any instructions concerning the liturgy had to be given in the vernacular. The author of the selection cited here was an Anglo-Norman cleric ("Jeremy") who wrote his little book around the middle of the twelfth century. The original version, since lost, was probably written in French and designed for the nobility in England who at that time still retained the speech of the 1066 invaders.

Somewhat over a century later, perhaps during the last decade of the thirteenth century, the book was translated into English, presumably for what by that time may have been a wider audience of literate folk. According to the editor of this rare document, few if any significant changes were made in the first translation. Later English versions reflected changes in forms of worship.

The book is designed to aid a devout person without a knowledge of

Latin in following the priest at mass. Along with explanations of the priest's movements and prayers and frequent injunctions to repeat the Our Father, or the Hail Mary and Creed, the author has suggested additional prayers. A few typical examples are given here. The emphasis of the book is on "mass hearing" and being present at the consecration and elevation of the Host. One of the prayers asks God to "receive this service and solemn sacrifice, for the priest and for all of us present here now or in the future, to hear this mass or to worship, to see the consecration or to pray . . ." There are no directions for receiving communion by the layman during the mass.

A few lines from the beginning and the end are presented in the original Middle English version (Text B).[1] The text is in rhymed octosyllabic couplets, not always regular, and including a few passages in other meters. Presumably, it was thought that an uncomplicated verse form would be easy to follow and perhaps to memorize. In short, the author's purpose was didactic, and content was more important than poetic elegance.

About two thirds of the entire text is given here in a modern English adaptation from the edition by T. F. Simmons, *The Lay-Folks' Mass-Book*, Early English Text Society, no. 71 (London, 1879), Text B, pp. 1–60, by Mary Baldwin. Wherever possible the original simple rhyme scheme has been preserved.

> Tho worthyest thing, most of godnesse,[1]
> In al this world, [*hit*] is tho messe.
> In alle tho bokes of holy kyrc,
> thate holy men, th*a*t tyme, con wyrc,
> tho m[*esse is p*]raysed mony-folde;
> tho [*vertus mi*]ght neu*er* be [*t*]olde,
> for if [*thousand*] clerkes d[*id nogh*]t ellis,
> Aft*er* th*a*t [*tho boke*] tellis,
> bot tolde [*tho vertus of*] messe sy*n*gynge,
> and tho [*p*ro*fet of m*]esse herynge,
> yit shuld tha[*i never tho*] fift parte
> for all thaire *wit* & alle thaire arte,
> telle tho v*er*tu [*me*] des & p*a*rdoun
> to hom that [*with devocyo*]un
> In clennes [*and in gode ent*]ent
> dos worship [*to*] this sacr*a*ment.

> The thing whose worth none can surpass
> In all this world is holy mass.
> The books of holy church, so well
> Written by holy men, all tell
> Its goodness and its worth are such
> Its virtues can't be praised too much.

1. With th and y substituted for the corresponding Middle English letters.

If a thousand clerks, as this book tells,
Devoted themselves to nothing else
But teaching the virtue of singing it,
Of hearing mass the great profit,
Still they, for all their wit and art,
Could never tell the fifth small part
Of virtue, pardon and reward
For those who with a devout heart,
With purity and good intent
Give worship to this sacrament.
    A book I read by Jeremy,
A holy man well known to be
A pious man and most devout,
Who in this volume thus speaks out.
He says that you should take good care
At mass, not to chatter there;
And illustration adds for you
Why chattering is wrong to do.
    Another part that this book has
Teaches how to hear the mass.
When the priest speaks, or if he sings,
Listen, and turn from other things;
But when the priest prays privately,
Then your prayers too should silent be,
And what I from the book will learn
I shall for you to English turn.

The Prayers Before Mass

    When the altar is arrayed,
The priest, his preparations made,
Takes the chasuble from the altar
In both his hands, he does not falter,
And moving just a little down,
Over his vestments puts it on.
Then all men kneel; the priest still stands
And up to God he holds his hands,
And then before the mass begins
Himself he humbles for his sins.
To all the folk he does confess
For all his sins, both more and less;
Also the clerks as well to him
Shrive themselves of all their sin
And ask from God His forgiveness
Before beginning to hear the mass.
Those the priest absolves straightway
Who shrive themselves, both clerk and lay,
Confessing to God what they did ill,
Whether aloud or keeping still.

Therefore, kneeling on your knee
As you beside you others see,
Shrive yourself of all your sins,
Beginning when the priest begins
As I will write for you to say.
Join your hands when thus you pray,
And to your prayer for absolution
Add *Pater* and *Ave*, and in conclusion,
Before you rise repeat the *Creed*,
The better for mercy from God to plead.
This prayer is a *Confiteor*
For those who have no Latin lore:

[An English version of the *Confiteor Dei omnipotenti* (I confess
to Almighty God), etc., follows]

The Introit

Then, when you have said your *Creed*
You should stand up, and with all speed,
For when all have confessed their sins,
The office of the mass begins,
And then the priest turns with his hand
His book at the altar's southern end.
And while you are still standing there
I wish that you would say this prayer:

O God, because of your goodness,
At the beginning of this mass,
Grant to all who shall it hear,
Of conscience to be clean and clear.
The priest, Lord, who the mass will say,
From all temptation save this day;
May he be clean in deed and thought,
May evil spirits hurt him not,
May he complete this sacrament
With a pure heart and good intent.
First, may this mass honor you,
Lord of all our succor true,
And your mother, maiden clean,
The saints with their devotion keen.
To all who hear it, grant soul's health,
Help and grace and ample wealth.
To everyone we have in mind,
Kin and friends of any kind,
Good Lord, grant them, for this mass,
Of all their sins, your forgiveness.
Give rest and peace that ever last

To souls who from this earth have passed.
To all of us your comfort send,
And bring us joy that will not end. Amen.

The Gloria

When in the mass on holy days
Or great feasts, as a special praise,
The *Gloria* is said or sung,
Say you then in English tongue:

[The *Gloria in Excelsis Deo* (Glory to God in the Highest), etc.,
followed by Collects and Epistle]

When the *Gloria* is finished, then
Kneel down on your knees again.
Whether mass be sung or said,
Repeat the *Pater* in your head
Till deacon or priest the Gospel read:
Then stand up and take good heed.

The Gospel

The priest will now his book bring forth
To the end of the altar at the north,
And with his thumb, if you will look,
He makes a cross upon the book,
And then another upon his face.
And now he has great need of grace,
Because an earthly man will read
The words of Christ, God's Son indeed.
Both they who hear and they who read
Of good teachers have great need,
How they should read, how they should hear
The words of God, so loved and dear.
All men should have a mighty awe
When they hear Scripture speak God's law,
And love as well, for that sweet Lord
Who sends us comfort with His word.
But now since hearing is our concern,
A way to listen you should learn.
One way suits those who can read,
Rude folk other teaching need.
Cross yourself, as you prepare
To hear the Gospel, standing there,
Then listen well, as I have said,
And pray the while the book is read:

In the name of the Father, Son, and Holy Ghost,
The one true God and Lord of Hosts,
May I welcome God's holy word
With glory and praise to you, O Lord.

Do not speak while the Gospel is read,
But think on Him who for you bled,
Meanwhile saying in your mind
The prayer that you here written find:

Grant me your grace, O Jesus mine,
And to amend grant will and time,
To keep your word and do your will,
To choose the good and leave the ill,
And that it so may be,
Good Jesus, grant to me. Amen.

This prayer should often be repeated
Until the Gospel is completed;
When the reading to an end has come,
Make a cross and kiss your thumb.

The Creed

At this time, if the Creed is said,
In place of Latin say instead
The Creed that I will write for you
In English, that is best to do.
When the Creed is not said, say nothing else,
But follow along as this book tells.
And now be sure you take good heed,
For here is written your English Creed.

[An English version of the Apostles Creed follows]

The Offertory Prayer

After that, the next thing,
Comes the time of offering.
Offer or not, it's up to you,
But how to pray I would you knew.
While you are standing, what to say
Is written next, to help you pray:

O Jesus, born in Bethlehem,
To you came there the three wise men.
They offered myrrh, incense and gold

And you received them, as is told,
And well you guided them all three
Home again to their country.
So these gifts that here we offer,
And the prayers that now we proffer,
Take, O Lord, as praise to you,
And be our help in all we do.
Keep all perils far away,
And grant our good desires today,
All our misdeeds for us amend,
In all our needs your succor send. Amen.

The Lavabo *and the* Orate Fratres

Say *Pater noster* as you stand
While the priest washes his hands.
    After that, the priest bows down
Before the altar, then turns around,
And with low voice he asks of you
To pray to God as he will do.
Pay close attention to the priest
When he turns, then strike your breast,
And think because of all your sin
You are not worthy to pray for him;
But when you pray, God sees your will,
And if it is good, forgives the ill.
With hope, then, in God's love you may
Answer the priest aloud and say:

    May the Holy Ghost come unto you
    And guide your works in all you do,
    Your heart and voice and all your ways,
    Unto God's worship and His praise.

The Secret Prayer

    Turning, the priest will then proceed
The prayers in his book to read;
At this time, kneel and say the prayer
That next in black is written here.
Much your prayer it will enhance
To raise your hands with reverence,
And with devotion hold them there
While you say this simple prayer: . . .
. . . .
Then while the priest prays privately,
You say your *Pater* silently.

The Preface and the First Part of the Canon

From where he stood, his prayer done,
To the altar's center the priest will come,
And bid all men, as he stands there,
To lift up then, as you will hear,
Heart and body and every part.
Listen well with all your heart
When he begins *per omnia*
And when he says *Sursum corda.*
At the end he says *Sanctus* thrice,
And *in excelsis* he says twice.[2]
Then as soon as he is through
See that you are ready too;
Say silently in your own mind
The prayer to God that you here find: . . .
. . . .
When you have said this, bend your knee
Before God in true piety.
Thank God for all His favors then
And pray as well for every man
Of each estate and each degree,
As holds the law of charity;
Therefore you should not delay
But say your prayer in this way:

Honored may you be, O Lord,
Worshipped always and adored.
I thank you Lord, as well I should,
For more than I can know of good
That from you I have received
Since the time I was conceived:
Life and limbs you have me lent,
My very mind you have me sent,
You have kept me with your grace
From many perils in many a place;
All my life and all my living
I have wholly of your giving;
You bought me dearly with your blood
And died for me upon the rood; . . .
. . . .
O Lord, protect your holy church,
And bishops, priests and simple clerks,
That they be kept in all good works;

2. "World without end . . .; Lift up your hearts . . .; Holy, holy, holy . . .; Hosanna in the highest."

The king, the queen, lords of the land,
That they maintain with even hand
Their proper state in all goodness
And rule the folk in righteousness.
Our kinsmen, those who wish us well,
Our friends, tenants, servants, all,
Old men, children and all women,
Merchants, craftsmen, and the tillmen,
Rich and poor men, great and small,
Lord, I pray you for them all,
That they be helped in health to dwell
And good and holy life as well.
To all who lead a wretched life
In slander, misfortune, or strife,
In sickness, in prison, or on the sea,
Disowned, in exile, in poverty,
To all of them send better days
Unto your worship and your praise. . . .
. . . .

The Consecration and Elevation of the Host

When consecration time is near,
A small bell ringing you will hear.
Then should you do reverence
To Christ Jesus' real presence
That can loose all baleful bonds.
Kneel and hold up both your hands
At the elevation: you behold
Christ himself, whom Judas sold;
Who then was scourged, put on the rood,
And for mankind there shed His blood;
And died and rose and went to heaven,
And yet shall come to judge us even
According as each man has done,
That same is He you look upon.
Look on this sacred mystery
Of holy church most reverently;
Behold this truth, believe it well,
Lest you in darkness ever dwell.
While you kneel there you should say
What prayer you wish, in your own way.
Each man should pray as best he knows,
And each a different prayer will choose.
One short prayer is all you need,
Then add a *Pater* and a *Creed*.
If no prayer you have in mind,

I set one here that you may find;
But though I write it here for you,
Change it if it suits you to.

May I praise you, O my king,
May I bless you, O my king,
    For each gift and every good
May I thank you, O my king;
Jesus, all my joy you bring.
        Jesus, you have spilled your blood
        And died for me upon the rood.
Jesus, grant to me your grace
To sing a song unto your praise.

Continuation of the Canon

Then when you have said the *Creed*,
The short prayer I bid you read
That next is written in black lettering:
It will help you for your bettering:

Lord, as you can, and as you will,
Have mercy on me, who have done ill.
I am content my will to bend
To accept whatever you may send.
Your mercy, Jesus, I implore,
And hope to have it all the more
Since you your own assurance gave
That what we ask for we shall have;
You bid us ask for what we need:
That I be saved I humbly plead.
And give me wit and wisdom right
To love you, Lord, with all my might.

The prayer that follows should be said
For all your friends who are now dead;
And for all Christian souls, that they
Receive God's mercy, you should pray. . . .
            . . .

The Lord's Prayer

The *Pater noster* you should pray
Until you hear the priest to say
Per omnia saecula aloud;
Then you stand up with the crowd;
For he will say, so you can hear,

To God in heaven the Lord's Prayer.
Listen to him with good will;
While he is speaking, you keep still,
But answer at *temptacionem:*
Sed libera nos a malo, Amen.[3]
To teach you this there is no need;
Who knows it not is dull indeed.
At this time you should say no other
Prayer except the *Our Father*
In Latin as you hear the priest recite it,
And then in English as now I write it:

> Our father, that is in heaven,
> Blessed be thy name to neven [name].
> Come to us thy kingdom.
> In heaven and earth thy will be done.
> Our daily bread grant us today,
> And our misdeeds forgive us aye;
> As we do to them that injure us,
> So too have mercy upon us,
> And lead us into no tempting,
> But shield us from all wicked thing. Amen.

The Agnus Dei (*Lamb of God . . .*)

When you can hear the priest again,
Stand and listen to him then.
He says *Agnus* thrice, and at the end
Asks God to us His peace to send.
If you are out of charity
In you that peace may not now be;
And so it will be good for you
To pray for charity anew.
When the priest the pax will kiss,
Kneel you down and pray then this:

[A prayer for love of God and man follows, to be said while the priest consumes the consecrated elements]

> During the rinsing by the priest,[4]
> Say your *Pater*, that is best.
> When the priest is finished, then
> Stand up on your feet again.
> The missal then the clerk removes

---

3. *. . . Et ne nos inducas in tentationem. Sed libera nos a malo* (and lead us not into temptation, but deliver us from evil).
4. Of the chalice, etc.

To the south of the altar as it behooves.
The priest then turns, if you will look,
To read the prayers in his book.
And so you should without delay
The following kind of prayer say:

Jesus, my king, to you I pray,
Have pity on us all this day,
And hear our prayers in this place,
Good Lord, for your holy grace.
Keep me and all whom you here find
From injury of any kind
That may befall in any way
In the deeds we do today,
Whether going, home abiding,
Sitting, standing, walking, riding.
If sudden chance should come to us
Otherwise than we would choose,
May this mass then for us become
Confession and viaticum.
And, Jesus, by your dear wounds five,
Teach us a righteous way of life. Amen.

When you have finished, I recommend
The *Pater noster* until the end,
For mass is not all finishèd
Till *Ite, missa est* is said.[5]
And so when you the *Ite* hear,
Or *Benedicamus* meets your ear,
The mass is done, but you should stay,
And this prayer of thanksgiving say.
Then truly, in God's holy name,
You may return from whence you came.

God be thanked for all His works,
God be thanked by priests and clerks,
God be thanked by every man,
And I thank God as best I can
For His great goodness beyond price,
And this day for this sacrifice.
With all the prayers said here today
That God be pleased I humbly pray.
I bless myself in God's good name
And mindful of whence the blessing came.
In nomine patris et filii et spiritus sancti. Amen.

5. The Latin words of dismissal (or *Benedicamus Domino*).

How you at mass your time should spend
I have now told, and I will end.
It will be good for you to turn
The pages of this book, and learn
The explanation, part by part,
And the prayers to get by heart.
  There surely is no need to prove
That all should honor and should love
The mass, above all things the best,
And in this world the worthiest.

How thou at tho messe thi tym shuld spende
Haue I told: now wil I ende.
tho robryk is gode vm while to loke,
tho praiers to con with-outen boke.
hit is skille with-outen doute,
that ilk mon [the] messe loue & loute,
for of alle in this world, then is tho messe
tho worthiest thing, most of godnesse.

Chronology

325	Council of Nicea
410	Sack of Rome by the Visigoths
430	St. Augustine of Hippo d.
431	Council of Ephesus
451	Council of Chalcedon
440–61	Pope Leo I
543 (c.)	St. Benedict of Nursia d.
590–604	Pope Gregory I
735	Bede the Venerable d.
768–814	Charlemagne
858–67	Pope Nicholas I
910	Foundation of the Monastery of Cluny
1049–54	Pope Leo IX
1073–85	Pope Gregory VII
1095	First Crusade preached by Pope Urban II
1098	Foundation of the Monastery of Cîteaux
1122	Concordat of Worms ending the Investiture Controversy
1123	First Lateran Council (Pope Calixtus II)
1139	Second Lateran Council (Pope Innocent II)
1140 (c.)	The *Decretum* of Gratian
1150 (c.)	*The Four Books on the Sacraments* of Peter Lombard
1153	St. Bernard of Clairvaux d.
1179	Third Lateran Council (Pope Alexander III)
1215	Fourth Lateran Council (Pope Innocent III)
1221	St. Dominic d.
1226	St. Francis of Assisi d.
1245	First Council of Lyons (Pope Innocent IV)
1274	Second Council of Lyons (Pope Gregory X)
1274	St. Thomas Aquinas d.

Index

Abbots, Benedictine rule on, 72–73
Abelard, Peter, 205, 206
Absinthe (beverage), 175
Adam of St. Victor, 238–240
Admonitio generalis (Charlemagne), 115–119, 144
  Something to Priest, Something to People, 117
  To All, 118–119
  To the Clergy, 116, 117–118
Adonus, Archibishop of Vienne, 198
Against Heresies (St. Irenaeus of Lyons), 18–20
Agobard, 152
Alaric, King, 51
Alberic, Abbot, 177, 178
Albigensian Crusade, 277, 292, 300, 301, 380, 391
Alcuin of York, 110, 112, 115, 152
  Letter to Charlemagne, 120
  Preface and Additions to the Roman Mass, 145–148
Alderic (deacon), 203
Alexander I, St., 19
Alexander I, Pope, 203
Alexander III, Pope, 278, 285–286, 289, 292, 319
Alexander IV, Pope, 388
Alexandria, patriarchate of, 2, 311
Alfred the Great, 96
al-Hakim, Caliph, 219
All Glory Laud and Honor (Theodulf of Orléans, 121, 130–131
Alleluia (chant), 153, 237
  Benedictine Rule on, 85
  sequence (melody), 113
Alwic (cleric), 198
Amalar of Metz, 112–113, 237
  Liber officialis, 152–158, 237

Amalarius of Metz (Cabaniss), 152
Ambrose of Milan, St., 6, 7, 50, 201, 210, 212, 214
  Hymn for Sunday Lauds, 42–43
Ambrosian hymns, 6, 42–44
Amiet, R., 145
Anacletus, St., 19
Anastasius, Patriarch of Antioch, 96
Anastasius, the Bibliotecarius, 150
Anastasius, Bishop of Thessalonica, 197
Anastasius II, Pope, 111
Anicetus, St., 20
Anthony of the Desert, St., 68
Antioch, patriarchate of, 2, 311
Antipopes, 168
Apologists, 7, 18, 30–34
Apostolic fathers, meaning of, 7
Apostolic Fathers, The, 10, 13, 28
Apostolic Tradition (St. Hippolytus), 34–36
Apostolical Constitutions, 36–39
Aquinas, St. Thomas, 45, 206, 367, 369–380
  hymns of, 379–380
  Summa contra gentiles, 369
  Summa theologica, 369–378
Ardo Smaragdus, 131–134
Arianism, 3–4, 236
  condemned, 3
Aristotle, 206, 281, 369
Arius, Bishop of Libya, 3
Arnold of Brescia, 168, 247
Arnold, Matthew, 357
Arsenius, Bishop, 150
Asceticism, 6, 68
Athanasius of Alexandria, St., 4
Augustine of Canterbury, St., 109, 134

Augustine of Hippo, St., 7, 192,
    200, 207, 212, 213, 214, 216,
    233
  City of God, 50–67, 111
  Confessions, 42, 50
Augustinian Friars, founded, 279
Augustus, Emperor, 1
Averroës, 281

Bacon, Roger, 324
Badilo (monk), 234
Baker, H. W., 44
Baldwin, Mary, 401
Baptism:
  Didache on, 28–29
  early descriptions of, 28–34
  Justin Martyr on, 30–32
  Lent, 4
  liturgy of Eucharist and, 4
Barmby J., 40, 96, 193, 198
Basil the Great of Caesarea, St., 68
Basil of Cappadocia, St., 6
Battle of Vices Against Virtues,
    The (Rutebeuf), 393–395
Beguinages (semi-religious order),
    280, 335, 343
Benedict of Aniane, St., 69, 112
  Concordia regularum, 134
  innovations to Benedictine Rule,
    131–134
Benedict of Nursia, St., 6, 68–95
Benedictine monasticism, 131–134,
    165
  Rule of St. Benedict, 68–95, 112,
    165, 178, 179, 180, 181, 243
Berengar of Tours, 207
Bernard of Clairvaux, St., 168–169,
    170, 177, 205, 239, 276, 277,
    281, 398
  On Consideration, 168–169, 247–
    275
  Sermons on the Virgin Mary,
    243–247
Bernard of Pisa, see Eugenius III,
    Pope
Besant de Dieu (Guillaume le
    Clerc), 391–392
Bèze, monastery of, 224
Birth of Western Economy, The
    (Latouche), 118
Bishop, Edmund, 145

Bishops:
  apostolic succession of, 2, 18–20
  Early Church canons on, 20–22,
    23
  liturgy for consecration of, 34–
    36
  Pastoral Rule, 95–108
Blessed Caprasius, Bishop, 234
Blessed William, the confessor, 233
Bonhomme, Brother, 367
Boniface, St., 109, 112
Boniface VIII, Pope, 193, 199, 278
Book of Pastoral Rule and Selected
    Epistles of Gregory the
    Great, 96
Book of the Pilgrim, 229–236
Bourbon, Étienne de, 395, 396–397
Bright, W., 25
Brittain, F., 42
Brown, S. M., 335
Bruno of Olmütz, Bishop, 385–389
Burgundio of Pisa, 206
Byzantine Church, 293, 306
  cultural differences between
    West and, 1–2
  schism (867–70), 162

Cabaniss, A., 152
Calixtus II, Pope, 177
Canons:
  beginning of, 3
  on bishops, 20–22, 23
  Carolingian Age, 111–112
  Central Middle Ages, 188–205
  classical period, 188
  Decretum, 166, 188–205
  Early Church, 3–4, 20–23
  High Middle Ages, 299–323
  See also names of councils
Canticle of Brother Sun (St. Fran-
    cis of Assisi), 356–357
Canticle of Canticles, 239
Carmelites, founded, 279
Carolingian Age, 109–163, 164, 165,
    166, 276
  ecclesiastical organization under
    royal authority, 115–144
  liturgical documents, 112–113,
    144–158
  re-emergence of the Papacy,
    158–163

Carta caritatis (Cistercian order), 177, 315–316
Cassian, John, 68, 90
Cassinum (Montecassino), 69
Cassiodorus, 212
Caswell, E., 357, 379
Catechumens, 36
  baptism of, 4, 6
  meaning of, 4
Catharism, 277, 292, 300, 363
Caxton, William, 398
Celestine I, St., 192, 320
Celibacy, 164, 192–197, 199
Celtic churches, 134
Central Middle Ages (900–1150), 164–275
  Bernard of Clairvaux, 243–275
  canon law, 188–205
  liturgy, 237–242
  monastic reforms, 164–165, 170–181
  papal reforms, 165–166, 181–187
  popular religion, 217–236
  Sacrament theology, 205–217
Cesarius, St., 231, 395, 396
Chadwick, Henry, 34–35
Charlemagne, 115, 120, 225 229
  administrative skill of, 110
  Admonitio generalis, 115–119, 144
  Epistola generalis, 144–145
  Letter from Alcuin to, 120
  Letter to Pope Leo III, 119–120
Charles Martel, 109
Charter of Love (Cîteaux monastery), 177, 315–316
Chartres, cathedral school of, 166
Chartularium universitatis Parisiensis, 367–369
Cheney, C. R., 283, 287, 324
Christian Latin Poetry (Raby), 241
Christian Rite and Drama in the Middle Ages (Hardison), 242
Christianity:
  Carolingian Age, 109–163
  Central Middle Ages (900–1150), 164–275
  High Middle Ages (1150–1300), 276–412
  Patristic period, 1–108
Christmas hymns, 44–45

Christological heresies, 3
Chrodegang of Metz, St., 112
Cistercian order, 168
  Benedictine Rule and, 177–181
  Carta caritatis, 117, 315–316
  early days of, 177–181
  Exordium, 177–181
  popes, 169, 247
Cîteaux, monastery of, 165, 177
  compared to Cluny, 177
  conversi (farm laborers), 177, 179
City of God, The (St. Augustine of Hippo), 50–67, 111
Clairvaux, monastery of, 168, 177
Clare, St., 279
Claudius Ephebus, 12–13
Clement of Rome, St., 18, 19, 149, 320
  Letter to the Corinthians, 10–13
Clementines (John XXII), 278
Cletus, St., 10
Cluny, monastery of, 165, 217
  compared to Cîteaux, 177
  customs of, 170–176
Cluny III (church), 170
Cluny Under St. Hugh (Hunt), 170
Collus, D. A., 383
Columban, St., 69
Compostela pilgrimage, 167
  Book of the Pilgrim on, 229–236
Concord of Discordant Canons (Gratian), 159, 166, 188–205, 206, 278
  Distinctions, 188, 189–198
Concordia regularum (St. Benedict of Aniane), 134
Conferences (Cassian), 68
Confessions (St. Augustine of Hippo), 42, 50
Consecrated host, elevation of, 280
Constantine (missionary), *see* Cyril, St.
Constantine I, Emperor, 1, 3
Constantine V, Emperor, 120
Constantine VIII, Emperor, 224
Constantinople (see), 23, 311
  ascendancy as a patriarchate, 2
Constitution for the Jews, 299, 320–321

Constitutions (Raymond of Peñafort), 363–367
Constitutions of the Dominican Order, The (Galbraith), 364
Consuetudines (Ulrich), 170–176
Contra Nicetam (Humbert of Moyenmoutier), 195
Conversi (farm laborers), 177, 179
Corbie, monastery of, 152
Corpus Christi, Feast of, 280, 379
Corpus Juris Canonici (ed. Friedberg), 189
Correspondence of Pope Gregory VII, The, 183
Coulton, G. G., 384
Council of Aachen, 134
Council of Carthage I, 205
Council of Chalcedon, 3, 4, 25
   final statement of faith, 27–28
Council of Clermont, 167
Council of Constantinople I, 3
   canons of, 23
Council of Constantinople II, 3
Council of Constantinople III, 3
Council of Ephesus, 3, 4
Council of London, 332
Council of Lyons I, 278, 338
Council of Lyons II, 278, 384
Council of Nicea I, 3, 303
   canons of, 20–23
Council of Nicea II, 3, 111
Council of Oxford, 327, 332, 334
Council of Rheims, 262
Council of Seville, 204
Council of Tarragona, 202
Council of Trent, 4
Councils and Synods (Popwicke and Cheney), 324
Creed of Athanasius, 328
Creed of Chalcedon, 27–28
Creed of Nicea, *see* Nicene Creed
Creytens, R., 364
Cross of Charles, 230
Crusades:
   beginning of, 167
   indulgence, 300–303
   "theology," 167
   See also names of crusades
Cults:
   saint, 166
   Virgin Mary, 280
Cyril, St., 113, 149, 150

Damasus I, St., 41
Dante Alighieri, 395
De consideratione (St. Bernard of Clairvaux), 168–169, 247–275
De sacramentis (Hugh of St. Victor), 206
Decretals, Pope Gregory IX, 278, 287, 288, 324, 388
Decretum, *see* Concord of Discordant Canons
Description of Visitations (Grosseteste), 327–328
Dictatus papae (Pope Gregory VII), 181–183
Didache, 28–30
   on Baptism, 28–29
   on Eucharist, 29–30
Diego of Osma, Bishop, 363
Diocletian, Emperor, 202
Dionysio-Hadriana (papal decrees), 111, 115
Dionysius, St., 290
Dionysius Exiguus, 111
Disciplinary Decrees of the Ecumenical Councils, The, 198, 299
Dix, Gregory, 34
Dominic, St., 278, 279, 363
Dominican order, 386
   documents, 363–380
   founded, 279
   Third Orders, 280
Donaldson J., 37
Donation of Constantine, 112
Donna del paradiso (Todi), 358–363
Downside Review (publication), 176
Drama of the Medieval Church, The (Young), 242
Duckett, Eleanor, 152
Due process (ecclesiastical court), 313–315
Dvornik, F., 150

Eales, S. J., 243
Early Church, *see* Patristic period
Early Medieval Theology (trans. McCracken), 121
Easter season, 167
   catechumens, 4, 6

Easter Sequence, The (Wipo),
    237–238
Ebbo of Rheims, Bishop, 134
Ecclesiastical History (Bede), 40
Ecclesiastical organization:
    development of, 2–3
    Patristic period, 10–23
    under royal authority, 115–144
Ecumenical Councils:
    canons (Patristic period), 20–23
    decrees of, 6–7
    number of, 3
    See also names of councils
Edict of Milan, 1, 2
Einhard, 110, 111
Eleutherius, St., 20
Ellard, G., 145
Emerton, E., 183
Ennodius, St., 182
Epistola generalis (Charlemagne),
    144–145
Essays in Criticism (Arnold), 357
Etsi animarum (papal bull), 388
Etymologies (Isidore of Seville),
    189
Eucharist, sacrament of:
    as being a "transubstantiation,"
        299–300
    common meal, 5
    Didache on, 29–30
    earliest description of, 5
    Fore-mass, 36–39
    Jewish tradition and, 5
    Justin Martyr on, 32–34
    liturgical development, 6
    offering of thanks, 5–6
    penance and, 4, 5
    in private homes, 5
    St. Paul on, 5
Eugenius III, Pope, 168, 169, 206,
    247, 248, 320
Eusebius of Caesarea, 3
Eutropius of Saintes, St., 230
Eutyches, 25
Evaristus, St., 19
Excommunication, 165, 280, 321
    of 1054, 195
Exomologesis practice, 5
*Exordium coenobii et ordinis
    Cisterciensis,* 177–181

Fahy, B., 344, 350, 356
Faith of Conques, St., 229, 230, 234
Falls, Thomas B. 31
Feltoe, C. L., 190, 195, 197
Feudalism, 164, 277
First Crusade, 167
First Crusade, The (Krey), 225
First Lateran Council (1123),
    277–278
Flavian Bishop of Constantinople,
    4, 25–27
Fliche, A., 281
Florentius, Brother, 367
Fore-mass, development of, 36–39
Formosa, Bishop, 150
Fornication, penance for, 138–139
Fortunatus (delegate), 12–13
Fortunatus, Bishop Venantius,
    45–47, 379
Four Books of Sentences (Lom-
    bard), 166, 205–217
Fourth Crusade, 292, 306
Fourth Lateran Council (1215),
    177, 277, 279, 281, 292–344
    canons of, 299–323
        implementation of, 323–334
    convoked, 278, 293–295
    Innocent III and, 292–299
    Letter of Convocation, 293–295
    opening sermon, 295–299
    on the sacraments, 280
Francis of Assisi, St., 278, 279, 350
    Canticle of Brother Sun,
        356–357
Franciscan order, 324, 381, 386
    founded, 279
    rift over poverty rule, 281
    Rule of the Third Order,
        350–356
        abstinence, 351–352
        burying the dead, 354–355
        correction, dispensation,
            officers, 355–356
        daily life, 351
        fasting, 352
        first rule of, 350
        meeting each month, 353–354
        prayer, 352–353
        sacraments, other matters, 353
        special mass, 353
        visiting the sick, 354–355

Franciscan order (*Continued*)
    Rule of 1223, 344–350
    Third Orders, 280
    writings, 344–363
Franks, 1, 109
Frederick II, Emperor, 276, 380
Friars preachers, provisions for,
    367–369
Friedberg, A., 189, 195, 199, 203
Fulk of Toulouse, Bishop, 363

Galbraith, G. R., 364
Gallican rite, 112, 144
Gamer, H. M., 135
Gasquet, Cardinal Francis A., 69
Gelasian sacramentaries, 40
Gelasius I, Pope, 40, 145, 161, 192
Genesius, St., 231
Germanic tribes, 1
Giles, St., 229, 231, 232–233
Glaber, Rodulfus, 217–225
Glagolitic alphabet, 149
Glimm, F. H., 10, 28
Glimm, F. X., 10, 28
Gloria (prayer), 37
Golden Legend, The (Voragine),
    397–400
Good Friday liturgy, 45
Good works, Benedictine rule on,
    74–76
Gorze, monastery at, 165
*Gospel According to Marks of
    Silver*, 389–390, 392
Gratian, 159, 166, 188–205, 206, 278,
    313
Greek language, 6, 34, 151
Greek rite, 237
Gregorian chants, 40
Gregorian reform, 165
Gregorian *Sacramentary*, 40
    Pope Hadrian I and, 145
    Preface and Additions to the
        Roman Mass, 145–148
Gregory of Nazianzen, St., 96
Gregory I, St., 1, 7, 109, 184, 196,
    198
    extant letters of, 96
    liturgy and, 40–42
    on the Pastoral Rule, 95–108
Gregory VII, Pope, 165–166,
    181–187, 198

Gregory VII, Pope (*Continued*)
    Dictatus papae, 181–183
    Letters, 183–187
Gregory IX, Pope, 276, 278, 287,
    288, 324, 338, 344, 350
Gregory X, Pope, 384
    letter from Bishop Bruno of
        Olmütz to, 385–389
Grosseteste, Bishop Robert,
    323–334
    Descriptions of Visitations,
        327–328
    Instructions to Archdeacons,
        324–327
    Statutes for the Diocese of
        London, 328–334
    Memoranda, 381–383
        to the Papal Notary, 383
        to Pope Innocent IV and
            the Cardinals, 381–383
Guibert of Nogent, 225–227
*Guide to pèlerin de St. Jaques
    de Compostelle, Le* (ed.
    Viellard), 229
Guillaume le Clerc, 391–392
Guillaume de Saint-Amour, 394
Gundricus, Bishop, 150

Hadrian I, Pope, 111, 115, 119, 145
Hadrian II, Pope, 149
Halitgar of Cambrai, 134–143
Hanssens, J. M., 152
Harding, Stephen, 177
Hardison, O. B., Jr., 242
Harduin of the Franciscans,
    Brother, 340
Hartrenft, C. D., 196
Haskins, Clare Allen, 390
Hebrew language, 151
Henry IV, Emperor, 181, 183
    excommunicated, 165
Heresy, 277, 299–300
    beginning of, 3–4
    Christological, 3
    Crusade indulgence and, 300–303
    meaning of, 3
    Trinitarian, 3–4
    See also names of heresies
Herlihy, D., 280, 398
High Middle Ages (1150–1300),
    276–412
    Dominican documents, 363–380

High Middle Ages (*Continued*)
  Fourth Lateran Council, 292–344
  Franciscan writings, 344–363
  Innocent III and, 287–299
  literature of protest, 380–395
  priests and laymen, 395–412
Hilary of Poitiers, St., 230, 236
Hilary, St., 192
Hincmar of Rheims, 159
Hippo, siege of, 50
Hippolytus, St., 34–36
Hispana (papal decrees), 111, 112
Historarium libri quinque (Glaber), 217–225
Historie de l'église (eds. Fliche and Martin), 281
History of Sozomen (trans. Hartranft), 196
Holy Cross monastery (Poitiers), 45
Homicide, penance for, 137–138
Honan, Daniel, 51
Honoratus, St., 231
Honorius III, Pope, 279, 344–345
Hormisdas, St. 192
Hubert of Canterbury, Archbishop, 283–287
Hugh, Abbot, 170, 171
Hugh of St. Victor's, 206, 209
Humbert of Moyenmoutier, Cardinal, 195
Humbert de Romanis, 384–385
Humility, Benedictine rule on, 78–82
Hunt, Noreen, 170
Hyginus, St., 19
Hymn on Christ's Passion (Fortunatus), 45
Hymn for Compline, 44
Hymn for Every Hour (Prudentius Clemens), 44–45
Hymn for Palm Sunday (Theodulf of Orléans), 130–131
Hymn for Sunday Lauds (St. Ambrose of Milan), 42–43
Hymns:
  Ambrosian, 6, 42–44
  of Aquinas, 379–380
  Carolingian Age, 113, 121, 130–131
  Christmas, 44–45

Hymns (*Continued*)
  dedicated to Virgin Mary, 280
  meter, 45
  Palm Sunday, 121, 130–131
Hymns Ancient and Modern, 44

Ignatius of Antioch, St., 13–18
Ignatius of Constantinople, St., 162
Immaculate conception, doctrine of, 243
Indulgences, 385
  crusades, 300–303
  money accepted for, 387
Innocent I, St., 192
Innocent II, Pope, 168
Innocent III, Pope, 276, 277, 278, 319, 321, 363, 381
  Fourth Lateran Council, 292–299
  Letter of Convocation, 293–295
  Letter to Archbishop Hubert of Canterbury, 283–287
  Letter to the Bishop of Ely, 287–292
Innocent IV, Pope, 276, 324, 388
  Robert Grosseteste's memoranda to, 381–383
Institutes, The (Cassian), 68
Instructions to Archdeacons (Grosseteste), 324–327
Investiture controversy, 165–166, 183
Iona, monastery at, 109
Ireland:
  monasticism in, 68, 69
  Scoti (monks), 109
Irenaeus of Lyons, St., 18–20
Irenaeus (Roberts and Rambaut), 18
Isidore of Seville, St., 111, 189, 192, 204
Isidoriana-Hispana (papal decrees), 111, 112

James the Apostle, St., 167
  Compostela shrine, 229–236
James of Zebidee, St., 233
Jebuin, Bishop of Châlons, 218–219
Jeremy (cleric), 400–412
Jerome, St., 7, 41, 192
Jerusalem:
  destruction of (A.D. 70), 2
  pilgrimages to, 167

Jerusalem, patriarchate of, 2, 311
Jews, 7, 168, 186, 217, 219–221, 225,
    238, 257, 319–323
  common meal tradition, 5
  Constitution for, 299, 320–321
  converts, 29, 323
  massacred, 168
John of Angély, St., 230
John the Apostle, St., 18, 20, 31
John Chrysostom, St., 212, 214
  sermon of, 47–50
John of Damascus, St., 7, 206
John VIII, Pope, 149
  Letter to Svatopluk of Moravia,
    150–151
John XXII, Pope, 278
John, Bishop of Palermo, 205
John, Bishop of Ravenna, 96
John, Bishop of Syracuse, 40
John (priest of Haudricourt), 336,
    337
John of Bray, 341–342
John of Montluçon, 339–340
John of Morgneval, 340
John of Neuilly-en-Thelle, Master,
    340
Judicial ordeal, practice of, 308
Justin Martyr, 30–34
  on Baptism, 30–32
  on Eucharist, 32–34
Justina (mother of Valentinian), 42
Justinian, Emperor, 1, 69

Kay, G. B., 359
Knowles, Dom David, 176
Krey, A. C., 225
Kyrie Eleison, 40–41, 86, 237

Latin fathers, 7–8
Latin language, 6, 34, 113, 381
  as liturgical language, 149–152
Latouche, R., 118
Lay investiture, banning of, 165
Lay-Folks' Mass-Book (Jeremy),
    400–412
  Agnus Dei, 410
  Benedicamus, 411
  Consecration and Elevation of
    Host, 408–409
  Continuation of the Canon, 409
  Creed, 405
  Gloria, 404

Lay-Folks' Mass-Book (Continued)
  Gospel, 404–405
  Introit, 403–404
  Lavabo and Orate Frates, 406
  Lord's Prayer, 409–410
  Offertory Prayer, 405–406
  Prayers before Mass, 402–403
  Preface and First Part of Canon,
    407–408
  Secret Prayer, 406
Le vites, defined, 2
Légendes de Constantin et de
    méthode, Les (Dvornik),
    150
Lehmann, P., 390
Leidrad, Bishop, 152
Lent, 21, 170
  baptism (Early Church), 4
  Benedictine rule on, 91–92
Leo I, Pope, 40, 145, 161, 184, 190,
    193, 195, 197, 215
  Letter to Flavian, Bishop of Con-
    stantinople, 4, 25–27
  Tome (letter), 4, 25–27
Leo III, Pope, 120
  letter from Charlemagne to, 119–
    120
Leo IV, Pope, 192
Leo IX, Pope, 195
Leo III, Emperor, 162
Leonard of Limoges, St., 229, 230,
    233, 234–235
Letter from Alcuin to Charle-
    magne, 120
Letter to Archbishop Hubert of
    Canterbury (Innocent III),
    283–287
Letter to the Bishop of Ely (Inno-
    cent III), 287–292
Letter from Charlemagne to Pope
    Leo III, 119–120
Letter of Convocation (Pope In-
    nocent III), 293–295
Letter to the Corinthians (St.
    Clement of Rome), 10–13
Letter to Flavian, Bishop of Con-
    stantinople (Pope Leo I),
    25–27
Letter of Pope John VIII to Svato-
    pluk of Moravia, 150–151
Letter of Pope Stephen V to
    Svatopluk (885), 151–152

Letter to the Romans (St. Ignatius
of Antioch), 14–18
Letters (St. Ignatius of Antioch),
13–18
To the Romans, 14–18
To the Trallians, 13–14
Letters (Pope Gregory VII), 183–
187
to Bishop Otto of Constance,
183–185
A Call to the Faithful to Protect
the Church from Enemies,
185–187
Letters (Pope Nicholas I), 112,
158–163
To the Bishops of Gaul, 158–161
To the Emperor Michael, 162–
163
*Letters and Sermons of Leo the
Great, The* (trans. Feltoe),
190
Leutard (heretic), 218–219
Liber extra (Gregory IX), 278
Liber officialis (Amalar of Metz),
152–158, 237
criticism of, 152
De tabulis, 156
Eclogae de officio missae, 153–
154
Entrance of the Bishop, 154–156
On the Offertory, 156–158
Liber sancti Jacobi, 229–236
Liber sextus (Boniface VIII), 278
Licinius, Bishop of Cartagena, 96
*Life of Benedict of Aniane and
Inda* (Ardo Smaragdos),
131–134
Life of Constantine (St. Cyril), 150
Life in the Middle Ages (Coulton),
384
*Life and Works of St. Bernard of
Clairvaux, The* (ed. Mabil-
lon), 243
Lindisfarne, monastery at, 109
Linus, St., 10, 19
Liturgy, 34–36
Canon (anaphora), 35–36
Carolingian Age, 112–113, 144–
158
Central Middle Ages, 237–242

Liturgy (*Continued*)
consecration of a bishop, 34–36
Epistola generalis (Charle-
magne), 144–145
Good Friday, 45
Gregory the Great and, 40–42
interpretation; symbolism and
allegory, 152–158
Kiss of Peace, 35
languages, 6, 34, 113, 149–152
Latin language and, 149–152
local variations, 112
meaning of, 4
music, 6, 37, 42–47, 113, 237–240
Offertory, 35
Patristic period, 28–50
Preface and Additions to the
Roman Mass, 145–148
religious drama and, 167, 241–242
sacraments and, 28–50
sequence, 237–240
Slavonic, 113, 149–150, 151, 152
Trope, 240–241
Logos, defined, 3
Lombard, Peter, 166, 319, 370
Four Books of Sentences, 205–
217
Lombards, 1, 69, 96
Louis I (the Pious), Emperor, 110,
111, 112, 131, 164
Louis II (the German), King, 149
Louis IX, King, 334

Mabillon, Dom J., 243
McCracken, G. E., 121
McNeal, E. H., 181
McNeill, J. T., 135
Magic, penance for, 140–141
Magnus, Albertus, 369
Manichaean sect, 50, 195
Marcellinus (friend of Augustine),
51
Marriage, sacrament of, 319
Martin of Tours, St., 45, 229–230,
233, 235–236
Martin, V., 281
Mary, *see* Virgin Mary
Mary of Le Puy, St., 229
Mary Magdalen of Vézelay, St.,
229, 234

Mass:
  early eucharistic liturgy and, 6
  elevation of consecrated host,
    280
  Lay-folks' Mass-book, 400–412
    Agnus Dei, 410
    Benedicamus, 411
    Consecration and Elevation of
      Host, 408–409
    continuation of the Canon, 409
    Creed, 405
    Gloria, 404
    Gospel, 404–405
    Introit, 403–404
    Lavabo and Orate Frates, 406
    Lord's Prayer, 409–410
    Offertory Prayer, 405–406
    Prayers before Mass, 402–403
    Preface and First Part of
      Canon, 407–408
    Secret Prayer, 406
  and priest with back to congre-
    gation, 113
Master Alcuin Liturgist (trans.
  Ellard), 145
Mauger, Master Peter, 283, 284,
  286, 287, 381
Maurice, Emperor, 96
Maurice of Sully, 205
Maximus, Bishop, 214, 234
Medieval Culture and Society
  (Herlihy), 280, 398
Medieval Handbooks of Penance,
  135
Memoranda (Grosseteste), 381–383
  to the Papal Notary, 383
  to Pope Innocent IV and the
    Cardinals, 381–383
Memorandum to Pope Gregory X
  (Bruno of Olmütz), 385–389
Methodius, St., 113, 149, 151
Metropolitan archbishop, jurisdic-
  tion of, 2–3
Michael III, Emperor, 149
  Pope Nicholas I letter to, 162–
    163
Middle Ages, 164–412
  See also Central Middle Ages;
    High Middle Ages
Migne, J. P., 152
Miracles, 166
Moerbeke, William, 369

Molesme, monastery at, 177
Monahan, Grace, 51
Monastic Agreement of the Monks
  and Nuns of the English Na-
  tion, The (trans. Symons),
  242
Monasticism:
  Carolingian Age, 112, 131–134
  Central Middle Ages, 164–165,
    170–181
  Dominican documents, 363–380
  essence of, 6
  Franciscan writings, 344–363
  in Ireland, 68, 69
  Patristic period, 6, 68–95
  reforms, 170–181
  Rule of St. Benedict, 68–95, 112,
    165, 178, 179, 180, 181, 243
  Third Orders 280
Monica, St., 50
Monophysite heresy, 4, 25
Montescassino, 112
Monumenta Germainiae historica,
    Leges II, 115
Moravian language, 149
Moslems, 109, 168, 229, 281, 292
Mozarabic rite, 112
Munro, D. C., 117, 144, 395
Mysticism, 168

Neale, J. M., 44, 45, 130
Neoplatonism, 50
Nestorianism, 4
Nestorius, 4
Nicene Creed, 24
  promulgated, 3
Nicetas, Abbot, 195
Nicholas I, Pope, 112, 149, 164,
    190, 192 198
  Letters, 112, 158–163
Nicholas of St-Laurent, 336
Notker of St. Gall, 237
Notre Dame, cathedral school of,
    205

Obedience, Benedictine rule on,
    76–77
Odilo, St., 171, 217
Oldoric, Bishop of Orléans, 224
On the Orthodox Faith (St. John
  of Damascus), 206

On the Statues (St. John Chrysostom), 47–50
Opus tripartitum (Humbert de Romanis), 384–385
Order of Friars Minor, 279
Order of Friars Preachers, 279
Ostrogoths, 1, 69
O'Sullivan, J., 335
Otto of Constance, Bishop, 183–185
Our Lady's Tumbler, 280
Oxford Book of Medieval Latin Verse (ed. Raby), 44
Oxford University, 324

Pachomius, 68
Pahfnucius, 196
Palm Sunday hymns, 121, 130–131
Pange, lingua (Aquinas), 379–380
Pange lingua gloriosi (Fortunatus), 45–47, 379
Pantin, W. A., 383
Papacy:
  Bernard of Clairvaux on, 247–275
  monastic popes, 169, 247
  re-emergence of, 158–163
  reforms, 165–166, 181–187
  See also names of popes
Papal legates, precedence of, 181
Paraliturgical ceremony, 167
Paris, cathedral school of, 166
Parodie im Mittelalter, Die (Lehman), 390
Paschal I, St., 198
Pastoral Rule (Gregory the Great), 95–108
Patriarchates, 2, 311
  eucharistic liturgical variants, 6, 34
Patristic period, 1–108, 193
  bishop as pastor, 95–108
  monasticism, 6, 68–95
  organization of Early Church, 2–3, 10–23
  Respublica Christiana concept, 6, 50–67
  sacraments and liturgy, 28–50
  statements of faith, 24–28
Paucapalea, 188
Paul, St., 7, 19, 20, 50, 231
  on the Eucharist, 5

Paul the Deacon, 110, 144
Peace of God, 167
Peace movements, 167, 217
Pelagius II, Pope, 96
Penance, sacrament of, 4, 5, 206, 209–216
  books (penitentials), 134–144
  eucharistic liturgy and, 4, 5
  exomologesis practice, 5
  public, 5, 22–23, 134
Penguin Book of Latin Verse, The, 42, 359
Penitentials, 134–144
People's Crusade, 168
Percival, H. R., 20, 24, 25, 27
Perjury, penance for, 139–140
Peter, St., 2, 10, 13, 19
Peter Damiani, St., 170–171
Peter of Mincy, Master, 343
Peter of Moissac, St., 229
Peter, Subdeacon of Sicily, 193
Peter (priest at St-Valéry), 337
Peter Lombard and the Sacramental System (Rogers), 206
Pharisees, 29
Philip, King of the Gauls, 233
Photius, Patriarch, 149, 162
Pilgrimages, 168, 217
  to Compostela, 167, 229–236
  concept of, 6
  to Jerusalem, 167
  to Rome, 165, 167
  to shrines, 167
Pippin III (the Short), King, 109, 112, 144, 145
Pius I, St., 19
Plato, 50
Platonism, 50
Polybius, Bishop of Tralles, 13–14
Polycarp, Bishop of Smyrna, 18, 20
Popes and the Jews in the Middle Ages, The (Synan), 299
Popular religion, 217–236
  guide for pilgrims, 229–236
  Histories (Glaber), 217–225
  report of Urban II's speech at Clermont, 225–229
Popwicke, F. M., 324
Preaching, resurgence of, 279–280
Preface and Additions to the Roman Mass (Alcuin of York), 145–148

Protest literature, 380–395
    Gospel According to Marks of
        Silver, 389–390
    Memoranda (Grosseteste), 381–
        385
    Opus tripartitum, 384–385
    parody, 389–390
    to the Papal Notary, 383
    to Pope Innocent IV and the
        Cardinals, 381–383
    in vernacular poetry, 391–395
Prou, M., 217–218
Provisions for the Friars Preachers
    at the University of Paris,
    367–369
Prudentius Clemens, Aurelius, 44–
    45
Pseudo-Isidorian (forged decre-
    tals), 112, 159, 203, 290
Public penance, 5
    canons on, 22–23
    end of, 134
Purgatory, 387

Quatuor libri sententiarum (Four
    Books of Sentences), 166,
    205–217
Quem quaeritis (religious drama),
    241–242
Quem quaeritis trope, 240–241

Raby, F. J. E., 44, 45, 130, 237, 239,
    241, 357 379
Radegund, St., 45
Rambaut, W. H., 18
Raoul Glaber, Les cinq lires de ses
    histoires (ed. Prou), 218
Rasoir, Master Gervais, 340
Rastislav, Prince of Moravia, 149
Raymond of Peñafort, 363–367
Raynaldus, Archbishop of Ace-
    renza, 321
Record of Visitations (Rigaud),
    334–344
Redemption, anniversary of
    (1033), 217, 221–222
Register (Gregory the Great), 96
Register of Eudes of Rigaud, The
    (ed. O'Sullivan), 325
Regula magistri, 68–69
Regularis concordia, 242

Relics, 113
    miracles associated with, 166
Religious drama, 241–242, 280
    origin of, 167
Renaissance, Carolingian, 110–112
Renaissance of the Twelfth Cen-
    tury, The (trans. Haskins),
    390
"Renclus de Moiliens," 392–393
Respublica christiana, concept of,
    110–111, 276
    Augustine on, 50–67
    meaning of, 6
Rheims, cathedral school of, 166,
    205
Rigaud, Archbishop Eudes, 334–
    344
Rite, meaning of, 4
Robert, King of France, 224
Robert of Grainville, 341
Robert of Manières, 339
Robert the Monk, 227–229
Robert of Puys, 337
Robert Grosseteste (Stevenson),
    381
Robert Grosseteste, Scholar and
    Bishop (Pantin), 383
Roberts, A., 18
Rogers, Elizabeth F., 206
Roland, 225, 229, 230–231, 236
Roman Empire, 1
Roman Penitential (Halitgar), 134–
    144
    Directions to Confessors, 136–
        137
    Prescriptions of Penance, 137–
        144
        of fornication, 138–139
        of homicide, 137–138
        of magic, 140–141
        of perjury, 139–140
        of polluted animals, 143–144
        of sacrilege, 141–142
        of theft, 140
        of things offered to idols, 143
        of things strangled, 143
        of various topics, 142
    Prologue, 135–136
Romans de Carité, 392–393
Romanus, St., 236

Rome:
  pilgrimages to, 165, 167
  republican movement, 247
  Visigoth sack of (410), 51
Rome, see of, 2, 23, 311
  Dictatus on, 181–183
  primacy of, 2, 13, 40, 159
Rothad of Soissons, Bishop, 159
Routiers (mercenary soldiers), 308
Rule of St. Benedict, 68–95, 112,
    165, 178, 179, 180, 181, 243
  abandonment of liturgical addi-
    tions, 177
  Cistercian monks and, 177–181
  innovations to, 131–134
  Instruments of Good Works,
    74–76
  Observance of Lent, 91–92
  Of the Amount of Food, 88–89
  Of Clothes and Shoes, 93–94
  Of Daily Manual Labor, 90
  Of Divine Office at Night Time,
    82
  Of the Measure of Drink, 89
  On Alleluia, 85
  On Celebration of Vergils, 83–
    84, 85
  On Humility, 78–82
  On Matins, 84–85
  On Obedience, 76–77
  On Order of the Community,
    94–95
  On Order of Psalms, 86–88
  On Psalms, 82–83, 86–88
  On Saying Divine Office, 85–86
  On Silence, 77–78
  On Taking Counsel of Brethren,
    73–74
  On the Weekly Reader, 88
  Perfection, 95
  Prologue, 69–72
  Reception of Guests, 92–93
  Role of the Abbot, 72–73
  Speaking after Compline, 89–90
Rule of St. Benedict, The (trans.
    Gasquet), 69
Rule of the Third Order, 350–356
  Abstinence, 351–352
  Burying the Dead, 354–355
  Correction, Dispensation,
    Officers, 355–356
  Daily Life, 351

Rule of the Third Order
    (Continued)
  Fasting, 352
  First Rule, 350
  Meeting each Month, 353–354
  Prayer, 352–353
  Sacraments, other Matters, 353
  Special Mass, 353
  Visiting the Sick, 354–355
Rule of 1223, 344–350
Rusticius, Bishop of Narbonne,
    195
Rutebeuf, 381, 393–395

Sabat mater, 357–358, 359
Sacramentary (liber sacramen-
    torum), 40
Sacraments:
  Council of Trent on, 4
  Fourth Lateran Council on, 280
  liturgy and, 28–50
    apostolic tradition, 34–36
    apostolical constitutions, 36–39
    Didache, 28–30
    Gregory the Great, 40–42
    Justin Martyr, 30–34
  meaning of, 4
  number of, 4
  theology of, 205–217
Sacrilege, penance for, 141–142
St. Bénigne at Dijon (monastery),
    217
St. Bernard's Treatise on Consider-
    ation, 248
Saint Justin Martyr (Falls), 31
St. Victor (abbey), 205, 238–239
Saint cults, 166
Saturninus, St., 233
Schisms, 162
Schola cantorum, founding of, 40
Schroeder, H. R., 299
Scoti (Irish monks), 109
Scudder, Vida, 40
Second Lateran Council (1139),
    193, 198–199, 278
Selected Epistles of Gregory the
    Great (Barmby), 40
Selected Letters of Pope Innocent
    III Concerning England
    (1198–1216), 283
Semple, W. H., 283, 287

Sequence:
  Alleluia, 113
  development of, 237–240
Sequence for the Nativity of the Virgin Mary (Adam of St. Victor), 238–240
Sermon:
  literature, 395–397
  Patristic period, 47–50
  of St. Bernard of Clairvaux, 243–247
  of St. John Chrysostom, 47–50
Sermons on the Virgin Mary (St. Bernard of Clairvaux), 243–247
Seven Ecumenical Councils, The, 20
Shrines, 229–236
  miracles associated witht, 166
  pilgrimages to, 167
Silence, Benedictine rule on, 77–78
Simmons, T. F., 400–412
Simon, Abbot of Marcherous, 341
Simony, 164 165, 312
Siricius, St., 111, 192
Sixtus I, St., 19
Slavonic language, 149
Slavonic liturgy, 113, 149–150, 152
  arguments against use of, 151
Solidarity concept of, 6
Song of Roland, 167
Soter, St., 20
Source Book of Medieval History, A, 181
Spirit of Protest in Old French Literature, The (trans. Wood), 391
Statutes of Bishop Robert Grosseteste for the Diocese of Lincoln, 328–334
Stephan V, Pope, 151–152
Stephan VI, Pope, 203
Stephans, W. R. W., 47
Steps of Humility, The (St. Bernard of Clairvaux), 243–247
Stevenson, F. S., 381
Sully, Bishop Maurice de, 395
Summa sententiarum, 206
Summa contra gentiles (Aquinas), 369
Summa theologica (Aquinas), 369–378

Sunday, ceremonial development of, 6
Superstition, 166, 277
Sylvester I, St., 192
Symons, T., 242
Synan, E. A., 299
Synod of Toledo, 322

Te Deum Laudamus, 338
Telesphorus, St., 19
Teutonicus, Albertus, 367
Thatcher, O. J., 181
Theft, penance for, 140
Theodore, Archbishop of Canterbury, 134
Theodoric, King, 1, 69
Theodosius, Emperor, 1, 47
Theodulf, Bishop of Orleans, 110, 120–131, 134
  Hymn for Palm Sunday, 121, 130–131
  Precepts to the Priests of His Diocese, 120–130
Third Lateran Council, 278, 290, 292, 294, 303, 305, 319
Third Orders, 280
Thomas of Canterbury, St., 396
Thorndike, L., 367
Timothy, St., 19
Tithes, 311
Titus, Emperor, 2
Todi, Jacopone da, 357, 358
Tome letter (Pope Leo I), 4, 25–27
Toulouse, Count of 277
Trajan Emperor, 20
Transubstantiation 299–300, 369
Treatise on the Apostolic Tradition of St. Hippolytus (ed. Chadwick), 34–35
Trinitarian heresies, 3–4
Trope:
  development of, 240–241
  meaning of, 240–241
Trophime, St., 231
Truce of God, 167
Ugolino, Cardinal, *see* Gregory IX, Pope
Ulrich, 170–176
University of Bologna, 205
University of Paris, 367–369

University Records and Life in the Middle Ages (trans. Thorndike), 367
Urban II, Pope, 167, 177, 183, 198, 286
    speech at Clermont, 225–229
Usury, 277, 319, 321

Valentinian, Emperor, 42
Valerius Vito, 12-13
Vandals, 50
Venerable Bede, 40
Venice Rule, 350–356
Vexilla regis prodeunt (Fortunatus), 45–47
Victricius, Bishop of Rouen, 194
Viellard, Jeanne, 229
Villon, François, 394
Virgin Mary:
    cult, 280
    devotions to, 168, 280
    hymns dedicated to, 280
    St. Bernard's sermons on, 243

Visigoths, 1, 51
Vitry, Jacques de, 395, 396
Voragine, Jacobus de, 397–400

Walsh, Gerald, 13, 51
Watts, W., 42
Wiching, Bishop, 151
Wilkinson, E. M., 118
William, Abbott of St. Bénigne, 217
William of St-Laurent, 336
Wipo, 237–238
Wood, Mary M., 391, 392, 394
Works of St. John Chrysostom, The, 47
Writings of St. Francis of Assisi, With Introduction and Notes by P. Hermann, O.F.M. (trans. Fahy), 344

Young, K., 242

Zosimus, Pope, 192, 231

DOCUMENTARY HISTORY OF WESTERN CIVILIZATION
Edited by Eugene C. Black and Leonard W. Levy

ANCIENT AND MEDIEVAL HISTORY OF THE WEST

Morton Smith: ANCIENT GREECE *

A. H. M. Jones: A HISTORY OF ROME THROUGH THE FIFTH CENTURY
Vol. I: The Republic
Vol. II: The Empire

Deno Geanakoplos: BYZANTINE EMPIRE *

Marshall W. Baldwin: CHRISTIANITY THROUGH THE THIRTEENTH CENTURY

Bernard Lewis: ISLAM TO 1453 *

David Herlihy: HISTORY OF FEUDALISM

William M. Bowsky: RISE OF COMMERCE AND TOWNS *

David Herlihy: MEDIEVAL CULTURE AND SOCIETY

EARLY MODERN HISTORY

Hanna H. Gray: CULTURAL HISTORY OF THE RENAISSANCE *

Florence Edler de Roover: MONEY, BANKING,
AND COMMERCE, THIRTEENTH THROUGH SIXTEENTH CENTURIES *

V. J. Parry: THE OTTOMAN EMPIRE *

Ralph E. Giesey: EVOLUTION OF THE DYNASTIC STATE *

J. H. Parry: THE EUROPEAN RECONNAISSANCE: Selected Documents

Hans J. Hillerbrand: THE PROTESTANT REFORMATION

John C. Olin: THE CATHOLIC COUNTER REFORMATION *

Orest Ranum: THE CENTURY OF LOUIS XIV *

Thomas Hegarty: RUSSIAN HISTORY THROUGH PETER THE GREAT *

Marie Boas Hall: NATURE AND NATURE'S LAWS

Barry E. Supple: HISTORY OF MERCANTILISM *

Geoffrey Symcox: IMPERIALISM, WAR, AND DIPLOMACY, 1550-1763 *

Herbert H. Rowen: THE LOW COUNTRIES *

C. A. Macartney: THE HABSBURG AND HOHENZOLLERN DYNASTIES
IN THE SEVENTEENTH AND EIGHTEENTH CENTURIES

Lester G. Crocker: THE AGE OF ENLIGHTENMENT

Robert and Elborg Forster: EUROPEAN SOCIETY IN THE EIGHTEENTH CENTURY

REVOLUTIONARY EUROPE, 1789-1848

Paul H. Beik: THE FRENCH REVOLUTION *
David L. Dowd: NAPOLEONIC ERA, 1799-1815 *
René Albrecht-Carrié: THE CONCERT OF EUROPE
John B. Halsted: ROMANTICISM
R. Max Hartwell: THE INDUSTRIAL REVOLUTION *
Mack Walker: METTERNICH'S EUROPE
Douglas Johnson: THE ASCENDANT BOURGEOISIE *
John A. Hawgood: THE REVOLUTIONS OF 1848 *

NATIONALISM, LIBERALISM, AND SOCIALISM, 1850-1914

Eugene C. Black: VICTORIAN CULTURE AND SOCIETY
Eugene C. Black: BRITISH POLITICS IN THE NINETEENTH CENTURY
Denis Mack Smith: THE MAKING OF ITALY, 1796-1870
David Thomson: FRANCE: Empire and Republic, 1850-1940
Theodore S. Hamerow: BISMARCK'S MITTELEUROPA *
Eugene O. Golob: THE AGE OF LAISSEZ FAIRE *
Roland N. Stromberg: REALISM, NATURALISM, AND SYMBOLISM:
Modes of Thought and Expression in Europe, 1848-1914
Melvin Kranzberg: SCIENCE AND TECHNOLOGY *
Jesse D. Clarkson: TSARIST RUSSIA: Catherine the Great to Nicholas II *
Philip D. Curtin: IMPERIALISM *
Massimo Salvadori: MODERN SOCIALISM

THE TWENTIETH CENTURY

Jere C. King: THE FIRST WORLD WAR *
S. Clough, T. and C. Moodie : ECONOMIC HISTORY OF EUROPE:
Twentieth Century
W. Warren Wagar: SCIENCE, FAITH, AND MAN:
European Thought Since 1914
Paul A. Gagnon: INTERNATIONALISM AND DIPLOMACY BETWEEN THE WARS, 1919-1939 *
Henry Cord Meyer: WEIMAR AND NAZI GERMANY *
Michal Vyvyan: RUSSIA FROM LENIN TO KHRUSHCHEV *
Charles F. Delzell: MEDITERRANEAN FASCISM, 1919-1945
Donald C. Watt: THE SECOND WORLD WAR *

* In preparation